Programming Languages for Business Problem Solving

Programming Languages for Business Problem Solving

Shouhong Wang

Hai Wang

Auerbach Publications
Taylor & Francis Group
Boca Raton   New York

Auerbach Publications is an imprint of the
Taylor & Francis Group, an **informa** business

Auerbach Publications
Taylor & Francis Group
6000 Broken Sound Parkway NW, Suite 300
Boca Raton, FL 33487-2742

© 2008 by Taylor & Francis Group, LLC
Auerbach is an imprint of Taylor & Francis Group, an Informa business

Library of Congress Cataloging-in-Publication Data

Wang, Shouhong.
   Programming languages for business problem solving / Shouhong Wang and Hai Wang.
      p. cm.
   Includes bibliographical references and index.
   ISBN 978-1-4200-6264-9 (alk. paper)

   1. Business--Computer programs. 2. Programming languages (Electronic computers) 3. Problem solving--Computer programs. 4. Management information systems. I. Wang, Hai, 1973- II. Title.
   HF5548.2.W2993 2008   005.13--dc22   2007021973

Visit the Taylor & Francis Web site at
http://www.taylorandfrancis.com

and the Auerbach Web site at
http://www.auerbach-publications.com

Contents

Preface

In the information technology era, the computer literacy of managers becomes more and more crucial for business success. Students in management information systems (MIS) must acquire fundamental theories of information systems and essential practical skills in computer applications. They must also develop the ability for life-long learning in information technology during their business education.

In the information technology era, the education for MIS students is quite challenging. Generally speaking, we would like to develop students who are more business oriented and problem driven in applying computer technology. Instead of teaching technical details (such as syntax and less-commonly used commands) and computational algorithms, we focus on the matching of business problems and computer solutions.

Interestingly, more than two decades after so-called fourth-generation computer languages proliferated in 1980s, the information industry still heavily relies on third-generation computer languages such as C, C++, Java, VB.NET, etc. In fact, in the modern computer age, there is a great variety of computer languages. A brief summary of computer languages commonly used in the MIS field is shown in the figure on the next page.

To meet the challenge of the ever changing computer technology, we must teach core components of computer technology in business and encourage students to develop their ability to learn independently.

This textbook is designed for business undergraduate MIS majors who study computer problem solving and programming for business. To avoid unnecessary overlap with the components of computer applications to the business fields covered in other courses, this book excludes word processing, databases and spreadsheets, which are expected to be taught in other information systems courses. The emphasis of this textbook is placed on computer languages that are commonly used in today's information systems for business, including

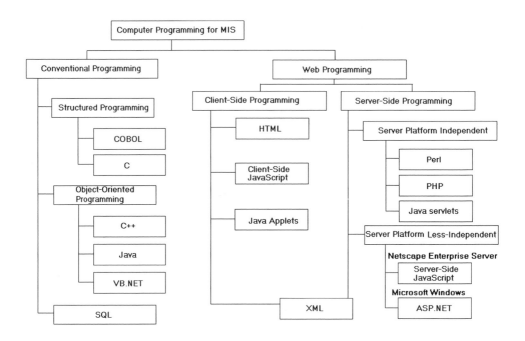

COBOL, C, C++, HTML, JavaScript, Java, VB.NET, Visual Basic for Applications, Perl, PHP, ASP.NET, XML, and SQL. This textbook consists of eleven chapters. It can be used for two computer programming courses for MIS majors: one is an introductory programming course, and the other is a Web application development course that focuses on server-side programming. The instructor may choose several chapters for a one-semester course, depending upon the needs. Overall, this book is a survey handbook of programming languages for MIS majors.

Chapter 1 provides an overview of COBOL which is old, but is still one of the most popular computer languages used in management information systems. It begins by describing the concepts of data files. Data file processing is not only the central part of COBOL, but also important for all third-generation computer languages. In this chapter, student will learn three organization structures of data files, and their applications to business data process. Using an example of payroll processing, this chapter explains the use of core statements of COBOL in business data processing. The appendices of this chapter provide manuals for running COBOL programs on mainframe.

Chapter 2 explains C++ and object-oriented programming. C++ are more likely to be used in software development instead of in business applications directly; nevertheless, the concept of object-oriented programming of C++ has been generally applied to all fields of business computing. Through several examples, students will learn basic skills of object-oriented programming.

Chapter 3 introduces tools of Web page development—HTML and JavaScript. In this chapter, students will learn how to develop Web pages by applying these so-called client-side programming tools, and will understand the source behind Web pages.

Chapter 4 discusses the modern computer language Java. Java covers a huge computational spectrum. In this chapter, students will learn Java applets, standard

Java programming (AWT and non-AWT), and Java servlets. The focal point of this chapter is placed on the computing capability of Java in the Internet computing environment.

Chapter 5 introduces Visual Basic (VB) and the concept of graphical user interface. VB.NET is becoming one of the most popular computer languages in MIS computing. Through several business application examples, this chapter explains core features of VB.NET.

Chapter 6 is an extension of Chapter 5. It provides an overview of Visual Basic for Applications (VBA), which is integrated in Microsoft spreadsheets (Excel) and databases (Access). Through this chapter, students will learn how to use Visual Basic for Applications to integrate Excel spreadsheets and develop decision support systems.

Chapter 7 introduces Perl for CGI programming. Students will learn typical examples of Perl programming, and understand the principles of the use of Perl to implement Web-based business applications based on the conventional CGI technology.

Chapter 8 introduces PHP script. Students will learn typical examples of PHP programming, and understand the unique features of PHP to implement Web-based business applications.

Chapter 9 introduces ASP.NET, the Web application development environment of the Microsoft platform. Students will learn major features of ASP.NET which are similar to Java servlets, CGI programming, or PHP in terms of Web application development, as well as unique features of ASP.NET.

Chapter 10 introduces XML. Students will learn typical examples of XML programming, and understand the application context of XML and its structure. The concepts of XHTML and XBRL are also introduced in this chapter.

Chapter 11 introduces SQL. Students will learn major features of SQL for querying and updating the databases. The role of SQL in Web applications is also briefly introduced through an ADO.NET example.

This textbook makes a balance between the classical information system languages, namely, COBOL and C++, and other modern computer languages such as Java and ASP.NET. Through the study of these computer languages, students will learn the migration of computer languages. The book introduces many key concepts of procedural programming languages in Chapters 1 and 2 for beginners. To avoid unnecessary duplications, other chapters do not repeat these key concepts in detail while applying them to examples. The book summarizes the six key concepts shared by all procedural programming languages on the last pages of the book. This summary is particularly useful for students who might not start with Chapters 1 and 2, but need to understand these concepts during the study of other chapters.

Students who use this book are expected to develop practical skills as well as have a bird's-eye view of computer programming. The objective of this book is that students will understand the characteristics of traditional file processing in legacy information systems, the philosophies of structured programming and object-oriented programming, the means of multimedia presentations on the Internet, the concept of human–computer interface design and decision support systems, and the basics of Web-based business applications for

Key Knowledge Elements	Requirements of IS Education (IS'02—Competency Level and Body of Knowledge Elements)	COBOL (Legacy File Processing) SQL (Database query)	C (Classical Function-Oriented) C++ (Classical Object Oriented)	HTML JavaScript PHP Java Applets (Web Applications—Client-Side)	Java Servlets APS.NET Perl XML (WebApplications—Server-Side)	VB.NET Java (AWT) (Graphical User Interfaces)
File processing	4 1.2.1 Formal problems and problem solving	×				
Simple data types	4 1.2.4 Abstract data types	×	×	×	×	×
If-then control	4 1.2.1 Formal problems and problem solving	×	×	×	×	×
Loop	4 1.2.1 Formal problems and problem solving	×	×	×	×	×
Function orientation	3 1.2.4.4 Modules and coupling	×	×	×		
Object orientation	3 3.3.6 Object-oriented methodologies		×	×	×	×
Web page development	4 3.9.7 Software development			×	×	
Client-server computing	3 3.1.2 Systems concepts			×	×	
Graphical user-computer interfaces	4 3.9.6 Human-computer interfaces			×	×	×
Environments of languages	3 1.3.7 Programming languages, design, implementation	×	×	×	×	×

e-commerce. Upon completion of the courses, students should be able to write computer programs in these computer languages to solve simple business problems related to information systems. More importantly, students will have developed the ability to learn details of these programming languages and new programming languages by themselves.

The relationships between the key knowledge elements offered in individual languages and the general requirements of IS education is summarized in the table earlier in this section. As shown in the table, the IS2002 model curriculum <http://www.is2002.org/> defines computer literacy as a set of knowledge elements related to problem solving using computer technology. Most knowledge elements listed in the table, such as abstract data types, modules and coupling, software development, human–computer interfaces, object-oriented methodologies, and programming languages can be acquired only through learning these computer languages.

In this textbook, a huge amount of material about computer languages that are commonly used in the modern MIS computing field are boiled down to a practical workable volume. Students must use this textbook fully. The textbook includes many practical computer programming examples. Reading these examples is necessary, but not sufficient. To learn computer programming, students must perform hands-on practices on computers. Students are required to conduct several programming projects for the courses. In order to learn the syntax and programming techniques through the textbook examples before they start working on a project for a language, students ought to edit (type and think!) these programming examples by themselves, run these programs, and examine the execution results. In many cases, students should read additional relevant reference books and manuals about these computer languages to complete course projects in creative ways. Similar to learning human natural languages, students are always encouraged to learn more about programming languages beyond a single textbook.

In summary, this textbook is to teach students "how to walk," and students are supposed to learn "how to run."

Finally, the first author would like to thank the faculty members and students of Earle P. Charlton College of Business, University of Massachusetts Dartmouth, who have encouraged the teaching–learning approach of "one-course-to-many-languages" for management information systems majors since 1998.

Shouhong Wang, PhD
University of Massachusetts, Dartmouth
<swang@umassd.edu>

Hai Wang, PhD
Saint Mary's University,
Halifax, Nova Scotia
<hwang@smu.ca>

List of Credits

Alpha VMS COBOL, VMS C, and VMS C++ are trademarks of Hewlett-Packard and COMPAQ.
 PowerTerm for Windows is a trademark of ERICOM Software.
 Windows, MS-DOS, Notepad, WordPad, Windows Explorer, Internet Explorer, Visual Basic, Visual Basic for Applications, Excel, Access, Jscript, Active Server Pages (ASP), Window Media Player, .NET, VB.NET, C#, ASP.NET, Visual Studio .NET, Visual Web Developer 2005 Express Edition, are trademarks of Microsoft Corporation.
 Java, J2SE, Java 2 SDK, JDK, JSWDK, and Javascript are trademarks of Sun Microsystems.
 Netscape is trademark of Netscape Communications Corporation.
 ActivePerl is a trademark of ActiveState Tool Corp.
 PHP is copyrighted by The PHP Group.
 Apache is copyrighted by The Apache Software Foundation
 EasyPHP is copyrighted by EasyPHP.
 XML is a trademark of World Wide Web Consortium (W3C).

Typographical Conventions

Certain typographical conventions are adopted throughout the book.

Bold text is used to set off important words or concepts.

`Mono-space` text is used for computer language code. The numerical line numbers marked in computer programs are used for explanations, and should not be typed for programming.

`[Mono-space]` text is used to indicate menu items, or general terms of user-defined statements. The brackets [ ] should not be typed for programming.

Mono-Space text is used to indicate general names of variables and arguments in syntax descriptions.

<u>Underlined</u> text is used to indicate user-typed commands in the operating system.

Compilers/Interpreters Used for the Programs in This Book

COBOL: VMS COBOL
C/C++: VMS C/C++
HTML: Netscape or Microsoft Internet Explorer
JavaScript: Netscape or Microsoft Internet Explorer
Java Applets, Free-Standing Java: JDK (for Windows)
Java Servlets: JDK and JSWDK (for Windows)
VB.NET: Microsoft .NET 2005
Visual Basic for Application: Microsoft Excel
Perl: ActivePerl (for Windows)
PHP: EasyPHP
ASP.NET: Microsoft .NET 2005
XML: Microsoft Internet Explorer
SQL: Microsoft Access, and Microsoft .NET 2005

Chapter 1

COBOL and File Processing

1.1 Introduction to COBOL

Before the early 1960s, no language was specifically suited to business tasks. In 1960, **C**ommon **B**usiness **O**riented **L**anguage (COBOL) was developed by Conference on Data Systems Languages (CODASYL). COBOL was a great success. In fact, a significant proportion of software in many management information systems (MIS) was written in COBOL and is still in use. Such systems are called **legacy systems** in that they are too valuable to discard but they represent a drain on information systems resources in maintenance and reengineering. COBOL has been standardized by American National Standard Institute (ANSI). Knowledge of COBOL is definitely an asset for business students who pursue their major in information systems.

Traditionally, COBOL is a file processing language. However, COBOL on most mainframe computers can be a **host language** of a **database management system**; namely, programmers are able call up functions of a database management system to manipulate databases in a COBOL program. This book focuses on COBOL for file processing.

Typically, COBOL programs run on mainframe computers, as illustrated in Appendix 1.2. However, there have been PC versions of COBOL compilers. NetCOBOL (previously called Fujitsu COBOL) is one of them, which is available on the Internet and can be downloaded free of cost.

1.2 Legacy Information Systems

Before the 1970s, MIS were usually built on mainframe computers. Such computing environment is called monolithic computing. In monolithic computing,

1

the mainframe computer processes all information for the business, although there might be many dummy terminals linked to the computer. The computer languages used in that period are known as **third generation computer languages** (3GL), such as COBOL and PL/1. 3GL have simple human-computer interfaces and limited built-in computational functions. A programmer who is using 3GLs must learn the syntax of the language, and describe detailed procedures to instruct the computer to perform a processing task. Today, in the year 2007, many enterprises are still using computer programs developed 30–40 years ago. This is because these computer programs are still useful and valuable. These information systems built in the 1960s and 1970s are called **legacy systems** as has been defined earlier.

The issues of legacy systems are not easy to solve. The reality is that the information industry still needs people to maintain legacy systems by manipulating 3GL. For the purpose of electronic commerce education, it is imperative that MIS students have essential knowledge and practical programming skills of third generation languages. By learning 3GL (typically, COBOL), students understand what is taking place within the computer during processing of business information. Practical programming skills are certainly beneficial for students in lifelong learning and job selection.

COBOL, FORTRAN, BASIC, APL, PL/1, and C are a few of the many 3GL. Third generation computer languages are flexible to use, and have been the foundations of computer applications. In fact, **fourth generation computer languages** (4GL) are built upon third generation languages, and many spreadsheets and database management systems are commonly implemented in C.

One of the common characteristics of 3GL is **file processing**, which is important for MIS. In business, people need to process huge volumes of data, such as personnel data, customer data, and inventory data. Because the CPU memory is limited and volatile, these data must be stored on a secondary storage medium such as disk. However, it takes much longer time to read or write data on secondary storage than it takes in the CPU memory. We will describe how these data are organized into files and processed. File is the simplest form of data storage, and is the basis for **data base**. In database courses you will learn more about the differences between file processing systems and database systems.

1.2.1   File, Record, Data Item, and Key

Terms related to data processing that are commonly used in the field are:

File A collection of a set of records. Note that, the term file is often overloaded. For example, a computer program is stored on disk as a "file." However, in this section, we use file exclusively for **data file**, but not computer program file.

- **Record** A description of a single transaction or entity in a repetitive file. A record is a collection of a set of data items.
- **Data Item**, or **Field**, or **Attribute** A description of a single characteristic of a transaction or entity. The three terms are interchangeable.

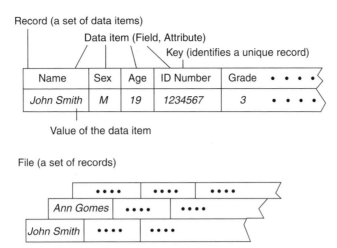

Figure 1.1   File, record, data item, and key.

- **Key** A data item, or a group of data items, that uniquely identifies a record in a file.
- **Data** Individual facts, or the value of a data item.

The hierarchy representing the relationship between file, record, data item, and key is illustrated in Figure 1.1.

1.2.2   Tape and Disk

Because CPU memory is limited and temporary, computer programs and data must be stored on secondary storage. Paper, magnetic tape, magnetic disk, and optical disk are some of the many forms of secondary storage. Magnetic disk is the most commonly used second storage media. Second to disk, magnetic tape is also often used in mass data storage. Conceptually, a magnetic tape for computers is similar to a cassette. Figure 1.2 illustrates the two major secondary storage devices.

1.2.3   Three Basic File Organizations

1.2.3.1   Sequential File

In a sequential file, records are stored in physically adjacent locations on the storage medium (e.g. tape, disk, paper printout) as depicted in Figure 1.3.

To find a particular record, the computer has to search the file by checking the records one by one, starting at the beginning of the file, until it finds the desired record or reaches end of file (EOF) in the case of failure.

Advantages:

1. Saves space.
2. No record key is required.

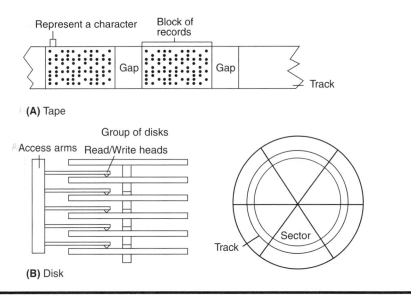

Figure 1.2   Tape and disk.

3. Efficient when all of the records are sequentially processed (e.g. payroll processing).
4. Can be implemented on any media.

Disadvantages:

1. It would take a long time to find a particular record.
2. It is difficult to update. For example, it is difficult to insert a record.

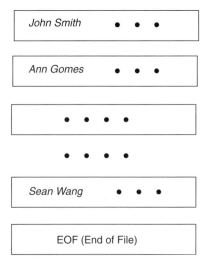

Figure 1.3   Sequential file.

1.2.3.2   Random File

A random file organization allows immediate, direct access to individual records in a file. The essence of random accessing is the ability to quickly produce an address from a record's key. Note that random files are only for disk, not for tape or paper.

The fundamental component of data access in the random file organization is the conversion of the record key of a record to the address of the record on the disk though a formula called **hashing function**.

The feature of hashing functions can be explained with an example. However, hashing functions used in real systems are much more complicated than the example given. Here, hashing function is defined as:

Address of record = remainder of [Record Key/111]

Suppose there is a record with its Record Key = 4567. Then,

Address of record = remainder [4567/111] = 16

That is, this record (its key value = 4567) is stored to the location with the address 16. Later, if one wants to find a record with the key = 4567, then the computer will quickly calculate the address according to the hashing function and immediately find it at this address.

Conflict Problem

No matter how sophisticated a hashing function is, there always exist synonyms, or conflicts; that is, several key values map onto the same address. For example, in the above case of hashing function,

```
Key 4567    ==>   Address 16
Key 349     ==>   Address 16
Key 1126    ==>   Address 16
      . . . . . .
```

To solve this problem, data structure techniques of pointer and overflow area are commonly used in dealing with conflict. Figure 1.4 briefly illustrates the solution.

You will learn that COBOL supports random files, and it can handle conflict automatically.

Advantages:

1. It can access an individual record very fast.
2. It is efficient in updating (e.g., adding and modifying records).

Disadvantages:

1. Sequential access is impossible.
2. A record key is necessary.

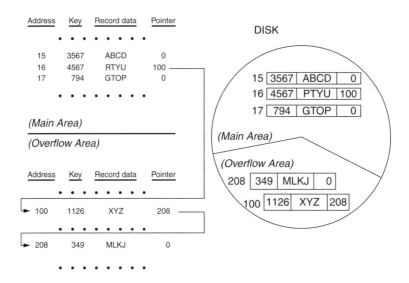

Figure 1.4   Conflict and its solution in random files.

3. Wastes spaces.
4. Synonyms make the process slower.

1.2.3.3   Indexed File

An indexed file keeps an index table which associate record keys with addresses. An index table is comparable to a content table in a textbook (see Figure 1.5).

An index table may be sorted based on a sequence of the record key values if needed. Usually, an index table is small and can be manipulated in the CPU memory. Hence, the conversion of a record key to the address of the record takes little time. However, if a data file is extremely large, then its index table will be so large that the index table itself is a disk file supported by a "second level" index table.

Advantages:

1. It can be used in both sequential and random access. Processing speed is fairly good for both.
2. It is efficient in adding a record, sorting and updating the file.

Disadvantages:

1. A record key is necessary.
2. If the data file is huge, then several levels of index tables are needed, and processing will be slow.

COBOL provides functions to support all of these three file organizations. COBOL programmers do not design the access mechanism in detail; that is, programmers do not define hashing functions for a random file and do not

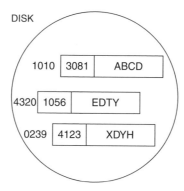

Index Table

Record Key	Address of Record
3081	1010
4123	0239
1056	4320
. . . .	. . . .

DISK

1010 | 3081 | ABCD

4320 | 1056 | EDTY

0239 | 4123 | XDYH

Figure 1.5   Index table in an indexed file.

build an index table for an indexed file. They only write sentences in a COBOL program to declare what organizations of files are being used.

1.2.4   Types of Business Data Files

An information system usually uses many data files for business processes. Some of the major types of files in business data processing are elaborated.

1.2.4.1   Master Files

A master file stores permanent data for the firm. For example, an employee file in the payroll system, a student file in the registration system, and an inventory file in the warehouse system are all master files. Master files can be read, modified, and appended, but can never be deleted from the system. Usually, a master file can be processed not only sequentially, but also randomly. For instance, the marketing department not only needs to quickly find a particular customer from the customer master file, but also would like to print out an entire list of all the customers. Thus, the organization for a master file is usually an indexed file.

1.2.4.2   Transaction Files

A transaction file stores day-to-day business operational data. An order log, which records date of order, number of the item to be ordered, amount of order, etc., in the order processing system is a transaction file. A transaction file is used to update a master file. Usually, a transaction file must be processed from the first record to the last one. Also, no record key is usually involved in transaction file. Hence, a transaction file is usually a sequential file. In principle, transaction files are temporary.

1.2.4.3   Reference Files

Reference files provide reference data. For example, tax rate tables and zip code tables are reference files. These are permanent data files and are usually random files.

1.2.4.4   Backup Files

For the purposes of security and archive, a data file is often saved to a backup file from time to time. The created backup file is occasionally used for system recovering or auditing. To save space, the sequential organization is used for backup files.

1.2.4.5   Working Files

In processing a huge amount of data, CPU memory may not be large enough. Hence, to use the second storage as an extended memory, the programmer must create working files. Working files are temporary. All the three basic file organizations may be used for working files. Few working files are used in a simple computer program.

1.2.4.6   Report Files

Report files are different from other types of files discussed earlier, in that report files are used to present information for humans, and are stored (or printed) on paper. Physically, the organization of a report files is always sequential.

1.2.5   Design of Organizations of Files

As discussed earlier, each of the three organizations of data files has its advantages and disadvantages. The design of the organization of a file always depends upon the business application context. However, there are general match relationships between the types of data files and organizations, as summarized in Figure 1.6. For instance, a master file is commonly an indexed file, but can also be a random file if sequential access is not required.

1.3   General Structure of COBOL—Four Divisions

A COBOL program is organized like the English language, but is much formalized. It is divided into four divisions, each of which must be dealt with in order.

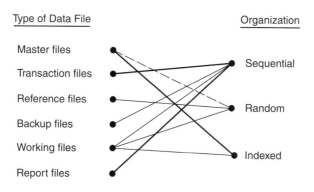

Figure 1.6   Select the organization for a data file.

1. **IDENTIFICATION DIVISION** shows the name of the program, and may give any other documentation deemed necessary.
2. **ENVIRONMENT DIVISION** describes the hardware configuration, and specifies the data files.
3. **DATA DIVISION** describes the data structure of files and working storage used in the program. The formats of data records are described in this division. Working storage in the main memory is also defined in this division.
4. **PROCEDURE DIVISION** expresses the program execution logic. The previous three divisions do not cause explicit actions of execution. Only this division contains the processing instructions.

The following is a toy-example COBOL program. The program in Listing 1.1 is to display "HELLO, WORLD!" on the computer screen. This example is used to explain some concepts of COBOL.

```
IDENTIFICATION DIVISION.
PROGRAM-ID.     EXAMPLE1.
ENVIRONMENT     DIVISION.
DATA            DIVISION.
PROCEDURE       DIVISION.
DISPLAY-MY-MESSAGE.
    DISPLAY     "HELLO, WORLD!".
    STOP RUN.
```

Listing 1.1   Simple COBOL example.

1.4   COBOL Words

A COBOL program is a set of **COBOL words** and **symbols**. A legal COBOL word consists of character (A–Z), digits (0–9), and hyphens (-). It must contain at least one character, and must be no longer than 30 letters. All characters in a COBOL word must be in capital. A legal COBOL word must not contain a space, and must not start with or terminate with a hyphen. A COBOL symbol could be +, −, *, /, \$, etc. Any COBOL word and symbol must be surrounded with spaces.

COBOL words are of two types, **reserved words** and **user-defined words**. COBOL reserved words have specific meanings and represent specific features or functions. In the example of Listing 1.1, those in bold font (just for the purpose of illustration) are COBOL reserved words, whereas, user-defined words are **program-name**, **data-names**, and **procedure-names**, defined by the programmer. A list of commonly used COBOL reserved words is shown in Appendix 1.1. Reserved words cannot be used as user-defined words. To avoid misuses of reserved words, we often use digits (0–9) and hyphens (-) in addition to alphabetic characters (A–Z) for user-defined words.

One of the characteristics of COBOL is self-documenting. COBOL requires very precise structure, whereas, users may define data names and procedure names as naturally as possible.

1.5   COBOL Program Format—Positioning, Spacing, and Punctuation

In COBOL, each sentence must be written in a specific format. For instance, a certain type of sentence must be written from a certain column, and each sentence must end with a **period**. In the standard COBOL coding form, any COBOL sentence starts after positions 8 except for a comment line which must have an asterisk sign (*) in position 7. Some sentences even start after position 12. However, many computer editors, such as the VMS Editor on Alpha computer, changed the rules and made online editing easier (see Appendix 1.2).

To improve the readability of the program, programmers often insert comment lines in the program (see an example in Listing 1.2 where the first column is assumed to be position 7). During compiling, computer ignores those comment lines.

```
*******************************
 IDENTIFICATION DIVISION.
 PROGRAM-ID.    MYCBL1.
*******************************
 ENVIRONMENT    DIVISION.
 *                              *
 * (SELECT FILES HERE)          *
 *                              *
*******************************
 DATA           DIVISION.
 *                              *
 * (DEFINE DATA STRUCTURE HERE) *
 *                              *
*******************************
 PROCEDURE      DIVISION.
 DISPLAY-MY-MESSAGE.
```

```
     DISPLAY    "HELLO, WORLD!".
     STOP RUN.
******** E N D ***************
```

Listing 1.2   Documenting COBOL programs by inserting comment lines.

Some important selected rules of COBOL programming are:

1. A word should not exceed 30 characters (no space), and should not begin or end with a hyphen.
2. At least one blank space must appear between words, or between a word and an arithmetic operator.
3. Each sentence must be ended with a period, and it must be followed by at least one blank space.

1.6   Typical Examples of COBOL Programs

Remembering syntax and rules through rote memorization is the most tedious method of learning computer languages. "Reading and programming" is the best method to learn COBOL. The first step of learning COBOL is to read several typical COBOL programs. To provide typical COBOL programs, four examples of COBOL program for a payroll processing system are given in Listings 1.3, 1.4, 1.5, and 1.6. After each of the example programs, we provide detailed explanations for the COBOL sentences used in the program.

The purpose of the first COBOL program in Listing 1.3 is to build an indexed file for employees. Once the employee master file has been built, it can be used for queries and other data processing. The second COBOL program in Listing 1.4 is to create a sequence data file that records each employee's work hours. These two programs in our examples are actually data entry support programs. The third COBOL program in Listing 1.5 manipulates the data files created by the previous two programs for payroll processing. The fourth COBOL program in Listing 1.6 is a maintenance program that is used to make modifications to the master file. The relationships between the COBOL programs and the data files are depicted in Figure 1.7.

1.6.1   Build a Master File

To build a master file for a COBOL application, one must create a COBOL program to allow the user to do data entry. The computer program accepts the data from the keyboard, and then writes them to the disk. Since a master file is usually used for various purposes, the organization of master file should be indexed.

```
1     IDENTIFICATION     DIVISION.
2     PROGRAM-ID.        EMPLOYEE.

3     ENVIRONMENT        DIVISION.
4     CONFIGURATION      SECTION.
5     SOURCE-COMPUTER.   ALPHA.
```

```
 6     INPUT-OUTPUT        SECTION.
 7     FILE-CONTROL.
 8         SELECT  EMPLOYEE-FILE
 9          ASSIGN TO "EMP.DAT"
10            ORGANIZATION IS INDEXED
11            ACCESS MODE IS DYNAMIC
12            RECORD KEY IS EMPLOYEE-ID.

13     DATA               DIVISION.
14     FILE               SECTION.
15     FD  EMPLOYEE-FILE
16         LABEL RECORDS ARE STANDARD.
17     01  EMPLOYEE-RECORD.
18         02   EMPLOYEE-ID        PIC X(2).
19         02   EMPLOYEE-NAME       PIC X(30).
20         02   EMPLOYEE-ADDRESS    PIC X(30).
21         02   EMPLOYEE-PAY-RATE   PIC 99.

22     WORKING-STORAGE    SECTION.
23     01  W-EMPLOYEE-ID             PIC X(2)  VALUE "00".

24     PROCEDURE          DIVISION.
25     MAIN-PROCEDURE.
26         PERFORM INITIALIZE-PROCESS.
27         PERFORM ACCEPT-DATA-PROCESS
28                UNTIL W-EMPLOYEE-ID = "99".
29         PERFORM TERMINATION-PROCESS.
30         STOP    RUN.

31     INITIALIZE-PROCESS.
32         OPEN  OUTPUT  EMPLOYEE-FILE.
33         DISPLAY  "INPUT EMPLOYEE ID NUMBER (2 DIGITS):".
34         ACCEPT W-EMPLOYEE-ID.

35     ACCEPT-DATA-PROCESS.
36         MOVE  W-EMPLOYEE-ID  TO  EMPLOYEE-ID.
37         DISPLAY  "INPUT EMPLOYEE NAME (30 LETTERS):".
38         ACCEPT  EMPLOYEE-NAME.
39         DISPLAY  "INPUT EMPLOYEE ADDRESS (30 LETTERS):".
40         ACCEPT  EMPLOYEE-ADDRESS.
41         DISPLAY  "INPUT EMPLOYEE PAY RATE (2 DIGITS):".
42         ACCEPT  EMPLOYEE-PAY-RATE.
43         WRITE   EMPLOYEE-RECORD
44            INVALID KEY DISPLAY "INVALID KEY ERROR!".
45         DISPLAY "INPUT NEXT EMPLOYEE ID NUMBER (2 DIGITS):".
46         ACCEPT W-EMPLOYEE-ID.

47     TERMINATION-PROCESS.
48         CLOSE  EMPLOYEE-FILE.
49         DISPLAY  "THANK YOU FOR DATA ENTRY!".
```

Listing 1.3   Example of COBOL program: build a master file.

Note that the line numbers in the program are just for references, and must not be typed in the program. Before we learn detailed syntax of COBOL statements, we explain how the COBOL program in Listing 1.3 works.

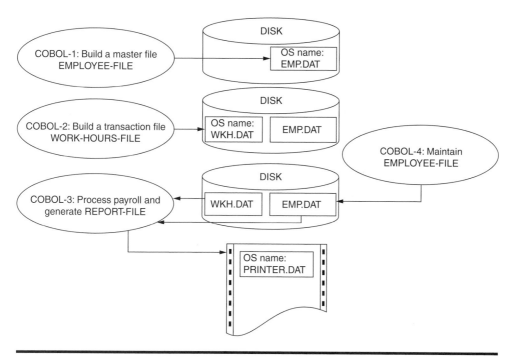

Figure 1.7   Payroll processing example.

Lines **1–2** are the IDENTIFICATION DIVISION. In this case, only one statement of PROGRAM-ID is used for the documentation purpose.

Lines **3–12** are the ENVIRONMENT DIVISION which defines the computing environment of this program. Lines **4–5** indicate the computer on which this program is run. These sentences are used only for documentation. This is because COBOL has many "dialects" on different types of computers.

Lines **6–12** are the INPUT-OUTPUT SECTION and describe input–output devices needed for this program. In this simple program, only one paragraph FILE-CONTROL is used.

Lines **8–12** is one sentence. It maps the master file we would like to build onto the disk. Lines **13–23** are the DATA DIVISION. There are two sections in this example. FILE SECTION defines the data structure for each data file. In this example, only one data file is used, and thus only one file definition (FD) statement is applied. For each FD, there is a description of data structure, starting from the record level (01) and ending with the lowest level of data elements. When the computer program is executed, it opens a buffer in the CPU memory to hold one (only one) record.

WORKING-STORAGE SECTION (lines **22–23**) describes data structures for working storage. When the computer program is executed, it opens "rooms" in the CPU memory to hold data. In this example, only one "room" is defined.

Lines **24–49** are PROCEDURE DIVISION and list all instructions for the computer to execute. In other words, the previous three divisions enables the computer to do preparations, and only this division instructs the computer to take procedural actions.

Lines **25–30** are the top-level module. Line **25** is the paragraph name. Lines **26–30** are instructions that instruct the computer to do three tasks and then shut down.

The first task is named INITIALIZE-PROCESS. When the computer executes line **26**, the execution sequence turns to line **31** where the paragraph name INITIALIZE-PROCESS is located. In this paragraph, the computer does three sub-tasks: opens the data file, displays a message for the user, and accepts a data item from the keyboard and stores it in the working storage named W-EMPLOYEE-ID. After line **34**, the **execution sequence** returns to the line right after line **26** to perform the next task. A detailed explanation about execution sequence is given in Section 1.6.10.

Lines **27** and **28** are one sentence. This sentence describes the second task as a "loop". Loop means that the computer must repeat a job until a certain condition is satisfied. In this example, the computer must repeat ACCEPT-DATA-PROCESS again and again until W-EMPLOYEE-ID becomes "99". When the computer execution sequence reaches this sentence, it turns to line **35**, where the paragraph ACCEPT-DATA-PROCESS starts.

Line **36** instructs the computer to move the component of W-EMPLOYEE-ID to the room for EMPLOYEE-ID in EMPLOYEE-RECORD. EMPLOYEE-ID can never be "99" in this case because the paragraph ACCEPT-DATA-PROCESS will not be executed once W-EMPLOYEE-ID contains "99".

Lines **37–42** are the dialog between the computer and the user and allow the user to input data of each of the employee. The data is held in the room for EMPLOYEE-RECORD.

Lines **43–44** are one sentence to instruct the computer to write an EMPLOYEE-RECORD to the disk. Note that the computer writes one record each time.

Lines **44–45** are a pair of sentences for the computer-user dialog, and allow the user to enter W-EMPLOYEE-ID for the next record. Remember that the computer is still under the control of the loop. If W-EMPLOYEE-ID is not equal to "99", the computer will repeat paragraph ACCEPT-DATA-PROCESS and allow the user to enter another employee's data. However, if the user enters "99" to W-EMPLOYEE-ID, the computer execution sequence escapes from the loop, and turns to the line right after line **28**.

Line **29** instructs the computer to perform the third task, TERMINATION-PROCESS. The computer execution sequence jumps to line **47** where the TERMINATION-PROCESS paragraph is located.

Line **48** instructs the computer to close the data file and release the disk file.

Line **49** is a message for the user that the computer program has been executed successfully.

One important concept of programming to learn is that the computer execution sequence is not the same as the order of programming code lines. In COBOL, except for the first paragraph, the order of other paragraphs in PROCEDURE DIVISION is trivial. The computer can find the required paragraph anywhere by searching the paragraph name. For example, one may put the entire paragraph TERMINATION-PROCESS (lines **47–49**) before the INITIALIZE-PROCESS. This does not change the result of execution by any means. This concept is essentially true for other computer languages as well.

The statements of the COBOL program listed earlier are described in more detail in the following sections.

1.6.2 Identification Division

Identification division provides identifying information about the program, such as program name, author, date, organization, and security notation. Most of them are just for documentation. Only the **PROGRAM-ID** paragraph is required to include a program name. In some COBOL versions, the program name should not be longer than eight characters.

1.6.3 Environment Division

COBOL has many dialects. Environment division provides information about the computer on which this program is working. The specifications of the environment division for a PC COBOL might be different from that for a program on the Alpha mainframe. The environment division commonly has two sections: the configuration sections and input–output section.

1.6.4 Configuration Section

CONFIGURATION SECTION makes annotations of the source computer (for compiling) and object computer (for execution) for the self-documentation purpose. This section is optional, that is, it can be omitted.

1.6.5 Input-Output Section and File-Control

The **INPUT-OUTPUT SECTION** must be included if the program uses a data file. For an **indexed data file**, the syntax of this section is:

```
INPUT-OUTPUT SECTION.
FILE-CONTROL.
    SELECT [data file name] ASSIGN TO [implementor name]
        ORGANIZATION IS INDEXED
        ACCESS MODE  IS  DYNAMIC
        RECORD KEY   IS [key name].
```

We put general terms of user-defined words or statements in [ ]. The bracket [ ] should not be typed for programming. Several points are worth noting.

1. One **SELECT** sentence corresponds to one data file used in one COBOL program.
2. The data file name will be used as an "internal name" of the present program. The internal name is used for programming. The implementor name is an "external name" of the data file. It is used for the operating system of the computer and is never cited in the program elsewhere.
3. The precise format of the implementor varies from computer to computer. This is probably the only "non-standard" part of COBOL.

4. The SELECT sentence must begin in the position indented at least 4 column. The SELECT sentence is one single sentence, and has one and only one period.
5. If the data file is indexed and the **ACCESS MODE** statement is omitted, then the access mode is sequential. In this case, when entering the records during the data entry, one must maintain that the values of the record key are in the strict increasing order.
6. The record key name must be defined later in the file description (FD).

For a **sequential file**, the syntax of this section is:

```
INPUT-OUTPUT SECTION.
FILE-CONTROL.
    SELECT [data file name] ASSIGN TO [implementor name].
```

In other words, if the data file is sequential, the **ORGANIZATION** statement can be omitted, and subsequent statements are not relevant. For a print file, the organization is always sequential.

1.6.6   Data Division

Data division describes the data structure of the data files and the working variables that are used in the program. It contains several sections such as file section, working storage section, screen section, and linkage section. We study file section and working storage section in this book.

1.6.7   File Section and FD

The **file section** includes file description (**FD**) statement and the data structure for the file record. FD statement has the following syntax.

```
FD    [disk file name]
      LABEL RECORDS ARE STANDARD.

FD    [printer file name]
      LABEL RECORDS ARE OMITTED.
```

Note that one FD statement corresponds to one data file selected in the SELECT statement, and the `data file name` in the two corresponding statements must be identical. The statement `LABEL RECORDS ARE STANDARD` or `LABEL RECORDS ARE OMITTED` is trivial in practice, but must be included. Also note that the FD statement is a single sentence, and the second line for the FD statement must be indented in the format.

An FD sentence is followed by a data structure for the data record. The entire file description paragraph (i.e., FD and the data structure) actually instructs the computer to open "rooms" (or **a buffer**) in the CPU memory to accommodate a data record. Note that COBOL communicates with the secondary storage (tape, disk, or printer) only through the "rooms" defined in FD (not "rooms" defined in WORKING-STORAGE).

1.6.8 *Data Structure and Picture*

In COBOL, data records and working variables (see WORKING-STORAGE) are described in the hierarchy style. **Level numbers** describe the relationships that exist among the data fields within a data record or a working variable. A **group item** is a field that can be further decomposed, and an **elementary item** cannot be decomposed. The level number 01 denotes the record or working variable as a whole, any level number from 02 to 49 can be used for a sub-group item or an elementary item. The level numbers must be in the increasing order, but might not be continuous. In typing, level 01 should not be indented, while other levels should be indented arbitrarily. For example,

```
01 EMPLOYEE-RECORD.
    02 EMPLOYEE-ID              PIC X(2).
    02 EMPLOYEE-NAME.
        05 EMPLOYEE-LAST-NAME   PIC X(20).
        05 EMPLOYEE-FIRST-NAME  PIC X(10).
    02 EMPLOYEE-ADDRESS         PIC X(30).
. . . . . .
```

where EMPLOYEE-NAME is a group item and should not be specified by PIC, and EMPLOYEE-LAST-NAME and EMPLOYEE-FIRST-NAME are the elementary items within EMPLOYEE-NAME. Figure 1.8 illustrates the COBOL descriptions of different data structures.

Generally, the programmer assigns a unique user-defined word to each of the data items. With one exception, the **FILLER** statement defines a data item that is not referenced elsewhere in the present program. You may use whatever name for the data item which is never cited in the present program. You will find later that the use of FILLER is much convenient.

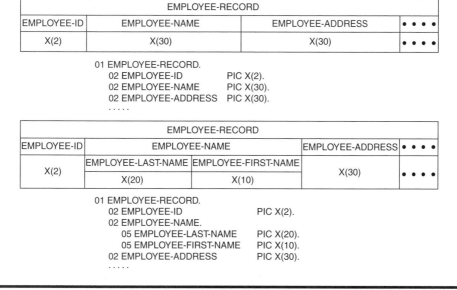

Figure 1.8   COBOL descriptions of record hierarchy.

For each of the elementary item (not for any group item), a **PICTURE (PIC)** statement is used to describe the **size** and **type** of the data field.

1. **9** indicates that the field is a **numeric** item. The numeric item can be used for calculation and exhibition.
2. **X** indicates that the field is a **character** item and cannot be computed.
3. The number within ( ) indicates the size of the field. For instance, QUANTITY PIC 9(3) means the data item QUANTITY can hold three digits. PIC 999 and PIC 9(3) are equivalent.
4. **V** means an **implied decimal point** for a computable numeric data item. For example,

   ```
   02    PAY-RATE        PIC 999V99.
   ```

   means the data item PAY-RATE can hold three digits before the decimal point and two digits after the decimal point, and this data item can be used for calculation. Note that the decimal point does not actually exist in the data item to save the CPU memory or disk space.
5. The **VALUE** statement initializes the content of a data item. Note that, without the initialization by using the VALUE statement, the initial content in a data item is unpredictable.
6. **Numeric editing symbols** specify the features of displayed or printed numeric data items, but they are not used for computable numeric data items. Major numeric editing symbols include:

   Z - Zero suppression with blank space replacement.
   * - Zero suppression with asterisk replacement.
   $ - Dollar sign. One $ sign is used for a fixed position, and two or more $ signs are used for floating.
   . - Explicit decimal point.

For instance,

```
02    PAY-RATE-P     PIC ZZ9.99.
```

means that PAY-RATE-P is a displayed or printed data item. It cannot be used for calculation.

Table 1.1 shows examples of the use of these data type symbols.

Table 1.1   COBOL Data Types

Data Type and Size	Usage of the Data Item ABC	Suppose ABC Holds Real Value 12.34, the Displayed Feature of ABC
ABC PIC 999V99	Holds data in CPU or on secondary storage (disk) for computation	01234
ABC PIC 999.99	Print for the user	012.34
ABC PIC ZZ9.99	Print for the user, suppress zeros	12.34
ABC PIC $$$9.99	Print for the user, add $ sign	$12.34
ABC PIC ***9.99	Print for the user, add * sign	**12.34

1.6.9   WORKING-STORAGE Section

The **WORKING-STORAGE** section defines any data items that do not appear in the data files but will be used for data manipulation. Actually, this section instructs the computer to open "rooms" in the CPU memory to accommodate these temporary data items. The need for working storage can be illustrated using a simple example. Suppose we want to exchange the contents of two data items, or variables (see Figure 1.9, "BEER" and "WATER"). One cannot perform this task unless a third data item (i.e., "WORKING-BOTTLE") is used.

Practically, COBOL programmers often make a large WORKING-STORAGE section to trade the simplicity of the PROCEDURE DIVISION.

1.6.10   PROCEDURE DIVISION

The PROCEDURE DIVISION contains the logic required to solve the problem. All instructions for procedural execution are included in this division. During the execution of the procedure of a program, instructions are executed in a sequence, called **execution sequence**, in which they are **encountered** (but not in the order they are listed). Some statements, such as PERFORM and IF-ELSE, control the execution sequence as will be discussed later in this chapter.

In **structured programming** the procedure division is composed by **modules**, or **procedures**, or COBOL **paragraphs**. A paragraph must be named by a user-defined word. A paragraph name should not be indented, but the COBOL command lines within a paragraph must be indented for at least four columns. The design and fragmentation of paragraphs is a kind of "art" work. The structure of the entire procedure division can be depicted using a **structure diagram** (**structure chart**). Traditional flowcharts of programming are not recommended in this book. We will return to structure diagrams later in this chapter. To make the program more readable and maintainable, usually, each paragraph has no more than 20 lines of COBOL sentences. In fact, the structured programming principle is widely applied for other third generation languages such as C.

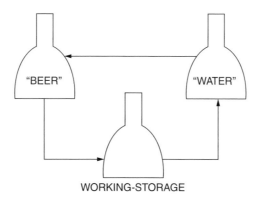

Figure 1.9   Need for working storage.

1.6.11   PERFORM Statement

The **PERFORM** statement controls the execution sequence. Two formats of the PERFORM statement are learned in our example. The first format is:

```
PERFORM [paragraph name].
```

This PERFORM statement causes the computer to execute the paragraph defined by the programmer just one time. After the execution of the entire paragraph, the computer returns back and executes the COBOL sentence next to this PERFORM statement. The second format is:

```
PERFORM [paragraph name]
      UNTIL [condition].
```

This PERFORM statement causes the computer to execute the paragraph repeatedly **until** the condition specified in the UNTIL sub-sentence becomes satisfactory. We call it **loop** (see Figure 1.10). In our example, the conditions

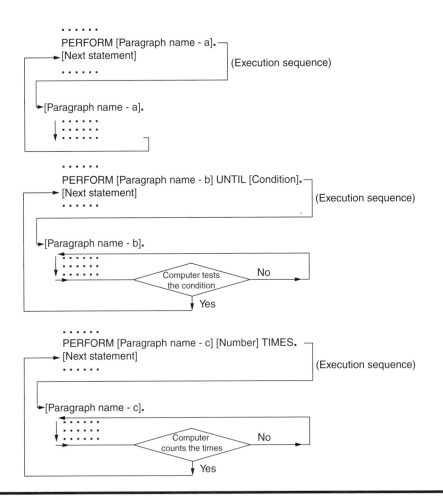

Figure 1.10   PERFORM and loop.

specified in the PERFORM statements are more likely to be related to the ACCEPT or READ statements.

Besides the above formats, the following form of loop is also often used.

```
PERFORM [paragraph name] [number] TIMES.
```

The power of the execution loop makes it possible that a few computer instructions can cause many execution steps. To indicate the execution loop in the structure chart, we put a circle on the link between the modules (seen later in the chapter, in Figure 1.14).

1.6.12   STOP RUN Statement

STOP RUN terminates the program execution and returns computer control to the operating system.

1.6.13   OPEN and CLOSE Statements

OPEN makes one or more files ready for processing. An **INPUT** file is used for read-only and an **OUTPUT** file is used for write-only. An **I-O** (stands for input-output) file can be used for "read" and "write". **CLOSE** terminates one or more files. Their syntax is:

```
OPEN  [type of access] [data file name].
CLOSE [data file name].
```

1.6.14   DISPLAY Statement

The **DISPLAY** statement displays information on the screen. It is often coupled with ACCEPT to implement simple user-computer interactions. Its syntax is:

```
DISPLAY [data item].
```

When you let the computer display an exact string on the screen, the string must be specified in quote. Note that

```
DISPLAY "OK".
```

and

```
DISPLAY OK.
```

are different. The first sentence means to display the exact **string** OK on the screen. The second sentence means to display the component currently held in the data item (or **variable**) named OK.

1.6.15   ACCEPT Statement

The **ACCEPT** statement allows the user to enter data from the keyboard into the computer. Its syntax is:

```
ACCEPT [data item].
```

Note that, in standard COBOL, the user must use the correct data format (size and type) to enter computable data item through ACCEPT. For example, suppose the program defines that

```
. . . . . .
      02    ITEM-PRICE      PIC    999V99.
. . . . . .
      ACCEPT   ITEM-PRICE.
. . . . . .
```

when the program is executed and you want to enter the actual value of 7.00 for ITEM-PRICE, you must type 00700 for it. Other formats for entering this value, such as 7, 700, $7, 7.00, $7.00, are all incorrect and will cause serious problems in calculation.

1.6.16 MOVE Statement

The operation of moving data from one "room" in the CPU memory to another is done with the **MOVE** statement. The syntax of the MOVE statement is:

```
MOVE [data item name 1, or specific value] TO [data item name 2].
```

Precisely speaking, the MOVE statement carries out a coping function. This is illustrated in Figure 1.11.

Again, note the difference between

```
MOVE    ABC    TO    XYZ.
```

and

```
MOVE    "ABC"  TO    XYZ.
```

The first sentence means to copy the components currently held in the data item named ABC to the data item named XYZ, but the second sentence means to let the data item named XYZ have the exact string ABC.

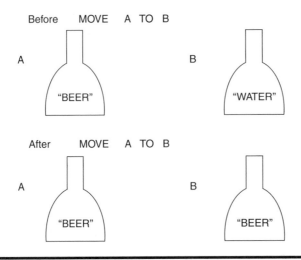

Figure 1.11   MOVE statement copies data.

1.6.17   WRITE a Record to the Disk File

The **WRITE** statement is used to transfer a record from the CPU memory to an output device (e.g., disk). Logically, only one record (not entire data file) is written to the output device once the WRITE statement is encountered. For a sequential file, its syntax is:

```
WRITE [record name].
```

For random access (the file organization could be indexed or random), the syntax is:

```
WRITE [record name]
      INVALID KEY [action when the key cannot be found].
```

1.6.18   Walk-Through a Procedure Division of a COBOL Program

Some may find that COBOL programming is tedious, but a COBOL program can probably be understood quite well by beginners due to its self-documentation style. To fully understand the structured COBOL programming, we walk-through the procedure division of the program in Listing 1.3.

In COBOL, each paragraph in the program is a **module**. The **execution sequence** of a COBOL program within a module is sentence by sentence. However, when a paragraph name is encountered in a PERFORM statement, the execution sequence shifts from the current module (calling module) to the called module. After the called module is executed completely, the execution sequence returns back to the calling module right after the PERFORM statement if the PERFORM statement is not a loop. A called module in turn contains a PERFORM statement(s), this module then becomes a calling module. If a PERFORM statement is a loop, it is executed repeatedly until a certain condition is satisfied. In principle, the execution "thread" can be infinitely long. The execution is ended when the execution "thread" reaches STOP RUN.

The following rules can be used for tracing the execution sequence of a COBOL program:

1. The execution sequence starts with the first line in the first paragraph in the PROCEDURE DIVISION.
2. Within a paragraph, the computer executes sentences one by one.
3. A PERFORM statement can call a paragraph, and the execution sequence shifts from the current paragraph (calling module) to the new paragraph (called module). If the PERFORM statement makes a loop, the called module is executed as many times as specified in the PERFORM statement or a certain condition is satisfied.
4. After the execution of the called paragraph as instructed by the PERFORM statement in the calling module, the execution sequence returns back to the calling paragraph. The computer then executes the next sentence after the PERFORM statement.

Note that the principle of the above-stated rules is also applicable for most other computer languages.

Now we examine the COBOL program of Listing 1.3 once again to see the happenings within the computer. MAIN-PROCEDURE (line **25**) is the top module of the program. This module specifies that this COBOL program performs three tasks: INITIALIZE-PROCESS (line **26**), ACCEPT-DATA-PROCESS (lines **27–28**), and TERMINATION-PROCESS (line **29**). Among the three, ACCEPT-DATA-PROCESS is a loop depending upon the value of W-EMPLOYEE-ID inputted by the user. Three modules correspond to the three tasks, as specified in the program. Start with the sentence PERFORM INITIALIZE-PROCESS (line **26**). The program thread goes to INITIAL-IZE-PROCESS module (lines **31–34**). In this module, the computer is directed to open an output file named EMPLOYEE-FILE (line **32**). The data structure of this file is defined in the FILE SECTION. **Operation 1** (marked with [1]) in Figure 1.12 illustrates the open operation.

The program then directs the computer to display a message and let the user to input an employee number, as shown by **operations 2 and 3** in Figure 1.12. After the user inputs data, the INITIALIZE-PROCESS (lines **31–34**) is completed. The program execution sequence returns to the upper module MAIN-PROCEDURE and goes to the next sentence PERFORM ACCEPT-DATA-PROCESS UNTIL W-EMPLOYEE-ID = "99" (lines **27–28**). The computer checks the value of W-EMPLOYEE-ID to see if the computer should perform the module ACCEPT-DATA-PROCESS (lines **35–46**) (**operation 4**). If the value of

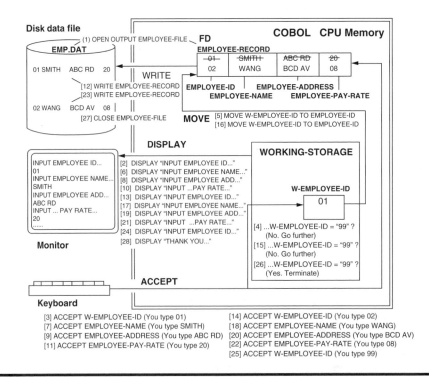

Figure 1.12   Walk-through the COBOL procedure in Listing 1.3.

W-EMPLOYEE-ID is not "99", then the program execution sequence jumps to the paragraph ACCEPT-DATA-PROCESS (lines **35–46**). In this module, the computer makes MOVE, DISPLAY, and ACCEPT operations, as illustrated by **operations 5–11** in Figure 1.12. After one EMPLOYEE-RECORD has been filled, the computer writes the record to the disk file, as illustrated by **operation 12** in Figure 1.12. The computer then lets the user to input the employee number for the next record, as illustrated by **operations 13–14**. With the new employee number, the program execution sequence returns to the upper level module MAIN-PROCEDURE again to check if the computer needs to perform ACCEPT-DATA-PROCESS repeatedly (see line **28**). This is illustrated by **operation 15**. In the example shown in Figure 1.12, the computer repeats the module ACCEPT-DATA-PROCESS (lines **35–46**), as illustrated by **operations 16–25**. This process repeats until the value of W-EMPLOYEE-ID is equal to "99", as illustrated by **operation 26**. Once the second task of ACCEPT-DATA-PROCESS (it is a loop) terminates, the program execution sequence goes to the third task TERMINATION-PROCESS (line **29**) and jumps to the TERMINATION-PROCESS module (lines **47–49**). In this module, the computer is directed to do two jobs: close the disk file (**operation 27**) and display a message to indicate the program operates successfully (**operation 28**).

1.6.19   Build a Transaction File

Now we examine the second example COBOL program that builds a transaction file. In this example, the transaction file records the work hours of the employees. A transaction file is different from a master file in many aspects. First, a transaction file does not contain permanent data other than foreign keys. For example, the work hours file can have employee numbers and the worked hours of this employee, but never contains employee names, employee addresses, etc. Second, a transaction file is used only once for data processing. For example, the work-hour file records the worked hours for the current week. After the processing of the current week payroll, it is no longer used again. Third, a transaction file is usually of sequential organization.

```
1     IDENTIFICATION    DIVISION.
2     PROGRAM-ID.       WORKHOUR.

3     ENVIRONMENT       DIVISION.
4     CONFIGURATION     SECTION.
5     SOURCE-COMPUTER.  ALPHA.

6     INPUT-OUTPUT      SECTION.
7     FILE-CONTROL.
8          SELECT   WORK-HOURS-FILE
9                   ASSIGN TO "WKH.DAT"
10                  ORGANIZATION IS SEQUENTIAL.

11    DATA              DIVISION.
12    FILE              SECTION.
13    FD   WORK-HOURS-FILE
```

```
14          LABEL RECORDS ARE STANDARD.
15      01  WORK-HOURS-RECORD.
16          02  EMPLOYEE-ID          PIC X(2).
17          02  WORK-HOURS           PIC 99.

18      WORKING-STORAGE   SECTION.
19      01  W-EMPLOYEE-ID            PIC X(2)  VALUE "00".

20      PROCEDURE           DIVISION.
21      MAIN-PROCEDURE.
22          PERFORM INITIALIZE-PROCESS.
23          PERFORM ACCEPT-DATA-PROCESS
24                  UNTIL W-EMPLOYEE-ID = "99".
25          PERFORM TERMINATION-PROCESS.
26          STOP    RUN.

27      INITIALIZE-PROCESS.
28          OPEN  OUTPUT  WORK-HOURS-FILE.
29          DISPLAY  "INPUT EMPLOYEE ID NUMBER (2 DIGITS):".
30          ACCEPT W-EMPLOYEE-ID.

31      ACCEPT-DATA-PROCESS.
32          MOVE  W-EMPLOYEE-ID  TO  EMPLOYEE-ID.
33          DISPLAY  "INPUT EMPLOYEE'S WORK HOURS (2 DIGITS):".
34          ACCEPT  WORK-HOURS.

35          WRITE   WORK-HOURS-RECORD.
36          DISPLAY  "INPUT NEXT EMPLOYEE ID NUMBER (2 DIGITS):".
37          ACCEPT W-EMPLOYEE-ID.

38      TERMINATION-PROCESS.
39          CLOSE  WORK-HOURS-FILE.
40          DISPLAY  "THANK YOU FOR DATA ENTRY!".
```

Listing 1.4   Example of COBOL program: build a transaction file.

At this point, you should be able to understand the above program because the structure of this program is the same as that of the program in Listing 1.3. The only significant difference between the two programs is the organizations of data files. Since the transaction file has to be processed for every record in the file, it should be designed as a sequential file to make the process efficient. Lines **8–10** specify the organization of the sequential data file.

After you build a file by inputting your data, you can view the data through an operating system command. For example, if you input two records for the work-hour file on Alpha mainframe and use $TYPE WKH.DAT to bring the records up on the screen, you will see the two records such as,

```
0124
0534
```

Each record has two data fields as defined in lines 16–17 in Listing 1.4. The first two characters represent the employee's ID, and the second two digits represent the work hours for that employee. Note that a disk file is used for computer processing. It may be viewed by a computer programmer for diagnosis, but is not really used for a non-technical user to read. In a COBOL disk file, there shall be no decimal points, nor space between the data fields to save space.

1.6.20   Data Processing

Next, we study the third program of the example. This program is to process the two data files and generate a payroll report.

```
1      IDENTIFICATION    DIVISION.
2      PROGRAM-ID.        PAYROLL.

3      ENVIRONMENT        DIVISION.
4      CONFIGURATION      SECTION.
5      SOURCE-COMPUTER.   ALPHA.

6      INPUT-OUTPUT       SECTION.
7      FILE-CONTROL.
8          SELECT   EMPLOYEE-FILE
9                   ASSIGN TO "EMP.DAT"
10                  ORGANIZATION IS INDEXED
11                  ACCESS MODE IS DYNAMIC
12                  RECORD KEY IS EMPLOYEE-ID-1.

13         SELECT   WORK-HOURS-FILE
14                  ASSIGN TO "WKH.DAT"
15                  ORGANIZATION IS SEQUENTIAL.

16         SELECT   REPORT-FILE
17                  ASSIGN TO PRINTER.

18     DATA              DIVISION.
19     FILE              SECTION.
20     FD  EMPLOYEE-FILE
21         LABEL RECORDS ARE STANDARD.
22     01  EMPLOYEE-RECORD.
23         02  EMPLOYEE-ID-1      PIC X(2).
24         02  EMPLOYEE-NAME      PIC X(30).
25         02  EMPLOYEE-ADDRESS   PIC X(30).
26         02  EMPLOYEE-PAY-RATE  PIC 99.

27     FD  WORK-HOURS-FILE
28         LABEL RECORDS ARE STANDARD.
29     01  WORK-HOURS-RECORD.
30         02  EMPLOYEE-ID-2      PIC X(2).
31         02  WORK-HOURS         PIC 99.

32     FD  REPORT-FILE
33         LABEL RECORDS ARE OMITTED.
34     01  REPORT-RECORD          PIC X(80).

35     WORKING-STORAGE    SECTION.
36     01  GROSS-PAY              PIC 9(4)V99.
```

```
37    01   NET-PAY                  PIC 9(4)V99.
38    01   TAX                      PIC 9(4)V99.
39    01   EOF-FLAG                 PIC XXX   VALUE SPACES.

40    01   HEAD-LINE.
41         02    FILLER    PIC X(10) VALUE "EMP.ID".
42         02    FILLER    PIC X(20) VALUE "EMPLOYEE NAME".
43         02    FILLER    PIC X(10) VALUE "WORK HOURS".
44         02    FILLER    PIC X(10) VALUE " GROSS PAY".
45         02    FILLER    PIC X(10) VALUE "       TAX".
46         02    FILLER    PIC X(10) VALUE "  NET PAY".

47    01   MONTHLY-PAYROLL-RECORD.
48         02    EMP-ID-R     PIC X(2).
49         02    FILLER       PIC X(8)  VALUE SPACES.
50         02    EMP-NAME-R   PIC X(20).
51         02    FILLER       PIC X(8)  VALUE SPACES.
52         02    WK-HOURS-R   PIC 99.
53         02    FILLER       PIC X(3)  VALUE SPACES.
54         02    GROSS-PAY-R  PIC $$$$9.99.
55         02    FILLER       PIC X(3)  VALUE SPACES.
56         02    TAX-R        PIC $$$$9.99.
57         02    FILLER       PIC X(3)  VALUE SPACES.
58         02    NET-PAY-R    PIC $$$$9.99.

59    PROCEDURE          DIVISION.
60    MAIN-PROCEDURE.
61       PERFORM INITIALIZE-PROCESS.
62       PERFORM 01-DATA-PROCESS
63            UNTIL EOF-FLAG = "YES".
64       PERFORM TERMINATION-PROCESS.
65       STOP    RUN.

66    INITIALIZE-PROCESS.
67       OPEN  INPUT EMPLOYEE-FILE
68             INPUT WORK-HOURS-FILE
69             OUTPUT REPORT-FILE.

70       MOVE  HEAD-LINE   TO  REPORT-RECORD.
71       WRITE REPORT-RECORD.
72       READ  WORK-HOURS-FILE
73            AT END  MOVE  "YES"  TO  EOF-FLAG.

74    01-DATA-PROCESS.
75       MOVE  EMPLOYEE-ID-2 TO EMPLOYEE-ID-1.
76       READ  EMPLOYEE-FILE
77            KEY IS EMPLOYEE-ID-1
78        INVALID KEY DISPLAY "RECORD IS NOT FOUND: ERROR!".

79       PERFORM 02-CALCULATE-PAYMENT.
80       PERFORM 02-WRITE-A-PAYROLL-RECORD.
81       READ  WORK-HOURS-FILE
82            AT END  MOVE  "YES"  TO  EOF-FLAG.

83    02-CALCULATE-PAYMENT.
84       COMPUTE  GROSS-PAY = EMPLOYEE-PAY-RATE * WORK-HOURS.
```

```
85              IF   GROSS-PAY > 1000
86                   COMPUTE  TAX = GROSS-PAY * 0.25
87              ELSE
88                   COMPUTE  TAX = GROSS-PAY * 0.20.
89              COMPUTE  NET-PAY = GROSS-PAY - TAX.

90    02-WRITE-A-PAYROLL-RECORD.
91         MOVE EMPLOYEE-ID-2   TO   EMP-ID-R.
92         MOVE EMPLOYEE-NAME   TO   EMP-NAME-R.
93         MOVE WORK-HOURS      TO   WK-HOURS-R.
94         MOVE GROSS-PAY       TO   GROSS-PAY-R.
95         MOVE TAX             TO   TAX-R.
96         MOVE NET-PAY         TO   NET-PAY-R.
97         MOVE MONTHLY-PAYROLL-RECORD  TO  REPORT-RECORD.
98         WRITE  REPORT-RECORD
99                AFTER ADVANCING  2  LINES.

100   TERMINATION-PROCESS.
101        CLOSE  EMPLOYEE-FILE
102               WORK-HOURS-FILE
103               REPORT-FILE.
104        DISPLAY "PAYROLL REPORT IS GENERATED IN PRINTER.DAT".
```

Listing 1.5   Example of COBOL program: data processing.

The above COBOL program manipulates the two data files (employee master file and work-hours transaction file) built by the previous two programs, and generates a payroll report. Let us examine to see how it works.

Lines **8–15** map the two disk data files to the disk. Lines **16–17** map the print file to the printer.

Lines **22–26** specify the data structure for EMPLOY-RECORD, and lines **29–31** specify the data structure for WORK-HOURS-RECORD. Note that since no single COBOL word is allowed to describe two different things within one COBOL program, we must use two different words for employee ID in the two records. This is the reason we use EMPLOYEE-ID-1 in line 23, and EMPLOYEE-ID-2 in line 30.

Lines **32–34** define the print data file. Since only 80 columns are available on one page of print paper, we use 80 spaces for a print record.

Lines **35–58** define six units of working storage. The first four are elementary data items, and the last two are group items. HEAD-LINE specifies the heading which will be printed on the top of the payroll report. MONTHLY-PAYROLL-RECORD will hold data for one record which will be printed on the payroll report. Changes to the two group items will change the appearances of the heading or printed records.

Lines **61–64** instruct the computer to perform three tasks before it shuts down.

The first task is implemented by lines **66–73**. Lines **67–69** open the three files. Line **70** gets the heading of the report. Line **71** writes the heading from the report record to the print file. Line **72** reads a record from the work-hours data file.

The second task is a loop specified by lines **62–63**. Line **63** means that the loop is executed until the end of the work-hours file has been reached. Remember, line **72** has read one record from the work-hours data file. If the work-hours data file is empty, the second task will never be executed. The second task is implemented by lines **74–82**. Line **75** gets the key (employee ID) from the work-hours record. This key is then used to find the employee record in the employee mater file, as stated by the sentence in lines **76–78**. Lines **77–78** mean that if the employee record cannot be found in the master file, the computer will display an error message to indicate that some one worked for hours but his/her record is not in the master file. If the program displays the error message, the payroll report becomes invalid.

Line **79** instructs the computer to do a sub-task, 02-CALCULATE-PAYMENT. The computer execution sequence then turns to line **83**. Lines **84–89** are the procedure of payment calculation. Line **84** gets gross pay. Lines **85–88** determine tax holding. Note that the tax depends on the amount of gross pay. Line **89** obtains net pay. These data of gross pay, tax, and net pay are held in the corresponding "rooms" of working storage. After line **89**, the computer execution sequence returns to line **80**.

Line **80** instructs the computer to perform the second sub-task 02-WRITE-A-PAYROLL-RECORD. The execution sequence jumps to line **90**. Lines **91–96** dump the calculated data items to MONTHLY-PAYMENT-RECORD for formatting. Now, MONTHLY-PAYMENT-RECORD is ready to print out. Line **97** moves the entire payment record to the buffer of the print file. Finally, lines **98–99** write the print record to the print file. The computer execution sequence returns to line **81** to read the next data record from the work-hours file. Line **82** means the computer has to find out whether the end of the work-hours file has been reached.

Remember that the computer is now in the loop. If the end of the work-hours file has not been reached, then lines **74** through **82** have to be repeated, as specified in lines **62–63**. Of course, when the computer repeats the loop, the two sub-tasks specified by the two paragraphs after line **83** and line **90** are also repeated accordingly. Note that the times of repeating the process should be equal to the number of records in the work-hours file.

After the loop, the computer executes line **64**, and the sequence jumps to line **100**. Lines **101–103** are one sentence to close the three files. Finally, line **104** shows a message for the user to indicate the successful execution of the program if no error message has been displayed.

The payroll report might be printed on the default printer immediately after the execution of the above-listed program, or might be stored on the disk as a printer file named "PRINTER.DAT", depending upon the system setting. If your system setting is the latter case, see the instructions in Appendix 1.2 to print the report.

Additional COBOL statements involved in Listing 1.5 are as explained in the following.

1.6.21 *READ Statement*

Once an input or input-output file is open, data can be read from the disk file by using the **READ** statement. Logically, only one record (not the entire file) is read from the secondary storage into the CPU each time when READ is encountered. Two formats of the READ statement are learned from Listing 1.5. For sequential access (the file organization could be sequential or indexed), the syntax of the READ statement is as follows:

```
READ [file name]
     AT END [action when EOF has been reached].
```

For random access (the file organization could be indexed or random), the syntax of the READ statement is as follows.

```
READ [file name]
     KEY IS [key field name]
     INVALID KEY [action when the key cannot be found].
```

1.6.22   IF-ELSE Statement

The IF-ELSE statement is to select an action(s) conditionally. Its syntax is:

```
IF [condition (is true)]
   [action 1]
ELSE
   [action 2].
```

Note that:

1. One and only one period is needed.
2. The ELSE part can be omitted if no action is taken when the tested condition is false.

The IF-ELSE statement controls the computer execution sequence. The logic of IF-ELSE statement is illustrated in Figure 1.13.

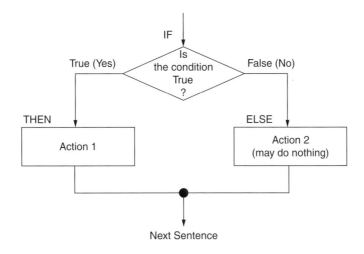

Figure 1.13   IF-ELSE statement controls the execution sequence.

1.6.23   COMPUTE Statement

Although many English style arithmetic operations, such as ADD, SUBTRACT, MULTIPLY, and DIVIDE are available in COBOL, the **COMPUTE** statement is the most powerful and convenient instruction for arithmetic calculations. The syntax of the COMPUTE statement is:

```
COMPUTE [data item name] = [arithmetic formula].
```

It means, calculate the specified arithmetic formula and place the result into the target data item. This fashion is employed in any other computer languages (e.g., C). An arithmetic formula is an expression of arithmetic calculations in a manner similar to day-to-day algebraic notation. It consists of two or more data item names and one or more operator symbols. The operator symbols include + (addition), − (subtraction), * (multiplication), / (division), and ** (exponentiation). In COBOL, sophisticated scientific calculation operations beyond the above-stated ones are not available. Note that any user-defined word and operator symbol must be surrounded with spaces.

1.6.24   WRITE a Record to the Printed Report

The syntax of the **WRITE** statement for sending a record to the printer file is:

```
WRITE [output record name]
      AFTER ADVANCING [number of lines spaced] LINES.
```

The programmer can control line spacing for the report by using the AFTER statement.

1.6.25   Maintenance

The fourth program of the example is maintenance. This COBOL program is a maintenance program. Using this program, the user is allowed to make modifications to the employee master file. Again, its data file name on the disk is "EMP.DAT".

```
1    IDENTIFICATION    DIVISION.
2    PROGRAM-ID.       MAINTAIN.

3    ENVIRONMENT       DIVISION.
4    CONFIGURATION     SECTION.
5    SOURCE-COMPUTER.  ALHPA.
6    INPUT-OUTPUT      SECTION.
7    FILE-CONTROL.
8        SELECT    EMPLOYEE-FILE
9                  ASSIGN TO "EMP.DAT"
10                 ORGANIZATION IS INDEXED
11                 RECORD KEY IS EMPLOYEE-ID
12                 ACCESS MODE IS DYNAMIC.

13   DATA             DIVISION.
14   FILE             SECTION.
15   FD  EMPLOYEE-FILE
```

```
16          LABEL RECORDS ARE STANDARD.
17     01   EMPLOYEE-RECORD.
18          02   EMPLOYEE-ID         PIC XX.
19          02   EMPLOYEE-NAME        PIC X(30).
20          02   EMPLOYEE-ADDRESS     PIC X(30).
21          02   EMPLOYEE-PAY-RATE    PIC 99.

22     WORKING-STORAGE    SECTION.
23     01   W-EMPLOYEE-ID            PIC X(2)  VALUE "00".
24     01   W-FLAG                   PIC X(2)  VALUE SPACE.

25     PROCEDURE          DIVISION.
26     MAIN-PROCEDURE.
27          PERFORM INITIALIZE-PROCESS.
28          PERFORM MODIFY-RECORDS
29               UNTIL W-EMPLOYEE-ID = "99".
30          PERFORM TERMINATION-PROCESS.
31          STOP    RUN.

32     INITIALIZE-PROCESS.
33          OPEN  I-O EMPLOYEE-FILE.
34          DISPLAY "EMPLOYEE ID (2 DIGITS) FOR MODIFICATION:".
35          ACCEPT W-EMPLOYEE-ID.

36     MODIFY-RECORDS.
37          MOVE SPACE          TO    W-FLAG.
38          MOVE W-EMPLOYEE-ID   TO    EMPLOYEE-ID.
39          READ EMPLOYEE-FILE
40               INVALID KEY   PERFORM ADD-A-RECORD
41                             MOVE  "AD"  TO  W-FLAG.
42          IF W-FLAG = SPACE    PERFORM CHANGE-A-RECORD.

43     CHANGE-A-RECORD.
44          DISPLAY   "EMPLOYEE NAME IS:    ".
45          DISPLAY    EMPLOYEE-NAME.
46          DISPLAY   "NEW NAME (30 LETTERS):".
47          ACCEPT     EMPLOYEE-NAME.
48          DISPLAY   "EMPLOYEE ADDRESS IS:   ".
49          DISPLAY    EMPLOYEE-ADDRESS.
50          DISPLAY   "NEW EMPLOYEE ADDRESS (30 LETTERS):".
51          ACCEPT     EMPLOYEE-ADDRESS.
52          DISPLAY   "EMPLOYEE PAY RATE IS:   ".
53          DISPLAY    EMPLOYEE-PAY-RATE.
54          DISPLAY   "NEW EMPLOYEE PAY RATE (2 DIGITS):".
55          ACCEPT     EMPLOYEE-PAY-RATE.
56          REWRITE    EMPLOYEE-RECORD
57              INVALID KEY DISPLAY "ERROR ON RECORD KEY!".
58          DISPLAY "EMPLOYEE ID (2 DIGITS) FOR MODIFICATION:".
59          ACCEPT     W-EMPLOYEE-ID.

60     ADD-A-RECORD.
61          DISPLAY   "ADD A NEW RECORD OF EMPLOYEE ...".
62          DISPLAY   "INPUT EMPLOYEE NAME (30 LETTERS):".
63          ACCEPT     EMPLOYEE-NAME.
64          DISPLAY   "INPUT EMPLOYEE ADDRESS (30 LETTERS):".
65          ACCEPT     EMPLOYEE-ADDRESS.
```

```
66          DISPLAY    "INPUT EMPLOYEE PAY RATE (2 DIGITS):".
67          ACCEPT     EMPLOYEE-PAY-RATE.
68          WRITE      EMPLOYEE-RECORD
69             INVALID KEY DISPLAY "ERROR ON RECORD KEY!".
70          DISPLAY "EMPLOYEE ID (2 DIGITS) FOR MODIFICATION:".
71          ACCEPT     W-EMPLOYEE-ID.

72   TERMINATION-PROCESS.
73          CLOSE      EMPLOYEE-FILE.
74          DISPLAY    "THANK YOU FOR THE MODIFICATIONS !".
```

Listing 1.6   Example of COBOL program: maintenance.

We examine how this program works. The part before line **27** is straightforward. Lines **28–29** specify the loop to perform MODIFY-RECORDS repeatedly, depending on the W-EMPLOYEE-ID inputted by the user.

Line **33** opens the I-O file. It means that the file can be used for reading and rewriting (see line 56).

Line **37** makes sure that W-FLAG is "spaces" at the beginning. Line **38** gets the employee ID which is initially entered by the user (line **35**). Lines **39–41** find the employee record from the master file. If the employee record cannot be found, then the computer performs the task of ADD-A-RECORD and sets W-FLAG to "AD". If this is the case, the computer execution sequence turns to line **60**, and executes lines **61** through **69** to allow the user to do data entry. Lines **70–71** get the next employee ID. This data item is used to determine whether the loop should be ended (line **29**).

Line **42** means that the computer has found the employee record specified by the inputted employee ID, and should execute CHANGE-A-RECORD. The execution sequence turns to line **43**.

Lines **44–55** allow the user to retype the data for this employee record. Lines **56–57** are one sentence. It uses REWRITE to overwrite the old record. Lines **58–59** get the next employee ID. Again, this data item is used to determine whether the loop should be ended (line **29**).

In this program, only the REWRITE statement is new to learn.

1.6.26   REWRITE a Record to the Disk File

The **REWRITE** statement is used to rewrite a record from the CPU memory to the disk. To change a record, one must first READ the record in the program. Note that in the OPEN statement, I–O must be used to indicate that the file is used for input as well as output.

For a sequential file, the syntax of REWRITE is:

```
REWRITE [record name].
```

For random access (the file organization could be indexed or random), the syntax is:

```
REWRITE [record name]
        INVALID KEY [action when the key is not valid].
```

1.7   Computing Context of COBOL Programming

To assist students in understanding COBOL programs, we use Figure 1.14 to illustrate common operations of file processing in the COBOL dominion. We have used a part of this COBOL dominion diagram to walk-through the COBOL program in Listing 1.3 and show the steps in Figure 1.12. Students are encouraged to use this diagram to walk-through another COBOL program step by step following the instructions in the procedure division.

After learning a typical COBOL programs, students need to write their own COBOL programs by imitating them. For instance, students may create an inventory system by modifying the four example COBOL programs. The first COBOL program can be redesigned to build an inventory master file. The second program can be rewritten for a batch of orders. The third program can be modified to print inventory-processing information. The modified COBOL programs are then compiled and executed. Through the process of debugging the programs, students become familiar with the COBOL world. If students have further questions or intend to learn more about COBOL, they should read additional COBOL textbooks and manuals.

1.8   Use 3GL

While many PC versions of COBOL provide good programming environment, typical COBOL on mainframes as a 3GL is not user friendly. Generally speaking, one has to go through several steps to make a COBOL program work. They include:

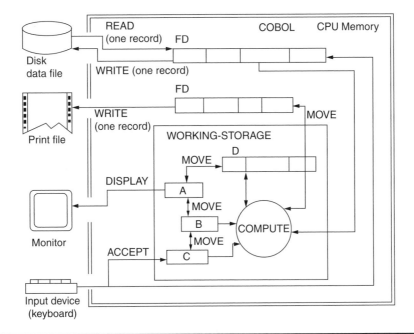

Figure 1.14   File processing in the COBOL dominion.

1. **Edit**   Using a computer Edit program, the programmer enters the COBOL program into the computer. Some PC versions of COBOL provide their own Editors, whereas others use the DOS Edit program. In the latter case, the programmer must follow the format of COBOL programs rigorously.
2. **Compile**   A compiler is a computer software that translates the source (human readable) code of the program into machine-language (object) code. After compiling a COBOL program, the compiler shows error messages to indicate the problems in the program.
3. **Link**   The object code generated by the compiler must be linked into an executable program. This step is often combined with step 4 and executed by the computer automatically.
4. **Run**   The compiled and linked program is executed. Note that even if the program has been compiled correctly, the program does not necessarily run correctly. The user must test the running results.

1.9   Debugging

It is hard to write and edit a COBOL program for once without any errors. The task of finding errors (bugs) is called debugging. Debugging is difficult and time consuming. Generally, there are two types of errors in programming: syntax errors and logic errors (runtime errors). One should also pay attention to operational errors.

1.9.1   Syntax Errors

Usually, the COBOL compiler can detect a syntax error. After compiling, the compiler provides error messages if the program contains syntax errors. The following heuristics would be useful in debugging.

1. The error messages are usually vague. They merely tell that there are errors related to the sentences indicated, but may not tell what exactly the errors are. For beginners, it might not be a good idea to try to interpret error messages.
2. If you have a hundred lines of error messages after compiling, it does not mean that the program has a hundred errors. Read the first error message, find the errors related to this message, and fix it. You then compile the modified program again.
3. An error message might indicate a specific line of code that contains errors. However, the real error may or may not be in this line. You should inspect the previous line, the next line, and all words and lines related to this line. That is why debugging is difficult and time consuming.
4. Common syntax errors are:
   - typos of misspelling a COBOL word, (e.g., ENVIROMENT DIVISION.);
   - omitting a period or having an extra period, (e.g., FD.);
   - missing space or having an extra space, (e.g., PIC X (2).);
   - violating programming format, (e.g., typing DISPLAY from the first column);
   - violating PIC definition, (e.g., 02   FILLER PIC X(3) VALUE "TOO BIG".)

- using a reserved COBOL word for a user-defined word, (e.g., 02 SPACE PIC X(5).); and
- using an undefined user-defined word.

1.9.2   Logical Errors

After a clean compile without a single error message, you can link the OBJ file. Errors may, although not commonly, occur during the link operation. After a clean link, you can run the EXE program. Logical errors or runtime errors often occur when the computer performs wrong operations or not as directed. To debug logical errors, you should use data samples to test the program based on the output of the program.

1. Exercise every possible option and check the computer outputs to see if the program does only as directed. IF statements must be examined. For instance, in the payroll example, you should use various sample data that result in different tax rates applied for tax calculations to check if the program performs correctly.
2. A program might produce unexpected results or even terminate with crash. It might be caused by wrong data types, inconsistent formats of data files, or illegal calculations (e.g., a number is divided by zero).
3. If a program is "dead", you must terminate it through interruption (e.g., by punching [Ctrl + C] simultaneously). This is more likely caused by a "dead" loop. You should check PERFORM... UNTIL ... statements and IF ... ELSE ... statements.

1.9.3   Operational Errors

An execution of a COBOL program might terminate with crash, even though the program itself does not have any syntax error or logical error. This is usually caused by incorrect operations. Typical operational errors are:

1. Try to open a data file which does not exist.
2. Try to open a data file with an incompatible format.
3. Input data with a wrong format (e.g., type 5, instead of 005, for a data item defined by PIC 999.).

1.10   Design and Documentation of 3GL Programming

There are many tools available to assist computer programmers in designing and documenting the information systems implemented in 3GL. A 3GL can be structured, object oriented, and a hybrid of the two. COBOL is a structured programming language. One of the tools for structured programming is **structure chart**. A structure chart is a hierarchy chart on which the computer program functions are represented as modules and the sequence of the execution of these modules can be traced. For instance, the COBOL program in Listing 1.5

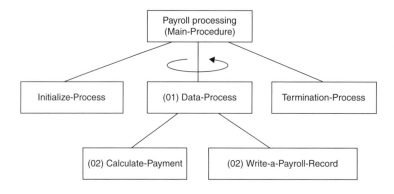

Figure 1.15   Structure chart for the COBOL program in Listing 1.5.

can be modeled in Figure 1.15. The execution sequence of modules follows the rule "**from top to down and from left to right**." The circle on the link between the two modules indicates the execution loop.

Before writing a COBOL program, the programmer should draw a structure chart to compose the structure of the program. The structure chart is a blueprint for the program, and should be modified frequently along debugging the program. The final version of the structure chart must match the product program.

The structure chart of a program is an important document for programmers. To make changes to a program, one must read the structure chart to understand the program. For instance, if one wants to make changes to the formula of calculation of tax holding in Listing 1.5, the only module needed to be changed is 02-Calculate-Payment. Changing any other module in this case is irrelevant. Apparently, structure charts are very useful for **software maintenance**.

1.11   Differences between 3GL and 4GL

The typical manner of MIS based on 3GL before the PC revolution is **batch processing**, as shown in Figure 1.16a. In batch processing, data is grouped together as source file before being inputted into the computer for processing. A job submitted to the computer might be processed a few hours or even a few days later depending on the job schedule for the CPU. The output is created when the job is processed. Usually, the output is generated in the central computing center and then distributed to the user by mail. For example, in a typical batch processing system for payroll, data entry clerks use keypunch machines to code the original data of work hours onto punched cards, or use key-to-tape or key-to-disk machines to enter the data onto tapes or diskettes. These punched cards, tapes, or diskettes are then read by the computer and stored into a transaction file waiting for the busy CPU which is supposed to do many things "simultaneously" for the organization. Once the CPU is available for the payroll

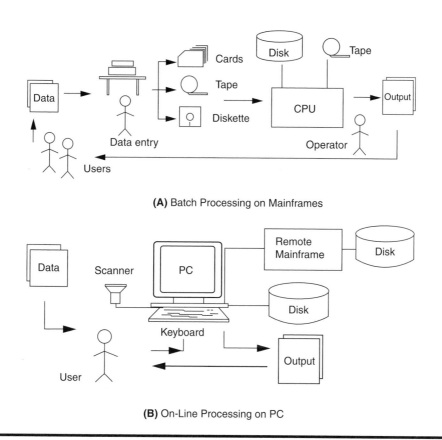

(A) Batch Processing on Mainframes

(B) On-Line Processing on PC

Figure 1.16   Information process approaches.

processing, the transaction file and the employee master file are processed by the computer programs, and checks and other reports are generated. These outputs are delivered to the payroll departments.

Due to the low prices of PC, and input and or output devices, the process approach on PC is different from the traditional one on mainframes. It is called **on-line processing**.

1. The user of the PC is the operator of the PC at the same time.
2. The PC is dedicated to a job each time.
3. The PC can be linked to a mainframe through the network, and presents the user-computer interface.
4. Data is entered into the PC directly from the keyboard or scanner.
5. The outputs of the computer, including the printout and screen display, are easy to access by the user.

The process approach of MIS on PC is shown in Figure 1.16b.

As observed in this chapter, 3GL are tedious. **4GL** tend to be less procedural than 3GL. It means that a 4GL provides many built-in functions that are commonly used in a type of application. The user of the language does not need to do programming for these functions from scratch. Hence, 4GL allow the user to

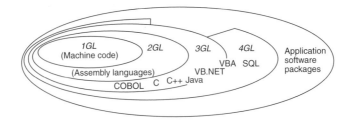

Figure 1.17   The build-on relationship between languages and software in MIS.

instruct the computer on **what** to do rather than **how** to do it. Structure Query Language (SQL), which will be discussed later in this book, is a typical 4GL.

Originally, 4GL is referred to a category of computer languages which are close to the high-level human natural languages. However, the concept of 4GL has been changed to a certain degree since a variety of computer software were developed. This change has blurred the boundary between 3GL, 4GL, and **application software packages**.

The major characteristics of 4GL that are unique to 3GL are:

1. Good human-computer interfaces.
2. Menu, icon, and natural-language-like commands.
3. Graphics.
4. Database functions.
5. User friendly; that is, the user can easily learn and use it.

Computer applications software packages are prewritten, commercially available computer programs for a very specific type of applications that eliminate the need for writing programs. A software package is often called **off-the-shelf software**. For example, QuickBooks is an accounting software package. Compared with spreadsheet software, the user of QuickBooks is allowed to perform accounting processes without writing any programs. The build-on relationship between the four generations of computer languages and business application software packages is shown in Figure 1.17.

1.12   Self-Review Exercise

1. A sequential disk file is as follows:

```
Linda...
Jone...
John...
Oldman...
Youngman...
Mark...
EOF (End of File)
```

To find the record of Youngman, how many times does the computer have to read a record from the disk?

2. A hashing function is:
   Address of record = Remainder of [Record key/19].
   Suppose that a Record Key is 379. What is the address of this record?

3. An indexed file on disk and its index table are as follows:

Disk File

Address	Data
43	Pen
20	Paper
05	Diskette
10	Watch
. . . .	. . . .

Index Table

Record Key	Address
20	14
130	43
43	10
14	29
. . . .	. . . .

Find the data of the record with the key value of 43.

4. What file organization best fits each of the following cases of file processing? Why?

   A. Inventory master file for a warehouse.
   B. Order transaction file for a bookstore.
   C. Student master file for the registrar's office.
   D. White pages of residence listings for a telephone company.
   E. Book listings for a library.
   F. Bit map for a picture.
   G. Time schedule table.
   H. Backup file for a student master file.

5. Name five master files, five transaction files, three reference files, and five report files in your day-to-day life.
6. Explain the file organizations used for the files you identified in Question (5).
7. Run the four COBOL programs in Listings 1.3, 1.4, 1.5, and 1.6. Input a test data set and print out the report.
8. Show the execution sequence of the following program fragment, and predict the result of the data item A.

```
. . . . .
13        MOVE ZERO TO A.
14        MOVE 1 TO B.
15        PERFORM SECTION-A.
16        PERFORM SECTION-B UNTIL B = 3.
17        PERFORM SECTION-C.
18        DISPLAY A.
. . . . .

32   SECTION-A.
33        PERFORM SECTION-D.
34        COMPUTE A = A + 1.
35   SECTION-B.
36        COMPUTE B = B + 1.
          PERFORM SECTION-D.
37        COMPUTE A = A + B.
38   SECTION-C.
39        PERFORM SECTION-D.
40        COMPUTE A = A + 2.
41   SECTION-D.
42        COMPUTE A = 2 * A.
. . . . .
```

9. Follow the execution sequence, line by line, of the program procedural logic in Listing 1.5.

10. Combine the four COBOL programs in Listings 1.3, 1.4, 1.5, and 1.6 into a single COBOL program. Draw a structured diagram for the combined COBOL program. Discuss the advantages and disadvantages of the combination.

11. Read the following COBOL program and complete it by filling the blanks.

```
1    _____        DIVISION.
2    PROGRAM-ID.          COMMIS.
3    _____        DIVISION.
4    CONFIGURATION        SECTION.
5    SOURCE-COMPUTER.     ALHPA.
6    _____        SECTION.
7    FILE-CONTROL.
8        SELECT  _____
9          ASSIGN TO "TEAM.DAT"
10         ORGANIZATION IS INDEXED
11         ACCESS MODE IS DYNAMIC
12         RECORD KEY IS SALESMAN-ID-A.
13       SELECT   MONTHLY-SALES-FILE
14         ASSIGN TO "SALES.DAT"
15         ORGANIZATION IS SEQUENTIAL.
16       SELECT   COMMISSION-REPORT
17         ASSIGN TO PRINTER.
18    _____               DIVISION.
19   FILE              SECTION.
20   FD   SALES-PERSON-FILE
21        LABEL RECORDS ARE STANDARD.
22   01  _____.
23        02  SALESMAN-ID-A            PIC X(2).
```

```
24         02   SALESMAN-NAME              PIC X(30).
25         02   SALESMAN-ADDRESS          PIC X(30).
26         02   SALESMAN-COMMISSION-RATE  PIC 99.
27    FD   MONTHLY-SALES-FILE
28         _____.
29    01   MONTHLY-SALES-RECORD.
30         02   SALESMAN-ID-B             PIC X(2).
31         02   MONTHLY-SALES             PIC 99.
32    FD   _____
33         LABEL RECORDS ARE OMITTED.
34    01   COMMISSION-RECORD             PIC X(80).
35    WORKING-STORAGE  SECTION.

36    01   COMMISSION-BEFORE-TAX         PIC 9(4)V99.
37    01   COMMISSION-AFTER-TAX          PIC 9(4)V99.
38    01   TAX-DEDUCTION                 PIC 9(4)V99.
39    01   EOF-SIGN                      PIC XXX     VALUE SPACES.
40    01   TITLE-LINE.
41         02   FILLER   PIC X(10)  VALUE "SLM-ID".
42         02   FILLER   PIC X(20)  VALUE "SALESMAN NAME".
43         02   FILLER   PIC X(12)  VALUE "SALES".
44         02   FILLER   PIC X(12)  VALUE " CMS+TAX".
45         02   FILLER   PIC X(12)  VALUE " TAX DED".
46         02   FILLER   PIC X(12)  VALUE "   CMS-PAY".
47    01   MONTHLY-COMMISSION-RECORD.
48         02   SALESMAN-ID-R             PIC X(2).
49         02   FILLER                    PIC X(8) VALUE SPACE.
50         02   SALESMAN-NAME-R           PIC X(20).
51         02   FILLER                    PIC X(8) VALUE SPACE.
52         02   MONTHLY-SALES-R           PIC 99.
53         02   FILLER                    PIC X(3) VALUE SPACE.
54         02   COMMISSION-BEFORE-TAX-R   PIC $$$$9.99.
55         02   FILLER                    PIC X(3) VALUE SPACE.
56         02   TAX-DEDUCTION-R           PIC $$$$9.99.
57         02   FILLER                    PIC X(3) VALUE SPACE.
58         02   COMMISSION-AFTER-TAX-R    PIC $$$$9.99.
59    _____          DIVISION.
60    _____.
61         PERFORM START-PROCESS.
62         PERFORM 01-COMMISSION-PROCESS
63              UNTIL EOF-SIGN = _____.
64         PERFORM _____.
65         STOP    RUN.
66    _____.
67         OPEN   INPUT SALES-PERSON-FILE
68              INPUT MONTHLY-SALES-FILE
69              _____  COMMISSION-REPORT.
70         MOVE  TITLE-LINE   TO  COMMISSION-RECORD.
71         WRITE COMMISSION-RECORD.
72         READ  MONTHLY-SALES-FILE
73              AT END      MOVE "FIN" TO EOF-SIGN.
74    01-COMMISSION-PROCESS.
75         MOVE  SALESMAN-ID-B  TO  SALESMAN-ID-A.
76         READ  SALES-PERSON-FILE
```

```
77                  KEY IS _____
78                  INVALID KEY DISPLAY "SALES PERSON IS MISSING!".
79          PERFORM  02-CALCULATE-COMMISSION.
80          PERFORM  02-PRINT-A-COMMISSION-RECORD.
81          READ  MONTHLY-SALES-FILE
82                  AT END     MOVE _____ TO EOF-SIGN.
83      02-CALCULATE-COMMISSION.
84          COMPUTE   COMMISSION-BEFORE-TAX =
85                  SALESMAN-COMMISSION-RATE * MONTHLY-SALES.
86          COMPUTE   TAX-DEDUCTION = COMMISSION-BEFORE-TAX * 0.2.
87          COMPUTE   COMMISSION-AFTER-TAX =
88                  COMMISSION-BEFORE-TAX - TAX-DEDUCTION.
89      02-PRINT-A-COMMISSION-RECORD.
90          MOVE SALESMAN-ID-B      TO   SALESMAN-ID-R.
91          MOVE SALESMAN-NAME      TO   SALESMAN-NAME-R.
92          MOVE MONTHLY-SALES      TO   MONTHLY-SALES-R.
93          MOVE COMMISSION-BEFORE-TAX TO COMMISSION-BEFORE-TAX-R.
94          MOVE TAX-DEDUCTION             TO TAX-DEDUCTION-R.
95          MOVE COMMISSION-AFTER-TAX   TO COMMISSION-AFTER-TAX-R.
96          MOVE MONTHLY-COMMISSION-RECORD  TO COMMISSION-RECORD.
97          WRITE _____
98                  AFTER ADVANCING   2    LINES.
99      CLOSE-PROCESS.
100         CLOSE _____
101               _____
102               _____.
103         DISPLAY "COMMISSION REPORT IS PRINTER.DAT!".
```

12. Describe the purpose of the COBOL program in Question 11. Draw a structure diagram for the above COBOL program.

13. Answer the following questions:
    A. How many files are used in the COBOL program in Question 11?
    B. Explain **specifically** why the organizations of the disk files are so designed.
    C. Suppose you apply the operating system command $TYPE and find the sample data of the disk files as follows:

    TEAM.DAT

12Jame	Garden	30
03Ann	Park	40
05Tim	Lake	50

    SALES.DAT

    0510
    0308

    If you run the COBOL program in Question 11, how many times does the program perform the following sentences or paragraphs?

    START-PROCESS
    STOP RUN
    01-COMMISSION-PROCESS
    02-PRINT-A-COMMISSION-RECORD

14. Given the sample data in Question 13, write the expected **print result** (on the printer) generated by the COBOL program in Question 11.
15. Given the program in Question 11 and the sample data in Question 13, walk through the program step by step using the diagram in Figure 1.12.
16. Develop a COBOL program that uses features or functions that are not mentioned in this textbook.
17. Discuss your experiences in debugging computer programs.
18. Develop a COBOL project to solve a business data processing problem that:
    A. Creates a master file.
    B. Creates a transaction file.
    C. Manipulates the data in the transaction file against the master file.
    D. Generates a well-organized print report.
    E. Maintains the data files.

Appendix 1.1   Commonly Used COBOL Reserved Words

ACCEPT	ACCESS	ADD	ADVANCING
AFTER	ALL	AND	ARE
ASSIGN	AT	BEFORE	BY
CALL	CLOSE	COBOL	COMP
COMPUTATIONAL	COMPUTE	CONFIGURATION	CONTROL
COPY	COUNT	DATA	DATE
DAY	DEBUGGING	DELETE	DISPLAY
DISK	DIVIDE	DIVISION	DYNAMIC
ELSE	END	END-IF	ENTER
ERROR	EXIT	FD	FILE
FILLER	FIRST	FOR	FROM
GO	HEADING	ID	IDENTIFICATION
IF	IN	INDEX	INDEXED
INITIALIZE	INPUT	INPUT-OUTPUT	INTO
INVALID	IS	I-O	I-O-CONTROL
JUST	JUSTIFIED	KEY	LABEL
LAST	LESS	LINE	LINES
MERGE	MODE	MODULES	MOVE
MULTIPLY	NEXT	NO	NOT
NUMBER	OBJECT-COMPUTER	OF	OFF
OMITTED	ON	OPEN	OPTIONAL
OR	ORDER	ORGANIZATION	OTHER
OUTPUT	PAGE	PERFORM	PIC
PICTURE	PLUS	POSITION	POSITIVE
PRINTING	PROCEDURE	PROGRAM	PROGRAM-ID
QUEUE	RANDOM	RD	READ
RECORD	RECORDS	RELEASE	RENAMES
REPORT	REPORTING	RETURN	REWIND
REWRITE	RUN	SEARCH	SELECT

SEQUENTIAL	SET	SORT	SOURCE-COMPUTER
SPACE	SPACES	START	STOP
SUM	TABLE	TAPE	TEST
THAN	THEN	THROUGH	THRU
TIME	TIMES	TO	TRUE
TYPE	UNTIL	UP	USE
VALUE	VALUES	WHEN	WITH
WORDS	WORKING-STORAGE	WRITE	ZERO
ZEROES	ZEROS		

Appendix 1.2   Instructions for Using COBOL on Mainframe

COBOL is usually available on any mainframe computer. To use your PC with the Windows operating system to access COBOL on the mainframe through the network, you need to find a **terminal emulator for Windows** (e.g., **PowerTerm** for Windows). The terminal emulator can emulate terminals of various types and allow the user to access programs and data on the mainframe. However, within the terminal emulator's environment, the user still uses the traditional operating system commands. The following is the procedures for using COBOL on the mainframe.

1. Find the icon or menus of the terminal emulator for Windows on your PC screen. Click it, and enter you ID and password. You should see a prompt sign **$** on the screen.
2. **$ EDIT** [program-file-name.COB] You define the program-file-name with the extension name [.COB] for COBOL program (e.g., EDIT W.COB).
3. Edit your COBOL code.

Note that the editor for COBOL may not request eight spaces to start a sentence. Also, avoid Tab key in source programs. You may insert comment lines in the program by using asterisk (*) in the first column of the line. For example:

4. When you finish the editing COBOL code, type **Ctrl+Z** (simultaneously Ctrl key and Z). You should see a prompt sign * on the screen.
5. * **EXIT** to exit the editor. Your program is automatically saved to the program file you have defined.
6. **$ COBOL** [program-file-name.COB] Compile your COBOL program (e.g., COBOL W.COB).
7. If no error message appears, then you link the object code in the [.OBJ] program file. Type

   $ LINK [program-file-name.OBJ] (e.g., LINK W.OBJ).

Otherwise you must return to editor and debug the COBOL program.

8. If no error message appears, the run the [.EXE] code. Type

   $ RUN [program-file-name.EXE] (e.g., RUN W.EXE).

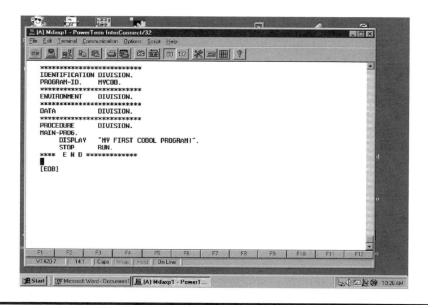

Figure Ch1-A2-1   Editing COBOL program.

Otherwise you must return to editor and debug the COBOL program.

9. If your COBOL program generates a sequential data file (or indexed data file in many mainframe computers), you may view the data file. Type: **$ TYPE** [data-file-name.DAT] (e.g., TYPE EMP.DAT) allows you to view the disk file "EMP.DAT".

10. If your COBOL program has a printer file, type:

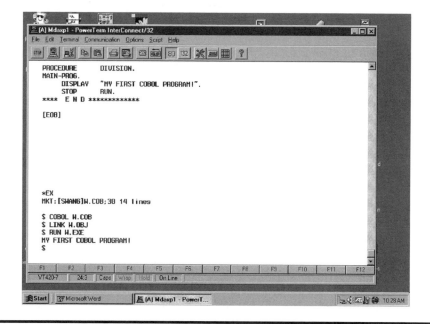

Figure Ch1-A2-2   Use the terminal emulator to access COBOL.

$ <u>TYPE PRINTER.DAT</u> to show the printer file on the screen.

11. You may use **$<u>DIR</u>** to view your files, use **$<u>DEL</u>** to delete files.
12. To print the source code or the printer file on the local printer, you may use **Microsoft Notepad**. To do so, use $TYPE command to bring the file to the screen and drag the part you want to print, then use [COPY] function of the emulator (on the top menu) to copy the part you would like to print, and [PASTE] to Notepad. Through Notepad you can print on the local printer.

Note that, using $<u>PRINT</u> command, one can print files on the central printer of the mainframe (but not locally); for example:

$<u>PRINT</u> [program-file-name.COB] to print the source code on the mainframe printer.
$<u>PRINT PRINTER.DAT</u> to print the printer file on the mainframe printer.

13. Before you leave the computer, you type **$<u>LO</u>** to log out.
14. If you want to copy your programs or data files, you may use **Microsoft Notepad (do not use any word processing software)**. Use the [COPY] function of the emulator to copy the part you would like to download, [PASTE] to Notepad, and then [SAVE AS] the Notepad file to the local disk. Be sure to select [All Files] in the [Save As Type] box in Notepad, and type the right extension name (e.g., W.COB). You may use the reverse procedure to copy back your program.

You may use FTP to download or upload programs and data files, as follows:

- Click [Start] on the Window, and [Programs], and then [WS_FTP]
- Click [WS_FTP95 LE] and bring the WS_FTP window up.
- Click [Connection] if the Session Properties window is not displayed.
- Type in the Profile Name (e.g., <u>alpha</u>, depending upon the computer in your organization) and Host Name (e.g., <u>umassd.edu</u>, depending upon the definition in your organization) and your ID and password, then click [OK].
- Select the files and location you want to transmit between the Local System and the Remote System.
- Be sure that you use "ASCII" mode to transmit your COBOL programs.
- Click the direct button in the middle of the window to perform the transmission.

Appendix 1.3   Guideline for COBOL Project Report

1. Front page.

Course name
Title of the project
Group members (names and ID)
Date

2. Text.
    Introduction and the problem to be solved
    Application of COBOL
    Discussion of the advantages and the disadvantages of COBOL

3. Diagrams.
    Structured diagrams of the COBOL programs

4. Source code of the COBOL programs.

5. Examples of test data.
    (Note that the examples must be original; that is, they are not edited using word processing.)

6. Samplers of printout.
    (Note that the printout must be original; that is, they are not edited using word processing.)

7. Operation manual for the users of the COBOL programs.
    (You need to tell the user about the rules in using your COBOL executable programs, such as how many digits for a particular data item, how to end the program, etc. However, you do not need to tell the user how to edit and compile your programs.)

Chapter 2

C++ and Object-Oriented Programming

2.1 Introduction to Object-Oriented Programming

Object-oriented programming (OOP) was first discussed in the late 1960s by those working with the SIMULA language. By the 1970s it was an important part of the Smalltalk language developed at Xerox. Meanwhile, the rest of the world bumbled along with languages like COBOL, and used functional decomposition methods to address problems of programming. OOP did not become a popular method until the 1980s. Currently, the basic philosophy of OOP has been extended to systems development. Three changes in computer applications have occurred over the past decade and are key factors as we enter the information technology era.

1. The underlying concepts of an object-oriented approach have had decades to mature, and attention has gradually shifted from issues of coding to issues of design and analysis.
2. The underlying technology for building object-oriented systems has become much more powerful. Object-oriented languages such as Java have become popular.
3. The systems built today are more "object-oriented" than the systems built in the 1970s and 1980s. Functional complexity is less of a concern than it was before; modeling "objects" has become a subject of higher priority. The networking, multimedia, client-server, and mobile computing environments require object-oriented systems.

This chapter explains the basic concepts of the object-oriented approach and provides the necessary knowledge for students to meet the challenges of **object-oriented analysis** (OOA). The characteristics of the object-oriented approach are described with examples. These examples are written in **C++**. To help students to understand these simple examples, it is essential to understand a little about **C** language before we learn C++. There are several reasons of doing so. First, C++ was migrated from C. In fact, C and C++ share many fundamental syntax features. When we learn C, we are in fact learning C++ as well. As C language has been a commonly used language, it is believed that the benefit of knowing C language would be far beyond what we initially desired. Second, we will study and compare two programming methodologies: **structured programming** (or **function-oriented programming**) and OOP. C is a typical structured programming language, whereas C++ is a typical OOP language. To provide a comparative view of the two programming methodologies, this chapter introduces the two sister languages. You will learn that the internal structure of operations within those classes created by C++ is often best built using the traditional structured programming techniques.

C and C++ are third generation languages, and have been standardized by ANSI (American National Standard Institute). To use C and C++, one must edit the source program code, compile the program, and link and run the executable code in the way similar to that used for COBOL. There are many free C and C++ compliers available on the Internet, which allow students to download for learning purposes.

2.2   Tour of C Language

C is a "mid-level" language. Compared to low-level languages (assembly languages), C programs are easier to write and take fewer instructions. They allow the programmer to take full advantage of the built-in capacities of the computer. Compared to high-level languages (e.g., COBOL), C programs are more compact and efficient; they provide the programmer with flexibility in writing a set of programmed instructions.

Let us examine C programming style. Suppose we want to display "Hello, World !" on the screen. The C program could be written as follows:

```
/* C Programming Example */
# include<stdio.h>
main()
{
 printf("Hello, world ! \n");
}
```

Listing 2.1   Example of C program.

A simple C program like this without involving external functions can also be a C++ program. Several notations and statements are essential and are explained in the following sections:

2.2.1 C/C++ Keywords

A C or C++ program is a set of C or C++ words and symbols. Commonly, a C/C++ word contains characters and underscores (_). C and C++ are case sensitive. For instance, "Word" and "word" are two different words in C and C++. C and C++ have their reserved words, called **keywords**, which implement specific features and may not be used as user-defined words such as variable names. Commonly used keywords in C and C++ are listed in Appendix 2.1.

2.2.2 Comment Statements

Comment statements are enclosed in pairs of /* */ (for C) or after // (for C++) to explain the logic of the program for humans. The computer compiler simply ignores comments.

2.2.3 Preprocessor

A #include statement is a **preprocessor**. A preprocessor tells the C (also, C++) compiler to look for a **header** file (library) before processing the program and to place the contents of the file in the program. In the example mentioned earlier, the C compiler looks for file <stdio.h> for input–output purposes. You may read programmer manuals to determine what header files (libraries) should be included in your program. As beginners, you may simply include <stdio.h>, <iostream.h>, <stdlib.h>, <string.h>, and <math.h> in any cases. Including unnecessary header files does not cause problems other than wasting the CPU memory.

2.2.4 Structure of a C Program, Functions, and Their Arguments

The elemental module of a C program is a **function**. In Listing 2.1, there are two C functions: main() and printf(). The function main() is special and execution begins with this function. Every C (also, C++) program has one and only one main(). **Functions** specify the type of operations a C program will perform, while **argument** (or **parameter**), which is placed in parenthesis after the function name, indicate what type of information is to be passed to the function.

There are two types of functions: C **standard functions** and user-defined functions. The procedures of C standard functions have been built in the C/C++ libraries, and the programmer is allowed to use them (e.g., printf()). **User-defined function** is explained in Section 2.3. Note that the concepts of function and argument (or parameter) presented in this chapter are universally applicable to all procedural computer languages.

A pair of braces indicate a functional body (a group of instructions): { is used to begin the functional body, whereas } marks the end of the functional body. A functional body (e.g., a loop) can be nested within another functional body.

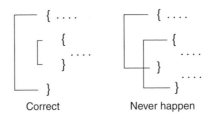

Correct   Never happen

Figure 2.1   Nested functional body.

Braces must be balanced (see Figure 2.1). The specific location of a brace is not important.

If a function body is simple that it has only one sentence, the pair of braces may be omitted.

2.2.5   Statements and Semicolon

A complete C (also, C++) statement (instruction) ends in a **semicolon**. However, a semicolon after an end-brace } may be omitted if the omission causes no ambiguity.

2.2.6   Data Type

Data type must be declared before a variable is used in the program. Important types of data include `int` for integers (e.g., 1, 2, 3), `float` for floating point numbers (e.g., 1.0, 3.14, 0.699), and `char` for characters (e.g., "a", "b", "D") and `strings` (e.g., "John Smith").

```
int a, b, c;        This defines the three variables a, b, c as integers
float x;            This defines variable x as a floating point number
char k;             This defines variable k as a character

char Customer_Name[32];
```

This defines `Customer_Name` as a string variable that can hold up to 31 characters. Strings are discussed in detail later in the chapter.

Data type for a variable can be declared anywhere in the program, but it is usually declared at the beginning of the program module (the main program, function, or class), or right before the variable is used at the first time in this module.

2.2.7   Arithmetic Operations

The symbols of **arithmetic operations** are similar to that in most other languages, for example:

```
x=5;                Let x equal to 5
x=a+b;              Let x get the value of a plus b
```

```
x=a-b;                    Let x get the value of a minus b
x=a*b;                    Let x get the value of a times b
x=a/b;                    Let x get the value of a divided by b
x=pow(a,b);              Let x gets the value of a^b (power)
```

There are some special operations in C (also, C++); for example:

```
y=x++;                    It means y=x+1
y=x--;                    It means y=x-1
```

To avoid confusion with "minus" and hyphen, we often use the underline sign "_" to make a single word in C.

2.2.8　*for Loop*

The **for loop** provides a repetition structure handling the details of counter-controlled repetition. A typical for-loop structure is:

```
for(int [counter]=1; [counter]<=[final value of the counter];
  [counter]++)
  { [repetition actions] };
```

The following is an example of for-loop:

```
1   #include<stdio.h>

2   main()
3   {
4     int i;
5     for (i=1; i<=10; i++)
6     printf("%4d %4d \n", i, i*i);
7   }
```

Listing 2.2　Example of for-loop.

In this example, i is the for-loop control variable (counter). (i=1; i<=10; i++) means that the initial value of i is 1, and the for-loop increments i by 1 (i.e., i++) each time. The repetition continues as long as i is less or equal to ten. In other words, the process (printf in this case) continues ten times.

2.2.9　*printf() Statement with Conversion Specifiers and Free Format Input–Output*

In the above example, in the printf() statement there are "%" symbols which are called **conversion specifiers**.

%d　Print an integer number; e.g., %4d is to print an integer number up to 4 digits.

%f　Print a floating point number; e.g., %4.2f is to print 4 digits before the decimal point and 2 digits after the decimal point.

%s　Print a character string.

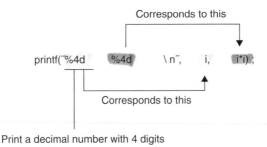

Figure 2.2   Format of command Printf.

%u   Means free format.

\n   means "advance the cursor to the beginning of the next line."

The relationship of the arguments in the `printf` statement is briefly illustrated in Figure 2.2.

Note that in C++ simple commands, cout (for screen output) and cin (for keyboard input) are available for free format input–output operations, as illustrated in the C++ examples later in this chapter.

2.2.10   *if Statement*

The **if statement** is used to choose among alternative courses of actions. The general syntax of the **if-else** structure is:

```
if ( [condition] ) { [action_1] ; }
else        { [action_2] ; };
```

Note that an action in an if statement can also be another if statement, as shown in the following example (C++).

```
 1 #include<stdio.h>
 2 #include<iostream.h>

 3 main()
 4 {
 5 float gross_income, state_tax, federal_tax;

 6 cout << "Input a number for gross income ...\n";
 7 cin >> gross_income;

 8 if( gross_income==0.0 )
 9       federal_tax=state_tax=0.0;
10 else
11     {
12       if( gross_income<=10000.0 )
13       {
14       federal_tax=gross_income*0.15;
15       state_tax=(gross_income-federal_tax)*0.05;
16       }
```

```
17      else
18      {
19      federal_tax=gross_income*0.25;
20       if((gross_income<=25000.0)&&(gross_income>10000.0))
21              state_tax=(gross_income-federal_tax)*0.08;
22          else
23              state_tax=(gross_income-federal_tax)*0.10;
24      }
25      };
26 printf("Federal tax is %5.2f \n", federal_tax);
27 printf("State tax is %5.2f \n", state_tax);
28  }
```

Listing 2.3   Example (C++) of if statement.

The complex if statement illustrated implements the following decision logic:

	Conditions			
	gross income =0	*gross income =(0,10k]*	*gross income =(10k,25k]*	*gross income >25k*
federal tax rate	0	15%	25%	25%
state tax rate	0	5%	8%	10%

Note that, in the if statement, the double equality (==) is used for testing the equality condition. In the condition expression, && stands for "**and**". "**or**" is represented by ||.

2.2.11   String and String Processing

In management information systems, data processing more often involves string (character) processing. Strings are stored as **arrays** of data type char. Suppose we use a 15-character string, we need to declare an array

```
char mystring[16];
```

as one space of the array is reserved for the null character ('/0'). In addition, since the index of an array begins with 0, which often causes confusion, we usually declare an array with two spaces longer than what is required. Two major operations are commonly used in string processing: **string copy** (strcpy) operation and **string comparison** (strcmp) operation. The syntax of strcpy is:

```
strcpy([destination string], [source string]);
```

This means to copy the source string to the destination string. The strcmp operation returns a value, which is explained as follows:

```
strcmp([string-1], [string-2]);
```

It returns 0 if the two strings are identical, 1 if string-1 is greater than string-2, and –1 if string-1 is less than string-2.

A string can be passed to a function for processing, or can be returned from a function. However, when you write a receiving function or a returning function for string processing, you must place asterisk (*) before the string parameter and the returning function. You will see more examples of string processing in the C/C++ programs shown in the following sections.

2.3 Functional Approach

2.3.1 Functional Decomposition

To model a system, we have to break the complex system down into subsystems or modules. There are two major types of decomposition approaches: the functional approach and the object-oriented approach. Traditional structured analysis and structured programming follows the functional decomposition approach, as we learned in using COBOL. Functional decomposition can be described using the diagram shown in Figure 2.3.

Functional decomposition is adopted in all procedure-oriented programming such as COBOL, FORTRAN, and C. In C programming, a subroutine, or a module, is defined as a **function**. Functional decomposition makes the program maintenance easier. Hence, the size of a function is usually small (e.g., 20 lines) to maintain readability of the program. A good programming practice never produces a large program (e.g., 100 lines) without dividing into readable functions.

2.3.2 User-Defined Functions

To explain how to write functions in C, we give a simple example in Listing 2.4. In this program, the main program calls the function that calculates the average value of two numbers, and then prints the result.

```
 1 # include<stdio.h>

 2 float avg(float, float); /* function avg is float type */

 3 main()
 4 {
 5  float x, y;
 6  float a;

 7  x=10.0;
 8  y=15.0;

 9  /* call function avg using arguments x and y */
10  a=avg(x,y);
11  printf("The average is : %f . \n", a);
12 }

13 /* function of avg() */
```

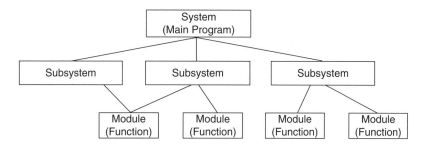

Figure 2.3   Functional decomposition.

```
14 float avg(float amt1, float amt2)
15 {
16  float answer;
17  answer=(amt1 + amt2) / 2.0;
18  return(answer);
19 }
```

Listing 2.4   Main program calls function avg( ).

The following is an explanation of how the program works. Line **2** defines the prototype of the function used by this program. avg is the user-defined function name. Lines **4–12** are the main program.

Lines **5–6** define the types of variables used in this main program. Lines **7–8** assign values to x and y.

Line **10** calls function avg, bringing values of x and y to the function, and gets a value from avg back to a. The computer execution sequence then turns to line **14**. The computer plugs values of x to amt1 and y to amt2, and executes lines **15** through **19**.

Line **16** defines a **local variable** for this function. Local variables are only valid within this function. Line **17** makes calculations. Line **18** returns the result value back to the calling function. The computer execution sequence returns to line **10** (the main program). Line **11** prints the result

```
The average is 12.5000.
```

on the screen, and the program is ended.

2.3.2.1   Declaration of User-Defined Functions

The programmer should make declaration statements to indicate the **prototypes** of the functions that are used in the present program after the preprocessor and before the main(). The general syntax is:

```
[function type] [function name] (data types of arguments);
```

The type of the function depends on the type of the data that returned by the function. Each function can have **arguments** to receive data passed from the outside of the function. These concepts are illustrated further.

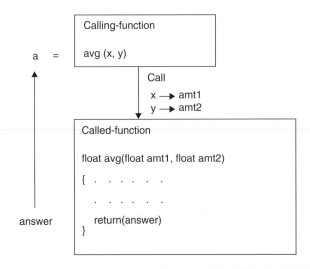

Figure 2.4   Call a user-defined function.

2.3.2.2   Called-Function and Calling-Function

The programmer must specify the declared functions using C. The specified function body is called **called-function**. For example, in Listing 2.4, the body of float avg(float amt1, float amt2) is a called-function. If one C program has two or more called-functions, the order of the called-functions in the program is not important. To use the function, there must be one statement outside the called-function, called **calling-function**, that calls the called-function. In Listing 2.4, avg(x,y) is the calling-function. The calling-function passes the corresponding **value** for each of the arguments (or parameters) to the called-function for processing. If the called-function **returns** a result to the calling-function, the type of the return value is the **type of the function**. If there is no return value, the return type (and thus the type of the function) is **void**. Note that the order of the parameters in the calling-function must be the same as the order of the arguments in the called-function, and the data type of the parameter in the calling-function must match the data type of the corresponding argument in the called-function. Figure 2.4 shows how a user-defined function works.

2.3.3   Example of Multiple Functions of C Program

Listing 2.5 shows a C program that prints out a table of monthly payments given the loan terms and interest rates. It uses for-loops, if-else statement, and multiple **function-calls**.

```
1   /* This is a C program to printout the monthly payment */
2   /* given a term loan and annual interest rates      */

3   #include<stdio.h>
4   #include<stdlib.h>
5   #include<math.h>
```

```
 6   int GetLoanTerm(int); /* These four are functions */
 7   float GetMonthlyIntRate(float);
 8   float CalculateMonthlyPayment(float, int, float);
 9   void PrintMonthlyPayment(int, float, float, int);

10   main()
11   {
12    int i, j;         /* for-loop counters */

13    int LoanTermYears;
14    int LoanTermMonths;
15    float LoanAmount;
16    float AnnualIntRate;
17    float MonthlyIntRate;
18    float MonthlyPayment;

19   /* Define the loan amount  */
20   LoanAmount=1000.0;

21   /* Print out a heading     */
22   printf("** MONTHLY PAYMENT FOR $%5.0f LOAN ** \n", LoanAmount);

23   /* The main program uses two for-loops  */

24   for (i=1; i<4; i++) { /* generates years of loan term */
25    LoanTermYears=i;

26     for (j=1; j<6; j++) { /* generates annual interest rate */
27       AnnualIntRate=0.045+0.005*j;

28       /* Change years to months */
29       LoanTermMonths = GetLoanTerm(LoanTermYears);

30       /* Change annual interest rate to monthly interest rate */
31       MonthlyIntRate = GetMonthlyIntRate(AnnualIntRate);

32       /* Calculate monthly payment */
33       MonthlyPayment =
34   CalculateMonthlyPayment(LoanAmount,LoanTermMonths,MonthlyIntRate);

35       /* Printout the table     */
36       /* print a line each time   */
37       /* j is a flag to control the format */
38   PrintMonthlyPayment(LoanTermYears,AnnualIntRate,MonthlyPayment,j);
39     }
40   }
41   }

42   /* Four functions are defined as follows */

43   /* (1) Change years to months */
44   int GetLoanTerm(int L_T_Y)
45   {
46    int L_T_M;
47    L_T_M = 12.0 * L_T_Y;
```

```
48   return(L_T_M);
49   }

50   /* (2) Change annual interest rate to monthly interest rate */
51   float GetMonthlyIntRate(float A_I_R)
52   {
53    float M_I_R;
54    M_I_R = A_I_R / 12.0;
55    return(M_I_R);
56   }

57   /* (3) Formula of the calculation of monthly payment */
58    float CalculateMonthlyPayment(float Loan, int Term, float Int_Rate)
59   {
60    float Payment;
61    Payment =
62   (Loan*pow((1+Int_Rate),Term)*Int_Rate)/(pow((1+Int_Rate),Term)-1);
63    return(Payment);
64   }

65   /* (4) printout an item, the Flag controls the format */
66   void PrintMonthlyPayment(int Term, float Int_Rate, float Pay, int Flag)
67   {
68    if(Flag==1)
69     {printf(" %2d-YEAR %1.4f %5.2f \n", Term, Int_Rate, Pay);}
70    else
71     {printf("     %1.4f %5.2f \n", Int_Rate, Pay);};
72   }
73   /* END of the program */
```

Listing 2.5   Example of C program with multiple function-calls.

The functioning of the programme is explained as follows. Lines **6–9** define four functions used in this program. Lines **10–41** are the main programs. Lines **12–18** define the types of variable used in this main program. Line **20** assigns a value to LoanAmount. Line **22** prints a heading for the printout on the screen.

Lines **24–40** are a for-loop. It generates data for the loan terms up to 3 years.

Lines **26–39** are another for-loop embedded in the first for-loop. This for-loop generates data for five different interest levels. Within this loop, line **27** generates annual interest rate. Since this program is to display monthly payment for a loan, and the loan term is usually expressed in year, we must change the number of years to the number of months. Line **29** calls the function GetLoanTerm to make a conversion. The computer execution sequence turns to line **44**. After lines **45–49**, the loan term has been changed to months, and the execution sequence returns to line **31**.

Line **31** calls the function GetMonthlyInRate to convert annual interest rate to monthly interest rate. The execution sequence turns to line **51**. After lines **52–56**, the interest rate has been converted into monthly interest rate, and the execution sequence returns to line **33**.

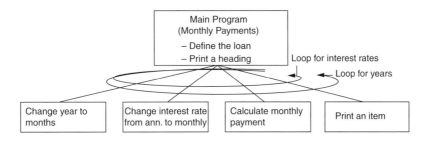

Figure 2.5   Structure diagram for the C program in Listing 2.5.

Lines **33–34** obtain monthly payment by calling the function `Calculate-MonthlyPayment`, and the execution sequence jumps to line **58**. Lines **59–64** complete the calculation and return the result back to line **33**.

Next, line **38** calls `PrintMonthlyPayment` function to print monthly payment. The execution sequence turns to line **66**. Note that this function does not return any value, and is of the void type. The logic defined in lines **67–72** is to make the printout formatted. For beginners, it might not be straightforward.

After each time of the iteration, the computer updates the values of the control counters. Remember that the computer is under the control of the two embedded loops. In other words, the computer repeats the procedure again and again for 15 times. Each time, new data is generated and printed on the screen.

The order of these functions in the program is trivial. As long as a necessary function is included in the program, the computer can find it anywhere by searching the function name in accordance with the program logic.

The structure diagram for the C program of Listing 2.5 is demonstrated in Figure 2.5.

Using procedure computer languages, one is able to easily implement the decomposed functions of the system. However, in the software engineering field, people found that functional decomposition approach has disadvantages, including:

1. Interfaces between functions are often too complicated.
2. Modules are often difficult to reuse because the partition of functions is very much arbitrary.
3. The separation of data from the processing makes computation in the networking environment inefficient.

The object-oriented approach is considered to have advantages over the function-oriented approach in these aspects.

2.4   Object-Oriented Approach

2.4.1   *Object and Class*

The elementary unit in object-oriented methods is **object**. It has been found that decomposition of a system based on objects is more natural than functional

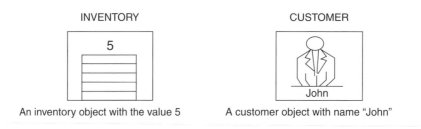

INVENTORY   CUSTOMER

5

John

An inventory object with the value 5   A customer object with name "John"

Figure 2.6   Examples of object.

decomposition. OOP has been proved to be effective in the networking environment. Figure 2.6 shows examples of objects.

A set of objects that have common characteristics is defined as a **class**. For example, INVENTORY is a class; CUSTOMER is a class. Classes are organized into hierarchies in which the subclass **inherits** the properties of its superclass(es). Figure 2.7 shows examples.

An object encapsulates its data descriptions (or **attributes**) and the operations that apply to it. There are two types of operations in the object. An operation that manipulates the encapsulated data in the object is called a **method**. The operation procedure that sends **messages** to other object(s) is called a **request for service**. Inheritance provides an explicit method for identifying and representing common attributes (see Figure 2.8).

Suppose we have already written some programs for the parent class; then we do not have to write similar programs for the child class (subclass) for the same manipulations. This is the importance of inheritance.

To analyze, design, and make documentation of the structures of object-oriented programs, system specialists need diagrammatic tools just like structure diagrams for function-oriented programs. Since object-oriented methods became popular in the late 1980s, there have been a great variety of analysis and design techniques or tools for object-oriented methods. The proliferation of techniques in the object-oriented area has caused confusion in all information technology and computer software-related fields. Recently, **Universal Modeling Language** (**UML**) has been promoted to become a "standard" tool for OOA and design. However, the complete version of UML is hard to learn for beginners. In this book, we use its variation, a simplified version of OOA and design tool for OOP, as shown in Figure 2.9. Object class, inheritance,

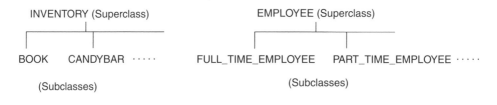

INVENTORY (Superclass)   EMPLOYEE (Superclass)

BOOK   CANDYBAR · · · · ·   FULL_TIME_EMPLOYEE   PART_TIME_EMPLOYEE · · · · ·

(Subclasses)   (Subclasses)

Figure 2.7   Superclass and subclass.

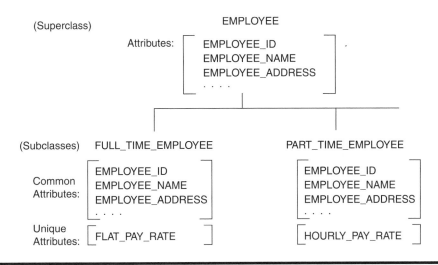

Figure 2.8   Inheritance.

request for service, and return data flow associated with messages can be represented by the shown elementary constructs.

2.4.2   Descriptions of Class, Object, Method, and Message

The elementary unit of **OOP** is object, which packages data and the operations that apply to the object. An object may include a number of unique storage locations for a set of attributes or variables together with a set of procedures (methods) which manipulate those variables. In C++, the objects belonging to the same class are described by a class definition. A class is generally constructed as shown in Listing 2.6 (it is not a program).

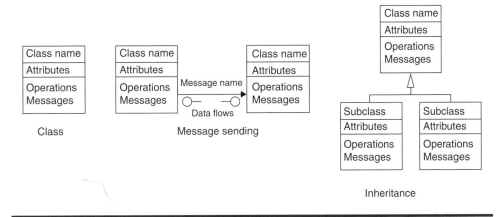

Figure 2.9   OOP diagram constructs.

```
class class_name_identifier
{
private:
 data and methods
 // The data and methods cannot be accessed directly
public:
 data and methods
 // The data and methods can be accessed directly
};
```

Listing 2.6   Class description format in C++.

For example, we may use the following C++ programming to describe the class called `inventory_ex` (see Listing 2.7).

```
1 // This code defines the class called inventory_ex
2 // File invent.h

3 class inventory_ex
4 {
5 private:
6   // Attributes

7     unsigned int inventory_value;

8 public:
9   // A constructor initialized to 4

10  inventory_ex() { inventory_value=4; };

11  // Methods of the object class

12  void increment() { inventory_value++; };
13  void decrement() { inventory_value--; };
14  unsigned int access_value() { return inventory_value;};
15 };
```

Listing 2.7   `Inventory_ex` class description (invent.h).

In the above simple example, line **3** defines the name of the class. This class has only one attribute, or variable, `inventory_value`. In the public section, the class is initialized by the **constructor**, and assigned the number 4 in this example (line **10**). There are three **operations** (or **methods**) in this class. The first operation is named increment (line **12**). Its function is to increase the value of the class by 1. The second is named decrement (line **13**). Its function is to decrease the value by 1. The third operation simply returns the value of `inventory_value`. Several new concepts are discussed further.

2.4.2.1 `public` and `private` Statement

`public` means that the variable or methods in this part is accessible to objects of any other class, and `private` means that the variable or method in this part is accessible only to objects created from the current class.

2.4.2.2 Constructor

Constructor is a specific method that always has the same name as the class. A constructor can have its own operation, as shown in Listing 2.8, or can be replaced by an independent method as shown in Listing 2.10. The constructor initializes the values of the attributes of the object declared. Generally, there are three ways to implement a constructor:

1. Assign values directly by using assign statements.
2. Accept values from the users (keyboard), or
3. Read disk files/database.

To focus on the major features of C++, we do not discuss disk files/database in this chapter.

2.4.2.3 Scope Resolution

To avoid the instance where many classes have methods with the same name and parameter list, we use the double colon (::) to indicate the **scope resolution**, as shown in Listing 2.8.

```
1   // This code defines the class called inventory_ex in a slightly
2   // different way
3   // File invent.h

4   class inventory_ex
5   {
6   private:
7    // Attribute of the class
8    int inventory_value;

9   public:
10   // A constructor initialize the object
11   // It is actually defined in an independent procedure

12   inventory_ex::inventory_ex()
13   {
14    InitInventory();
15   };

16   // Operation for the constructor
17   void inventory_ex::InitInventory()
18   {
19    int w;
20    // Get the data from the keyboard
21    cout << "Please enter a number for one inventory object: \n";
22   cin >> w;
23   inventory_value=w;
24   };

25   // Methods of the object class
26   void inventory_ex::increment() { inventory_value++; };
```

```
27   void inventory_ex::decrement() { inventory_value--; };
28   int inventory_ex::access_value() {return inventory_value;};
29   };
```

Listing 2.8   Another example for the `inventory_ex` Class.

The program in Listing 38 is almost the same as that in Listing 2.7, except for the use of scope resolution and the use of input–output commands to accept a value from keyboard for `inventory_value`. Note that some versions of C++ compliers do not support scope resolution.

2.4.2.4   Declare an Object

Once a class has been defined, a program (the main program or other classes) can declare an object of this class using the statement:

```
class_name object_name;
```

As seen in the example of Listing 2.9 (Lines 8 and 9), part 1 and part 2 are two objects of the class `inventory_ex`.

2.4.2.5   Message Sending

Unlike the functions (or subroutines) in the structured function-oriented approach, an object module allows other module to use its individual methods (i.e., not necessarily all of the methods) through the message sending.

The statement:

```
object_name.method_name;
```

defines message sending. Note that the variables cannot be accessed or modified from outside the object unless **messages** are used and sent to the object. These messages may result in the execution of one or more methods contained in the object.

The program in Listing 2.9 shows how to declare objects, and how a program sends messages to objects and acquires information from those objects. Remember that every C++ program has one main program. The main program is stored in a program file with extension name **.cpp** (see Line 2 in Listing 2.9).

```
1   // A programm that uses the class inventory_ex
2   // File main.cpp

3   # include<stdio.h>
4   # include<fstream.h>
5   # include"invent.h"

6   main()
7   {
8   inventory_ex part1;   // part1 is an object of inventory_ex
9   inventory_ex part2;   // part2 is an object of inventory_ex
```

```
10  part1.increment(); // a message
11  part2.decrement(); // a message
12  printf("\n part-1 = %u ", part1.access_value() ); // a message
13  printf("\n part-2 = %u ", part2.access_value() ); // a message

14  }
```

Listing 2.9   Program that uses the `inventory_ex` Class (main.cpp).

We examine how the above C++ program works with the class defined in **Listing 2.7**.

Line **5** instructs the computer to find the header file for the class used by this program. When writing a program to use classes defined before, one has to include files containing these classes. In our example, the `invent.h` file defining the `inventory_ex` class is included. Note that this header file is developed by the user (i.e., it is not standard library), and is cited by using quotation marks.

Line **8** defines an object of the class `inventory_ex`. It is named `part1`. The computer execution sequence turns to the `inventory_ex` class (Listing 2.7) and creates an object. Conceptually, the object `part1` has its own value of the attributes and can perform operations independently. Upon the creation of the `part1` object, the computer executes the constructor of the class for this object. In this case, the initial value of the attribute `inventory_value` is set to 4 (line **10** of Listing 2.7).

Similar to line 8, line 9 creates another object, named `part2`. In this case, the initial value of the attribute `inventory_value` of `part2` is also set to 4. At this point, the computer holds two objects of the class `inventory_ex`.

Line **10** in Listing 2.9 is a message sent to the object `part1` to request the operation increment. The computer execution sequence turns to line **12** in Listing 2.7 for this object. Remember that the attribute `inventory_value` of `part1` is initially set to 4. After execution of line **12** in Listing 2.7, `inventory_value` of `part1` becomes 5.

Look back to line **11** in Listing 2.9. It sends a message to the object `part2` to request the operation decrement. The computer execution sequence turns to line **13** in Listing 2.7 for the object `part2`. Its initial value of `inventory_value` is 4. It becomes 3 after the decrement operation.

Line **12** in Listing 2.9 is to print data on the screen. It contains a message to the object `part1` to request `access_value`. The computer execution sequence turns to line **14** in Listing 2.7, and returns `inventory_value` of the object `part1` to the message sender for printing.

Line **13** in Listing 2.9 does a similar job as line 12, but requests `access_value` for the object `part2`, and prints the returned value of `inventory_value` of `part2` on the screen.

Thus, the output of the main program and the class defined in Listing 2.7 is:

```
part-1 = 5
part-2 = 3
```

The execution process can be depicted in Figure 2.10.

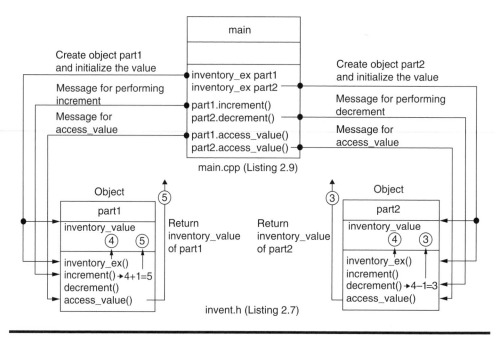

Figure 2.10   Walkthrough programs of Listing 2.9 and Listing 2.7.

Through this subsection, we have learned the important features of OOP that are different from features of function-oriented programming.

2.5   Example of C++ Program with One Object Class

The syntax of C++ is very similar to C except for those descriptions related to class. In this section we learn C++ through a typical example with a small scale (Listings 2.10a and 2.10b). Note that, in C programs, the main program and functions are stored in the same program file (with extension name .c), but in C++ the main program (with extension name .cpp) and classes (with extension name .h) should be stored in separate program files.

Students should learn how to write C++ programming, and understand that, using the object-oriented development approach, one can implement a system (in C++) directly based on an OOP design result, provided that the design is done in sufficient detail. In this small example, the user is supposed to input a discount rate for the grocery store and print out a flyer. The OOP diagram for this example is shown in Figure 2.11.

```
1 // **** Main program for advertisement (file: ad.cpp) ****
2 #include<stdio.h>
3 #include<stdlib.h>
4 #include<math.h>
5 #include<iostream.h>
6 #include<string.h>
7 #include"grocery.h"
```

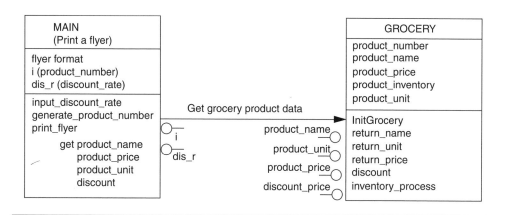

Figure 2.11   Example of OOP design—grocery store.

```
 8 // The header file of the class GROCERY used is included
 9 // The main program is to manipulate the GROCERY objects
10 // and print a flyer based on the current discount rate

11 main()
12 {
13   float dis_r; // for discount rate
14 // The program asks the user to input the current discount rate
15 printf("Please input discount rate ... in percentage. \n");

16 cin>> dis_r;
17 printf( "\n");

18 // Display the headlines of the flyer

19 printf("\n");
20 printf("\n");
21 printf("    My Small Grocery Store at UMD  \n");
22 printf("    ***************************** \n");
23 printf("\n");
24 printf("        Regular Price   Sale Price \n");
25 printf("\n");

26 // Manipulates the available Grocery objects
27 // In this case, we assume we have only 5 items

28 for (int i=1; i<=5; i++) {

29   GROCERY Grocery;
30   Grocery.InitGrocery(i);

31  // Notice the spaces in the following printf sentence

32  printf ("%s      ",
33             Grocery.ReturnGrocery_Product_Name());

34  printf("%4.2f ", Grocery.ReturnGrocery_Product_Price());
```

```
35  printf("/ %s   ",
36              Grocery.ReturnGrocery_Product_Unit());

37  printf("%4.2f ", Grocery.Grocery_Discount(dis_r));
38  printf("/ %s \n", Grocery.ReturnGrocery_Product_Unit());
39    }
40 }
```

Listing 2.10a   Example of C++ program—grocery store (main program ad.cpp).

```
 1 // **** Class GROCERY definition ****
 2 // File is "grocery.h"

 3 class GROCERY

 4 // Class declaration
 5 {
 6    private:
 7 // Attributes
 8      int   Grocery_Product_Number;
 9      char  Grocery_Product_Name[20];
10      float Grocery_Product_Price;
11      float Grocery_Product_Inventory;
12      char  Grocery_Product_Unit[5];

13    public:

14    GROCERY ()
15     {

16 // Constructor is actually implemented by the method
17 //  void InitGrocery(int) depending on G_N
18   };

19 // Operations
20 // The following procedure simulates the system to read a
21 // database/data file which records information of the
22 // grocery products.
23 // One may substitute this procedure by using database/files

24    void InitGrocery(int G_N) {

25     Grocery_Product_Number=G_N;

26      if (Grocery_Product_Number==1)
27        { strcpy(Grocery_Product_Name, "Milk   ");
28                                        // put spaces in
29            Grocery_Product_Price=2.59;
30            Grocery_Product_Inventory=300.0;
31            strcpy(Grocery_Product_Unit, "Oz ");
32                                        // put a space in
33        };
34      if (Grocery_Product_Number==2)
35        { strcpy(Grocery_Product_Name, "Egg   ");
36                                        // put spaces in
```

```
37                  Grocery_Product_Price=1.89;
38                  Grocery_Product_Inventory=800.0;
39                  strcpy(Grocery_Product_Unit, "Dzn");
40          };

41          if (Grocery_Product_Number==3)
42             { strcpy(Grocery_Product_Name, "Beef   ");
43                                              // put spaces in
44                Grocery_Product_Price=2.99;
45                Grocery_Product_Inventory=150.0;
46                strcpy(Grocery_Product_Unit, "Lb ");
47                                              // put a space
48          };

49          if (Grocery_Product_Number==4)
50             { strcpy(Grocery_Product_Name, "Bean   ");
51                                              // put spaces in
52                Grocery_Product_Price=1.09;
53                Grocery_Product_Inventory=100.0;
54                strcpy(Grocery_Product_Unit, "Lb ");
55                                              // put a space
56          };

57          if (Grocery_Product_Number==5)
58             { strcpy(Grocery_Product_Name, "Melon  ");
59                                              // put spaces in
60                Grocery_Product_Price=1.59;
61                Grocery_Product_Inventory=100.0;
62                strcpy(Grocery_Product_Unit, "Pc ");
63                                              // put a space
64          };

65  }

66 // Next are methods of the GROCERY class ...
67  // Return Name

68   char *ReturnGrocery_Product_Name()
69        {return Grocery_Product_Name;};

70  // Return Unit

71   char *ReturnGrocery_Product_Unit()
72        {return Grocery_Product_Unit;};

73  // Return Price

74 float ReturnGrocery_Product_Price()
75        {return Grocery_Product_Price;};

76  // Calculate Price after discount

77   float Grocery_Discount(float Discount_Rate) {
78     float Price_After_Discount;
79       Price_After_Discount=
```

```
80              Grocery_Product_Price*(1-Discount_Rate*0.01);
81       return(Price_After_Discount);
82    };

83   // Process Inventory
84   float Grocery_Inventory_Process(float Inventory_Change)
85   {
86       Grocery_Product_Inventory=
87              Grocery_Product_Inventory+Inventory_Change;
88       return(Grocery_Product_Inventory);
89    };
90   };
```

Listing 2.10b   Example of C++ program—grocery store (class grocery.h).

We examine how the program in Listing 2.10b works. Lines **8–12** define attributes of the GROCERY class. Lines **14–18** are the constructor. It is empty in this case. The actual "constructor" is implemented by an independent procedure named InitGrocery to initialize the values of attributes for the created objects of this class. It is specified in lines **24** through **65**.

As discussed earlier in this chapter, there are several ways to initialize the object. Typical business applications use disk data files (similar to that discussed in the chapter of COBOL) or databases. In this example, we simplify the issue and use the program to assign values to these attributes based on the identification of each object created. Line **25** assigns the Grocery_Product_Number with G_N which is brought up by the request message to the object. Lines **26–33** means that if G_N (the identification for the object to be created) is equal to 1, then the Grocery_Product_Name is assigned with "Milk", and so on. Line **28** is a notation that explains we would like to put some spaces in to make all the product names are of the same length. Similarly, lines **34–40** initialize the object with Grocery_Product_Number of 2, and so on.

There are six methods in this class. These methods are all easy to follow. As examined before, the order of these methods in the program of the class is not important.

We now examine the program in Listing 2.10a to study its functioning. Line **7** includes the program file for the GROCERY class. Line **13** defines a variable for discount rate. Lines **15–16** allow the user to input the discount rate. Lines **19–25** print out the heading for the discount flyer.

Lines **28–39** define a for-loop. The for-loop instructs the computer to do five times. For each time, it creates an object of Grocery (line **29**). When the computer encounters line **30**, the execution sequence turns to line **24** in Listing 2.10b. Line **25** in Listing 2.10b means that the identification of the object is brought by i, the control counter of the for-loop in the main program.

Return to the main program in Listing 2.10a. Within the for-loop, lines **32–33** print the product name which is obtained through the message. Line **34** prints the price before the discount. Lines **35–36** print the unit. Line **37** prints the price after the discount. The price after discount is obtained through the message sent to the object (see line **77** in Listing 2.10b).

Note that, in this example, method `Grocery_Inventory_Process` of `GROCERY` class is never used by the main program. In other words, a method built in a class may not be used by a particular program, but is ready for use. As an exercise, students may expand this main program by using this method for inventory processing.

From this example, we understand the differences and relationships between function-oriented and object-oriented approaches, including:

1. Using the OOP approach, a module is a class that encapsulates data and methods into a single software fragment. In the function-oriented approach, data and functions are separated. Definitions of object classes are natural, but definitions of functions are more or less artificial.
2. In OOP, a method is actually a "function" within the class. Within a method, we still use principles of "structured programming." From this view, the object-oriented paradigm encompasses the function-oriented paradigm.
3. From the view of computer execution, a called-function must be executed from the beginning to the end of the function module, but a message-evoked class might be used partially. In other words, in OOP, not every method defined in a class must be used for a particular application. The object-oriented approach is beneficial for **software reuse** because of such good features.

In the following sections, we will learn more about OOP.

2.6 Example of C++ Program with Two Object Classes

In this section, we present an example with two object classes. The program is supposed to produce an invoice of the book order upon the user types in an order number. There are two classes in this program: order and book. Using our OOP design method, the program is expressed in an OOP diagram as shown in Figure 2.12.

In this example, the main program obtains information of the order to be invoiced from the ORDER class, and then finds the book information pertinent to this order from the BOOK class. The **association** between the two objects (order and book) is the **data linkage** `Book_Number` accompanied with the messages, as shown in Figure 2.12 by the shaded data items. This linkage is implemented by one sentence in the main program shown in Listing 2.11a, line **32**.

```
1 // **** Main program for invoicing (file: invoice.cpp) ****

2 #include<stdio.h>
3 #include<stdlib.h>
4 #include<math.h>
5 #include<iostream.h>
6 #include<string.h>
7 #include"order.h"
8 #include"book.h"

9 // The header files of the classes ORDER and BOOK are included
```

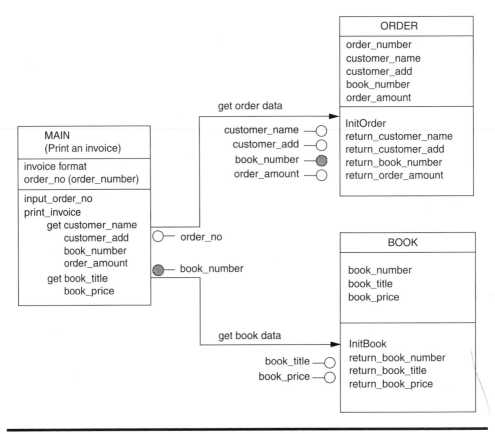

Figure 2.12   Example of OOP design—book order processing.

```
10 // The main program is to manipulate the ORDER and BOOK objects, and

11 // print an invoice based on the user inputed order number

12 main()
13 {
14   int order_no; // for order number

15 // The program asks the user to input the order number for the invoice
16 // In this illustrative case, we assume we have only 3 orders

17 printf("Please input the order number (1 or 2 or 3) for invoicing... \n");
18 cin>> order_no;
19 printf( "\n");

20 // Display the headlines of the flyer

21 printf("\n");
22 printf("\n");
23 printf("       UMD Campus Book Store Invoice   \n");
24 printf("       ***************************** \n");

25 printf("\n");
26 // The following procedure manipulate the ORDER and BOOK objects
```

```
27 ORDER Order;
28 Order.InitOrder(order_no);

29 printf("Customer Name:  %s \n", Order.ReturnCustomer_Name());
30 printf("Customer Address: %s \n", Order.ReturnCustomer_Add());
31 BOOK Book;
32 Book.InitBook(Order.ReturnBook_Number());

33 printf("Book Title:    %s \n", Book.ReturnBook_Title());

34 printf("Book Price:    $%4.2f \n", Book.ReturnBook_Price());

35 printf("Order Amount:   %u \n", Order.ReturnOrder_Amount());

36 printf("Amount Due:    $%4.2f \n",

37  Order.ReturnOrder_Amount()*Book.ReturnBook_Price());

38  printf("\n");
39 }
```

Listing 2.11a Example of C++ program—book order (main program invoice.cpp).

```
1 // **** Class ORDER definition ****
2 // File is "order.h"

3 class ORDER

4 // Class declaration
5 {
6  private:

7 // Attributes
8   int      Order_Number;
9   char     Customer_Name[20];
10   char     Customer_Add[20];
11   int      Book_Number;
12   int      Order_Amount;

13   public:
14    ORDER()
15    {
16 // Constructor is actually implemented by the method
17 //   void InitOrder(int) depending on Order_No
18    };

19 // Operations

20 // The following procedure simulates the system to read a
21 // database/data file which records information of the orders.
22 // One may substitute this procedure by using database/files

23    void InitOrder(int Order_No) {
24       Order_Number=Order_No;
```

```
25        if (Order_Number==1)
26              { strcpy(Customer_Name, "John     ");
27                strcpy(Customer_Add, "Westport ");
28                Book_Number=1234;
29                Order_Amount=10;
30              }
31        if (Order_Number==2)
32               { strcpy(Customer_Name, "Liz     ");
33                 strcpy(Customer_Add, "Eastport ");
34                 Book_Number=3456;
35                 Order_Amount=5;
36               }
37        if (Order_Number==3)
38               { strcpy(Customer_Name, "Bill    ");
39                 strcpy(Customer_Add, "Southport ");
40                 Book_Number=2345;
41                 Order_Amount=20;
42               }
43     }

44 // Next are methods of the ORDER class ...
45  // Return Customer Name

46  char *ReturnCustomer_Name()
47              {return Customer_Name;};

48  // Return Customer Address

49  char *ReturnCustomer_Add()
50              {return Customer_Add;};

51  // Return Book Number

52 int ReturnBook_Number()
53               {return Book_Number;};

54  // Return Order Amount

55 int ReturnOrder_Amount()
56               {return Order_Amount;};
57 };
```

Listing 2.11b   Example of C++ program—book order (class order.h).

```
1 // **** Class BOOK definition ****
2 // File is "book.h"

3 class BOOK

4 // Class declaration
5 {
6 private:
7 // Attributes
8  int   Book_Number;
9  char  Book_Title[30];
10  float  Book_Price;
```

```
11  public:
12   BOOK()
13    {
14 // Constructor is actually implemented by the method
15 //   void InitBook(int) depending on B_N
16   };
17 // Operations
18 // The following procedure simulates the system to read a
19 // database/data file which records information of the books.
20 // One may substitute this procedure by using database/files

21    void InitBook(int B_N) {
22        Book_Number=B_N;

23        if (Book_Number==1234)
24            { strcpy(Book_Title, "Programming    ");
25              Book_Price=29.59;
26            }
27        if (Book_Number==2345)
28            { strcpy(Book_Title, "Computers     ");
29              Book_Price=39.59;
30            }
31        if (Book_Number==3456)
32            { strcpy(Book_Title, "Systems Analysis ");
33              Book_Price=49.59;
34            }
35        if (Book_Number==4567)
36            { strcpy(Book_Title, "Data Bases    ");
37              Book_Price=59.59;
38            }
39    }

40 // Next are methods of the BOOK class ...

41  // Return Title
42  char *ReturnBook_Title()
43                {return Book_Title;};

44  // Return Price
45 float ReturnBook_Price()
46                {return Book_Price;};

47 };
```

Listing 2.11c   Example of C++ Program—book order (class book.h).

2.7   Example of C++ Program with Multiple Classes and Inheritance

In this example, we learn more about inheritance. This example is a payroll system. The system determines pay and produce a paycheck. There are two types of employee: full-time and part-time. The system determines pay based on time cards for part-time employees, but based on flat pay rates for full-time employees.

Using our OOP design method the payroll system is analyzed, and its OOP diagram is shown in Figure 2.13.

Several points are worth learning from this program.

1. OOP emphasizes data encapsulation. When the attributes are identified for each object, a data dictionary entry automatically results.
2. OOP emphasizes inheritance. In this case, both PARTTIMEEMPLOYEE and FULLTIMEEMPLOYEE could belong to the class EMPLOYEE. They share common data attributes and operations. Similar treatments could be applied to them.
3. OOP emphasizes service relationships between the modules (i.e., messages).

The OOP diagram in Figure 2.13 is translated to C++ program, as shown in Listing 2.12. Note that the main program and each of the classes should be stored in th eir own program file.

It will be observed that based on the OOP diagram, little expansion is needed to implement the software system. For instance, the object classes implemented in C++ are readily developed, corresponding to the object diagrams shown in Figure 2.13. All interactions between the objects are well defined by message sending.

Note that, in the C++ program of Listing 2.12, we use scope resolutions (e.g., EMPLOYEE::) to differentiate the methods with the same method names.

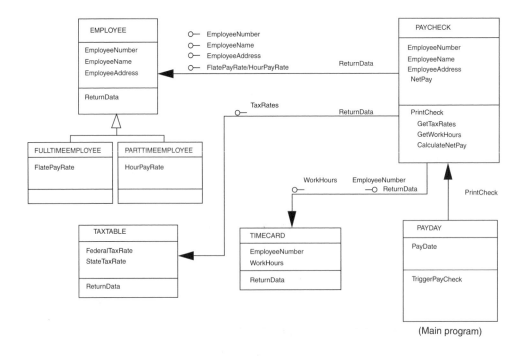

Figure 2.13   OOP design example with multiple classes and inheritance.

```
 1 // **** Main program (file: main.cpp) ****

 2 #include<stdio.h>
 3 #include<stdlib.h>
 4 #include<math.h>
 5 #include<string.h>
 6 #include<fstream.h>
 7 #include"paycheck.h"

 8  // In C++, a header file of the class used for this class is included
 9  // The main program is to simulate object PAYDAY to trigger PAYCHECK
10 void main()
11 {
12  int PayDay;
13  char TypeAgain;

14 // Get today's date
15    cout << "Enter today's date. Note that 7 is the payday. \n";
16   cin >> PayDay;
17 // If today is not the payday, the program does nothing
18    if (PayDay!=7) cout << "Sorry, today is not the payday! \n";
19 // If today is the payday, the program will print checks
20  if (PayDay==7) {
21 // Assume we want to print checks for all of the employees
22 // In this prototype, we assume there are 5 persons in the company
23 // This procedure could be modified for a specific case
24    for (int i=1; i<=5; i++) {
25 // Define an object Paycheck of Class PAYCHECK
26        PAYCHECK Paycheck;
27 // Message to Paycheck to print paychecks and get net pay amount as well
28        Paycheck.PrintRecord(i);
29    if (i<5)
30 { cout << "\n Do you need the next check ...(type y then enter)... \n";
31   cin >> TypeAgain;}
32    else
33 { cout << "Thank you for using this payroll system! \n"; };

34    }
35  }
36 }

37 // **** Class PAYCHECK ****
38 // File is "paycheck.h"

39 #include"timecard.h"
40 // TIMECARD class is used for this class, and its file is included

41 #include"employee.h"
42 // EMPLOYEE and its subclasses FULLTIMEEMPLOYEE and
43 // PARTTIMEEMPLOYEE are included

44 #include"taxtable.h"
45 // TAXTABLE class is used for this class, and its file is included

46 class PAYCHECK
```

```
47 {
48 // Attributes
49  private:
50   char EmployeeNumber[5],
51            EmployeeName[30],
52            EmployeeAddress[30];

53       float NetPay;
54    public:
55 // Operations
56        void PAYCHECK::PrintRecord(int i) {
57                float TimeWorked, PayRate, FedTaxRate, StateTaxRate;

58        strcpy(EmployeeNumber, GetEmployeeNumber(i));
59        strcpy(EmployeeName, GetEmployeeName(i));
60        strcpy(EmployeeAddress, GetEmployeeAddress(i));
61        TimeWorked=GetTimeWorked(EmployeeNumber);
62        PayRate=GetEmployeePayRate(EmployeeNumber);
63        FedTaxRate=GetFederalTaxRate();
64        StateTaxRate=GetStateTaxRate();
65 NetPay=CalculateNetPay(TimeWorked,PayRate, FedTaxRate, StateTaxRate);

66 // The following defines the check's format
67 printf("\n=======================================================");
68  printf("\n T H E   C O M P A N Y   B A N K   C H E C K");
69  printf("\n ******************************************* \n");
70 printf("Employee No.: %s \n", EmployeeNumber);
71 printf("Name:        %s \n", EmployeeName);
72 printf("Address:     %s \n", EmployeeAddress);
73 printf("Net Payment:                          $%5.2f", NetPay);
74 printf("\n==============================================\n");

75 }

76        char *PAYCHECK::GetEmployeeNumber(int i) {
77        char E_Number[5];
78        EMPLOYEE Employee;
79        Employee.InitEmployee(i);
80        strcpy(E_Number, Employee.ReturnE());
81        return(E_Number);
82        }

83        char *PAYCHECK::GetEmployeeName(int i) {
84        char E_Name[30];
85        EMPLOYEE Employee;
86        Employee.InitEmployee(i);
87        strcpy(E_Name, Employee.ReturnEN());
88        return(E_Name);
89        }

90        char *PAYCHECK::GetEmployeeAddress(int i) {
91        char E_Address[30];
92        EMPLOYEE Employee;
93        Employee.InitEmployee(i);
```

```
94        strcpy(E_Address, Employee.ReturnEA());
95        return(E_Address);
96        }

97        float PAYCHECK::GetTimeWorked(char *E_N) {
98        float TimeWorked;
99        TIMECARD TimeCard;
100       TimeCard.InitEmployeeNumber(E_N);
101       TimeWorked=TimeCard.ReturnData();
102       return(TimeWorked);
103       }

104       float PAYCHECK::GetEmployeePayRate(char *E_N) {
105       float PayRate;

106       FULLTIMEEMPLOYEE FullTimeEmployee;
107       FullTimeEmployee.InitFullPayRate(E_N);
108       PayRate=FullTimeEmployee.ReturnFullPayRate();

109       if (PayRate==0.0) {
110       PARTTIMEEMPLOYEE PartTimeEmployee;
111       PartTimeEmployee.InitHourPayRate(E_N);
112       PayRate=PartTimeEmployee.ReturnHourPayRate();
113       }
114       return PayRate;
115       }

116       float PAYCHECK::GetFederalTaxRate() {
117       TAXTABLE TaxRate;
118       return(TaxRate.ReturnFederalTaxRate());
119       }

120       float PAYCHECK::GetStateTaxRate() {
121       TAXTABLE TaxRate;
122       return(TaxRate.ReturnStateTaxRate());
123       }
124 float PAYCHECK::CalculateNetPay(float W_T, float P_R, float F_T, float P_T)
125 {
126 // Calculate net pay based on work time, pay rate, and tax rates
127 float NetPay;

128 if (P_R<=40.0) { NetPay=W_T*P_R*(1-F_T)*(1-P_T); }
129 // Suppose pay rate is less 40 for part time employee,
130 // otherwise the rate (must be greater than 40) is flat for FT employee
131 else      { NetPay=P_R*(1-F_T)*(1-P_T); };
132  return NetPay;
133 }
134 };
135 // **** Class EMPLOYEE and its subclasses FULLTIMEEMPLOYEE and
136 // PARTTIMEEMPLOYEE
137 // File is "employee.h"
138 class EMPLOYEE
139 {
```

```
140 // Attributes
141 // EMPLOYEE is a superclass (base class). Its attributes may be
142  // used by its subclasses (derived class), and use definition of
143 // 'protected'

144   protected:

145   char    EmployeeNumber[5];
146   char    EmployeeName[30];
147   char    EmployeeAddress[30];

148   public:
149  // Constructor

150   EMPLOYEE()
151  {
152 // The constructor is defined by void InitEmployee(int);
153  };

154 //  Operations

155 //  Function for the constructor
156 //  The following procedure simulates a search a database or data file
157 //  for EMPLOYEE information. One may use a database/data file search
158 //  procedure to substitute this function.

159   void EMPLOYEE::InitEmployee(int i) {

160       if (i==1) {
161               strcpy(EmployeeNumber, "123");
162               strcpy(EmployeeName, "Ann");
163               strcpy(EmployeeAddress, "A Street");};

164       if (i==2) {
165               strcpy(EmployeeNumber, "234");
166               strcpy(EmployeeName, "Bill");
167               strcpy(EmployeeAddress, "B Street");};

168       if (i==3) {
169               strcpy(EmployeeNumber, "345");
170               strcpy(EmployeeName, "Connie");
171               strcpy(EmployeeAddress, "C Street");};

172       if (i==4) {
173               strcpy(EmployeeNumber, "456");
174               strcpy(EmployeeName, "Dany");
175               strcpy(EmployeeAddress, "D Street");};

176       if (i==5) {
177               strcpy(EmployeeNumber, "567");
178               strcpy(EmployeeName, "Ed");
179               strcpy(EmployeeAddress, "E Street");};
180     }
181 // Methods
182  char *EMPLOYEE::ReturnE() { return EmployeeNumber; };
```

```
183  char *EMPLOYEE::ReturnEN() { return EmployeeName; };
184   char *EMPLOYEE::ReturnEA() { return EmployeeAddress; };
185 };

186 // Subclass FULL-TIME-EMPLOYEE
187 // Its superclass is EMPLOYEE
188 class FULLTIMEEMPLOYEE : public EMPLOYEE

189 {
190  private:
191    float FullPayRate;
192  public:
193    FULLTIMEEMPLOYEE()
194    {
195    // The constructor is defined by void InitFullPayRate(char);
196    }

197 // Operations
198 // Function for the constructor
199 // The following function simulates a database/data file function to
200 // retrieve the flat pay rate for full time employees.
201 // One may use a database/data file processing to substitute it.

202 void FULLTIMEEMPLOYEE::InitFullPayRate(char *EmployeeNumber) {

203 if (strcmp(EmployeeNumber, "123")==0) FullPayRate=1100.00;
204 if (strcmp(EmployeeNumber, "234")==0) FullPayRate=1300.00;
205 if (strcmp(EmployeeNumber, "345")==0) FullPayRate=1500.00;
206 if (strcmp(EmployeeNumber, "456")==0) FullPayRate=0.00;
207 if (strcmp(EmployeeNumber, "567")==0) FullPayRate=0.00;
208 }

209 // Methods
210    float FULLTIMEEMPLOYEE::ReturnFullPayRate() { return FullPayRate; }
211 };

212 // Subclass PART-TIME-EMPLOYEE
213 // Its superclass is EMPLOYEE

214 class PARTTIMEEMPLOYEE : public EMPLOYEE

215 {
216  private:
217    float HourPayRate;

218  public:
219    PARTTIMEEMPLOYEE()
220    {
221    // The constructor is defined by  void InitHourPayRate(char);
222    }

223 // Operations
224 // Function for the constructor
225 // The following function simulates a database/data file function to
226 // retrieve hour pay rates for part time employees.
```

```
227  // One may use a database/data file processing to substitute it.

228 void PARTTIMEEMPLOYEE::InitHourPayRate(char *EmployeeNumber) {
229      if (strcmp(EmployeeNumber, "456")==0) HourPayRate=10.00;
230      if (strcmp(EmployeeNumber, "567")==0) HourPayRate=12.00;
231     }
232 // Methods
233 float PARTTIMEEMPLOYEE::ReturnHourPayRate() { return HourPayRate; }
234 };
235 // **** Class TIME_CARD definition ****

236 // File is "timecard.h"

237 class TIMECARD
238 // Class declaration
239 {
240   private:

241 // Attributes
242   char EmployeeNumber[5];
243   float WorkHours;

244    public:
245 // Constructor

246 TIMECARD ()
247 {
248 // Initialize EmployeeNumber by void InitEmployeeNumber(char);
249 };

250 // Operations

251  void TIMECARD::InitEmployeeNumber(char *E_N) {
252     strcpy(EmployeeNumber, E_N);
253 }

254 // The following procedure simulates the system to read time cards
255 // or search a database/data file which records the work hours
256 // for each of the employees.
257 // One may substitute it with a procedure of the database system
258  float TIMECARD::ReturnData() {
259            if (strcmp(EmployeeNumber, "123")==0) WorkHours=32.5;
260            if (strcmp(EmployeeNumber, "234")==0) WorkHours=34.5;
261            if (strcmp(EmployeeNumber, "345")==0) WorkHours=35.0;
262            if (strcmp(EmployeeNumber, "456")==0) WorkHours=20.5;
263            if (strcmp(EmployeeNumber, "567")==0) WorkHours=37.5;
264     return WorkHours; }
265 };

266 // **** Class TAXTALBE ****
267 // File is "taxtable.h"

268 class TAXTABLE
269 {
```

```
270 // Attributes

271    private:
272    float FederalTaxRate,
273    StateTaxRate;

274 public:
275 // Constructor
276 // Practically, the taxtable could be a data file containing
277 // a matrix indexed by income range

278 TAXTABLE() {
279 FederalTaxRate=0.15;
280 StateTaxRate=0.10;
281 }

282 // Operations
283 // If a data file is practically used, the following methods
284 // can be procedures to retrieve tax rates
285    float ReturnFederalTaxRate() { return FederalTaxRate; };
286    float ReturnStateTaxRate() { return StateTaxRate; };
287 };
```

Listing 2.12   C++ program for the OOP design in Figure 2.13.

In the above C++ program, only the part of inheritance is a new subject. Line **188** defines the subclass FULLTIMEEMPLOYEE within class EMPLOYEE. Line **214** defines another subclass PARTTIMEEMPLOYEE within class EMPLOYEE. Note that the two subclasses share the same attributes (lines **145–147**, EmployeeNumber, EmployeeName, and EmployeeAddress), but have different pay rate. Line **191** defines the flat pay rate for FULLTIMEEMPLOYEE, and line **217** defines the hour pay rate for PARTTIMEEMPLOYEE.

2.8   Identify Classes for OOP Projects

In designing object-oriented programs, one must **identify classes**. The general rules for the determination of classes for object-oriented programs can be summarized as follows:

1. **Physiomorphic** object classes are physically existing entities; e.g., customer, student, and inventory.
2. **Event** object classes represent events of routine operations; e.g., ordering and credit approving.
3. **Document** object classes are information entities that enter the business process (e.g., orders), or information entities produced by the business process (e.g., online bill).

An attribute is not an object class. For example, Student_Name is not a class. It is an attribute of Student object class. A generic function is not an object class. For example, Calculate_Sum_of_Two_Number or Find_Future_Value is not an object class, but could be a method of a class.

2.9 Debugging

Debugging C/C++ programs is a difficult task. After compiling (build) a C/C++ program, the compiler will show error or warning messages if the program is not perfect. A warning message does not prevent you to run the program, but it might cause problems (e.g., loss of information when converting data types). Any error could be fatal. In a good programming environment, if you click an error item, the environment will move the cursor to the place where the error is caused. However, the real problem may not be exactly located. Also, an error-free condition is necessary, but it does not guarantee the correctives of your program.

Common syntax errors are:

- Typos of misspelling a word.
- Omitting a symbol (e.g., missing one side of brace or parenthesis).
- Violating format.
- Using an undefined user-defined variable.

Logical errors or runtime errors often occur when the computer performs wrong operations, not as you direct it. To debug logical errors, one should use data samples to test the program based on the output of the program.

1. Exercise every possible option to check the computer outputs to see if the program does only as you direct it. if statements are commonly examined to find possible options.
2. A program might terminate with crash. Usually, it is caused by wrong data types, wrong calculations (e.g., a number is divided by zero), a wrong size of an array, or wrong data file operations.
3. If a program is "dead," you must terminate it through interruption (e.g., by punching [Ctrl + C] simultaneously). A "dead" program is more likely caused by a "dead" loop. You should check for-loop statements and if statements.

Warning messages often appear after the compiling. For example, if the program involves data type conversion (e.g., convert a variable from integer to floating), the compiler will give a warning that some information might be lost during the conversion. Warning does not prevent the execution of the program.

2.10 Self-Review Exercise

1. Read the following C program and complete it by filling the blanks.

```
1 # include        <stdio.h>
2    float     Commission_Calculation( float );
3 main()
```

```
 4 {
 5     int      i;
 6 float sales;
 7 float commission_rate ;
 8 for (i=1 ;  i<=3 ;  i++)
 9 {
*10  sales=10.0*i;
 11  Commission_Rate=Commission_Calculation(sales);     describes format
*12    printf("The commission rate for sales of %2.2f is : %2.2f.\n",
```
(arrow pointing to %2.2f) describes format

```
 13    sales, Commission_Rate);
 14 }
 15 }
 16 float Commission_Calculation(float S)
 17 {
 18  float     C_R;
 19  if (S<=15)   { C_R=0.01; };
 20  if ((S>15) && (S<=25) )    { C_R=0.02; };
 21  if (S>25)    { C_R=0.01; };
 22  return   (C_R);
 23 }
```

main

Commission_calculation

2. Draw a structure diagram for the C program in exercise 1.

*3. Write the expected print result generated by the C program in exercise 1.

4. Read the following C++ program and complete it by filling the blanks.

* The commission rate for sales of 10.0 is 0.01.
The commission rate for sales of 20.0 is 0.02.
The commission rate for sales of 80.0 is 0.03.

```
 1 #include<stdio.h>
 2 #include<stdlib.h>
 3 #include<math.h>
 4 #include<iostream.h>
 5 #include<string.h>
 6 #include"customer.h"
 7 // The header file of the class CUSTOMER used is included
 8 main()
 9 {
10  float    credit;
11  printf( "Customer Name    Payment Due \n");
12  printf( "\n");
13  credit=100.0;
14  for (int i=1; i<=3; i++) {
15     CUSTOMER Customer;
16     Customer.   ConstCustomer(i);
17  printf ("%s    ", Customer.ReturnCustomer_Name());
18  printf("%4.2f \n", Customer.Customer_Due(credit));
19     } ;
20  }
```

```
 1 // **** Class CUSTOMER definition ****
 2 // File is "customer.h"
 3 class CUSTOMER
 4 // Class declaration
 5 {
 6    private:
 7 // Attributes
 8    int  Customer_Number;
```

```
 9     char  Customer_Name[20];
10     float  Customer_Balance;
11    char  Customer_Phone[15];

12 public:
13    CUSTOMER ()
14    {
15 // Constructor is actually implemented by the method
16 //    void ConstCustomer(int) depending on C_N
17       };
18 // Operations
19 // The following procedure simulates the system to read a
20 //database/data file which records information of customer
21  void ConstCustomer(int C_N) {
22        Customer_Number=C_N;
23        if (Customer_Number==1)
24            { strcpy(Customer_Name, "John    ");
25              Customer_Balance=200.0;
26              strcpy(Customer_Phone, "123-1234 ");
27            }
28        if (Customer_Number==2)
29            { strcpy(Customer_Name, "Anne    ");
30              Customer_Balance=-200.0;
31              strcpy(Customer_Phone, "123-2345 ");
32            }
33        if (Customer_Number==3)
34            { strcpy(Customer_Name, "Greg    ");
35              Customer_Balance=100.0;
36              strcpy(Customer_Phone, "123-7890 ");
37            }
38  }

39 // Next are methods of the CUSTOMER class ...

40  char  *  ReturnCustomer_Name()
41              {return Customer_Name;};

42  char  *ReturnCustomer_Phone()
43              {return Customer_Phone;};

44  float ReturnCustomer_Balance()
45              {return Customer_Balance;};

46  float Customer_Due(float CR) {
47     float  Due_Amount ;
48        if ((Customer_Balance+CR)<0)
49           { Due_Amount=(Customer_Balance+CR)*-1; }
50        else
51           { Due_Amount=0; };
52     return  (Due_Amount);
53 }
54   };                                  ↗ P.71
```

5. Draw an OOA diagram for the C++ program in exercise 4.

6. Write the expected print result generated by the C++ program in exercise 4.

7. Run the C++ program in Listing 2.10. Has the method `Grocery_Inventory_Process` of the GROCERY class ever been used in this program? Discuss the advantages of object-oriented modules.

8. Read the C++ program in Listing 2.11. Sketch the expected print result generated by the program.

9. Compare function-oriented approach and object-oriented approach.

10. Develop a C project that contains one main program and two or more functions.

11. Develop a C++ project that contains one main program and two or more classes.

Appendix 2.1   Commonly Used C and C++ Keywords

C and C++ Keywords

auto	break	case	char
const	continue	default	do
double	else	enum	float
for	goto	if	int
long	register	return	short
signed	static	struct	typedef
union	unsigned	void	while

C++ Only Keywords

catch	class	dynamic_cast	explicit
false	friend	new	operator
private	protected	public	static_cast
template	this	true	try
typeid	typename	using	

Appendix 2.2   Instructions for Using C++ on Mainframe

C and C++ are usually available on any mainframe computer. To use your PC with the Windows operating system to access C and C++ on the mainframe through the network, you need to find a **terminal emulator for Windows** (e.g., PowerTerm for Windows). The terminal emulator can emulate terminals of various types and allow the user to access programs and data on the mainframe. However, within the terminal emulator's environment, the user still uses the traditional operating system commands. The following is the procedures of using C and C++ on the mainframe.

Appendix 2.3   Guideline for C++ Project Report

1.   Front page
     Course name
     Title of the project

Step	C	C++
1. Log-in		
2. Start editing	$edit [filename.c] e.g., edit w.c	$edit [filename.cpp] for main program e.g., edit w.cpp $edit [filename.h] for class e.g., edit BOOK.h
3. Edit	Type code	Type code
4. Finish editing	Type Ctrl+z	Type Ctrl+z
5. Exit editing	* exit	* exit
6. Compile	$ cc [filename.c] e.g., cc w.c	$ cxx [filename.cpp] e.g., cxx w.cpp
7. Link	$ link [filename.obj] e.g., link w.obj	$ cxxl [filename.obj] e.g., cxxl w.obj
8. Run	$ run [filename.exe] e.g., run w.exe	$ run [filename.exe] e.g., run w.exe

(See **Instructions of Using COBOL on Mainframe** for $dir, $del, $print, copying files to Notepad, and uploading/downloading files.)

    Group members (names and ID)
    Date
2.   Text
    Introduction and the problem to be solved
    Application of C++
    Discussion of the advantages and the disadvantages of C++
3.   Diagrams
    OOA diagrams
4.   Source code of the C++ programs
5.   Examples of test data (must be original)
6.   Samplers of printout (must be original)
7.   Operation manual for the users of the C++ programs

Chapter 3

HTML, JavaScript, and Web Pages

3.1 Introduction to World Wide Web and the Internet

As a new information technology, the **World Wide Web** (**WWW** or the **Web**) has had a remarkable impact on business and organizations globally. The Web is the prototype for the "information superhighway." Using the Web, people create innovative ways of doing business and change existing business customs. To participate in this business revolution one must become familiar with the Web. This chapter provides essential knowledge for understanding the process of creating Web pages.

The **Internet** is a network of networks. It is a linkage of smaller networks each of which agrees to use the same communication rules (called a **protocol**) for exchanging information. The Internet protocol is a transmission control protocol/Internet protocol (**TCP/IP**). The Internet is a great place to acquire information from across the world. The user can also acquire computer software or even work on other computers located thousands of miles away. Major **Internet Operations** are summarized as follows:

Internet Operations	Purposes
E-mail	Exchange electronic messages
FTP (File Transfer Protocol)	Retrieve files from a computer elsewhere on the Internet
Telnet	Work on a computer elsewhere on the Internet (e.g., log on the UMD mainframe from your home)
World Wide Web	Transfer text, images, and sound on the Internet

To access the Internet, the computer must be linked to the Internet through an **Internet provider** (usually a local telephone company). Computers on the Internet play two types of roles: server and client. On the Internet, a **server** is a computer that manages its data including text, images, video clips, and sound. A server computer is set up by an individual or organization and it allows other computers to access its data. On the Web, a server is also called a **Web site**. A **client** is a PC that can access data on a server. On the Web, the software supporting the client operations is called a **browser**. Netscape Navigator and Microsoft Internet Explorer are the two most popular Web browsers. A browser uses a **graphical user interface** (**GUI**) which is supported by a local operating system, for example, Microsoft Windows.

The first page encountered when one visits a Web site is the **home page** of the site. From the home page one can explore other Web pages and other Web sites that have been linked to it. A Web home page is accessed by an address. In Web terminology, the address of a Web page is referred to as its **Uniform Resource Locator** (**URL**), because a URL is a standard means of consistently locating the Web page no matter where they are stored on the Internet. A URL for a Web page is defined by the letters **http**, which stands for **Hypertext Transfer Protocol**.

The documents available on the Internet make wide use of **hypertext** and **multimedia**. Using hypertext, the user can move from document to document by following hyperlinks. Hypertext and multimedia are often combined to create **hypermedia**. With hypermedia, a user can have an in-depth look at a Web page by clicking on a graphic image and hearing an audio clip, or clicking on a word and seeing animation.

3.2   Creating Web Pages Using HTML

There are many software packages available for creating Web pages. Like word processing software, these Web page authoring tools allow the user to use menus and function buttons to create Web pages, thereby releasing the user from tedious programming work. In fact, many word processing software packages can translate an ordinary document into a Web page. However, the basic tool for creating Web pages is the **Hypertext Markup Language** (HTML).

To use HTML to create a Web page, one needs to follow the following steps.

1.   Create your own folder (directory). Save your Web pages in this folder.
2.   Edit a text of HTML for the Web page. **Notepad** or **WordPad** in the Accessories group in the Windows operating system can be used for editing. The Web page developer can write a HTML text (see Listing 3.1 for an example of HTML), and save it to your folder as a file with the extension name **.html**, e.g., MyWebPage.html. If you use Notepad, make sure you choose [All Files] for [Save as type] when you save the file. If you use WordPad, you choose [Text Document] for

[Save as type], and may also want click the check box to set this
format as default. When you use WordPad to open a file, you need to
choose [All Documents] for [Files of Type] to view all files
in your folder.

3. Re-open the HTML text file in a Web browser. In Netscape or Microsoft
    Internet Explorer, click [File], [Open], and the HTML file you saved.
    The HTML file is opened and read by the browser. The Web page
    described by the HTML is then displayed on the screen. You can also
    open a Web page by clicking the icon of the Web page file you saved.

4. Make changes. If modification is required, the original HTML text file
    should be called up in the editor (Notepad or WordPad). After making
    modifications, you must save it before re-opening it in the Web
    browser.

The basic component of HTML is a **tag** which tells the browser how to
display data. HTML **container tags** are used in pairs to indicate the start and
end of a structure. For example:

```
<TITLE>Jonh Smith's Web Page</TITLE>
```

The tags <TITLE> and </TITLE> around the text inform the browser that
these words are the title of the Web page. **Empty tags** do not surround any
components. For example, <HR> causes a horizontal line, and does not hold
text.

Web pages have a particular structure which is stated as follows:

```
<HTML>
 <HEAD>
 . . . . . .
 </HEAD>
 <BODY>
 . . . . . .
 </BODY>
</HTML>
```

In this book, we learn most commonly used tags.

3.3   Simple Container Tags

Major simple container tags are presented below.

3.3.1   *<HTML>*

It indicates the document written in HTML.

3.3.2   *<HEAD> and <TITLE>*

These tags are used to identify the title of the document. The title of the Web
page will be displayed on the top of the browser window.

3.3.3 <BODY>

It is used to contain the main portion of an HTML document.

The BGCOLOR attribute controls the background color of the page. For example, <BODY BGCOLOR=LIGHTBLUE> makes a light blue background. One can also use a code to define the background color (e.g., <BODY BGCOLOR=00FFFF>).

The BACKGROUND attribute brings a background image for the Web page. For example, <BODY BACKGROUND="Marble.gif"> makes the image "Marble.gif" as the background if the image file is stored with the Web page.

3.3.4 Comments <!-- ... -->

You may put comments within pair <!-- and -->.

3.3.5 Headings <H1> ... <H6>

These tags indicate headings. HTML allows six different levels of headings. <H1> has the biggest font, and <H6> has the smallest font.

3.3.6 <P>

It indicates a new paragraph. <P ALIGN=CENTER> is used for centering a paragraph.

3.3.7 <I>

The text within the container tags is displayed in italics.

3.3.8 <DL><DT><DD>

HTML provides a variety of functions of formatting the document. <DL> <DT><DD> are a few of them. They stand for definition list, define term, and define definition, respectively.

3.3.9 <A>

The anchor tag <A> creates a link to another Web site. It can have **attributes**. HREF (hypertext reference) defines the target of the link to the URL. For example:

```
<A HREF="http://www.umassd.edu">UMD</A>
```

means that the user is allowed to access "http://www.umassd.edu" by clicking "UMD."

3.3.10 *<CENTER>*

All text and images within a <CENTER> container will be centered on the page.

3.4 Empty Tags

Major empty tags are presented below.

3.4.1 *<HR>*

<HR> causes a horizontal rule.

3.4.2 *
*

It adds a line break into the text.

3.4.3 *<IMG>*

One of the attractions of the Web pages is the integration of text and images. Web browsers support a wide variety of image formats. The two most popular formats are **GIF** (**.gif** files) and **JPEG** (**.jpg** files). JPEG files have a higher quality, but GIF files can be "animated" images. An animated GIF file has a series of images that are displayed in an order to form animation (e.g., rotation and motion). You can download images from the Internet by right-clicking the image you want to download and then click [Save As] on the displayed menu to save it.

Images can be inserted into a document by using <IMG> tag. Using <IMG> tag, you must include **attributes** in the tag. The ALIGN attribute indicates the position of the image. The SRC attribute defines the source of the image. The ALT (alternate) attribute contains a text that is displayed when the browser is unable to display the actual image.

Listing 3.1 shows a simple Web page example. This Web page is not well designed, and merely shows the basic features of some tags. Students are encouraged to learn more about the HTML through further reading, view the source code of well-designed Web pages, and design a fancy Web page for your project.

```
1  <HTML>
2    <HEAD>
3     <TITLE>A Web Page</TITLE>
4    </HEAD>
5  <BODY BGCOLOR="#FFFFF">
6    <H1>My First Web Page <BR> The Largest Heading</H1>
7    <H6>The Smallest Heading</H6>
8    <HR>
9    I am trying to learn HTML to create my own Web page. I start
10   with this toy example to see what it looks like.
```

```
11    <P>
12    Now I am going to put interesting information on my page.
13    I am using DL to define a list, DT to define a term, and DD to
14    define definition of the term.
15    </P>

16  <DL>
17    <DT>MIS 212
18    <DD>Programming and Business Problem Solving
19    <DT>MIS 315
20    <DD>Management Information Systems
21  </DL>

22    <P>
23    The real power of Web pages is the ability to create links. To
24    learn about <I>links</I>, go to the Web site for
25    <A HREF="http://www.taylorandfrancis.com/">Taylor & Francis</A>.
26    </P>

27    <P>
28    I can also put images and email addresses on my Web page.
29    </P>
30    <P ALIGN=CENTER>
31    <IMG ALIGN=MIDDLE ALT="T&F Logo"
32  SRC="http://www.taylorandfrancis.com/images/tandf_banner_top_logo.gif">
33    <A HREF="mailto:MyEmail@YourUniversity.edu">MyEmaiAddress</A>
34    </P>

35    </BODY>
36    </HTML>
```

Listing 3.1   Example of HTML code for a Web page.

The Netscape's presentation of the HTML Web page is shown in Figure 3.1.

3.5   Complex Container Tags

3.5.1   *<FORM>*

One of the most useful features of HTML is **FORM**. A form allows the user to fill out data and click a "**SUBMIT**" button that sends the data from the filled form to the server that hosts the Web page. To process the data sent from the form, the server must run a program. There are many types of programs that can process the client requests through FORM. Common Gateway Interface (CGI) programs are commonly used for this purpose. A CGI program can be written in Practical Extraction Report Language (**Perl**), C, or other languages. **Java Servlet** is another common approach to processing data submitted by FORM on the server's side. Perl and Java Servlet is discussed in the later chapters.

To collect a small amount of data submitted by FORM, it is possible to use the e-mail system but not build a program to handle the data. Note that the

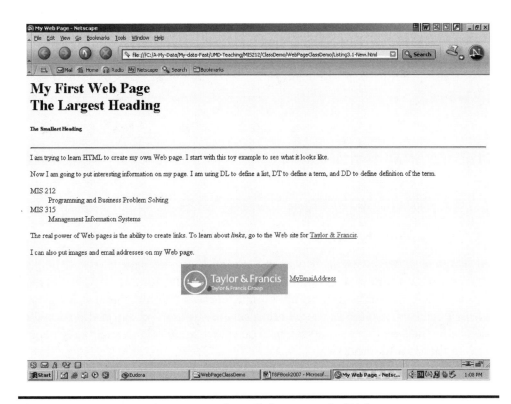

Figure 3.1   Netscape's presentation of the example Web page.

transmission of data through FORM highly depends upon the server that receives the data. It is no surprise if an e-mail server does not receive data filled in the FORM properly. Listing 3.2 shows an example of form. You may modify your e-mail address and then try the Web page. Also, you may insert lines 6–18 of Listing 3.2 into the HTML document in Listing 3.1 at the line right before </BODY> (line 35) to merge the two Web pages.

```
1    <HTML>
2    <HEAD>
3    <TITLE> My Form Web Page </TITLE>
4    </HEAD>
5    <BODY>
6    <H2> SEND DATA TO ME! </H2>
7    Please fill the form and submit it :
8    <BR>

9    <FORM ACTION = "mailto:MyEmail@U.edu" METHOD=POST>
10   Your Name: <BR>
11   <INPUT TYPE=TEXT NAME="name" SIZE=50> <BR>

12   Your Email Address: <BR>
13   <INPUT TYPE=TEXT NAME="email" SIZE=50> <BR>

14   Your Brief Comments: <BR>
```

```
15    <TEXTAREA NAME="comm" ROWS=4 COLS=50> </TEXTAREA> <BR>

16    <INPUT TYPE=SUBMIT VALUE="Submit the Data">
17    <INPUT TYPE=RESET VALUE="Start Over Again">

18    </FORM>
19    </BODY>
20    </HTML>
```

Listing 3.2   HTML code of a form.

Several attributes of FORM and related tags are explained below.

3.5.1.1   Attribute ACTION

The attribute ACTION points to the application that is to capture the data. The value of this attribute could be a CGI program on the remote server specified by a URL, or, in our example, an e-mail address. When you use an e-mail system to capture the data, the location of the captured data on the receiver's side is specified by the e-mail system. You may use an editor, such as Notepad, to open the data file and view it.

3.5.1.2   Attribute METHOD

The attribute METHOD instructs the browser to send the data back to the server. The value of the attribute could be GET or POST. GET is not recommended recently. In general cases, POST should be used.

3.5.2   <INPUT> and Its Attributes TYPE, NAME, SIZE, and VALUE

The INPUT tag is the tool to create actual input fields in a form. It has attributes such as TYPE, NAME, SIZE, and VALUE. The TYPE attribute specifies the type of the input field. TEXT and TEXTAREA are used for text-entry. RADIO is used for radio buttons. The NAME attribute of the INPUT tag specifies the label, or the name of the input field. The SIZE attribute specifies the size of the text-entry field.

SUBMIT is used to create a submission command button, and RESET is used to create a reset command button. The VALUE attributes give the labels on these command buttons.

3.5.3   FRAME and FRAMESET

One HTML Web page can host several sub-pages. The space on the screen for a sub-page is called **frame**. Using the <FRAMESET> and <FRAME> tags, the Web page designer sets frames and defines each frames, as shown in an example in Listing 3.3.

```
<HTML>
<FRAMESET COLS="25%, *">
    <FRAME SRC="Frame1.html">
    <FRAME SRC="Frame2.html">
</FRAMESET>
</HTML>
```

Listing 3.3   HTML code for setting frames.

In the example given earlier, the frames are set in columns. The left column occupies 25 percent of the entire screen width. The asterisk sign means that the rest of the screen is allocated to the right column. A frame can be set in rows when using the attribute ROWS for the tag. Within the <FRAMESET> container, the two frames are defined by using <FRAME> tags. The attribute SRC defines the two source Web pages for the sub-pages.

3.6   Publish the Web Page and Create Web Pages without Writing HTML

To publish Web pages on the Internet, one needs to get space on a Web server. You may rent space from a Web hosting provider (e.g., a local telephone company). Some Web hosting providers have their own Web standards and guidelines. If the Web is crucial for your business, you can create your own Web server by connecting a dedicated computer to the Internet.

Recently, many software packages, including word processing packages, are available to allow users to create Web pages without writing HTML. Nevertheless, the code of the Web pages for the Internet browsers is still HTML. After you download a Web page from the Internet using a browser (e.g., Netscape), you can view the HTML source code of the Web page by clicking the main menu [View] and then [Source Code]. By viewing the source code of various Web pages, you can learn more about HTML.

3.7   Introduction to JavaScript

A **script language** is embedded or interpreted by another program (e.g., HTML). It does not instruct the computer processor directly, and has limited functions. **JavaScript** is a script language and is directly interspersed with HTML statements. Microsoft's version of JavaScript is called **Jscript**. Originally, JavaScript was used to validate user input, but now it is used to accomplish a variety of tasks including client-side calculations, client-side lookup databases, create image maps, and personalize documents before they are displayed.

In terms of syntax, JavaScript is very similar to C and C++. A JavaScript program is contained between the <SCRIPT> and </SCRIPT> tags in the HTML program, with exceptions of **event handlers** as discussed later. JavaScript is entirely interpreted at run time. JavaScript can be put in either of two places in an HTML program: between <HEAD> and </HEAD> or between <BODY> or </BODY>. JavaScript is case-sensitive.

Listing 3.4 is a simple example of JavaScript program that displays a line of message in the Web page created by HTML. For illustration purpose, we use bold font for the part of JavaScript in the example.

```
 1 <HTML>
 2  <HEAD>
 3   <TITLE> Hello World Example of JavaScript </TITLE>
 4  </HEAD>
 5  <BODY>

 6   <SCRIPT>

 7   document.write("Hello, World! I am learning JavaScript!")

 8   </SCRIPT>

 9  </BODY>
10 </HTML>
```

Listing 3.4   JavaScript example "Hello, World!".

3.8   Typical Examples of JavaScript

Three major applications of JavaScript in Web pages (manipulating images, manipulating FORM, verifying input data of form, and processing cookies) are illustrated in this section through examples.

3.8.1   Image Manipulations

Listing 3.5 shows a simple example of manipulating images. Assume that there are two images, called photo1.jpg and photo2.jpg in the **JPEG** format. In this example, these two images are placed in the folder named images. This images folder and the HTML program are placed in the same folder. This JavaScript program implements an image rollover task described as follows: After opening the Web page, if the user uses the mouse to point to the image originally displayed in photo1, the user may click on the image to load the linked Web home page. However, when the user moves the mouse out from photo1, the image rollovers to photo2. When the mouse is moved back to the image, the image rollovers back to photo1. To test this program, one must make (or copy) two images in the JPEG format.

```
 1 <HTML>
 2  <HEAD>
 3   <TITLE>My Web Page of Image Rollover</TITLE>
 4  </HEAD>
 5  <BODY>
 6   <A HREF = "http://www.umassd.edu"
```

```
7   onMouseOver = "document.photo.src = 'images/photo1.jpg' "
8   onMouseOut = "document.photo.src = 'images/photo2.jpg' ">

9   <IMG SRC = "images/photo1.jpg" WIDTH=400 HEIGHT=300 NAME="photo">

10  </A>
11  </BODY>
12  </HTML>
```

Listing 3.5   Use JavaScript to manipulate images.

Running the above HTML and JavaScript program, you will see one of the two photos when you move the mouse over the location of the photo, and you will also see the other photo when you move the mouse out of the location. When you click the photo, you will be linked to the UMassD home page. If your program does not work, more likely you have incorrect image names or you have put the images in a wrong place. More details of the JavaScript related to this example are discussed below.

3.8.2   Object Classes and Their Methods and Attributes

JavaScript is a mixture of function-oriented and object-oriented paradigms. JavaScript has many predefined object classes that have been built in the JavaScript interpreter. These classes have built-in methods (equivalent to functions). In Listing 3.4, `document` is an **object**, and `write` is its **method**. Parameters or arguments are placed in the parenthesis of the method. The JavaScript sentence in Listing 3.4 directs the Web page (document) to write a message "Hello, World!". In Listing 3.5, `document` is an object, `photo` is an image object within the object `document`, and `src` (source) is an **attribute** of the object `photo`. Note that this image name (`photo`) is defined in the HTML tag `<IMG...NAME...>` (see line **9**). **value** is an attribute commonly used in various objects, as can be seen in the following several examples.

A basic hierarchy of object classes in the Netscape browser is shown in Figure 3.2.

Very much like C++, the general syntax of JavaScript statements related to the built-in classes is:

```
[Object Name].[Sub-object Name].[...].[Attribute Name or Method Name( )]
```

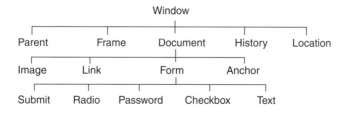

Figure 3.2   Basic hierarchy of object classes in Netscape.

e.g., `document.write()` in Listing 3.4, and `document.photo.src` in Listing 3.5.

3.8.3   Event Handler

Events are actions the user performs while visiting the Web page. Moving the mouse and submitting a form are examples of events. JavaScript deals with events, with commands called **event handlers**. Event handlers are usually applied within the HTML tags. Commonly used event handlers are:

Event Handlers	Event
onMouseOver	The mouse is moved over an object
onMouseOut	The mouse is moved off an object
onSubmit	The user submits a form
onBlur	The user closes the object
onClick	The user clicks the object
onFocus	The object becomes active
onSelect	The content of the object is selected

onMouseOver and onMouseOut are used in JavaScript in Listing 3.5. They instruct the computer to react in such a way that when the mouse is moved over the hyperlink "`http://www.umassd.edu`," the `photo` object becomes 'images/photo1.jpg' (see line **7**). When the mouse is moved out of the territory of the `photo` object defined in the HTML tag <IMG...WIDTH... HEIGHT...>, it becomes 'images/photo2.jpg' (see line **8**). Note that some event handlers (e.g., onBlur and onSubmit) may not work if the Web browser is not installed properly.

3.8.4   Verify Input on the FORM

Second JavaScript example is examined here. A major utility of JavaScript is to verify the input of the users. Listing 3.6 exhibits a JavaScript program that verifies the e-mail address typed by the user when he or she submits a FORM back to the Web server. The program assumes that if the text box for e-mail address on the FORM has not been filled, or the typed e-mail address string contains any illegal characters, such as slash, comma, space, colon, and semi-colon, then the computer signals error warning and asks the user to retype the e-mail address.

```
1  <HTML>
2  <HEAD>
3  <TITLE> My Form Web Page </TITLE>

4  <SCRIPT>

5  // Define a function for the action after verify the email address
```

```
 6 function VerifyForm(form) {

 7 // If VerifyEmailAdd function returns false based on typed
 8 // address then give alert
 9 // and move the cursor back to the email box and highlight it
10 // and return true (move on to the next task)

11  if (!VerifyEmailAdd(form.email.value)) {
12  alert("OOPS! Invalid email address. Please input again!")
13   form.email.focus()
14   form.email.select()
15   return false
16  }
17 return true
18 }

19 // Define a function to verify the email address types in the form

20 function VerifyEmailAdd(EmailString) {

21 // If the email address is empty, then give false

22  if (EmailString == "") {
23   return false
24  }

25 // Define five bad characters (incl. space) in illegal email address

26  BadChars = "/, :;"

27 // For each of the 5 bad characters (including a space), check the typed
28 // email address. If a bad character has been found, then give false
29   for (i=0; i<=4; i++) {
30     aBadChar=BadChars.charAt(i)
31     if (EmailString.indexOf(aBadChar,0) >= 0) {
32     return false
33   }
34  }

35 // Otherwise (i.e., the above two errors are not found), give true

36  return true
37 }

38 </SCRIPT>
39 </HEAD>

40 <BODY>
41 <H2> SEND DATA TO ME! </H2>
42 Please fill the form and submit it :

43 <BR>

44 <FORM onSubmit="return VerifyForm(this)"
45   ACTION="mailto:MyEmail@U.edu" METHOD=POST>
```

```
46 Your Name: <BR>
47 <INPUT TYPE=TEXT NAME="name" SIZE=50> <BR>

48 Your Email Address: <BR>
49 <INPUT TYPE=TEXT NAME="email" SIZE=50> <BR>

50 Your Brief Comments: <BR>
51 <TEXTAREA NAME="comm" ROWS=4 COLS=50> </TEXTAREA> <BR>

52 <INPUT TYPE=SUBMIT VALUE="Submit the Data">
53 <INPUT TYPE=RESET VALUE="Start Over Again">
54 </FORM>
55 </BODY>
56 </HTML>
```

Listing 3.6   Use JavaScript to verify typed e-mail address in the form.

We examine how the JavaScript program works. Lines **4–38** are the JavaScript program.

Line **6** defines a function called `VerifyForm`. This function has one argument called form. This means that the function works based on the brought-in form.

Lines **11–16** are one if statement. This statement calls another function named `VerifyEmailAdd`. Line **11** means that if `VerifyEmailAdd` returns "false," then the computer should signal an alert (line **12**), and move the cursor back to the e-mail text box and allow the user to retype an e-mail address (lines **13–14**). If the `VerifyEmailAdd` returns "true," then this function returns "true" back to the calling function (line **17**).

Lines **20–37** implement the function `VerifyEmailAdd` that verifies the e-mail address typed in the email text box in the FORM. The argument of this function is `EmailString`, which is supposed to be replaced by the value of the text box named "email" (line **11** and line **49**). Lines **22–24** let the function return "false" if the string is empty. Line 26 defines all illegal characters for any e-mail address. In this case, five bad characters (including space) are defined.

Lines **29–34** are a search procedure to find whether there is any bad character. Since we have defined five bad characters, the for-loop repeats five times. For each time, one character is selected for checking (line **30**). Lines **31–33** instruct the computer that if the selected bad character is found in the `EmailString`, then return "false."

If the e-mail string is not empty and no bad character has been found, then the computer executes line **36**, and returns "true" to the calling function.

Now we examine line **44**. This line means when the FORM is submitted, the computer passes **"this"** (the current form) to the function VerifyForm and executes the function. In line 44, **"return"** means the computer keeps calling the function until the called function returns "true."

Important features of JavaScript related to this example are discussed below.

3.8.5   Similarity and Dissimilarity of JavaScript and C/C++

The syntax of JavaScript is very similar to C/C++. In terms of function declaration and calling, JavaScript is of the style of C language. On the other hand,

JavaScript uses many built-in object classes. The use of built-in object classes in JavaScript is of the style of C++ language. JavaScript is case-sensitive. A comment line in a JavaScript program is placed after //, or within pair /* and */.

A few features of JavaScript programs are different from that of C/C++. In JavaScript, data types of variables are not needed to declare. The type of a variable is determined by the assignment. For instance, in Listing 3.6,

```
BadChars = "/, :;"
```

means that a string is assigned to the variable `BadChars`, and this variable automatically becomes the type of string.

In JavaScipt, a semicolon (;) is not needed after a sentence. JavaScript has its reserved words, that is, words that are not recommended for user-defined words (see Appendix 3.2).

In JavaScript, you can use "`function`" to define a user-defined object class. Compared with C++, JavaScript is weak in the object-oriented feature.

3.8.6   *Function and Calling a Function*

Similar to C, a **function** of JavaScript is a set of JavaScript statements that perform a specific task. A function can be called by another JavaScript statement. The format of a JavaScript function is:

```
function [user-defined function name](arguments) {
[statements of the function]
}
```

In Listing 3.6, `VerifyEmailAdd` is a function name, and `EmailString` is its argument. Similar to C, a JavaScript function can **return** a value back to the calling function. The value returned could be numerical or **Boolean** (true or false).

There are usually two ways to calling a function. One is to call a function within another function.

```
[called function name](passing arguments)
```

In Listing 3.6, function `VerifyForm` calls `VerifyEmailAdd` by passing the argument `form.email.value` to substitute `EmailString`.

The other way of calling a function is the use of an event handler.

```
[event handler]="[called function name](passing arguments)"
```

In Listing 3.6, `onSubmit` calls function `Submit` by passing the argument `this`. **this** represents the **current active object**. Since the function `Sumbmit` has argument `form`, `this` denotes the current active FORM in this case.

3.8.7   *String Processing*

JavaScript has **string** (character) object class that has many built-in methods. In Listing 3.6, `BadChars` is a string object, and `charAt()` is the method identifies the character at the position specified in parenthesis. In JavaScript, index of positions starts with 0. `EmailString` is also a string object, and `indexOf()` is another built-in method that finds a location of a sub-string in the string. `EmailString.indexOf(aBadChar,0)` means "to search `Email-String` from position 0 to find the location of the sub-string specified in `aBadChar`, and return the value of the location." If the search fails to find the sub-string, the entire string processing returns value −1.

Strings can be added together. In Listing 3.8, it is to be observed that:

```
document.cookie = "UserName=" + UserName + ";expires=" +
            expireDate.toGMTString()
```

It means that the string operation adds the four strings together and hands over the long string to `document.cookie`.

3.8.8 *If Statement*

The format of **if** statement of JavaScript is very similar to that of C. In Listing 3.6, `if(!VerifyEmailAdd(form.email.value))` means that if the function `VerifyEmailAdd` based on `form.email.value` is not "true" (i.e., it returns "false"), then the actions specified in the action statements will be taken.

3.8.9 *alert Statement*

alert statement is often used to alert the user with a warning message. It results in an alert window. The user can click the OK button to close the alert window.

Before we explain miscellaneous JavaScript statements, we examine the third example of JavaScript and cookies.

3.8.10 *Client-Side Calculation*

Next, we examine third JavaScript example. JavaScript allows the user on the client side to find more information from the Web page based on the inputted data on the FORM. In this example, the user inputs the weight of a package for the delivery, the days needed for transportation, and the destination, then finds the delivery service charges.

```
1 <HTML>
2 <HEAD>
3 <TITLE> FEE CALCULATION </TITLE>

4 <SCRIPT>
5 function CalPayment(form)
6 { form.Payment.value = "";
7    DeliveryWeight=eval(form.Delivery.value);
8    DeliveryDays=eval(form.Days.value);
```

```
 9  if(form.State[0].checked) {
10    form.Payment.value = DeliveryWeight * DeliveryDays * 1;
11  }
12  if(form.State[1].checked) {
13    form.Payment.value = DeliveryWeight * DeliveryDays * 2;
14  }
15 }

16 </SCRIPT>
17 </HEAD>

18 <BODY>
19 <H2>Estimate the delivery charge by yourself.</H2>
20 <FORM NAME="PAY">
21 <P> Input the weight of package for the delivery:
22 <INPUT TYPE=TEXT SIZE=10 NAME="Delivery"> lb<BR>
23 </P>
24 <P>Input the days needed for transportation:
25 <INPUT TYPE=TEXT SIZE=10 NAME="Days"><BR>
26 </P>
27 <P>Choose the destination State:</P>
28 <INPUT TYPE=RADIO NAME="State">In State<BR>
29 <INPUT TYPE=RADIO NAME="State">Out State
30 <BR></P>
31 <INPUT TYPE=BUTTON VALUE="Estimate Payment",
32 onClick="CalPayment(PAY)">
33 <INPUT TYPE=RESET VALUE="Reset">
34 <P>The delivery charge would be: $
35 <INPUT TYPE=TEXT SIZE=10 NAME="Payment"><BR>
36 </P>
37 </FORM>
38 </BODY>
39 </HTML>
```

Listing 3.7   Client-side calculation on the FORM.

In the above example, lines **20–37** implement the FORM. There are three textboxes. The first one (line **22**) is used for the user to input the weight of the package. The second one (line **25**) is used for the user to input the days for the delivery. The third one (line **35**) is used to display the calculation result. There are two radio buttons (lines **28–29**). The user is expected to select the delivery destination. The radio buttons are called "State," and only one of them can be activated. Thus, the JavaScript automatically assigns State[0] to the first radio button, and State[1] to the second radio button. Lines **31–32** implement a command button. On clicking this button, the JavaScript function CalPayment() is called. Note that the argument of this function is the name of the FORM.

Now we examine the JavaScript function CalPayment() programmed in lines **4–16**. Line **5** declares the function name. Line **6** makes the textbox for the answer empty. Line **7** captures the weight of the package for the delivery. The **eval** function converts the string in the textbox into a numerical number. Line **8** captures the days permitted for the delivery. Lines **9–11** calculate the service charge if the user selects "In State" using the radio button. Lines **12–14** calculate the service charge if the user selects "Out State."

3.8.11   JavaScript and Cookies

In Web computing, a **cookie** is a piece of information that a Web page gives to the user's browser when the two first meet. It contains information about the Web server and the Web pages visited, and is stored on the user's computer hard disk as a plain text file. On the other side, the remote server saves its part of the cookie and information about the user. The issue of cookie is controversial, since people prefer anonymous access of Web sites. Nevertheless, cookies exist, and a JavaScript programmer can perform many useful tasks with cookies. For instance, a Web server can remember the visitor's name.

A cookie is a text string with the following format:

```
[Cookie Name]=[Value of the cookie];
expires=expirationDateGMT;
path=[URL path];
domain=[site domain]
```

Only the first two lines are mandatory. The first line defines the cookie's name and its value. The second line defines the expiration date (the standard Internet time based upon **Greenwich Mean Time (GMT)**) after which the browser will automatically delete the cookie. The next two lines allow the programmer to store a URL and a domain value in the cookie.

The following JavaScript provides an example of cookie manipulations. In this example, two Web pages with HTML and JavaScript programs are involved. The first Web page (ABC1.html in Listing 3.8) allows the user to input his or her name. The inputted user's name is then written to a cookie that is in turn stored on the Web page's server. The second Web page (ABC2.html in Listing 3.9) uses the cookie created by the JavaScript program in the first Web page. In this case, when the user downloads the second Web page (note that, it must be stored on the same server as the first Web page), the JavaScript program in the second Web page will retrieve the user's name from the cookie and display it for the user.

If you run the program in Listing 3.8 on your local computer using Microsoft Internet Explorer, you can view the cookie in the folder C:/WINDOWS/ COOKIES. Using Netscape, cookies are stored in the folder C:/Program Files/Netscape/Users....

To control the computer's behavior with respect to cookies, the Web browser can be set to allow or disallow your computer to send a cookie to the server.

```
1  <HTML>
2  <HEAD>
3  <TITLE> Write a cookie based on a form </TITLE>

4  <SCRIPT>
5  expireDate = new Date
6  expireDate.setTime(expireDate.getTime() + (24*60*60*1000*365))
```

```
 7 // if the cookie is not empty then retrieve the user's name

 8 UserName = ""
 9 if (document.cookie != "") {
10   UserName = document.cookie.split("=")[1]

11 }

12 // write a cookie

13 function WriteCookie() {
14   UserName = document.CustomerForm.NameBox.value
15   document.cookie = "UserName=" + UserName + ";expires="
16     + expireDate.toGMTString()
17 }

18 </SCRIPT>
19 </HEAD>

20 <BODY>
21 <H3>ABC.COM is now adopting relationships marketing strategy!
22 </H3>

23 <P>We will keep your name in our customer file. Please visit
24 our company's E-store (ABC2.html), we will give you warmest
25 greetings!
26 </P>

27 <FORM NAME=CustomerForm>

28 Please Enter Your Name:

29 <INPUT TYPE=TEXT NAME=NameBox onBlur="WriteCookie()">

30 </FORM>
31 </BODY>
32 </HTML>
```

Listing 3.8   Use JavaScript to write a cookie to the server.

We examine how the JavaScript program stated in Listing 3.8 works. Line **5** defines the variable `expireDate`, which is an object of `Date` class. `Date` class is a built-in class in the JavaScript library. There are many standard methods of `Date` class. Line **6** uses two of these methods: `setTime` (to set new time) and `getTime` (to get the current time). In JavaScript, time is measured in milli-second. Line 6 sets the expire time one year ahead (i.e., 365 days per year, 24 hours per day, 60 minutes per hour, 60 seconds per minute, and 1000 milli-seconds per second).

Line **8** defines the variable `UserName`. Lines **9–11** retrieve the user name if the cookie for the user is not empty. Note that lines **9–11** ensure that the user's name previously stored in the cookie is not lost if the user does not input his or her name this time.

Lines **13–17** are the function WriteCookie. Line **14** obtains the user's name from the text box (note the FORM name in line **27** and the box name in line **29**). Lines **15–16** generate a string and write the string to the cookie.

In line **29**, the onBlur command instructs the computer to write a cookie when the user leaves the Web page.

The following examines how a JavaScript program retrieves the cookie.

```
1  <HTML>
2  <HEAD>
3  <TITLE> Read a cookie </TITLE>
4  </HEAD>

5  <BODY>
6  <H3> ABC.COM E-Store Web Page </H3>

7  <SCRIPT>

8  if (document.cookie != "") {
9  document.write("Hello," + document.cookie.split("=")[1] + "!")
10 }

11 </SCRIPT>

12 <H4>
13 Welcome to ABC.COM E-Store!
14 </H4>

15 </BODY>
16 </HTML>
```

Listing 3.9   Use JavaScript to read a cookie from the server.

In the JavaScript program in Listing 3.9, lines **8–9** retrieve the user's name stored in the cookie, and display it on the Web page.

Various JavaScript statements used in the previous examples are further explained as follows:

3.8.12 Miscellaneous JavaScript Statements

3.8.12.1 new Statement

new statement creates a new object. In Listing 3.8, line **5**, Date is a JavaScript predefined object class, and expireDate is a user-defined new object of Date (time string).

3.8.12.2 Miscellaneous Functions and Methods

There are a variety of methods in JavaScript.

In Listing 3.7, lines **7** and **8**, the eval() function evaluates the string in the input textbox and converts it to a numerical value. For instance, if you input "200+300" in the Delivery textbox, DeliveryWeight ends up with 500. This feature is powerful.

In Listing 3.6, line **13**, `focus()` is a method of text box object that moves the cursor to the text box. In line **14**, `select()` is also a method of text box object that highlight the text box.

In Listing 3.8, line **6**, `getTime()` is to get the current time from the time string. `setTime()` is to set a time string. In line **16**, `toGMTString()` is a method of `Date` that puts the `expireDate` into the standard Internet time string. The outcome of this method is a standard time string.

In line **10** of Listing 3.8 and line **9** of Listing 3.9, `split("=")` is a method of cookie object. It splits a cookie record into fields, where `cookieField[0]` is the cookie's name and `cookieField[1]` is the value of the cookie. The operation `document.cookie.split("=")[1]` finds the value of the cookie.

In Listing 3.8, line **15**, the statement `document.cookie = ...` actually writes the cookie to the user's disk and the server.

3.9   Debugging Source Codes of Web Pages

Web page browsers are more tolerant of errors in HTML and JavaScript programs than other language compilers or interpreters. That is, the program with errors can still run, although not perfectly. Usually, the browser can continue to interpret and execute HTML and JavaScript programs when an error is encountered and ignored by the user. In many cases of error, the browser dumps unexpected results on the Web page (e.g., a broken icon for an image) without fatal interruptions. Browsers provide built-in debugger functions. Common errors in HTML and JavaScript programming include:

Misspelling words
Missing a tag
Omitting symbols
Violation of formats
Incorrect URL
Incorrect folders for images
Incorrect image format (JPG or GIF)

After debugging a Web page written in HTML, JavaScript, as well as Java applets (Chapter 4), one should re-open the Web page file in the browser, instead of clicking the Web page icon or clicking the "refresh" button, to discharge the old programs.

3.10   Self-Review Exercise

1. Access an interesting Web page on the Internet, and view the HTML source code.
2. Create a Web page by using the HTML language. Include tags that are not mentioned in the textbook.

3. Create an electronic document by using a software package (e.g., Microsoft Word), and then convert it into an HTML document. View the HTML code and give comments.
4. Fill blanks in the following HTML and JavaScript program.

```
1  <HTML>
2  _____
3  <TITLE> Web Page with JavaScript </TITLE>
4  <SCRIPT>
5  // Define a function to verify the name types in the form
6  function VerifyName(NameString) {

7  // If the name is empty, then give false
8  if (_____ == "") {
9  return false
10 }

11 // Define 7 bad characters which are illegal in names
12    IllegalChar = "/, :;[]"
13 // For each of the 7 bad characters, check the typed name
14 // If a bad character has been found, then give false

15 for (i=0; i<=_____; i++) {
16    aBadChar=_____.charAt(i)
17    if (_____.indexOf(aBadChar,0) >= 0) {
18    return false
19    }
20 }

21 // Otherwise (the above two errors are not found), give true
22 return _____
23 }

24 // Define a function for the action after verify the name

25 function SubmitForm(_____) {

26 // If the verification returns false based on typed address
27 // then give alert
28 // and move the cursor back to the name box and highlight it
29 // and return true (move on to the next task)

30 if (!VerifyName(form._____.value)) {
31  alert("Ha-ha! Invalid name. Please input again!")
32  form._____.focus()
33  _____.name._____()
34  _____ false
35 }
36 return true
37 _____
38 _____
39 </HEAD>
40 _____
41 <H3> SEND YOUR INFORMATION BACK TO ME! </H3>
```

```
42 Please fill the form and submit it :
43 <BR>
44 <FORM onSubmit="return _____(this)"
45  ACTION="mailto:MyEmail@U.edu" METHOD=POST>
46 Your Name: <BR>
47 <INPUT TYPE=TEXT NAME="name" SIZE=50> <BR>
48 Your Address: <BR>
49 <INPUT TYPE=TEXT _____="address" SIZE=50> <BR>
50 Your Request: <BR>
51 <INPUT _____=TEXT NAME="request" _____=100> <BR>
52 <INPUT TYPE=SUBMIT _____="Submit Information">
53 <INPUT TYPE=RESET VALUE="Reset the Form">
54 _____
55 </BODY>
56 </HTML>
```

5. Fill in the blank in the following HTML and JavaScript program.

```
 1 <HTML>
 2 <HEAD>
 3 <TITLE> Set a cookie based on a form _____
 4 _____

 5 expireDate = new Date
 6 expireDate.setTime(expireDate.getTime()+(24*60*60*1000*365))
 7 StudentAddress = ""
 8 if (document.cookie != "") {
 9 StudentAddress = document.cookie.split("=")[1]
10 }

11 function SetCookie() {
12 StudentAddress = document._____.AddressBox.value
13  document.cookie = "StudentAddress=" + _____
14    + ";expires=" + _____
15 }

16 </SCRIPT>
17 _____

18 <BODY>
19 <H4>We will keep your address updated!
20 </H4>
21 <FORM _____=StudentForm>
22 Please Enter Your Address:
23 <INPUT TYPE=TEXT NAME=AddressBox onBlur="SetCookie()">
24 </FORM>
25 _____
26 </HTML>
```

6. Use JavaScript to verify a form.
7. Use JavaScript to manipulate an image.
8. Use JavaScript to manipulate a cookie.
9. Develop a Web page with business contents, one FORM, and components of JavaScript for verifying the FORM and client-side calculation.

Appendix 3.1 HTML Tag List

<!-- . . . -->	Comments
<A> . . . </A>	Anchor; creates a hyperlink (att: HREF)
<APPLET> . . . </APPLET>	Defines and triggers Java applet
<B> . . . </B>	Bold font
<BASE>	Defines the base URL for all relative URLs in the current document
<BIG> . . . </BIG>	Big font
<BLINK> . . . </BLINK>	Cause annoying blink text
<BODY> . . . </BODY>	Defines the body of an HTML document (att: BGCOLOR, BACKGROUND)
 	Break line
<CAPTION> . . . </CAPTION>	Creates a caption for a table
<CENTER> . . . </CENTER>	Centers the text
<DD> . . . </DD>	Indicates that the text is the definition part of a definition list
<DT> . . . </DT>	Indicates that the text is the term part of a definition list
<FONT> . . . </FONT>	Set font; (att: COLOR, SIZE)
<FORM> . . . </FORM>	Delimits a form
<FRAME> . . . </FRAME>	Delimits a frame
<FRAMESET>.</FRAMESET>	Set multiple frames
<Hx> . . . </Hx>	Headers, where x is a number 1–6 for the level
<HEAD> . . . </HEAD>	Delimits the document's head
<HR>	Horizontal rule
<HTML> . . . </HTML>	Contains the HTML document
<I> . . . </I>	Italic font
<IMG>	Inserts an image (att: ALIGN, ALT, SRC, HEIGHT, WIDTH)
<INPUT TYPE=CHECKBOX>	Creates a checkbox-input within a form
<INPUT TYPE=RADIO>	Creates a radio button within a form
<INPUT TYPE=IMAGE>	Creates an image input element within a form
<INPUT TYPE=SUBMIT>	Creates a submit button within a form (att: NAME, VALUE)
<ISINDEX>	Creates a searchable HTML document (att: ACTION and PROMPT)
<LI> . . .</LI>	List
<LINK>	Establishes a link
<P> . . . </P>	Delimits a paragraph
<PARAM>	Set parameters for Java applets
<S> . . . </S>	Causes struck
<SELECT> . . . </SELECT>	Creates a multiple-choice menu
<TABLE> . . . </TABLE>	Delimits a table; (att: ALIGN, BORDER, VALIGN, WIDTH)

`<TD> . . . </TD>`	Describes a table data cell
`<TITLE> . . . </TITLE>`	Creates the title
`<U> . . . </U>`	Underlines

Appendix 3.2   JavaScript Reserved Words and Other Keywords

JavaScript reserved words are

break	continue	else	false	for	function
if	in	new	null	return	this
true	var	void	while	with	

The following words are not reserved, but are not recommended to be used as user-defined words.

alert	Anchor	Area	Array	assign	blur
Button	Checkbox	close	Date	defaultStatus	
document	Element	focus	Form	Frame	frames
function	getClass	history	Image	JavaClass	length
Link	location	Location	Math	name	navigator
netscape	Number	Object	onClick	onSubmit	onError
onFocus	onLoad	open	Option	parent	Password
prompt	Radio	Reset	scroll	Select	status
String	Submit	sun	Text	top	valueOf
window	WINDOW				

Appendix 3.3   Guideline for Web Page Project Report

1. Front page
   Course name
   Title of the project
   Group members (names and ID)
   Date
2. Text
   Introduction and the purpose of the Web page
   Application of HTML, JavaScript
3. Source code of the HTML, JavaScript programs
4. A diskette which contains the Web page and all needed images and sounds. The Web page on the diskette must be workable; that is, one clicks the icon of the Web page on the diskette, the Web page should be displayed on the screen without an error.

Chapter 4

Java and Computing on the Internet

4.1 Web-Based Computing

The **World Wide Web** provides universal client-server applications. With this model, the clients and servers communicate using the **HTTP** protocol. This protocol defines a simple set of commands. The Web has been extended to provide more interactive forms of client-server computing. Now the typical client-server architecture has been extended into the **3-tier** architecture with Web servers in many organizations for electronic commerce. The common definition of 3-tier Web servers is client (tier 1), application server (tier 2), and database server (tier 3) (see Figure 4.1).

The Web client-server technology is also being used on private networks called **Intranets**. An Intranet is an internal corporate network that is developed using the Web client-server approach. Intranets can be either standalone enterprise networks or networks linked to the Internet but sit on the private side of a **firewall**. Intranets enable corporations to utilize the common Internet technology to link up with their suppliers, customers, and business partners.

4.2 Web Servers with Java-Style

Java is a computer language developed by Sun Microsystems. It is an object-oriented programming that is very similar to C++. Java became popular because of a Netscape Navigator plug-in that made it possible to sun small Java programs, knows as **applets**, within a www browser during the 1990s. Note that

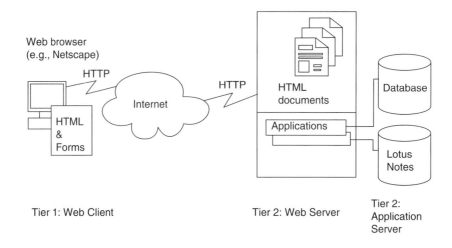

Figure 4.1   Web servers and the 3-tier architecture.

JavaScript is not Java but a completely different language designed by Netscape Communications Corporation.

Java was designed to be a complete computer language for computing on the Internet. Java employs a portable operating system environment so that the programmer is able to write portable components that can be distributed on the Web. Java has many subsets of languages. There are three major distinct ways of running a Java programming:

1. **Java application**: Like other computer languages such as C++, Java application can run as a **free-standing** program. It includes **Abstract Window Toolkit (ATW)**-based and **non-ATW programs**.
2. **Java applets**: Java introduces a unique model of client–server interaction for the Web. Using Java, one can write programs called applets that can be downloaded from a server into a Java compatible browser (e.g., Netscape) on the client side. Applets enable the distribution of executable content across the Web along with data.
3. **Java servlets**: Java servlets are Java programs that are executed on the server side. A Java servlet can response the user's request on the client side through a Web page, and send the execution results back to the client. Java servlets are secure, portable, and easy-to-use. It is a replacement for CGI programs.

4.3   Introduction to Java Applets

Java applets are a special type of small program that serves as an extension to an HTML document and provide better audio-visual effects. It is a small Java program that can be embedded in an HTML page. Applets are different from full-fledged Java application programs in that they are not allowed to access certain resources on the local computer (e.g., data files, modems, printers, etc.)

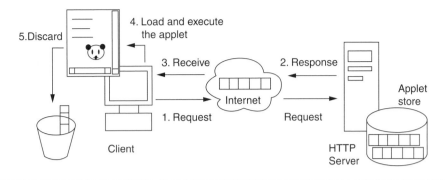

Figure 4.2   Java-style Web servers.

and are not allowed to communicate with other computers across the network. Figure 4.2 shows a Web client–server interaction mode that includes Java applets. As seen from the figure, Java applets allow the client to execute the program previously stored on the server, while the server becomes a warehouse of programs, data, and Web pages.

4.4   Run a Java Applet within a Web Page

To run a Java applet, you must compile the applet and obtain its class code, and create a Web page that uses this class. You can access **Java Development Kit** (Sun's **JDK**; in **J2SE**) to obtain the most current version of the Java compiler by downloading the latest JDK from Sun's Web site at `http://java.sun.com/` (see Appendix 4.1 for details). There are also software packages that provide better computing environments for Java programming.

Edit the following simplest Java applet.

```
1 import java.awt.Graphics;
2 public class HelloWorldApplet extends java.applet.Applet {
3   public void paint(Graphics g) {
4     g.drawString("Hello World! I am learning JAVA!", 5, 25);
5   }
6 }
```

Listing 4.1   Example of Java applet (HelloWorldApplet.java).

You may find that Java has the same style as C/C++. We briefly explain how the above Java applet works. Line **1** is a preprocessor to import the library. Line **2** is the heading of the Java applet. Lines **3–5** are the method `paint`. In Java applets, a text printed on the screen is graphics. In this case, g is an object of class `Graphics`. Line **4** uses a standard method of `Graphics` named `drawString` to print the string "Hello World ..." on the screen at the defined location (5, 25).

Save the source code file. Note that the file name must be the same name of the class defined in the Java program. In this example, you must use

`HelloWorldApplet.java`

for the file name (see Listing 4.1, line 2). Remember the folder that is used to save the Java applet.

Compile the Java applet as stated. You will obtain `HelloWorldApplet.class` file in the folder, if your source code is correct.

Next, edit the HTML program that uses the Java applet, as follows:

```
 1 <HTML>
 2 <HEAD>
 3 <TITLE>Hello to Everybody!</TITLE>
 4 </HEAD>
 5 <BODY>
 6   <P>My Java applet has been loaded and executed successfully!
 7 </P>
 8   <APPLET CODE="HelloWorldApplet.class" WIDTH=250 HEIGHT=45></APPLET>
 9 </BODY>
10 </HTML>
```

Listing 4.2   Example of HTML code that triggers a Java applet.

Note line **8**. An applet in the HTML program is referred to with the `<APPLET>` tag, and the `CODE` attribute is used to indicate the name of the compiled applet. You use the `WIDTH` and `HEIGHT` attributes to indicate the size of the applet. The browser (Netscape) uses these attributes to define how big a space to leave for the applet on the Web page. In this case, a box of 250 pixels wide and 45 pixels high is created. You should understand that your Java applet can be used flexibly by any HTML programs.

Save the HTML program to the same folder of the Java applet class file, with a filename

`[filename].html`

As an example, `HelloWorldApplet.html`.

Use a Web browser (Netscape or Internet Explorer) to open the Web page. You should be able to view the Web page as shown in Figure 4.3.

Note that the first line of the text displayed is the message brought up by the HTML code (see line **6** in the HTML program Listing 4.2), and the second line of the text (it is actually an image) is the execution result of the Java applet you programmed.

As we emphasized earlier, the HTML program and the Java class file used for the HTML program must be placed in the same folder if the HTML program does not specify otherwise. A typical layout of program files and data files is shown in Figure 4.4. In this layout, the project is placed in folder (e.g., `Project1`). The Java class file (in this case, `HelloWorldApplet.class`) and the HTML program (in this case, `HelloWorldApplet.html`) is placed in the same folder (e.g., `Project1`). There are also other folders such as `images` and `audio` where image data and audio data are placed, as discussed in detail later in this chapter.

4.5   Java Applet Programming

Now we discuss more about the characteristics of Java applets.

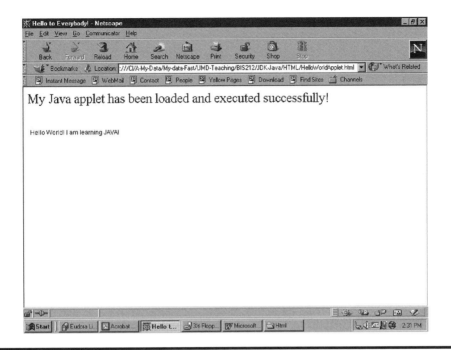

Figure 4.3   HelloWorldApplet shown in Netscape.

4.5.1   Similarity of Java Syntax and C and C++ Syntax

Much of Java syntax is virtually identical to that of C and C++. The concepts of **public** and **private**, syntax of **data types**, **if statement**, **for-loop**, and **arithmetic operators** are the same we learned from C and C++.

4.5.2   Difference between Java Applets and C++

There are a few differences between Java applets and C++ (and Java applications) programs.

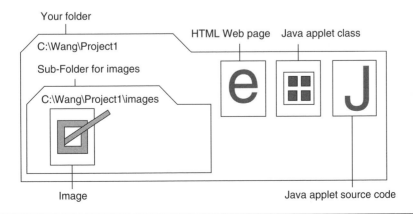

Figure 4.4   Typical layout of folders for a Web page with Java applets.

1. An applet has no `main` method.
2. An applet has no constructor. Instead, replace the constructor with a method named `init`, as discussed later in this subsection.

4.5.3 *import Statement*

The `import` statement includes the Java class library used for the present program. `awt` stands for **Abstract Window Toolkit** as mentioned earlier. AWT is discussed later in the chapter. You may follow program examples to use import statements.

4.5.4 *Heading of an Applet*

For each Java applet, the applet name must be defined as follows:

```
public class [applet name] extends java.applet.Applet
```

Again, the applet name in the heading must be used for the Java applet program file name.

4.5.5 *Methods and Parameters*

In Java (as in other OOP languages such as C++) a command instruction is a **method**. There are two types of methods in Java: those written by the programmer, and those pre-written in the Java libraries.

The concept of message sending in Java is the same as that in C++. If the method being used has been programmed outside the current class, the method name follows an object name to indicate the class where the method is programmed. Recall the example of the Java applet in Listing 4.2. This applet is to draw graphics (a string in this example) on the screen at a certain point (defined by (5, 25) in this case). `Graphics` is a **class**, g is an **object** of the `Graphics` class. `drawString` is a **method** of the `Graphics` class which has been defined in the Java library `java.awt.Graphics`.

A method often has a list of **parameters** (or **arguments**). In the example of Listing 4.2, (`"Hello World! I am learning JAVA!"`, 5, 25) is the parameters of the method `drawString`. In this case, the parameters mean that the text is drawn at the position 5 pixels from the left and 25 pixels from the top of the graphics box which is in turn defined by the HTML program (see Listing 4.2, line **8**).

4.5.6 *image*

Java supports two formats for images: **GIF** and **JPEG**. The GIF format (with the extension name `.gif`) is usually used for icons and graphics, and the JPEG format (with the extension name `.jpg`) is usually used for photos with high resolution.

To use images, the image names must be declared in the `Image` **type** statement. There are many library methods that can be used to process images. `getImg` is one of them. To get an image from the Internet, we use

```
[image] = getImage([URL]);
```

To get an image from a graphics file, we use

```
[image] = getImage(getCodeBase(), "[image file name]");
```

where `getCodeBase()` gives the **location of the present Java applet class**.

4.5.7 audio

Java supports playing audio clips. There are many formats of audio clips. Java supports the **AU** format (with the extension name `.au`). You can download audio clips from the Internet for exercises. If the format of the audio clip downloaded is not the AU format, you may double click on the icon of the audio clips to let **Windows Media Player** to play it, and meanwhile you can save it as the AU format by using the extension name `.au`.

To play an audio clip in a Java applet, one must declare an `AudioClip` object. `getAudioClip` is a library method that can be used to get an audio clip.

```
[audio clip]= getAudioClip(getCodeBase(),
"[audio clip file name]");
```

The methods `play` or `loop` can be used to specify how the audio clip is played. The method `play` plays the audio clip once, but `loop` plays the audio clip again and again until the applet is terminated.

4.5.8 Thread

In Java there is a special type of class, called **thread**. A `thread` object is an independent execution unit that can compete for system resources such as CPU time and disk files. When a Java program performs several tasks simultaneously it is called **multithreading** (or **parallelism**).

One of the advanced features of Java programming language is the support for concurrent programming. This can be an analogy of human information process. One can find that normally humans can do many different things "simultaneously" such as talking, listening, and driving. This is an explanation of the reason for the use of multiple threads. The Java package includes the Thread class that allows the Java program to execute multiple threads. On a multiprocessors machine, threads allow the program to use all of the available processors to do different tasks. On a uniprocessor computer, individual tasks could be placed into separate threads if some of them take a long time to complete, especially when the program instructs the processor to wait for disk or network access. Using multiple threads, the program runs faster because the CPU does not waste much time on waiting for resources. For instance, a user-computer interface can have its own thread that handles user input. This makes the program more responsive. Nevertheless, multiple threads might cause problems. For example, if more than one thread can access a piece of data, then the programmer must guarantee that simultaneous access does not corrupt that data. The Java community invents many techniques to solve such problems.

Applets often use `thread` to implement animation and perform periodic actions. When an applet uses a `thread` object, it must implement the `Runnable` interface. A thread will not become runnable until a program calls its `start` method explicitly. The `start` method calls the thread's `run` method automatically. The `run` method defines code that should be executed whenever a thread gets started. When a thread object is used, one must define the `interrupt` method explicitly to kill the thread.

4.5.9   Keywords `new` and `this`

In Java the keyword `new` allows the programmer to **create** a new object and **initialize** the object in one single statement. The keyword `this` represents the object that is **currently** working on.

4.5.10   `try` and `catch` Statements

Exceptions mean that something has gone wrong when the program is being executed. The use of exceptions makes the program more tolerant of system errors. In Java, exceptions are dealt by the `try`, `catch` pair, along with other statements. A typical control structure that consists of a "try block" and a "catch block" is as follows:

```
try { [a series of statements] }
catch (InterruptedException e) { [handle the exception] }
```

In the catch block, the action of handling the exception might be omitted.

4.5.11   `paint` and `repaint` Statements

The `paint` method is one of those methods which the programmer must write. It is **triggered by the browser** whenever the screen needs to be **painted**.

On the other hand, the `repaint` method is provided by the library, and the programmer uses it to notify the browser that the window has changed and it needs to be **repainted**.

4.5.12   Structure of Java Applets

An applet is always an object of `Applet` class. There are actually five methods the programmer can build when creating an applet. Each runs at a specific time in an applet's life.

1. init: The init method acts as a constructor. It is executed only once.
2. start: The start method is run after the init method completes and each time the user returns to the same Web page. A Java applet program never needs to call the method explicitly.
3. paint: Java applets commonly use the paint method to display messages in the window.
4. Interrupt: A web browser runs the interrupt method whenever a user moves away from a page which is invoking an applet.
5. destroy: A web browser runs the destroy method when the user leaves the web page window. In most cases, we do not need to explicitly define the method in a Java applet, as the web browser will destroy the applet.

A typical structure (not a program) of Java applets for animation and multimedia presentation is listed in Listing 4.3.

```
1 import [classes and methods];
2 . . . . .
3 import [classes and methods];

4 /* The import mechanism tells the Java compiler which  */
5 /* which files to search when it looks for classes     */
6 /* and methods in the library                          */

7 public class [user-defined class-name] extends java.applet.Applet

8 /* Write Applets with Threads for animation            */
9 /* Include the words implements Runnable               */

10     implements Runnable {

11 /* Define variables                                    */

12     Image [variable-name];
13     AudioClip [variable-name];
14     . . . . . .
15     Thread [thread-name];

16 /* Major Applet Activities I: Initialization method    */

17     public void init() {
18        [code for the initialization method]
19     }

20 /* Major Applet Activities II: Starting                */

21     public void start() {
22      if ([tread] == null) {
23         [tread] = new Thread(this);
24         [tread].start();
25      }
26     }

27 /* Major Applet Activities III: Stopping               */
```

```
28    public void interrupt() {
29     if ([tread] != null) {
30        [tread].interrupt();
31        [tread] = null;
32      }
33    }

34 /* Since we use Thread, we use run() to contain what    */
35 /* we want the Applet to do                            */
36 /* This part may be seen as an extended part of Start() */

37    public void run() {
38     [code for the run method]
39    }

40 /* Major Applet Activities IV: Painting or repainting   */

41    public void paint([parameter]) {
42      [code for the paint method];
43    }
44 }
```

Listing 4.3   Typical structure of Java applets.

4.6   Examples of Java Applets

Now we learn two typical Java applets for animation and audio play.

4.6.1   Animations

Listing 4.4 shows the Java applet which implements animation by painting two images alternatively. You may find samples of images and audio clips in the folders in JDK (e.g., C:\jdk2\demo\applets\animator\). You may also copy an image from a Web page by clicking the image using the right button of the mouse.

```
1 import java.awt.Graphics;
2 import java.awt.Image;
3 public class Animations extends java.applet.Applet

4 /* Write Applets with Threads for animation              */
5 /* Include the words implements Runnable                 */

6        implements Runnable {

7 /* Define variables                                      */

8        Image pictures[] = new Image[2];
9        Image CurrentImg;
10       Thread Mainthread;

11 /* Major Applet Activities I: Initialization method      */

12 /* Suppose there are two graphics in the folder "images/" */
```

```
13    public void init() {
14      String pics[] = { "T1.gif", "T2.gif" };
15      for (int i=0; i<2; i++) {
16         pictures[i] = getImage(getCodeBase(),
17            "images/" + pics[i]);
18      }
19    }

20 /* Major Applet Activities II: Starting              */

21    public void start() {
22      if (Mainthread == null) {
23          Mainthread = new Thread(this);
24          Mainthread.start();
25      }
26    }

27 /* Major Applet Activities III: Stopping             */

28    public void interrupt() {
29      if (Mainthread != null) {
30          Mainthread.interrupt();
31          Mainthread = null;
32      }
33    }

34 /* Since we use Thread, we use run() to contain what  */
35 /* we want the Applet to do                           */
36 /* This part may be seen as an extended part of Start() */

37    public void run() {
38       int i=0;
39       while (true) {
40          CurrentImg = pictures[i];
41          repaint();
42          try { Thread.sleep(500); }
43          catch (InterruptedException e) { }
44          if (i==0) i=1;
45          else i=0;
46       }
47    }

48 /* Major Applet Activities IV: Painting or repainting  */

49    public void paint(Graphics g) {
50         g.drawImage(CurrentImg, 10, 10,this);
51    }
52 }
```

Listing 4.4   Example of Java applet for animation.

We examine how the Java applet in Listing 4.4 works. Lines **1–2** import libraries. Again, beginners may follow typical examples to determine what libraries should be imported for their programs.

Line **3** is the heading. Line **6** is the standard statement of Java applets.

Lines **8–10** define variables. In this case, pictures[] is an array of two elements, and each element within the array are images. In Java applet, you define a thread for better control of locus of execution.

Lines **13–19** are the initialization method of the applet. Line **14** defines the name of the two images used in this program. Lines **15–18** are a for-loop to retrieve the two images. Note that lines **16** and **17** find the images based on the defined folder and the two images' names.

Lines **21–26** are the starting procedure. Line **23** assigns the thread, and line **24** starts the thread.

Lines **28–33** are the stopping procedure. This procedure simply stops the thread.

Lines **37–47** are the extension of the starting. Line **38** defines an index variable for the retrieved images. Lines **39–46** define a loop. Line **39** means that this loop is executed again and again until the thread is stopped. Line **40** assigns CurrentImg with the first of the two retrieved images. In line **41**, the command repaint forces the computer to redo line **49** painting. In this case the image stored in CurrentImg is painted. After painting, the computer execution sequence of this thread returns to line **42**.

Lines **42** and **43** are used in pair. Line **42** instructs the thread to "sleep" for 500 milliseconds. Line 43 is a standard procedure to deal with the exception. Lines **44–45** implement a **switch** through change the index of the two images. Remember that the thread is under the control of the loop. At the next time of the iteration, the other image will be displayed. In this way, the two images show up alternatively after 500 milliseconds each time. This is exactly the way of implementing animations.

The HTML code (called the **host HTML program**) that triggers the Java stated earlier applet is shown in Listing 4.5.

```
 1 <HTML>
 2 <HEAD>
 3 <TITLE>ANIMATION!</TITLE>
 4 </HEAD><BODY>
 5 <P>My Java applet for animation has been loaded!</P>
 6 <P>You may see the animation result ..........</P>
 7 <P>

 8 <APPLET CODE="Animations.class" WIDTH=300 HEIGHT=300></APPLET>

 9 </P>
10 </BODY>
11 </HTML>
```

Listing 4.5   HTML code that triggers the Java applet of animation.

4.6.2   Audio Playing

Listing 4.6 shows the Java applet which implements audio play by playing two pieces of sound, simultaneously.

```
 1 import java.awt.Graphics;
 2 import java.applet.AudioClip;
```

```
3 public class Audioplay extends java.applet.Applet

4 /* Write Applets with Threads for audio play          */
5 /* Include the words implements Runnable               */

6         implements Runnable {

7 /* Define variables                                    */

8         AudioClip soundpc1;
9         AudioClip soundpc2;
10        Thread Mainthread;

11 /* Major Applet Activities I: Initialization method    */
12 /* Suppose there are two audio clips in the folder "audio/" */

13        public void init() {
14            soundpc1 = getAudioClip(getCodeBase(),
15                    "audio/Sound1.au");
16            soundpc2 = getAudioClip(getCodeBase(),
17                    "audio/Sound2.au");
18        }

19 /* Major Applet Activities II: Starting                */

20        public void start() {
21            if (Mainthread == null) {
22                Mainthread = new Thread(this);
23                Mainthread.start();
24            }
25        }

26 /* Major Applet Activities III: Stopping               */

27        public void interrupt() {
28            if (Mainthread != null) {
29            Mainthread.interrupt();
30            Mainthread = null;
31            }
32        }

33 /* Since we use Thread, we use run() to contain what   */
34 /* we want the Applet to do              */
35 /* This part may be seen as an extended part of Start() */

36        public void run() {
37            while (true) {
38                soundpc1.loop();
39                soundpc2.play();
40                try { Thread.sleep(500); }
41                catch (InterruptedException e) { }
42            }
43        }

44 /* Major Applet Activities IV: Painting or repainting  */
```

```
45          public void paint(Graphics g) {
46              g.drawString("Sounds ... ... ...", 20, 10);
47          }
48 }
```

Listing 4.6   Example of Java applet for audio play.

You may find that the Java applet in Listing 4.6 is almost the same as that in Listing 4.4, except for two. First, the applet uses audio clips instead of images. Second, to simplify the program, the applet does not use a "switch" for the selection of the audio clips.

The HTML code that triggers the Java applet stated earlier is shown in Listing 4.7.

```
 1 <HTML>
 2 <HEAD>
 3 <TITLE>AUDIO!</TITLE>
 4 </HEAD><BODY>
 5 <P>My Java applet for audio has been loaded!</P>
 6 <P>You may hear the sound ..........</P>
 7 <P>

 8 <APPLET CODE="Audioplay.class"></APPLET>

 9 </P>
10 </BODY>
11 </HTML>
```

Listing 4.7   HTML code that triggers a Java applet of audio play.

The HTML code that triggers the two Java applets for multimedia display simultaneously is shown in Listing 4.8.

```
 1 <HTML>
 2 <HEAD>
 3 <TITLE>Animation and Audio!</TITLE>
 4 </HEAD>
 5 <BODY>
 6 <P>My Java applets for animation and audio has been loaded!</P>
 7 <P>You may see the animation as well as hear the sound......</P>

 8 <P>

 9 <APPLET CODE="Animations.class"></APPLET>
10 <APPLET CODE="Audioplay.class"></APPLET>

11 </P>
12 </BODY>
13 </HTML>
```

Listing 4.8   HTML code that triggers Java applets of animation with audio play.

4.6.3   Get Parameters from the HTML Program

The host HTML program can change the execution behavior of a Java applet through setting **parameters** for the Java applet. Let us take an example. Suppose we want the "HelloWorldApplet" Java applet to display the greeting message with a name specified by the host HTML program. The Java applet and the host HTML program are written as Listing 4.9 and Listing 4.10, respectively.

```
1 import java.awt.Graphics;
2 public class HelloApplet extends java.applet.Applet {
3   public void paint(Graphics g) {

4   String YourName = getParameter("Person");

5   g.drawString("Hello, " + YourName + "!", 5, 25);
6   }
7 }
```

Listing 4.9   Java applet gets a parameter from the HTML program.

```
1 <HTML>
2 <TITLE>Passing a Parameter to Java Applet </TITLE>
3 <BODY>
4 <P>
5 The Java applet gets the parameter of "Person" from the
6 HTML code, and displays the message ...
7 </P>
8 <APPLET CODE="HelloApplet.class" WIDTH=250, HEIGHT=45>

9 <PARAM NAME="Person" VALUE="Dr. Wang">

10 </APPLET>
11 </BODY>
12 </HTML>
```

Listing 4.10   HTML program sets the parameter for the Java applet.

Note lines **4–5** in Listing 4.9 and line **9** in Listing 4.10. Line **4** in Listing 4.9 declares a variable and uses `getParameter` to let the host HTML program set the parameter. Line **9** in Listing 4.10 uses the `PARAM` tag and the attributes `NAME` and `VALUE` in pair to set the parameter. Note that the name of the parameter specified in `<PARAM>` in the HTML and the name specified in `getParameter` in the Java applet must match identically. In this example, the name of the parameter is `Person`.

The formal syntax of these two correlated instructions is shown as follows:

4.6.3.1   `getParameter` *in Java Applet*

In the Java applet, `getParameter` obtains the value of the parameter ("Person" in the example of Listing 4.9) from the HTML and passes it to the internal variable ("YourName" in the example of Listing 4.9).

```
[type][internal variable] = getParameter("[parameter name]");
```

4.6.3.2 *<PARAM> Tag in Host HTML Program*

In the host HTML program, the PARAM tag defines the value of the parameter and passes it to the Java applet through the parameter.

```
<PARAM NAME="[parameter name]" VALUE="[value of the parameter]">
```

4.7 Java Applications (Free-Standing Java Programs)

As discussed in the previous sections, a Java applet is triggered from a Web page. Alternatively, **Java applications**, or free-standing Java programs, can run independently without the support of Web pages. They are just like C++ and other computer programs. All operating systems (DOS, UNIX, MacOS, and Windows) provide the facility to run Java applications. There are two types of Java applications: **ATW-based** and non-ATW programs. ATW-based Java applications employ the AWT, a Java library. ATW-based Java applications use **GUI** facilities, including windows, button, text box, combo box, scrollbars, etc. **Non-ATW** Java programs are of the traditional style, and are used for UNIX and DOS operating systems.

4.7.1 AWT-Based Java Applications

A typical structure (not a program) of AWT-based Java applications is listed in Listing 4.11.

```
 1 import java.awt.*;
 2 import java.awt.event.*;

 3 public class [class name] extends Frame implements ActionListener,
 4 WindowListener {

 5 // Variables

 6 Button [button name];
 7 TextField [textfield name];
 8 Scrollbar [scrollbar name];
 9 [other data type and variables];

10 // Main program

11 public static void main(String[] args) {
12  [class name] [object name] = new [class name]();
13  [object name].setSize([size]);
14  [object name].setVisible(true);
15  }

16 // Constructor

17 public [class name]() {
18  setTitle([title]);
19  setLayout(new FlowLayout());
20  [textfield object] = new TextField([size]);
```

```
21  add([textfield object]);
22  [textfield object].addActionListener(this);

23  [button object] = new Button([caption]);
24  add([button object]);
25  [button object].addActionListener(this);
26  this.addWindowListener(this);

27  [other code];
28  }

29  // Actions of command button

30  public void actionPerformed(ActionEvent event) {

31  if (event.getSource() == [button object]) {
32   [other code for actions];
33   repaint();
34   }
35   [other code];
36  }

37  // Close the window

38  public void windowClosing(WindowEvent event) {
39     System.exit(0);
40  }

41  // Empty WindowListener methods

42  public void windowIconified(WindowEvent event) {
43  }
44  public void windowOpened(WindowEvent event) {
45  }
46  public void windowClosed(WindowEvent event) {
47  }
48  public void windowDeiconified(WindowEvent event) {
49  }
50  public void windowActivated(WindowEvent event) {
51  }
52  public void windowDeactivated(WindowEvent event) {
53  }

54  // Paint/repaint method

55  public void paint(Graphics g) {
56   [code for paint method];
57  }
58  }
```

Listing 4.11   Typical structure of AWT-based Java applications.

Note that the Java program file name must be the same as the class name specified in the program. For example, the class name in the following example is PV, so you must save the program as PV.java (case-sensitive). After editing, click [Build] to compile the Java program. After compiling, you can run it as shown later in this section.

Before we learn new Java statements, we present an example of AWT-based Java application. In this example, the user is allowed to input the interest rate in the textbox, and click the button to obtain the calculation result of the present value.

```
1 // AWT-based Java applications - Free-standing Java programs

2 import java.awt.*;
3 import java.awt.event.*;

4 public class PV extends Frame implements ActionListener,
5 WindowListener {

6  Button Calc;
7  TextField IntRateField;
8  float IntRate;
9  float PValue;

10  public static void main(String[] args) {
11   PV pv = new PV();
12   pv.setSize(600, 400);
13   pv.setVisible(true);
14   }

15  public PV() {
16   setTitle("Present Value Calculation");
17   setLayout(new FlowLayout());

18   IntRateField = new TextField(10);
19   add(IntRateField);
20   IntRateField.addActionListener(this);

21   Calc = new Button("Calculate Present Value");
22   add(Calc);
23   Calc.addActionListener(this);
24   this.addWindowListener(this);

25   PValue = (float)100;
26   }

27  public void actionPerformed(ActionEvent event) {
28   Float IntRateObject = Float.valueOf(IntRateField.getText());

29   if (event.getSource() == Calc) {
30    IntRate = IntRateObject.floatValue();
31    PValue = 100 / (1 + IntRate);
32    repaint();
33    }
34   }

35  public void windowClosing(WindowEvent event) {
36    System.exit(0);
37   }
38  public void windowIconified(WindowEvent event) {
39   }
```

```
40  public void windowOpened(WindowEvent event) {
41  }
42  public void windowClosed(WindowEvent event) {
43  }
44  public void windowDeiconified(WindowEvent event) {
45  }
46  public void windowActivated(WindowEvent event) {
47  }
48  public void windowDeactivated(WindowEvent event) {
49  }

50  public void paint(Graphics g) {
51      g.drawString("*** Input interest rate in the text box," +
52      "and click the button to find out the present value ***", 50, 100);
53      g.drawString("Interest Rate is " + IntRate, 50, 150);
54      g.drawString("Present Value of $100 on the Date One Year Later is $"
55   + PValue, 50, 200);

56  g.drawString("Java Free-Standing Program runs ...", 50, 300);
57  }
58 }
```

Listing 4.12   Example of AWT-based Java application.

We examine how the above program works. Lines **1–2** import libraries. Line **3** is the heading. It says that PV is a class of **Frame**. Line **5** is a standard statement for AWT-based Java applications as discussed in detail later in this section. Lines **6–9** define 4 variables. Two of them are unique to non-AWT Java and C++. One is a button, and the other is text box.

Lines **10–14** are the main program. In AWT-based Java, the main program actually initializes an object of the class (PV in this case). In this case, it sets the size for the object of the PV frame class, named pv, and makes it visible.

Lines **15–26** define the PV class. Lines **16–17** set the title and layout of the frame. Line **18** creates the text box as a new object of text box. Line **19** adds this text box object to the frame. Line **20** makes this text box active. Lines **21–23** do the similar job for the button object. Since the button will result in an action, line **24** must be applied. Line **25** assigns a value to the variable PValue.

Lines **27–34** define the action for the command buttons. Line **28** defines an object type `Float` to catch the data by converting the character string in the text box to the object. Note that `Float` is a class, and it is different from `float` which is a data type. Lines **29–33** define the action when the user clicks the button named `Calc`. Lines **30–31** calculate the present value of 100 based on the interest rate inputted by the user in the text box. Line **32** forces the computer to repaint the window.

Lines **35–49** are standard statements, and most of them are empty in this case.

Lines **50–57** are the paint procedure, which is the same as we learned from Java applets.

Details of Java statements in the earlier example are further explained below.

4.7.1.1 Class `Frame` and Its Methods

An AWT-based Java application is an object (user interface) of class `Frame`. `setSize` and `set.Visible` are methods of `Frame` to initialize the size of the frame and show it on the screen. `setTitle` places a title in the title bar of the frame. `setLayout` sets particular layout (`FlowLayout`) to display the widgets (buttons, text boxes, scroll bars) in the order from-left to right.

4.7.1.2 ActionListener

In Java you can design buttons, scroll bars, and text boxes to implement a user interface. The program must be registered as an action listener (`Action-Listener` in particular) to response the actions from the user through these widgets (e.g., clicking the button). In this example, `addActionListener (this)` registers a listener to the current object.

4.7.1.3 WindowListener

An AWT-based Java application is supposed to be able to run in the Windows environment. Thus, it must be registered as a Window listener (`Window-Listener` in particular). As seen in the example program, there are many methods of Window listener, including `windowClosing`, `windowIconified`, `windowOpened`, `windowClosed`, `windowDeiconified`, `window-Activated`, `windowDeactivated`. Except for `windowClosing` where the library method `System.exit(0)` is used to destroy the window and terminate the Java program, most of these methods are empty. You must include them in the Java application, even though they are empty.

4.7.1.4 Main Program

As discussed earlier in this chapter, in Java the main program is a method of the main class. It has its arguments or parameters. The parameters are an array of `string`, called **args**. In an AWT-based Java application, usually these parameters are not used. However, in a non-AWT Java application, they are very useful. We will return to this later in the section of non-AWT Java applications.

4.7.1.5 Widgets

In designing a graphical user interface, widgets must be used. Widgets in Java include `Scrollbar`, `Label`, `Button`, `TextField`, etc.

4.7.1.6 Cast Operator

Often we need to convert values of a variable from one type to another. In Java, we use **cast operator** to implement the conversion. For example, in

```
PValue = (float)100
```

the cast operator (float) converts the integer 100 to a float number (100.00) for PValue. There always is a risk of losing information when converting a number.

4.7.1.7 String Processing

In Java, string processing is convenient. As seen in the example, the general format of the method g.drawString is:

```
g.drawString(["string"] + [variable], [location]);
```

4.7.1.8 Run AWT-Based Java Application

To run an AWT-based Java application in Windows, go to [Start], [Run], type CMD, and click [OK]. After the C:\> prompt, type

```
C:\>jview [project directory][java class name]
```

For example,

```
C:\>jview c:\BIS212\Project2\PV.class
```

When you run the above Java, you will have the Java-generated user interface shown in Figure 4.5.

4.7.2 Non-AWT Java Applications

Non-AWT Java applications are similar to C++ programs. Nevertheless, there are a number of significant differences. First, the main program in a C++ program

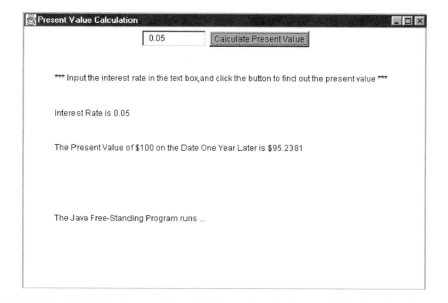

Figure 4.5   GUI generated by the AWT-based Java application.

is not defined in a class explicitly, but the main program in a non-AWT Java application is defined as a method of the main class explicitly. Second, in C++, classes are usually stored in header files separately. However, in Java applications, classes can be included in the main class. Non-AWT Java applications have the following structure.

```
 1 import java.io.*;

 2 public class [main class name] {

 3  public static void main(String[] args) {

 4     [main class name] [object name] = new [main class name]();
 5     [data type and variables];
 6     [object name].[main method]([parameters]);
 7  }

 8  private void [main method]([parameters]) {
 9    [code];
10  }

11 // additional class

12 public class [additional class name] {

13 // Attributes

14 [data types and variables];

15 // constructor

16    [code];

17 // methods

18    [code];
19  }
20  }
```

Listing 4.13   Typical structure of non-AWT Java application.

Again, the Java program file name must be the same as the class name you specified in the program. For example, the class name in the following example is GroceryJava, so you must save the program as GroceryJava.java (case-sensitive). After editing, click [Build] to compile the Java program. After compiling, you can run it as shown later in this section.

To make a comparison of non-AWT Java applications with C++ programs, we translate the C++ program in Listing 2.10 into Java applications. The Java application to print out the brochure of the grocery store is shown in Listing 4.14.

```
 1 // **** non-AWT Java application ****
 2 import java.io.*;

 3 public class GroceryJava  {
 4 public static void main(String[] args)  {
```

```
 5  System.out.println("  My Small Grocery Store at UMD  ");
 6  System.out.println(" ****************************** ");
 7  System.out.println(" ");
 8  System.out.println(" Regular Price   Sale Price ");
 9  System.out.println(" ");

10  GroceryJava grocery = new GroceryJava();

11  int dis_r=Integer.parseInt(args[0]);
12  grocery.MainMethod(dis_r);
13  }
14  private void MainMethod(int dis_r)  {
15   for (int i=1; i<=5; i++) {

16  // The following procedure manipulate the available
17  // Grocery objects, assuming we have only 5 items

18      GROCERY Grocery = new GROCERY();
19      Grocery.InitGrocery(i);

20  // Notice the spaces in the following sentence

21
22      System.out.println (
23       Grocery.ReturnGrocery_Product_Name()
24       + Grocery.ReturnGrocery_Product_Price()
25       + "  /  "
26       + Grocery.ReturnGrocery_Product_Unit()
27       + "    "
28       + (((float)(int)(Grocery.Grocery_Discount(dis_r)*100))/100
29       + "  /  "
30       + Grocery.ReturnGrocery_Product_Unit());
31   }
32  }

33  // **** Class GROCERY definition ****
34  public class GROCERY

35  // Class declaration
36  {
37   private

38  // Attributes

39      int     Grocery_Product_Number;
40      String  Grocery_Product_Name;
41      float   Grocery _Product_Price;
42      float   Grocery_Product_Inventory;
43      String  Grocery_Product_Unit;

44  // Operations
45      // The following procedure simulates the system to read a
46      // database/data file which records information of the
47      // grocery products. One may substitute this procedure
48      // by using database/files
```

```
49   public void InitGrocery(int G_N) {
50
51    Grocery_Product_Number=G_N;
52      if (Grocery_Product_Number==1)
53          { Grocery_Product_Name= "Milk ";
54                                   // put spaces in
55            Grocery_Product_Price=(float) 2.59;
56            Grocery_Product_Inventory=300;
57            Grocery_Product_Unit= "Oz ";
58                                   // put a space in
59        };
60      if (Grocery_Product_Number==2)
61          { Grocery_Product_Name= "Egg ";
62                                   // put spaces in
63            Grocery_Product_Price=(float) 1.89;
64            Grocery_Product_Inventory=800;
65            Grocery_Product_Unit="Dzn";
66        };
67      if (Grocery_Product_Number==3)
68          { Grocery_Product_Name= "Beef ";
69                                   // put spaces in
70            Grocery_Product_Price=(float) 2.99;
71            Grocery_Product_Inventory=150;
72            Grocery_Product_Unit="Lb ";
73                                   // put a space
74        };
75      if (Grocery_Product_Number==4)
76          { Grocery_Product_Name= "Bean ";
77                                   // put spaces in
78            Grocery_Product_Price=(float) 1.09;
79            Grocery_Product_Inventory=100;
80            Grocery_Product_Unit= "Lb ";
81                                   // put a space
82        };
83      if (Grocery_Product_Number==5)
84          { Grocery_Product_Name= "Melon ";
85                                   // put spaces in
86            Grocery_Product_Price=(float) 1.59;
87            Grocery_Product_Inventory=100;
88            Grocery_Product_Unit= "Pc ";
89                                   // put a space
90        };
91
92   }

93 // Next are methods of the GROCERY class ...

94 // Return Name
95 public String ReturnGrocery_Product_Name()
96        {return Grocery_Product_Name;};
97 // Return Unit
98 public String ReturnGrocery_Product_Unit()
99        {return Grocery_Product_Unit;};

100 // Return Price
```

```
101 public float ReturnGrocery_Product_Price()
102         {return Grocery_Product_Price;};

103 // Calculate Price after discount

104 public float Grocery_Discount(float Discount_Rate) {
105     float Price_After_Discount;
106     float Rate_After_Discount;
107   Rate_After_Discount = (float) (1-Discount_Rate*0.01);
108   Price_After_Discount=Grocery_Product_Price*Rate_After_Discount;
109 return(Price_After_Discount);
110  }

111 // Process Inventory

112 public float Grocery_Inventory_Process(float Inventory_Change)
113  { Grocery_Product_Inventory=
114     Grocery_Product_Inventory+Inventory_Change;
115   return(Grocery_Product_Inventory);
116  }
117  }
118 }
```

Listing 4.14   Non-AWT Java application (Java Code for the example of grocery store in Listing 2.10).

As has been discussed in AWT-based Java applications, the main program of Java defines the main class. This is also true in non-AWT Java applications. This feature of Java is unique to C++. However, this is only a formality. In fact, the object created by the main class triggers other classes in exactly the same way as that of a C++ main program. In other words, one can translate a C++ main program into a non-AWT Java program by changing the format.

We examine how the program works. Line **2** imports the library. Lines **3–118** define the main class. Remember that, in C++, the programs of classes cannot be placed within the main program. However, in non-AWT Java, the programs of classes used by the main class are included in the main class.

Line **4** is the standard heading for the main class. Lines **5–9** print the heading of the flyer. Line **10** creates an object of the main class. Line **11** defines a variable for the discount rate, and assigns a value through args. We will explain args later. Line **12** instructs the computer to execute a method in the main class.

Lines **14–31** define the method used in line **12**. This part is almost the same as that of the C++ main program.

Lines **34** through **117** are the class GROCERY. This part is the same as that of the C++ example explained earlier, with a few minor differences.

Important unique features of non-AWT Java applications are explained in the following section.

4.7.2.1   Run Non-AWT Java Application and args

A non-AWT Java application can be triggered by the operating system. To run a non-AWT Java application in Windows, go to [Start], [Run], type CMD, and click [OK]. After the prompt, type

```
C:\>jview [project directory][java class name][value of args]
```

For example,

```
C:\>jview c:\BIS212\Project3\GroceryJava 25
```

One may also use Sun's JDK. For example, suppose your non-AWT Java application (`GroceryJava.class`) is stored on Drive F, and the JDK locates in the folder `c:\jdk1.2.2\bin`, you can trigger the Java program by typing

```
c:\jdk1.2.2\bin> f:
F:> c:java GroceryJava 25
```

In the examples stated, 25 is the first argument (parameter) for the main program. In this example, the first argument is defined as `args[0]`, and thus `args[0]` is assigned with 25. Specifically in this case, 25 is the discount rate. Apparently, you can specify the discount rate by using the argument.

4.7.2.2   System.out.println

In non-AWT Java applications, you can use `System.out.println` to display a string on the screen. `System.out.println` seems to be easier to use than `printf` in C++.

4.8   Java Servlets

We have learned Java applets and understood the advantages of Java applets in Web-based applications. However, you may have found that downloading Java applets from the server takes a significant time. **Java servlets** solve this problem. Java servlets are executed on the server side, and send the execution results to the client side based on the client requests. More importantly, Java servlets allow the client to make a variety of processes on the server, such as database manipulations.

In many cases, the functions performed by Java servlets are quite similar to **CGI** applications (e.g., **Perl** programs), proprietary server application programming interfaces (**APIs**), server-side **JavaScript**, or Microsoft's **ASP.NET** (new version of Active Server Pages), which are generally called **server-side programming**. However, each of these techniques has its own characteristics, advantages, and problems as well. Generally speaking, the advantages of Java servlets are efficient (compared with CGI techniques), economic (no need for particular vendor or product at additional costs), and, more importantly, platform independent (i.e., executable in any operating systems). The major tasks of server-side programs are to response the user's requests on the client side, process data on the server, and generate **dynamic Web pages** that are sent to the client side through the Internet. Dynamic Web pages are different from **static Web pages**. A static Web page is an HTML document that the content is established at the time the page is created. It is located at a certain URL. Any user who accesses it will get the same information. The Web page changes only after a programmer update the HTML document. On the other hand,

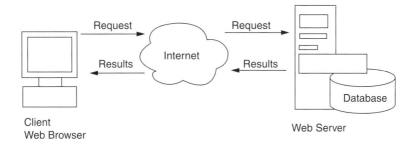

Figure 4.6   Execution cycle of a Java servlet.

a dynamic Web page is generated by a server-side program. It may not have an URL. It can provide different information depending upon the variables set by individual users on the client side.

Java servlets are executed entirely inside the **Java Virtual Machine**, which is created by the Java computing environment. In principle, Java servlets run on a server, but they can be tested on any stand-alone computer with an appropriate operating system. All examples discussed in this book are applied to a computer with the **Windows 2000** operating system. The cycle of a Web-based application with a Java servlet is illustrated in Figure 4.6.

4.8.1   Software Requirements of Java Servlets

To compile and execute Java servlets, the two most important software packages are the **JDK** and **Java Server Web Development Kit** (**JSWDK**). Both of these two development kits can be downloaded from <http://www.javasoft.com> with no cost provided the downloading follows the license agreements. In this book, all examples are demonstrated using version **JDK1.2.2** for JDK (Java™ 2 SDK, Standard Edition, Version 1.2.2) and **JSWDK-1.0.1** for JSWDK.

In the following discussion, we assume that the two development kits are installed in their folders:

```
C:\jdk1.2.2
C:\jswdk-1.0.1
```

Appendix 4.1 provides step-by-step instructions for setting a server with Windows (e.g., Windows 2000 Server) or a personal server on your PC with Windows (e.g., Windows 2000) for running Java servlets.

A programmer might not set a server, but must know the folder structure of the Java servlet server, as shown in Figure 4.7. To run Java servlets, the programmer must place Java servlet class files, HTML files, and data files in the corresponding folders (see Figure 4.7).

4.8.2   Edit and Compile Java Servlets

1. Create your own folder in the JDK folder, say, `c:\jdk1.2.2\MyJava` to hold your Java servlets programs. Use Notepad to edit the Java servlet. As an example,

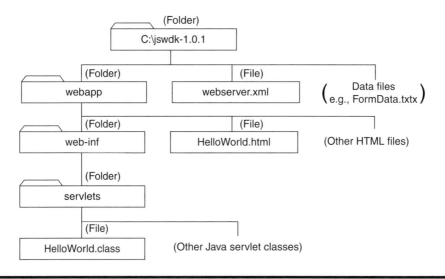

Figure 4.7   Configuration structure for the default server.

edit a Java servlet program as follows, and save it as `HelloWorld.java` into
your folder.

```
import java.io.*;
import javax.servlet.*;
import javax.servlet.http.*;
public class HelloWorld extends HttpServlet
  {
   public void doGet(HttpServletRequest request,
       HttpServletResponse response)
       throws IOException, ServletException
    {
      response.setContentType("text/html");
      PrintWriter out = response.getWriter();
      out.println("<html>");
      out.println("<head>");
      out.println("<title>Hello World!</title>");
      out.println("</head>");
      out.println("<body>");
      out.println("<h1>Hello World!</h1>");
      out.println("</body>");
      out.println("</html>");
      out.close();
    }
  }
```

Listing 4.15   Servlet HelloWorld.java program.

This program is explained in detail later in this section. Here, we continue
to make this servlet work.

2. Compile the Java servlet from `jdk1.2.2\bin` as follows.

```
C:\jdk1.2.2\bin>javac c:\jdk1.2.2\MyJava\HelloWorld.java
```

Or

```
C:\jdk1.2.2\MyJava>c:\jdk1.2.2\bin\javac HelloWorld.java
```

If everything has been set correctly, the class file, `HelloWorld.class`, will be generated in your folder (`MyJava`).

3. Move the `HelloWorld.class` file to the servlets folder.

```
c:\jswdk-1.0.1\webapp\web-inf\servlets
```

(see Figure 4.7).

4.8.3   Web Page That Triggers Java Servlet

As an example, we build an HTML file named `HelloWorld.html` for the default server, which is supposed to trigger a servlet named HelloWorld, as shown in Listing 4.16. You may use a different name for the HTML file, and design to trigger any other servlets through this Web page as discussed later in this section.

```
1 <HTML>
2 <HEAD>
3 <TITLE>This is a test of Java servlet</TITLE>
4 </HEAD>
5 <BODY>
6 <A HREF="../servlet/HelloWorld">
7         Trigger Java Servlet - HelloWorld</A>
8 </BODY>
9 </HTML>
```

Listing 4.16 Example of invoking the HelloWorld Servlet (HelloWorld. html).

In Listing 4.16, line **6** specifies the servlet to be triggered. The name of the servlet is HelloWorld. Later we will show how to build this servlet. Note that the folder "`../servlet/`" is not a physical folder. In fact, regardless of the physical folder the Java servlet is placed in, we always use this **logical folder** for Java servlet in the HTML program.

Place the HTML file within the `webapp` folder together with `web-inf`.

4.8.4   Trigger a Java Servlet

1. From Windows Explorer, find `startserver.bat` in the `jswdk-1.0.1` folder, and double click it to start the server. Two MS-DOS windows show up (see Appendix 4.1, Figure 4.A1.3). This indicates that the default server has been started. The URL address for the default server is:

```
http://localhost:8080/
```

where 8080 means the **port**. Note that, at present, we are using PC to run servlets. If we use a real server to run servlets, the URL should be different from this. For instance, if the real server has its IP address 134.88.127.2, then the URL address is:

```
http://134.88.127.2:8080/
```

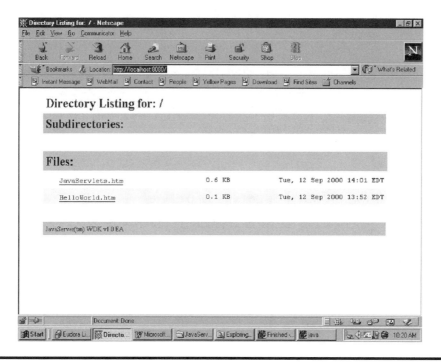

Figure 4.8   Access the default server (http://localhost:8080).

2. Start a Web browser, Netscape or Internet Explorer. Type `http://localhost:8080` in the URL Location box, and hit Enter. Figure 4.8 window will show up.

The default server lists all HTML files in the `webapp` folder. Click `Hello-World.html`. The Web page which allows you to trigger the HelloWorld servlet will be downloaded from the server (Figure 4.9).

3. Click the hyper link `Trigger Java Servlet - HelloWorld` to trigger the servlet. The triggered servlet then generates a dynamic Web page, and sends it back to the client side. The dynamic Web page will show up on the client's screen as in Figure 4.10.

In this example, the servlet is triggered from the Web page. However, you can trigger the servlet directly from the server by typing the URL `http//localhost:8080/servlet/HelloWorld`, as shown in the URL location in Figure 4.10.

In summary, there are two common ways to trigger servlets:

- Trigger a servlet from an HTML Web page, by clicking a hyper link or a button.
- Typing a servlet URL into a browser window.

4. Close the Web browser. Use Windows Explorer to find `stopserver.bat` in the `jswdk-1.0.1` folder, and double click it to stop the server. Note that the MS-DOS Java window disappears.

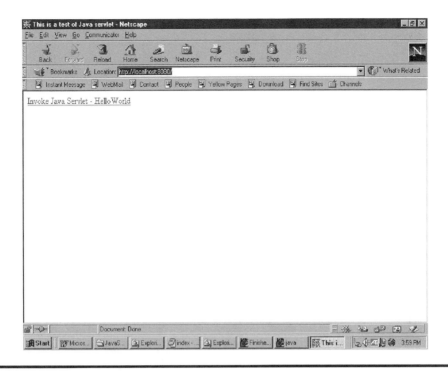

Figure 4.9   HelloWorld.html Web page.

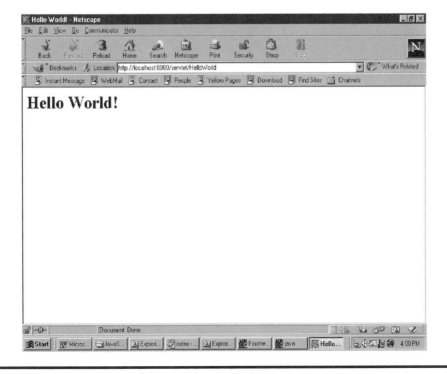

Figure 4.10   HelloWorld Servlet is triggered.

One of the advantages of Java servlets is that a Java servlet class resides in CPU after it is triggered, and will response to a later request very quickly. Compared with Java servlets, CGI based Perl is slow because each time the Perl program will be reloaded and re-interpreted in response to a request. If hundreds and thousands of clients access the server simultaneously, Java servlets are significantly faster than Perl. However, novice programmers must note that, when testing a Java servlet program after debugging, one must stop the server (by clicking `stopserver.bat`) first to discharge the servlet class, and then restart the server by clicking `startserver.bat`. In cases where the remote server is not controlled by the programmer, the program name must be changed (e.g., with a version number).

4.8.5 Structure of Java Servlets

A servlet is an object of `HttpServlet` class. There are actually three types of methods in a servlet. Each runs at a specific time in a servlet's life.

1. `init`: The `init` method creates and initializes the resources that the servlet will use to handle client requests. It is executed only once.
2. `service`: The `service` method handles all requests sent by the client. It is executed after the `init` method completes. Commonly used servlets are objects of the `HttpServlet` class, and the `HttpServlet` class has already implemented the `service` method for these servlets. When the `HttpServlet.service` method is executed, it will determine which specific methods will be further triggered to make responses to the client requests. These specific methods need to be programmed by the servlet programmer. We have learned from HTML that clients commonly use two methods to make requests from a Web page: GET and POST. Thus, two methods are commonly specified in servlets to handle clients' requests:

    `doGet()`: if the request method is GET
    `doPost()`: if the request method is POST

3. `destroy`: When a service is completed, the servlet executes the `destroy` method to release all resources it has used (e.g., close a database connection). In most cases, we do not need to explicitly define this method if the `init` method does not create any resources for the servlet.

A typical structure (not a program) of Java servlets is listed in Listing 4.17.

```
1 import javax.servlet.*;
2 import javax.servlet.http.*;
3 import java.io.*;
4 import java.util.*;
  . . . . .
5 import [other classes and methods];
6 public class [user-defined class-name] extends HttpServlet {

7 // initialization method
8  public void init(ServletConfig config)
```

```
 9          throws ServletException {

10 // Commonly, pass the ServletConfig object to the super class

11       Super.init(config);
12  }

13 // Process the HTTP GET request
14    public void doGet(HttpServletRequest request,
15       HttpServletResponse response)
16       throws ServletException, IOException {

17 // Code for the doGet method; typically

18      response.setContentType("text/html");
19      PrintWriter out = response.getWriter();
20      out.println("<HTML>");
21      out.println("<HEAD><TITLE> [Title] </TITLE></HEAD>");
22      out.println("<BODY>");

23      [Code for the body of the dynamic Web page]
24      [Other code for data processing on the server]

25      out.println("</BODY></HTML>");
26      out.close();
27    }

28 // Process the HTTP POST

29    public void doPost(HttpServletRequest request,
30         HttpServletResponse response)
31         throws ServletException, IOException {

32 // Code for the doPost method; typically

33      response.setContentType("text/html");
34      PrintWriter out = response.getWriter();
35      out.println("<HTML>");
36  out.println("<HEAD><TITLE> [Title] </TITLE></HEAD>");
37      out.println("<BODY>");

38      [Code for the body of the dynamic Web page]
39      [Other code for data processing on the server]

40      out.println("</BODY></HTML>");
41      out.close();
42    }

43 // Get Servlet information

44    public String getServletInfo() {
45      return "Servlet Information";
46    }
47 }
```

Listing 4.17   Typical structure of Java servlets.

4.8.6 Java Servlet Programming

In this subsection, we will learn more details of Java servlet programming. We first build a Web page as a client-server interface. As you will see, after the client Web browser downloads this Web page from the server, the client is able to trigger the Java servlets on the server by clicking hyperlinks or submit buttons. Then we discuss individual servlets in detail.

4.8.6.1 Web Page to Trigger Java Servlets

```
 1 <HTML>
 2 <HEAD>
 3 <TITLE> Trigger Java Servlets </TITLE>
 4 </HEAD>
 5 <BODY>

 6 <H1> Trigger Java Servlets on the Server </H1>
 7 <BR><HR>
 8 <H3> Hyperlink to Java Servlet "HelloWorld" </H3>
 9 <A HREF="../servlet/HelloWorld">
10          Trigger Java Servlet - HelloWorld</A>
11 <BR>
12 <HR>
13 <H3>Information of the Client's Request
14 </H3>
15  <FORM ACTION="../servlet/ClientRequestInfor" METHOD=POST>
16 <INPUT TYPE=SUBMIT VALUE="Get Information of Client Request">
17  </FORM>

18 <BR><HR>
19 <H3>Java Servlet saves data of FORM, and writes them to a file
20 </H3>
21 <FORM ACTION="../servlet/SaveForm" METHOD=POST>
22 Your Last Name: <BR>
23 <INPUT TYPE=TEXT NAME="lname" SIZE=50> <BR>
24 Your First Name: <BR>
25 <INPUT TYPE=TEXT NAME="fname" SIZE=50> <BR>
26 Your Email Address: <BR>
27 <INPUT TYPE=TEXT NAME="email" SIZE=50> <BR><BR>
28 Place Your Order: <BR>
29 Item:    <INPUT TYPE=TEXT NAME="item1" SIZE=10>
30 Quantity: <INPUT TYPE=TEXT NAME="Q1" SIZE=5> <BR>
31 Item:    <INPUT TYPE=TEXT NAME="item2" SIZE=10>
32 Quantity: <INPUT TYPE=TEXT NAME="Q2" SIZE=5> <BR>
33 Item:    <INPUT TYPE=TEXT NAME="item3" SIZE=10>
34 Quantity: <INPUT TYPE=TEXT NAME="Q3" SIZE=5> <BR>
35 <BR>
36 <INPUT TYPE=SUBMIT VALUE="Process the Order">
37 <INPUT TYPE=RESET VALUE="Start Over Again">
38 </FORM>

39 <BR><HR>
40 <H3> Search Online Yellow Page</H3>
41 <H4> Type the name of the person you want to find</H4>
```

```
42 <H5> (E.g., Wang)</H5>
43 <FORM ACTION="../servlet/SearchFile" METHOD=POST>
44 <INPUT TYPE=TEXT NAME="name" SIZE=50>
45 <BR>
46 <INPUT TYPE=SUBMIT VALUE="Search">
47 <INPUT TYPE=RESET VALUE="Reset">
48 </FORM>

49 </BODY>
50 </HTML>
```

Listing 4.18 Web page to trigger Java servlets on the server (JavaServlets. html).

The above HTML file (JavaServlets.html) must be placed in the right folder on the server, in our case, c:\jswdk-1.0.1\webapp\ (see Figure 4.7).

There are four parts in this Web page. Lines **6–10** are the first part. It is a hyperlink that triggers the HelloWorld servlet, as we have tested earlier. In Line **9**, "../servlet/" means the default logical folder of the servlet. Note that it is not a physical folder.

Lines **13–17** are the second part. It triggers ClientRequestInfo servlet. As we will learn, the servlet returns specific information relating to the client's request.

Lines **19–38** are the third part. In this part, the user on the client side sends an order through the FORM, and triggers SaveForm servlet. As we will learn later, the servlet saves the order data on the server's disk, and return a confirmation to the client.

Lines **40–48** are the fourth part. This part allows the user on the client side to search an online yellow page file using the SearchFile servlet. Later we will learn how the servlet searches the data file on the server and returns search result to the client.

4.8.6.2 Simple Servlet

In this subsection, we learn Java servlet programming through the HelloWorld servlet. For convenience, we re-list the servlet as follows:

```
 1 import java.io.*;
 2 import javax.servlet.*;
 3 import javax.servlet.http.*;

 4 public class HelloWorld extends HttpServlet {
 5  public void doGet(HttpServletRequest request,
 6     HttpServletResponse response)
 7     throws IOException, ServletException
 8  {
 9    response.setContentType("text/html");
10    PrintWriter out = response.getWriter();
11    out.println("<html>");
12    out.println("<head>");
13    out.println("<title>Hello World!</title>");
14    out.println("</head>");
15    out.println("<body>");
```

```
16    out.println("<h1>Hello World!</h1>");
17    out.println("</body>");
18    out.println("</html>");
19    out.close();
20  }
21 }
```

Listing 4.19   Servlet HelloWorld.java program.

In Listing 4.19, lines **1–3** are preprocessors to import the library. For HTTP Web applications, `javax.servlet.*` and `javax.servlet.http.*` are needed.

Line **4** is the heading of the Java servlet. Lines **5–7** declare the `doGet` method. In this simple Java servlet, there is no `init` method. Only method `doGet` is used to handle the client's request. Note that `doGet` is the default method to response the HTTP request. Since the hyperlink defined by lines **9–10** in Listing 4.18 does not specify what request method is used, the doGet method is used to response the request through the hyperlink. We will discuss doGet in detail later.

Line **9** is to set content type for the response. Note that this is the first thing we must specify. In most cases, we want to response the client's request by sending an HTML text file, and use `"text/html"` for the type.

Line **10** is to get the `PrintWriter` to write the HTML text file. This is implemented by calling `ServletResponse`'s `getWriter` method, and creating the object `out` for the writer.

Lines **11–18** print the HTML text file that will be sent back to the client in the `HttpServletResponse` object. Finally, line **19** closes the writer. The HTML document printed by the Java servlet is as follows:

```
<html>
<head>
<title>Hello World!</title>
</head>
<body>
<h1>Hello World!</h1>
</body>
</html>
```

Listing 4.20   Output of the Java servlet in Listing 4.19.

4.8.6.3   *HttpServlet*

There are two main servlet classes: `GenericServlet` and `HttpServlet`. The `HttpServlet` class is extended from `GenericServlet`, and is convenient to use for HTTP Web applications.

4.8.6.4   *doGet and doPost*

The `doGet` method handles client's GET request; typically through the hyperlink. The `doPost` method handles POST request; typically through the FORM submit button. The two methods are very similar.

```
doGet(HttpServletRequest request, HttpServletResponse response)
doPost(HttpServletRequest request, HttpServletResponse response)
```

Both methods receive HttpServletRequest object (request) and HttpServletResponse object (response). These objects represent client's request and response to the client, respectively. The HttpServletRequest object contains information sent from the client and the HttpServlet Response object contains information that will be sent back to the client.

4.8.6.5 *throws and Exceptions*

For some reasons, the servlet might not be able to execute a method. The throws clause is used to instruct that under certain circumstances the method will generate a specific exception. This would make the Java servlet more tolerant of errors. For example, the declaration:

```
public void doGet(HttpServletRequest request,
     HttpServletResponse response)
     throws IOException, ServletException
```

indicates that the doGet method can generate an IOException and Servlet-Exception.

4.8.6.6 *setContentType*

The setContentType method sets the content type for the response. A Java servlet sets content type only once. It must be set before writing to a writer or output stream.

4.8.6.7 *PrintWriter, getWriter, println, and close*

PrintWriter is a class of print writer for printing document. In the example of Listing 4.19, out is an object of PrintWriter.

getWriter is a method of ServletResponse class and let the servlet to get a writer.

println is a method of PrintWriter, and is used to print a line specified in the argument.

close method is used to release the print writer when the print task is completed.

4.8.6.8 *Information of the Client's Request*

Once the client triggers a Java servlet and makes a request, the HttpServlet-Request object holds information about the client's request. These pieces of information about client's request can be used for application programming.

The following Java servlet can be triggered by a request from the Web page of Listing 4.18 (lines 15–17). It will show several examples of information about the client request.

```
1 import java.io.*;
2 import javax.servlet.*;
3 import javax.servlet.http.*;

4 public class ClientRequestInfor extends HttpServlet {

5  public void doPost(HttpServletRequest request,
6          HttpServletResponse response)
7          throws IOException, ServletException
8  {
9    response.setContentType("text/html");
10   PrintWriter out = response.getWriter();

11   out.println("<html>");
12   out.println("<body>");
13   out.println("<head>");
14   out.println("<title>Information of Client</title>");
15   out.println("</head>");
16   out.println("<body>");
17   out.println("Your request method is:" +
18       request.getMethod());
19   out.println("<br>");
20   out.println("The Protocol is:" +
21       request.getProtocol());
22   out.println("<br>");
23   out.println("Your IP address is:" +
24       request.getRemoteAddr());
25   out.println("<br>");
26   out.println("Your host name is:" +
27       request.getRemoteHost());
28   out.println("<br>");
29   out.println("The requested session ID is:" +
30       request.getRequestedSessionId());
31   out.println("</body>");
32   out.println("</html>");
33   out.close();
34 }
35 }
```

Listing 4.21 Servlet ClientRequestInfor.java.

In line **18**, the getMethod method returns the HTTP method (i.e., GET or POST) used by the client request.

In line **21**, the getProtocol method returns a string representing the protocol used in the request. In line **24**, the getRemoteAddr method returns the IP address of the client. In line **27**, the getRemoteHost method returns the qualified host name of the client. In line **30**, the getRequestedSessionId method returns the session ID associated with the request.

4.8.6.9 Save FORM Data to the Server's Disk

One of the major advantages of servlets is the capability of data processing on the server. In this subsection, we demonstrate how a Java servlet can save the data that is sent by the user on the client side through a Web page FORM. The following program is the servlet `SaveForm.java` that responses an order from the client side.

```java
1 import java.io.*;
2 import java.util.*;
3 import javax.servlet.*;
4 import javax.servlet.http.*;

5  public class SaveForm extends HttpServlet
6 {
7 public void doPost(HttpServletRequest request,
8                    HttpServletResponse response)
9                    throws ServletException, IOException
10 {
11  response.setContentType("text/html");
12  PrintWriter out = response.getWriter();

13  out.println("<h2>Form has been submitted....</h2>");

14  // get values from the FORM

15  String lname = request.getParameter("lname");
16  String fname = request.getParameter("fname");
17  String email = request.getParameter("email");
18  String item1 = request.getParameter("item1");
19  String Q1 = request.getParameter("Q1");
20  String item2 = request.getParameter("item2");
21  String Q2 = request.getParameter("Q2");
22  String item3 = request.getParameter("item3");
23  String Q3 = request.getParameter("Q3");

24  // if there is an order
25  if ((Q1 != null && Q1.length() > 0) ||
26      (Q2 != null && Q2.length() > 0) ||
27      (Q3 != null && Q3.length() > 0))
28  {
29   out.println("Hi, " + fname);
30  }

31  // the FORM has an empty order
32  else {
33   out.println("No data has been entered.");
34  }

35  // a try-catch pair to write data to the server
36  try {

37   // define the name of the data file on the server
38      String outputFileName="Formdata.txt";
39   // get FileWriter ready
40   FileWriter fout = new FileWriter(outputFileName);

41   // write data to the file
42   // data items are separated by \n
43      fout.write(lname);
```

```
44        fout.write("\n");
45        fout.write(fname);
46        fout.write("\n");
47        fout.write(email);
48        fout.write("\n");
49        fout.write(item1);
50        fout.write("\n");
51        fout.write(Q1);
52        fout.write("\n");
53        fout.write(item2);
54        fout.write("\n");
55        fout.write(Q2);
56        fout.write("\n");
57        fout.write(item3);
58        fout.write("\n");
59        fout.write(Q3);
60        fout.write("\n");

61    // send a feedback message to the client
62    out.println("<h3>Your order is being processed ...</h3>");

63    // close the file-writer
64    fout.close();
65  }

66    // IO exception when the server has problems
67    catch(java.io.IOException e) {
68   out.println("Sorry, the server has problems with file.");
69   out.println("Please try again later.");
70    }

71    // complete the dynamic Web page
72   out.println("<p>back to <a href=../JavaServlets.html>Form</a>");

73    out.close();
74    }
75  }
```

Listing 4.22   Servlet SaveForm.java.

In the program in Listing 4.22, lines **1–4** import necessary libraries. Lines **15–23** retrieve the value of each request parameter. Note that the parameter names are corresponding to that defined in the FORM (see Listing 4.18, lines **23–34**).

Lines **25–34** are an if-else statement to make sure that the FORM contains order data.

Lines **36–67** implement a try-catch pair to handle possible exceptions. In this case, if the disk, for example, has problems, the program will not be crashed. Line **38** defines the file name for the data file. After this program is executed, you can find the data file in the folder C:\ jswdk-1.0.1\.

Line **40** declares a FileWriter to write data to a file. Its internal name is fout and its external name is Formdata.txt in this case.

Note that the program in Listing 4.22 overwrites the data file with the new FORM data. If you want to **append** the newly received data to the data file, line 40 must be changed to

```
FileWriter fout = new FileWriter(outputFileName, true);
```

Lines **43–60** write the captured data to the file. Note that we use a separator "\n" to separate data items. Finally, lines **64** and **73** close the FileWriter and PrintWriter, respectively, and the lines between specify the exception and complete the dynamic Web pages.

Note that, for the simplicity, we omit all quotation marks in the HTML tags of the dynamic Web page. In simple cases, this does not cause problems. In an example later in this chapter, we show that, to print a quotation mark, one must use \" coupled with + signs in the `println` statement.

When you start the Web site `JavaServlet.html` (see Figure 4.8), you will see a part of the Web page is a FORM which allows the user to place an order, as shown in Figure 4.11. After you enter the data and click the submit button, the request, along with the data, is sent to the server, and `SaveForm` Java servlet is triggered. The servlet stores the data on the server's disk, and sends a confirmation message back to the client, as shown in Figure 4.12.

The data file can be processed by other programs or software packages. Figure 4.13 shows the retrieval result by Excel spreadsheet.

In fact, Java servlets are able to process databases directly, if **Java database connectivity (JDBC)** is installed.

Next, we learn several Java statements which newly appear in Listing 4.22.

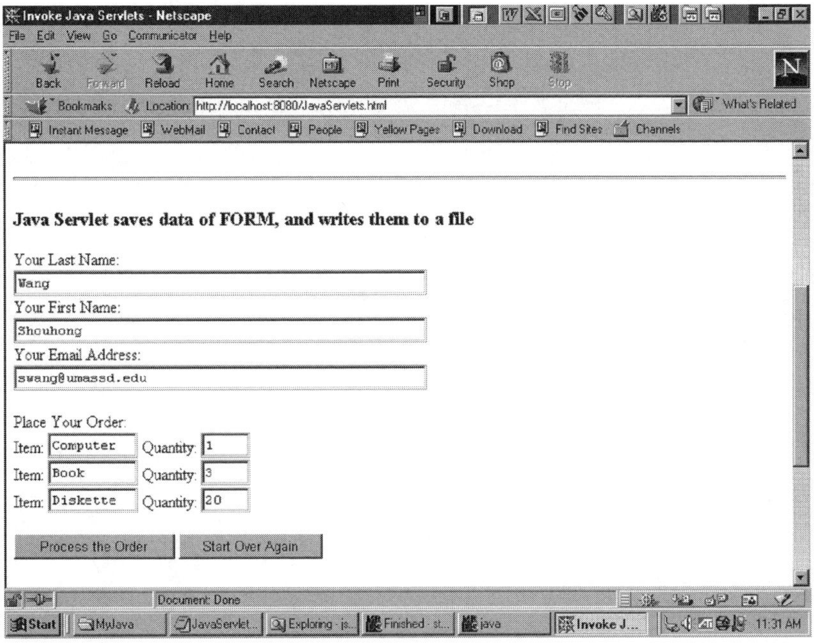

Figure 4.11 Input data through the FORM and trigger Servlet SaveForm.

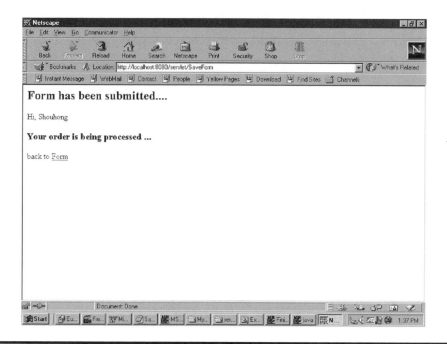

Figure 4.12   Servlet SaveForm sends a dynamic Web page back to the client.

4.8.6.10 *getParameter*

A Java servlet captures the FORM data through the `getParameter` method of the `request` class. The syntax of the `getParameter` method is

```
request.getParameter("[parameter name]")
```

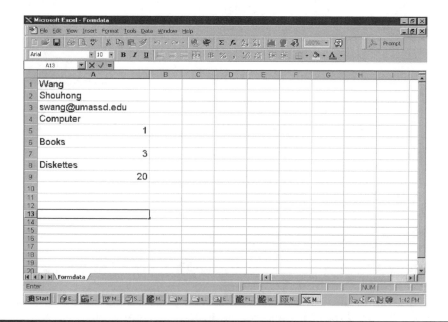

Figure 4.13   Data stored on the server and viewed by Excel spreadsheet.

where the argument [*parameter name*] is the corresponding parameter name specified by the FORM.

4.8.6.11   FileWriter, Write, and Close

FileWriter is a class of **writer** for writing disk files. In the example of Listing 4.22, fout is an object of FileWriter. To get a FileWriter, two arguments are needed: writer name and output file name.

FileWriter [*writer name*] = new FileWriter([*output file name*]);

write is a method of FileWriter, and is used to write a line specified by the argument to the disk file.

close method is used to release the file when the writing task is completed.

4.8.6.12   Read Data File from the Server

In this subsection, we will learn how a Java servlet can read and search a disk file on the server, and provide requested information for the client. In this example, suppose we have a YellowPage.txt file on the server's disk. The user on the client side is allowed to input a person's name and search the yellow page file to find this person's telephone number.

As an example, you may use Notepad to edit YellowPage.txt file as shown in Figure 4.14.

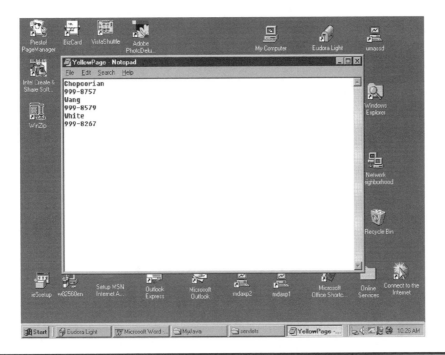

Figure 4.14   Text file (YellowPage.txt) used for Servlet SearchFile.

This file is then stored on the server's disk. In our case, we save it in the folder C:\jswdk-1.0.1\. The following is the SearchFile.java program.

```
1  import java.io.*;
2  import java.util.*;
3  import javax.servlet.*;
4  import javax.servlet.http.*;

5  public class SearchFile extends HttpServlet {
6   // define an object of BufferedReader class
7   private BufferedReader fin;
8   public void doPost(HttpServletRequest request,
9                      HttpServletResponse response)
10                     throws ServletException, IOException
11 {
12    response.setContentType("text/html");
13    PrintWriter out = response.getWriter();

14    // catch the name from FORM
15    String name = request.getParameter("name");

16    // make sure the name is entered
17    if (name != null && name.length() > 0)
18    {
19     out.println("<p>Search for " + name + "</p>");
20    }
21    else {
22     out.println("No name is entered.");
23    }

24    // a try-catch pair
25    try {
26    // define the file name for input
27    String inputFileName = "YellowPage.txt";
28    // define the BufferedReader name
29  fin = new BufferedReader(new FileReader(inputFileName));

30        // set a storage
31        String phone = null;
32        // read a line
33        String line = fin.readLine();
34    // a loop to read the file one line by one line
35    while (line != null) {
36      // if the name is found in the line
37      if (line.equals(name))
38      {
39      // find the phone number at the next line
40      phone = fin.readLine();
41      // finish the reading
42      line = null;
43      }
44      // otherwise read the next line
45      else {
46       line = fin.readLine();
```

```
47      }
48     }

49 // print the search result to the dynamic Web page
50 out.println("<P>" + name + "- phone number is " + phone + "</P>");

51     fin.close();

52     // exception
53     } catch(java.io.IOException e) {
54         out.println("YellowPage file is not available.");
55         out.println("Please try again later.");
56     }

57 out.println("<p>Back to <a href=../JavaServlets.html>Form</a>");
58         out.close();
59     }
60 }
```

Listing 4.23   Servlet SearchFile.java.

In the above program, lines **1–4** import libraries. Line **7** defines an object of BufferedReader. BufferedReader is able to read lines of text from a file.

Line **15** captures the name from the FORM to be searched. Lines **17–23** make sure that the name is entered. Line **25** and line **53** are a try-catch pair.

Line **27** defines the input file name (YellowPage.txt in this example). Line **29** defines the BufferedReader object fin in accordance with the input file name. Line **31** sets a variable to hold the search result of telephone number. Line **33** reads one line from the input file name.

Lines **35–38** are a while-loop to search the request information. If the requested name is found (line **37**), then read the next line to find this person's telephone number (line **40**) and terminate the while-loop (line **42**), otherwise keep reading the next line (line **46**).

Line **50** sends the search result back to the client. Line **51** closes the BufferedReader.

Lines **53–56** deal with exception if the disk file has problems for searching. Finally, line 58 closes the PrintWriter for the dynamic Web page.

Figures 4.15 and 4.16 show the execution of the example.

Several new statements are explained in the following section.

4.8.6.13   FileReader and BufferedReader

FileReader and BufferedReader classes are used to read disk files. The difference between these two **readers** is that BufferedReader reads one line each time, but FileReader reads a specified amount of data. We usually use BufferedReader especially when we search the file. The syntax of the definition of a BufferedReader object is

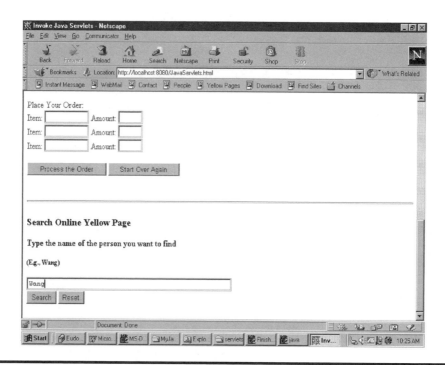

Figure 4.15   Input data and trigger Servlet SearchFile.

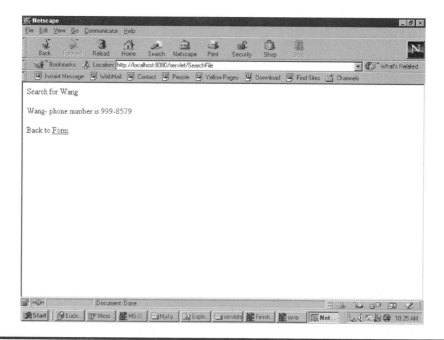

Figure 4.16   Servelt SearchFile sends a dynamic Web page back to the client.

```
[reader name] = new BufferedReader(new FileReader([input file name]))
```

The file reader should be closed after the use.

4.8.6.14 `readLine` Method

When a `BufferedReader` object is employed, the `readLine` method can be used to read one line from the disk file.

```
[target string] = [reader name].readLine();
```

4.8.6.15 `while` Loop

The `while` loop implements a repetition of actions when the condition is true.

```
while ([condition]) { [actions] }
```

4.8.6.16 Comparison of Strings

In Listing 4.23, line 37 involves a comparison of strings. Note the special syntax of comparison of strings in Java. The following prototype specifies the comparison of two strings in the `if` statement to test if they are the same.

```
if ([string-1].equals([string-2]))
```

4.8.6.17 Convert String to Numerical Number

Using `FileReader`, one is usually dealing with strings. To convert a string to a numerical number, a conversion method must be used. For example:

```
int aNumber = Integer.parseInt(aString)
```

converts `aString` to an integer number called `aNumber`.

4.9 Example of Web-Based Business Application Using Java Servlets

In this subsection, we present an example of Web-based business application of online auction. The following four programs/data files implement the application. The first HTML document (Listing 4.24) is the home page. It allows the client to start an auction. It triggers the first Java program (see Auciton.java in Listing 4.25). This Java program accesses the bidding historical data file (see BidData.txt in Listing 4.26), and generates a dynamic HTML document to the client. This dynamic HTML document is not a real HTML document that resides on the server, but is sent by the Java program to the client side. It contains a bidding form and allows the client to make a bid. It in turn triggers the second Java program (see Bid.java in Listing 4.27). The second Java program records the bid and updates the bidding historical data file.

```
<HTML>
<HEAD>
<TITLE> ABC Online Auction </TITLE>
</HEAD>
<BODY>
<H1> Welcome to ABC Online Car Auction </H1>
<IMG ALT=Auction Item SRC="images/Car.jpg">
<BR>
<FORM ACTION="../servlet/Auction" METHOD=POST>
<INPUT TYPE=SUBMIT VALUE="Go_Auction!">
</FORM>
</BODY>
</HTML>
```

Listing 4.24   Home Page of the application (HomePage.html).

```
import java.io.*;
import java.util.*;
import javax.servlet.*;
import javax.servlet.http.*;
public class Auction extends HttpServlet {
  private BufferedReader fin;

  public void doPost(HttpServletRequest request,
                     HttpServletResponse response)
                     throws ServletException, IOException
 {
     response.setContentType("text/html");
     PrintWriter out = response.getWriter();

     try {
      String inputFileName = "BidData.txt";

fin = new BufferedReader(new FileReader(inputFileName));
         int HighestBid = 0;
         String line = fin.readLine();
         while (line != null) {
            String Bid = fin.readLine();
            int BidNumber=Integer.parseInt(Bid);
            if (BidNumber>HighestBid)
            {
            HighestBid = BidNumber;
            line = fin.readLine();
            }
            else {
            line = fin.readLine();
            }
         }

out.println("<H2>" + "The Highest Bid is $" + HighestBid + "</H2>");
out.println("<br><br>");
    fin.close();
   } catch(java.io.IOException e) {
     out.println("The server is not available.");
```

```
        out.println("Please try again later.");
    }

out.println("<form action=../servlet/Bid method=post>");
out.println("Your Email Address: <br>");
out.println("<input type=text name=email size=50>");
out.println("<br><br>");
out.println("Your Bid (Number only, no $): <br>");
out.println("<input type=text name=bid size=50>");
out.println("<br><br>");
out.println("<input type=submit value=Go-Bidding!>");
out.println("</form>");

out.println("<p>Back to <a href=../HomePage.html>Home Page</a>");
out.close();
   }
}
```

Listing 4.25   First Java Servlet program of the application (Auction.java).

```
StartPrice
500
```

Listing 4.26   Data file used to record Bid Data (BidData.txt).

```
import java.io.*;
import java.util.*;
import javax.servlet.*;
import javax.servlet.http.*;

public class Bid extends HttpServlet
 {
  public void doPost(HttpServletRequest request,
                     HttpServletResponse response)
                     throws ServletException, IOException
  {
   response.setContentType("text/html");
   PrintWriter out = response.getWriter();

    String email = request.getParameter("email");
    String bid = request.getParameter("bid");

  if (bid != null && bid.length()>0)
   {out.println("<h2>Bid has been submitted....</h2>");

  try {

    String outputFileName="BidData.txt";

    FileWriter fout = new FileWriter(outputFileName, true);
    fout.write(email);
    fout.write("\n");
    fout.write(bid);
```

```
   fout.write("\n");
   out.println("<h3>Your bid has been recorded ...</h3>");
   fout.close();
   }

   catch(java.io.IOException e) {
   out.println("Sorry, the server has problems with file.");
   out.println("Please try again later.");
   }
 }
 else {out.println("No data has been entered.");}

   out.println("<p>Back to <a href=../HomePage.html>Home Page</a>");
   out.close();
  }
 }
```

Listing 4.27 Second Java Servlets in the application (Bid.java).

The Java servlet in Listing 4.25 generates a dynamic Web page with a FORM. Again, we omit all quotation marks in the generated HTML document for simplicity. However, in many cases, we must print quotation marks. To print a quotation mark for an HTML tag, one must use \" in the `println` statement. Here is an example.

```
out.println("<input type=submit value=" + "\"" + "Go Bidding!" + "\"" + ">");
```

4.10   Databases Connection and the Use of SQL

About 80 percent of Web applications are related to databases. Java servlets can access databases on the server through using Structure ouery Language (SQL). To do so, the Java servlet loads **JDBC** driver and then interacts with **Open Database Connectivity (ODBC)** driver, which further allows the servlet to connect to any ODBC compliant database and use SQL to access the database. To use Java servlets to access databases on the server with Windows operating system, you need to set **Data Source Names (DSN)** of the server, as detailed in the Appendix 4.1.

Next, we show an example of database connection and the use of SQL in Java servlets. Suppose we have Microsoft Access database named `Student.mdb` on the server. The database has a table called `tblStudent` which contains student records including data items such as `StudentID`, `StudentName`, `StudentAddress`, `StudentEnrolYear`, etc. The Java servlet in Listing 4.28 is able to connect to the database and display data through SQL. We will learn SQL in more detail in Chapter 10. Here we merely show a simple example.

```
import java.sql.*;
import java.io.*;
import javax.servlet.*;
import javax.servlet.http.*;
```

```
public class AccessDB extends HttpServlet {
public void doGet(HttpServletRequest request,
                  HttpServletResponse response)
  throws ServletException, IOException {

  response.setContentType("text/html");
  PrintWriter out = response.getWriter();
  out.print("<html><head>");
  out.print("</head><body>");

  out.print("<form action=\"");
  out.print( request.getRequestURI() );
  out.print("\" method=\"post\">");
  out.print("<input type=\"submit\" ");
  out.print("value=\"Display Student Records \"> ");

out.print("Display Student Records from MS Access Database</form>");
  out.print("</body></html>");
  out.close();
 }

public void doPost(HttpServletRequest request,
                   HttpServletResponse response)
  throws ServletException, IOException {

  response.setContentType("text/html");
  PrintWriter out = response.getWriter();

  out.print("<html><head>");
  out.print("</head><body>");
  out.print("<pre>");
  out.print("<font color=blue>ID\tStudentName \t\tYear \n");
  out.print("</font>");

  // System timing

  long time1 = System.currentTimeMillis();

  // connect to the database

  Connection connect = null;
  Statement statmt = null;
  ResultSet result = null;

  try {
   Class.forName("sun.jdbc.odbc.JdbcOdbcDriver");
   connect = DriverManager.getConnection("jdbc:odbc:Student");
   statmt = connect.createStatement();

  // Use SQL for query

   result = statmt.executeQuery
 ("SELECT studentID, StudentName, studentEnrolYear FROM tblStudent");

   // Read records and display them

   while(result.next()) {
    out.print(result.getObject(1).toString());
```

```
   out.print("\t");
   out.print(result.getObject(2).toString());
   out.print("\t\t");
   out.print(result.getObject(3).toString());
   out.print("\n");
  }
  out.print("<font color=blue>Thank you for using database! \n");
  out.print("</font>");

 } catch (SQLException e) {
  throw new
  ServletException("OOPS! Servlet Could not display records.", e);
 } catch (ClassNotFoundException e) {
  throw new
  ServletException("OOPS! JDBC Driver not found.", e);
 } finally {
  try {
   if(result != null) {
    result.close();
    result = null;
   }
   if(statmt != null) {
    statmt.close();
    statmt = null;
   }
   if(connect != null) {
    connect.close();
    connect = null;
   }
  } catch (SQLException e) {}
 }

 // System timing

 long time2 = System.currentTimeMillis();

 out.print("</pre>");
 out.print("<p>Process Time : ");
 out.print( (time2 - time1) );
 out.print(" ms.</p>");

 out.print("<p\"><a href=\"");
 out.print( request.getRequestURI() );
 out.print("\">Back</a></p>");

 out.print("</body></html>");
 out.close();
 }
}
```

Listing 4.28   Java Servlets Microsoft access database (AccessDB.java).

In Listing 4.28, the key part of database connection and data access is high-lighted in bold. As shown in Listing 4.28, there are several important steps for database manipulation.

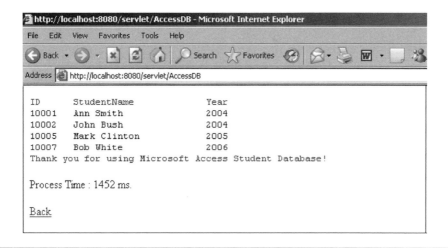

Figure 4.17 Database retrieval result of Listing 4.28.

1. The first step is to load JDBC/ODBC driver using `Class.forName()` method and define three types of objects for database manipulation: `Connection`, `Statement`, and `ResultSet`.
2. Second step is to make connection to the database using `DriverManager.getConnection()` method. The name of the database is provided here. Note that the real path to the database is defined in DSN.
3. Third step is to retrieve records from the database using the `Statement` and `ResultSet` objects. The SQL query is used here as arguments of the methods.
4. Fourth step is to display the data though the use of the `ResultSet` object and `getObject(n)` method.
5. Finally, you need to close the database connection.

Figure 4.17 shows the data records retrieved by the servlet.

4.11 Typical Scheme of Web-Based Business Applications

Examples of Web-based business applications include online shopping, online registration, online group discussion, online auction, online inquiry, etc. Despite the variety of the types of Web business applications, the programming scheme is almost the same. On the client side, the user can see one static Web page for logon, which is located at a known URL. This static Web page can trigger a server-side program that verifies the login and generates dynamic Web pages. A dynamic Web page either rejects the logon, or provides a main page for the application. The main page contains a form that allows the user to input data and trigger a server-side program to perform the application. Typically, the program manipulates data files on the server through searching, adding, deleting, and then generates a dynamic Web page as a response or confirmation for the user. This typical scheme is depicted in Figure 4.18.

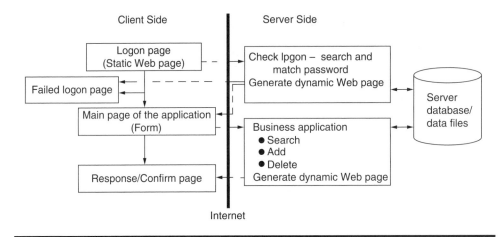

Figure 4.18   Typical scheme of Web-based business applications.

The scheme in Figure 4.18 could be expanded for a complicated application where the application is composed of several tasks. For example, online shopping has several tasks including browsing catalog, filling shopping cart, payment, etc. In this case, the main page of the application might contain several items of menus or forms. Each item of menus or forms will in turn trigger a server-side program that performs the particular task. A complicated task may in turn have several sub-tasks. For example, sub-tasks of payment include reviewing invoice, inputting credit card number, etc. Each sub-task is also supported by server-side programs.

4.12   Debugging Java Programs

When using Visual J++ for Java applets and Java applications, errors specified in the Task List window provide hints for debugging. Click an error item in the Task List window, the Visual J++ environment moves the cursor to the location where the error is caused. However, the real cause of the error might not be pointed out exactly. A clean Task List window after compiling is necessary, but does not guarantee an error-free program.

When using JDK and JSWDK for Java programs (including Java servlets), debugging may not be an easy task for beginners.

Common syntax errors are:

- Software environment has not been set properly.
- The class name and the program file name are not the same.
- Typos of misspelling a word.
- Omitting a symbol.
- Violating format.
- Using an undefined user-defined variable.

Logical errors or runtime errors often occur when the computer performs wrong operations or not as directed. To debug logical errors, you should use data samples to test the program based on the output of the program.

Common logical errors are:

- Images and audio files used by the Java applets are placed in wrong folders.
- The format of image or audio file is not supported by the Java applets.
- Wrong data types.
- Wrong calculations.
- A "dead" loop.
- When you debug Java servlets as server-side programs, you need to re-upload your programs to the server. If you use your personal server on PC, you need to re-start the server once you make changes to the program.

4.13   Self-Review Exercise

1. Download JDK from the Internet to your PC. Discuss the license agreement.
2. Read the following Java Applet and complete it by filling the blanks.

```
1 import java.awt.Graphics;
2 import _____;

3 public class Test3 extends _____

4    implements _____ {

5 /* Define variables                                    */
6     Image pics[] = new Image[2];
7     Image newimg;
8     Thread _____;

9 /* Major Applet Activities I: Initialization method */

10    _____ _____ init() {
11    String location[] = { "cartoon1.gif", "cartoon2.gif" };
12     for (int i=0; i<2; i++) {
13       pics[i] = getImage(getCodeBase(),
14         "gif/" + _____ );
15     }
16    _____

17 /* Major Applet Activities II: Starting                */
18     public void start() {
19        if (mythread == null) {
20            mythread = new Thread(this);
21            _____;
22        }
23     }

24 /* Major Applet Activities III: Stopping               */
25     public void interrupt() {
26        if (mythread != null) {
27            _____;
28            mythread = null;
29        }
30     }
```

```
31 /* We want the Applet to do                          */

32      public void run() {
33          int i=0;
34          while (_____) {
35              _____ = pics[i];
36              repaint();
37              try { Thread.sleep(500); }
38              catch _____
39              if (i==0) i=_____;
40              else i=0;
41          _____
42      }

43 /* Major Applet Activities IV: Painting or repainting */

44      public void paint(Graphics gr) {
45          _____.drawImage(_____, 10, 10, this);
46      }
47 _____
```

3. Read the following HTML, which is designed to use the Java Applet
    programmed in Question (2) for a Web page with animation, and fill in the
    blanks.

```
 1 <HTML>
 2 <HEAD>
 3 <TITLE>This is a test for Java Applet!</_____>
 4 </HEAD>

 5 <BODY>

 6 <P>I felt a little dizzy before the test ....
 7 </P>
 8 <P>But now I understand more about Java Applet ....
 9 </P>

10 <APPLET CODE ="_____" _____=400 _____=400></_____>

11 </BODY>

12 </_____>
```

4. Suppose "cartoon1.gif" and "cartoon2.gif" in the Java Applet (in Question (2))
    are two pictures as shown below,

cartoon1.gif

cartoon2.gif

and the Java class is placed in the folder (directory) `C:\jdk1.2\bin\myfile`,

    A. What folder should these two pictures be placed into?
    B. What folder should the HTML program (in Question (3)) be placed into?
    C. What does the Web page designed in Question (3) look like? (Specify the title, body…)

5. Develop a Java applet that plays animation with three or more cartoon pictures.
6. Develop a Java applet that plays audio clips.
7. Discuss the characteristics of Java computing.
8. Develop a Web page project that includes your HTML code and your Java applets.
9. Complete the following free-standing Java application program named `MyJava.java`.

```
 1 // AWT-based Java applications - Free-standing Java programs

 2 import _____.*;
 3 import _____.event.*;

 4 public class _____ extends Frame _____ ActionListener,
 5 WindowListener {

 6 Button _____;
 7 TextField RateField;
 8 float Rate;
 9 float FValue;

10 public static _____ main(String[] _____) {
11   MyJava _____ = new MyJava();
12   myjava.setSize(400, 300);
13   myjava.setVisible(true);
14   }

15 public _____() {
16   setTitle("Compute Future Value");
17   setLayout(new _____());

18   _____ = new TextField(10);
19   add(RateFiled);
20   _____.addActionListener(this);

21   Comp = new Button("Compute Future Value");
22   add(_____);
23   _____.addActionListener(this);
24   this.addWindowListener(_____);

25   FValue = (float)100;
26   }

27 public void actionPerformed(ActionEvent event) {
28 Float RateObject = _____.valueOf(RateField.getText());
```

```
29  if (event.getSource() == Comp) {
30   Rate = RateObject.floatValue();
31   FValue = 100 * (1 + Rate);
32   repaint();
33  }
34 }

35 public void windowClosing(WindowEvent event) {
36    System._____(0);
37 }
38 public void windowIconified(WindowEvent _____) {
39 }
40 public _____ windowOpened(WindowEvent event) {
41 }
42 public void windowClosed(WindowEvent event) {
43 }
44 _____ void windowDeiconified(WindowEvent event) {
45 }
46 public void windowActivated(WindowEvent event) {
47 _____
48 public void windowDeactivated(WindowEvent _____) {
49 }
50 public void paint(Graphics g) {
51  g.drawString("*** Input the interest rate," +
52       "and click the button", 30, 100);
53  _____("Interest Rate is " + Rate, 30, 150);
54  g.drawString("The Future Value of $100 is $" +
55       FValue, 30, 200);
56 }
57 }
```

10. Sketch the screen when the Java application program in Question (9) runs.

11. Complete the following Java servlet program, named SaveData.java.

```
 1 import java.io.*;
 2 import java.util.*;
 3 import _____
 4 import _____
 5 public class _____ extends HttpServlet
 6 {
 7  public void doPost(HttpServletRequest _____,
 8              _____ response)
 9              _____ ServletException, IOException
10  {
11    response._____("text/html");
12    _____ out = response.getWriter();

13    out.println("<h2>Form has been submitted....</h2>");
14    String name = request._____("name");
15    _____ email = request.getParameter("email");
16    String item1 = request.getParameter("item1");
17    String Q1 = request.getParameter("Q1");
18    String item2 = request.getParameter("item2");
19    String Q2 = request.getParameter("Q2");
20    String item3 = request.getParameter("item3");
```

```
21    String Q3 = request.getParameter("Q3");

22    if ((Q1 != null && Q1.length() > 0) ||
23        (Q2 != null && Q2.length() > 0) ||
24        (Q3 != null && Q3.length() > 0))
25    {
26      out._____("Hi, " + fname);
27    }

28    else {
29      _____.println("No data has been entered.");
30    }
31    try {
32      String _____="Formdata.txt";

33      _____ fout = new FileWriter(dataFileName);

34      _____.write(name);
35      fout._____("\n");
36      fout.write(email);
37      fout.write("\n");
38      fout.write(item1);
39      fout.write("\n");
40      fout.write(Q1);
41      fout.write("\n");
42      fout.write(item2);
43      fout.write("\n");
44      fout.write(Q2);
45      fout.write("\n");
46      fout.write(item3);
47      fout.write("\n");
48      fout.write(Q3);
49      fout.write("\n");

50    out.println("<h3>Your order is being processed ...</h3>");

51      _____.close();

52    }

53    catch(java.io._____ e) {
54    out.println("Please try again later.");
55    }
56      _____.close();
57    }
58    _____
```

12. Develop a project using free-standing non-AWT Java application.
13. Develop a project using free-standing AWT-based Java application.
14. Develop a project using Java servlets to save FORM data and read data from the server.
15. Write a Java servlet that contains SQL to access an Access database.
16. Using Java servlets, implement the following scenario.

A.   The company has its Web site (home page in HTML) on the server, and allows any clients to access the Web site using its URL.
B.   The home page is a log-in page that asks the client to enter user-ID and password. After the client enters the user-ID and password and clicks the log-in button, the server will check the user-ID and password against a disk file to see whether the user is permitted to enter the system.
C.   The client will receive a sorry message if the user-ID and password do not match. Otherwise, the client will see an online purchasing window with a greeting message. The dynamic Web page is generated by a Java servlet.
D.   After the client makes an online purchase, the purchasing data will be saved on the server. Also, a Java servlet will generate an invoice for this purchase back to the client.

Appendix 4.1   Set up Java Platform for JDK and Java Servlets on Computer with Windows Operating System

Note:

1.   When you download the free software kit, you must read and accept the License Agreement issued by the Sun Company.
2.   The following instructions and URL for downloading may vary depending on the time and actual Web site you are accessing.
3.   The following instructions may vary depending on the setting of your computer.
4.   Your computer could be a real server or a PC.

I. Download JDK

0.   Check your Drive C and make sure there is a storage space larger than 100MB.
1.   Start Netscape, and access `<http://java.sun.com/>`, and find [Download].
2.   Find [Java™2 Platform, Standard Edition (J2SE™)] section, and find [J2SE1.2.2 - Windows platform].
3.   Download the newest version of JDK (e.g., `jdk1.5.0_06` in 2006). In this book, we assume you download `jdk1.2.2-win32.exe`. Close Netscape.
4.   Install JDK1.2.2 by clicking the icon of `jdk1.2.2-win32.exe`, and following the displayed install instructions.
5.   Restart your computer. Now you should have folder `C:\jdk1.2.2` on C Drive.

If you are going to use Java servlets, you need to download JSWDK as follows.

6.   Start Netscape, and access `<http://java.sun.com/products/servlet/archive.html>`.

7. Find JavaServer™ Web Development Kit (JSWDK) 1.0.1 Release in the Archive.
8. Download it, choosing Windows platform. Close Netscape.
9. After downloading, setup the development kit. You should have folder `C:\jswdk-1.0.1` on C Drive.
10. Restart the computer.

Note that advanced version of JDK might require advanced hardware.

II. Run Java Programs Using JDK

JDK works in the CMD (or DOS) environment in the Windows operating systems. If you have your own JDK on C Drive, you are more likely to work under the directory

`C:\jdk1.2.2\bin`   (The number after `jdk` indicates the version.)

In the next example, you will learn how to create a simple Java applet, place it inside a Web page, and view the execution result of the applet. In the following steps, we use underline string to indicate what you need to type in the CMD environment in the Windows 2000 (or up) operating system ([`Start`], then [`Run`] and type cmd), or the DOS environment in the earlier version of Windows operating systems.

1. You may feel easy if you work on the Drive F. However, if you want to work on the Drive C, you must set up your own directory, say `HTML` (by typing `mkdir  HTML` under the current directory `C:\jdk1.2.2\bin >mkdir HTML`).

Because the browser reads HTML programs, it can find HTML files and your applets. To keep track of all related files, one should put all HTML files and applet code in the same directory (or folder).

We assume that you use the Drive F to hold all HTML files, Java applets, and folders of images and sound clips.

2. You enter the CMD environment (MS-DOS), and go to the JDK directory by typing

```
C:\>cd jdk1.2.2\bin
C:\jd1.2.2\bin >
```

Then minimize the CMD window.

Note that this step may not be required if the system has set the path for the Java compiler.

3. Start Notepad, and enter a Java program, as shown in Listing 4.1, to create a Java applet.
4. After editing, click [`File`] and [`Save As`]. Save the Java program on the Drive F. Give the file a name:

```
[filename].java
e.g., HelloWorldApplet.java
```

Note that the file name must be the same name of the class defined in your Java applet program.

5. Re-call the CMD window. Compile the applet using javac.

Note that you must make sure that the current directory of the Drive C is `C:\jdk1.2.2\bin`. To compile the Java applet, you should type

```
F:\>c: javac HelloWorldApplet.java
```

After compiling, you should now have a file called `HelloWorldApplet.class` on the diskette on the Drive F.

6. Open Notepad, edit an HTML program. This HTML program will trigger the Java applet and can be read by the Web browser Netscape.
7. Enter the HTML code, as shown in Listing 4.2, in the editing window.
8. Save the HTML file on the Drive F, with a filename

```
[filename].html
```

For example, `HelloWorldApplet.html`

9. Test the result of your applet using Netscape. In Netscape, you click [File] on the menu, and [open] the local HTML file (`HelloWorldApplet.html` in our example). Or, you may find the HTML file and click it directly. The expected result is shown in Figure 4.3.

III. Set a Server for Java Servlets

1. Software Requirements of Java Servlets

To compile and execute Java servlets, the two most important software packages are the **JDK** and **JSWDK**. Both of these two development kits can be downloaded from `<http://java.sun.com>` with no cost provided the downloading follows the license agreements. In this book, all examples are demonstrated using version **JDK1.2.2** for JDK and **JSWDK-1.0.1** for JSWDK.

In the following discussion, we assume that the two development kits are installed in their folders:

```
C:\jdk1.2.2
C:\jswdk-1.0.1
```

2. Set the Configuration Structure and Configuration Files

This section provides step-by-step instructions for setting a server with the Windows (e.g., Windows 2000 Server) or a personal server on your PC with Windows (e.g., Windows XP) for running Java servlets.

To set up the default server and let the server find the servlets, one needs to define **configuration structure** (folders and files) and **configuration files**.

One can copy configuration files from the servlet examples which come with the JSWDK package, open them with the text editor (Notepad or Wordpad) to view the contents, and then make necessary modifications as will be discussed.

Configuration structure and configuration files are related to the particular application. Here we give an example of setting configuration structure and configuration file so that you can follow for hands-on.

1. Download JSWKD. Suppose the folder (directory) where JSWDK was installed is

   ```
   C:\jswdk-1.0.1
   ```

2. Create a new folder for the applications within the folder C:\jswdk-1.0.1 . You may give any name to the folder. In our example, we use webapp for the application folder. If you use a different name, then all configuration files and applications related to this name should be modified correspondingly.

3. Find the original **webserver.xml** file in c:\jswdk-1.0.1. You may use Microsoft Internet Explorer, or WordPad to view it. It has a length comment text, but the following part is important.

```
<!DOCTYPE WebServer [
.......
<!ELEMENT Service (WebApplication*)>
<!ATTLIST Service
    id ID #REQUIRED
    port NMTOKEN "8080"
    hostName NMTOKEN ""
    inet NMTOKEN ""
    docBase CDATA "webpages"
    workDir CDATA "work"
    workDirIsPersistent (false | true) "false">
.......
```

Listing Ch4-A1-1a   Original `webserver.xml` in JSWDK.

Using WordPad, make modifications to webserver.xml as in the following. Note the word in bold font.

```
<!DOCTYPE WebServer [
......

<!ELEMENT Service (WebApplication*)>
<!ATTLIST Service

    id ID #REQUIRED
    port NMTOKEN "8080"
    hostName NMTOKEN ""
    inet NMTOKEN ""
    docBase CDATA "webapp"
    workDir CDATA "work"
    workDirIsPersistent (false | true) "false">
........
```

Listing Ch4-A1-1b   Change the webserver.xml for webapp.

This change sets your own document base instead of the default folder. After making the modification, save it. Note that, if you do not want to lose the original copy, you must keep an original copy in a different file name.

4. Create a folder named `web-inf` within `c:\jswdk-1.0.1\webapp`. This name must not be changed.
5. Within `webapp`, we need one HTML file for the servlets default server. When the client accesses the URL of the default server, the HTML file will be downloaded to the client Web browser. The client is then able to trigger Java servlets on the server through this HTML web page.
6. Create a folder named `servlets` within `web-inf`. You may use a different name for the folder, but must keep the specification in the HTML file (see Section 4.8.2, line 6 in Listing 4.16) consistent.

The configuration structure for the default server to run Java servlets is shown in Figure 4.7 in Section 4.8.1.

3. Set CLASSPATH Variables

To compile Java servlets and run the default server, we must set **CLASSPATH variables** in the DOS `autoexec.bat` file. To do so, click [`start`] on the Window, select [`Run`], type [`sysedit`], and click [`OK`]. In the AUTOEXEC. BAT window, add

```
set path=c:\jdk1.2.2\bin\;%PATH%
set classpath=c:\jswdk-1.0.1\lib\servlet.jar;%CLASSPATH%
set classpath=c:\jdk1.2.2\lib;%CLASSPATH%
set classpath=c:\jdk1.2.2\lib\tools.jar;%CLASSPATH%
```

as shown in Figure 4.A1.1. Close the window and click [`yes`] to save it. You must `Restart` the computer to make it effective.

4. Start and Stop the Server

If everything has been set correctly, you can click `startserver.bat` in folder `jswdk-1.0.1` to start your server, as shown in Figure 4.A1.2.

If you cannot start the server, you must miss some part of the configuration procedure. To stop the server, click the `stoptserver.bat` icon in Windows Explorer, and you will see a window that indicate finishing.

Note that, Java servlets reside in the server's memory. Thus, every time you debug a Java servlets program, you must restart the server to discharge the old version of the program.

IV. Set ODBC for Java Servlets

To allow Java servlets to access Microsoft Access databases, you must set ODBC for data sources.

1. Click [`Start`] and go to [`Control Panel`].
2. Find and click [`Administrative Tools`].

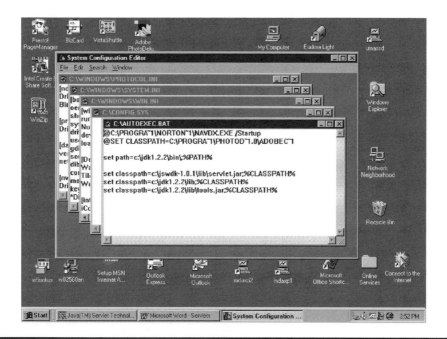

Figure 4.A1.1   Set CLASSPATH variables.

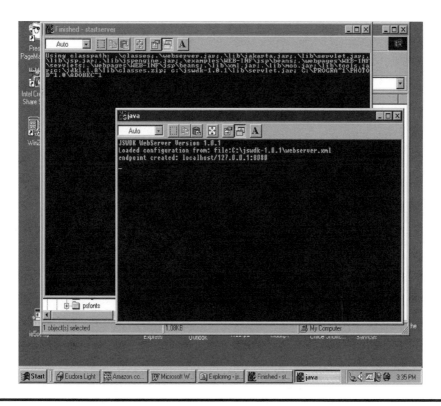

Figure 4.A1.2   Execute `Startserver.bat` from Windows Explore.

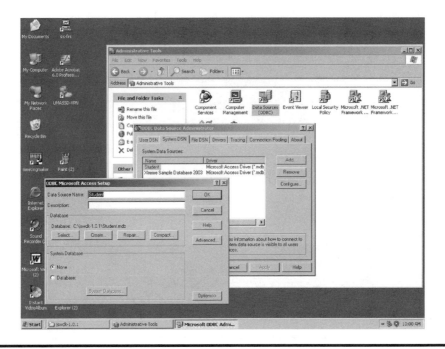

Figure 4.A1.3   Set ODBC DSN.

3. Find [Data Sources (ODBC)] and click it.
4. Find [System DSN] folder and open it.
5. Click [Add] button and add the database.
6. Type your DSN.
7. Click [Select] button and define the path to your database. Make sure the path appears on the ODBC setup pane.
8. Click all [OK] buttons and close panes. It is ready for testing the database connection.

Appendix 4.2   Use WS-FTP to Upload and Download Files

To upload your programs to the server, or download data files from the server, you can use WS-FTP.

After starting WS-FTP, you need to enter

■ Host Name/Address—the URL of the server
■ User ID—your user ID
■ Password—your password for connecting the server

To connect to the server, as shown in Figure 4.A2.1.

After you log-in to the server, you will see two sub-windows in WS-FTP. The left window shows your client's (local) side, and the right window shows the server's (remote) side, as shown in Figure 4.A2.2.

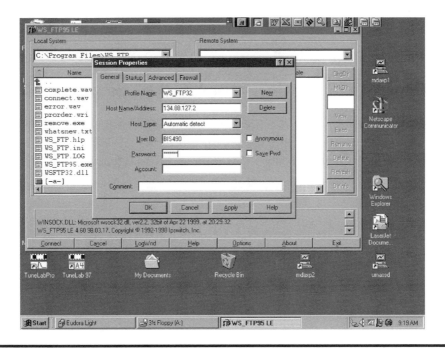

Figure 4.A2.1   Use WS-FTP to connect to the server.

Figure 4.A2.2   Uploading and downloading programs or data files.

To upload or download files, you need to:

- Choose corresponding folders on your local side and the server's side.
- Use the corresponding buttons to upload or download files.
- Select "ASCII" mode to upload or download programs and data files.

Working on the right window, you can also create or delete a folder on the server, and view programs or data files on the server. However, if you want to make changes to a file on the server, you must download it first, make changes on your PC, and then upload the updated file back to the server.

Appendix 4.3   Guideline for Web Page Integrating

HTML, JavaScript, and Java Applet Project Report

1. Front page
    Course name
    Title of the project
    Group members (names and ID)
    Date

2. Text
    Introduction and the purpose of the Web page
    Application of HTML, JavaScript, Java applets

3. Source code of the HTML, JavaScript, and Java applet programs
4. A diskette which contains the Web page and all needed images and sounds. The Web page on the diskette must be workable; that is, one clicks the icon of the Web page on the diskette, the Web page should be displayed on the screen without an error.

Appendix 4.4   Guideline for Server-Side Programming (Java Servlet) Project Report

1. Front page
    Course name
    Title of the project
    Group members (names and ID)
    Date

2. Text
    Introduction and the purposes of Java servlets
    Application of HTML and Java servlets

3. Source code of the HTML and Java servlet programs
4. Screen shots of the home Web site and dynamic Web pages that demonstrate the interactions between the client and server.
5. Test data files that are used for the application, inputted by the client, and stored on the server.

Chapter 5

Visual Basic and Graphical User Interface

5.1 Graphical User Interface

In business computer applications, such as order processing, payroll program, and billing, the users of computer programs require customized applications to accommodate the needs of the business processes in the organization as well as the individuals' preferences. One of the important aspects in business computer applications is the design of **GUI**.

A GUI allows the user to use a mouse to click on boxes for entering text, to click to buttons to initiate a process, and so forth. By using a GUI, the user can better control the execution of the computer application program.

Figure 5.1 shows an online price quote GUI. Through the GUI the customer is allowed to interact with the system to receive information.

Visual Basic is Microsoft's product. It provides tools that make it easier for the programmer to create good GUI. As most business applications require frequent modification, the programmer can change the user interface and processing scripts quickly. Visual Basic has several versions. In this book we introduce the recent version **VB.NET**. VB.NET is not totally compatible with the old versions of Visual Basic. VB.NET is one part of Visual Studio .NET which is a complete set of development tools for building comprehensive business applications including Web applications. Since it fits the .NET scheme, it loses many good features that are available in Visual Basic 6.0.

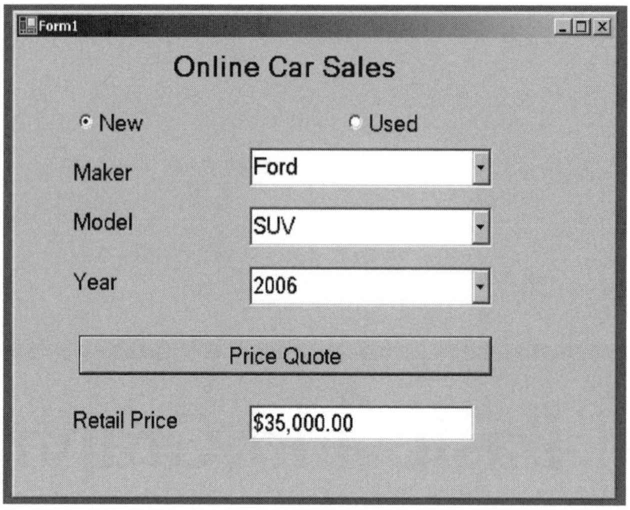

Figure 5.1   An example of a GUI.

5.2   VB.NET Environment

VB.NET provides a good **programming environment**, that is, a software tool specifically designed to facilitate the creation of new applications. One can use it to easily construct and test new applications. VB.NET provides two major facilities to the programmer:

1. A set of **development tools**, which enable the programmer to create elements for the GUI easily.
2. A programming language, which enable the programmer to specify how the computer performs the tasks required by the elements of the GUI.

Start Visual Studio .NET (clicking [Start] – [Programs] – [Microsoft Visual Studio .NET]), and open [New Project]. Your screen will look similar to that in Figure 5.2.

Choose [Visual Basic Project] in the left sub-window, and [Windows Application] in the right sub-windows. Use [Browse ...] button to choose the folder for your project, and type the project name. Click [OK] to open the design screen. After open [Toolbox], your screen will look similar to that shown in Figure 5.3.

As shown in Figure 5.3, there are several major components in the VB.NET environment.

1. **Menu bar:** It gives many functions needed to develop projects. The menu bar is similar to those in other Microsoft software.
2. **Tool bar:** It contains icons for some most frequently used functions specified in the Menu bar.
3. **Toolbox:** It is a collection of tools for the design of a GUI at design time. It allows the programmer to place **control elements** on the form.

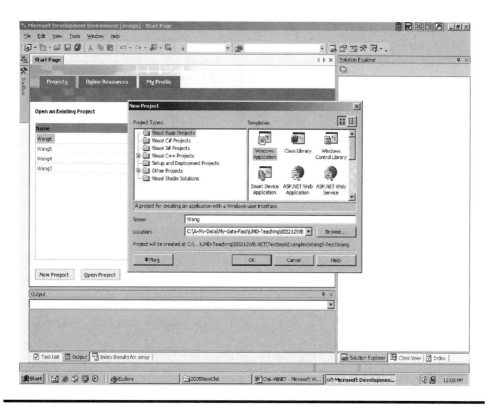

Figure 5.2   Start a VB.NET project.

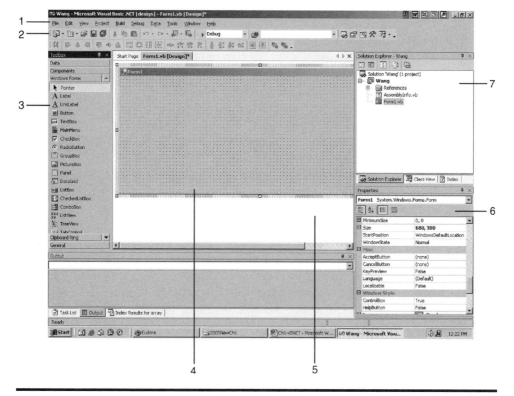

Figure 5.3   VB.NET environment.

4. **Form Window:** There are two modes for the Form Window. In **design mode**, the Form Window is a working space for the design of a GUI. In **run mode** (when you click [Debug] and [Start] in the Menu bar), it displays the GUI to the user at run time.

5. **Coding Window:** It allows the programmer to view and write VB.NET code for any element on the form. If it is not visible, one can double click on an element on the form.

6. **Properties Window:** It is used at design time to examine and change the settings for the properties of each element on the GUI.

7. **Solution Explorer Window:** It lists all the forms, classes, code modules, and resource files for The VB.NET project.

You may click [View] on the Menu bar to bring any sub-window up if it is not visible.

Note that, when you first launch VB.NET, the window on the screen might not be exactly the same as in Figure 5.3. You may use a mouse to reposition and drag theses small windows.

5.3 Event-Driven Programs and Brief Overview of VB.NET

In VB.NET, a GUI unit is a form. A form is a class, which can have attributes, methods, and subclasses. One of the major tasks of developing a GUI application using VB.NET is to write **event-driven** programs for these classes. In this section, we will learn how VB.NET works in implementing GUI. We use a toy example to show the essential steps in designing GUI by using VB.NET.

Suppose we are designing a GUI so that when the user clicks a message button, the window displays a message "Hello, World!" on the screen. We implement this by performing the following steps.

1. Work on [Form1.vb [Design]] Click the "**Label**" tool on the toolbox (the button marked "**A**"), and drag a space on the form to indicate where the message is supposed to displayed.

2. Bring the Properties Window up by clicking the icon on the toolbar, if it is not visible. Work on the Properties Window, and change the label Text to spaces by deleting "label1." The label has its default name "Label1" but does not have any text now (see Figure 5.4). Note that you may change the label name (e.g., to "MsgLabel"), using the Property Window. For programming, you need to cite the name correctly. For simplicity, we always use the default names of the control elements in our examples.

3. Click the [**Button**] tool on the toolbox (shown as a button). Draw a button on the form. You can resize the button. Bring the Properties Window up, and change the Text to "Get A Message." The command button has its default name "Button1," and its caption is "Get A Message" (see Figure 5.4). Change the font of the caption in the Property Window. Again, you may change the name of the button (e.g., to "MsgButton") in the Property Window.

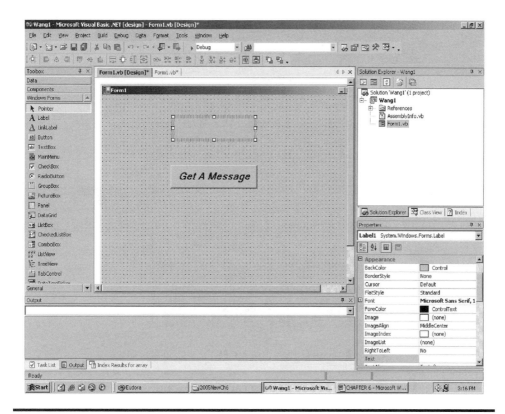

Figure 5.4 Create label and button.

4. Double click the [Get A Message] button on the form to bring the Code Window up. Now you can write an event-driven program in the Code Window for the "Get A Message" button to specify what will happen if the user click this button. You may find that Visual Basic has formatted the program and has **templates** such like

```
Public Class Form1
    Inherits System.Windows.Forms.Form
[Windows Form Designer generated code]
    Private Sub Button1_Click(ByVal sender As System.Object, _
        ByVal e As System.EventArgs) Handles Button1.Click

    End Sub
End Class
```

Since we want the GUI to display a message "Hello, World!" in the label box, we simply add a statement in the template as follows. We will return to explain the template later.

```
Private Sub Button1_Click(ByVal sender As System.Object, _
    ByVal e As System.EventArgs) Handles Button1.Click
    Label1.Text = "Hello, World!"
End Sub
```

The coding window shown in Figure 5.5. Note that in this statement Label1 is an object, Caption is the property of "Label1," and the statement

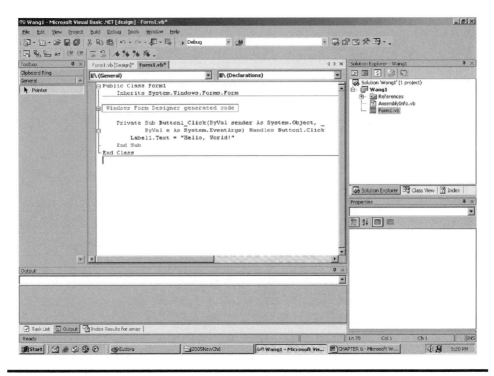

Figure 5.5   Write an event-driven program in the coding Window.

assigns "Hello, World!" to the Label. If you wish to change the default font for the message, you can manipulate Font in the Properties Window.

5. Run the program by click [Debug] on the Menu Bar, and then [Start]. Now you have the form in run mode. Notice the differences between design mode and run mode. If you click the [Get A Message] button, the GUI display "Hello, World!" in the label box, as shown in Figure 5.6.

    Note that run mode brings the **Immediate Window** up for debugging programs. If you want to make changes to the GUI (e.g., the font for the message), you have to return to the design mode.

6. Quit run mode by closing the run-mode window. Save the project in the folder you specified by clicking [File] and then [Save All]. Remember the name of the folder where you save the project. Next time you can retrieve the project after logging in VB.NET.

If changes to the application are required, the programmer must re-open the project, modify the project in design mode, and then run it.

5.4   Single-Form VB.NET Project

In this section we learn more features of computer programming with VB.NET. Suppose the program calculates monthly payment based on the amount of loan and the period of term. The GUI accepts these data from the user, and allows the user to select an interest rate from a **combo** menu, and then calculates the monthly payment. The design of Form1 is shown in Figure 5.7. In this form,

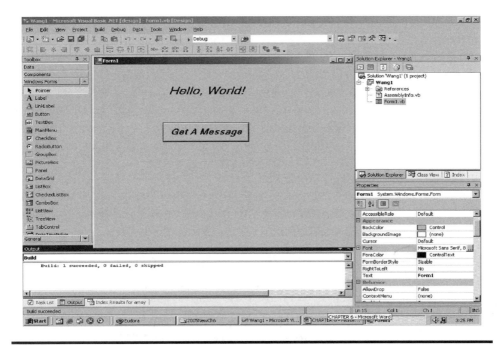

Figure 5.6   Run the event-driven program.

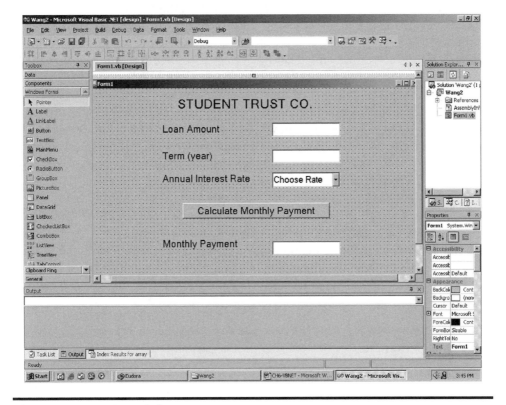

Figure 5.7   Design of the Form.

five Labels are created to simply display titles including "STUDENT TRUST CO.," "Loan Amount $," "Term(year)," "Annual Interest Rate," and "Monthly Payment." Two **TextBoxes** are created to catch the data, and the third TextBox is used to display the calculated monthly payment. The difference between TextBox and Label is that a TextBox can catch data as well as display data, but a Label can only display text. Besides, the Label "Annual Interest Rate," a **ComboBox** is created to show the alternative interest rates applied. Finally, a command Button is created for the user to find the answer. To write VB.NET programs, you must remember the names of these element objects (boxes and buttons).

Double click on the body of Form1 (other than any objects within the form), and bring the Coding Window up. You type in the following code in bold for adding items to ComboBox1 when the form is loaded.

```
1  Private Sub Form1_Load(ByVal sender As System.Object, _
2         ByVal e As System.EventArgs) Handles MyBase.Load
3      Dim InterestRate As Double
4      For InterestRate = 0.05 To 0.12 Step 0.005
5          ComboBox1.Items.Add(InterestRate)
6      Next InterestRate
7  End Sub
```

[Handwritten annotations: "for loop" bracketing lines 4–5; "initially set" pointing to 0.05; "once reached" pointing to 0.12; "increment by" pointing to Step 0.005]

Listing 5.1   Visual Basic codes for the combo menu.

The above example tells us how to load a ComboBox and how to write a **for-loop** in VB.NET. Lines **1** and **2** are the declaration of method Form1_ Load, and are displayed by the programming environment to allow you to define any thing you want the computer to execute during loading the form. In VB.NET, if a method does not return a value, it is called sub (subroutine), and if a method returns a value, it is called a **function**. A subroutine or function can have parameters to communicate with the request. We do not explain the parameters in this example because we do not use them. In VB.NET, if a line of code is too long to print, one may use a space followed by a underscore sign (_) to divide the line. Line **3** declares a variable used for this program. We will explain data types later in this chapter. Lines **4–6** are a for-loop. InterestRate is the **controller**. It is set initially to 0.05, and increases 0.005 each step. The for-loop is ended when InterestRate reaches 0.12. Line **5** instructs the computer to add an item to the ComboBox with the value of InterestRate. Line **6** defines the boundary of the for-loop.

Double click the designed command button in Form1, and bring the Coding Window up for the button. The following program is to catch the data from the text boxes and the combo menu, and calculate the payment by using a built-in function Pmt.

```
1  Private Sub Button1_Click(ByVal sender As System.Object, _
2          ByVal e As System.EventArgs) Handles Button1.Click
3      Dim LoanAmount, LoanTerm, InterestRate, MonthlyPayment As Double
4      LoanAmount = Val(TextBox1.Text)
5      LoanTerm = Val(TextBox2.Text)
6      InterestRate = Val(ComboBox1.Text)
```

↓ negative ✱
    sign

```
7    MonthlyPayment = -Pmt(InterestRate/12, LoanTerm*12, LoanAmount, 0, 0)
8    TextBox3.Text = Format(MonthlyPayment, "Currency")
9 End Sub
```

Listing 5.2   VB.NET code for the Button.

We examine how the program in Listing 5.2 works. Lines **1** and **2** are displayed by the programming environment to allow you to define the subroutine when the user clicks the command button. Line **3** declares four variables used in this program. Line **4** catches a value from `TextBox1` for `LoanAmount`. Line **5** catches a value from `TextBox2` for `LoanTerm`. Line **6** catches a value from `ComboBox1` for `InterestRate`. Line **7** calculates the monthly payment using function `Pmt`. `Pmt` is a built-in function in VB.NET. It returns the monthly payment based on the monthly interest rate, terms in months, loan amount, etc. If one wants to show the payment without a sign, a negative sign ✱ must be applied as payment is always negative in terms of balance. Finally, line **8** displays the monthly payment in `TextBox3` in the currency format (e.g., $30.08). Note that, `Format()` is a function that specify the format of the data item.

VB.NET provides many built-in calculation functions such as `Pmt`. To make the user easier to learn a variety of topics and functions, the .NET environment provides online help. Using online help (clicking [`Help`] and [`Index`]), the user is allowed to use keywords to search relevant topics. Figure 5.8 shows a screen shot of online help for the Pmt function.

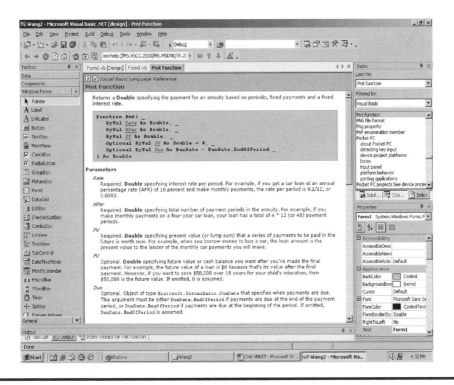

Figure 5.8   Online help for Pmt function.

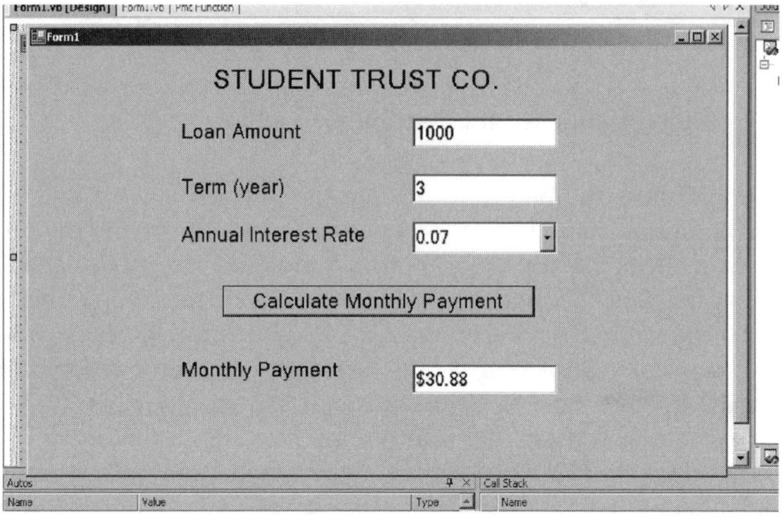

Figure 5.9   Expected result of the design.

Now you are ready to test the program. You can debug and run the application by clicking [Debug] - [Start] on the menu. If there is no typo in the program, the following execution result is expected (see Figure 5.9).

The user of the program is allowed to input data of loan amount and term in the respective text boxes, and select the annual interest rate by clicking the combo menu. Upon clicking the button [Calculate Monthly Payment], the program will give the number of monthly payment in the text box "Monthly Payment."

5.5   VB.NET Project with Multiple Forms

This section gives an example of VB.NET project with multiple forms. The GUI of this example allows the user to choose food items and input purchase, view the purchase summary, and print the receipt on the printer.

5.5.1   Design Forms

The programmer designs Form1 for the primary GUI as shown in Figure 5.10. To make the GUI attractive, the form is decorated with color background downloaded from <http://www.free-pictures-photos.com/>. Note that when you download images from the Internet, you must obtain permission and cite the source for acknowledgment.

On Form1 several combo boxes and text boxes are created to accept inputs from the user. A button is created to allow the user to view the order.

To display order information on the screen, click [PROJECT] on the menu and then [Add Windows Form]. Form2 is designed as shown in Figure 5.11. Several label boxes are employed to display information. To allow the user to

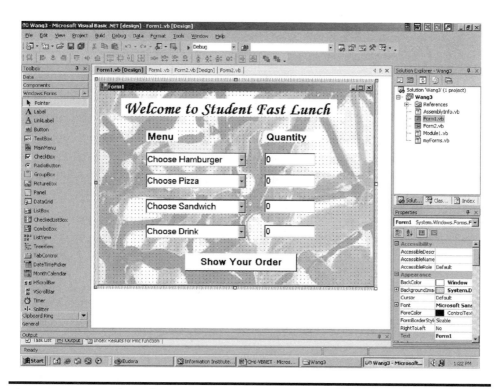

Figure 5.10   Design of Form1.vb.

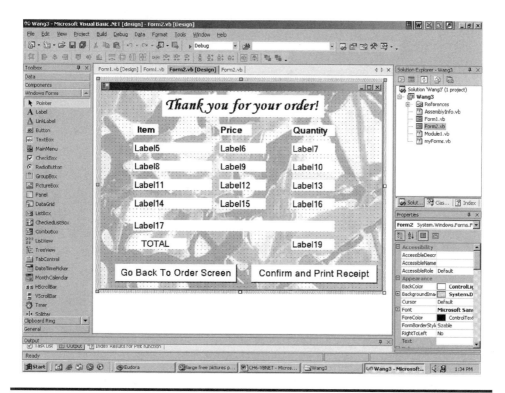

Figure 5.11   Form2.vb in design mode.

go back to Form1 and hide Form2, one button named [Go Back to Order Screen] is designed. The second button is to print a receipt for the user.

5.5.2   *Module*

To define global constants or variables, such as prices of the merchandises and sales tax rates which can be **shared** by all classes of the project, we need to use **Module.** Click [PROJECT] on the menu and then [Add Module]. The Code Window for the module is displayed. You can write code for the module, as shown in Figure 5.12. Note that you must use the keyword **Public** to define any shared constants and variables.

Type the following program into the Module. Note that, in Visual Basic, one can use an apostrophe sign for a comment line for the purpose of self-documentation.

```
1  Module Module1
2   ' At the Module level one can define constants or
3   ' global variables shared by all classes

4   ' The prices
5   Public Const CheeseBurger = 3.79
6   Public Const DeeterBurger = 5.89
7   Public Const ChickenBurger = 4.69
8   Public Const PepperoniPizza = 3.59
9   Public Const LowfatPizza = 3.69
10  Public Const PanPizza = 2.99

11  Public Const BBQTurkey = 3.49
12  Public Const ItalianSausage = 3.39
13  Public Const TunaMelt = 5.79

14  Public Const SpringWater = 0.99
15  Public Const IceTea = 1.49
16  Public Const Soda = 1.05

17  ' Sales tax rate might be applied
18  Public Const SalesTaxRate = 0.05

19  ' Module can also use used to build a reference to share
20  ' In this case, this allows to change Form2 from other forms

21  Sub main()
22      Dim Form2 = New Form2
23      Form2.ShowDialog()
24  End Sub

25 End Module
```

Listing 5.3   Code for Module1.vb.

In Listing 5.3, line **1** and line **25** are the pre-generated template. Lines **2–4** are notations. In VB.NET, a notation line starts with a single quotation mark ('). Lines **5–18** define the prices of merchandise and tax rate for all classes to share.

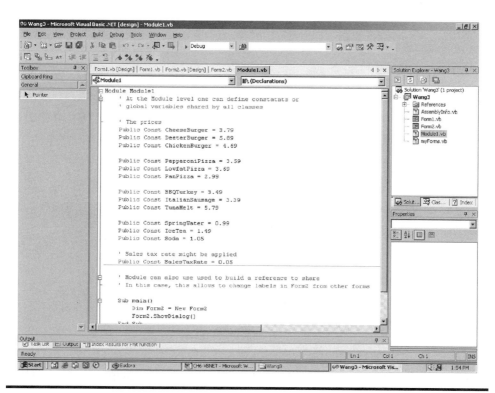

Figure 5.12   Write code for module.

In VB.NET, the elements (labels, textboxes, etc.) in a form are unable to be addressed from the outside of the form unless a dialog reference is built. Lines **21–24** serve this purpose so that the components of Form2 can be addressed from Form1 for changes (e.g., Form2.Label1="this string"). Thus, modules are also often used to store subroutines and functions that can be requested by any class within the project.

5.5.3   Class

A form is a class. However, in VB.NET, two forms do not share information unless a super class is created to make the two forms share throughout the application project. To create a class, click [Project] and [Add Class]. The code in Listing 5.4 is to make the two forms share each other so that one form can manipulate another form.

```
1  ' To create a class and make objects shared within the class
2  ' In this case, share Form1 and Form2 throughout the application

3  Public Class Class1
4      Public Shared Form1 As Form
5      Public Shared Form2 As Form
6  End Class
```

Listing 5.4   Code for Class1.

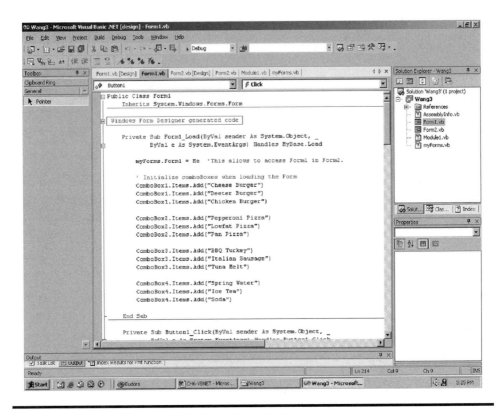

Figure 5.13   Write code in the coding Window.

5.5.4 Coding for Forms

Now we return to Form1 to write code for the class. Double click the form or Button1 in design mode, enter the Coding Window for the form, and write code as shown in Figure 5.13. Note that it is unnecessary to type the templates, and simply double click the element concerned to obtain its template.

The entire program for Form1 is shown in Listing 5.5.

```
1 Public Class Form1
2     Inherits System.Windows.Forms.Form
```

```
3 [Windows Forms Designer Generated Code]
```

```
4 Private Sub Form1_Load(ByVal sender As System.Object, _
5     ByVal e As System.EventArgs) Handles MyBase.Load

6 Class1.Form1 = Me 'This allows to access Form1 in Form2.

7 ' Initialize comboBoxes when loading the Form
8 ComboBox1.Items.Add("Cheese Burger")
9 ComboBox1.Items.Add("Deeter Burger")
10 ComboBox1.Items.Add("Chicken Burger")

11 ComboBox2.Items.Add("Pepperoni Pizza")
12 ComboBox2.Items.Add("Lowfat Pizza")
```

```
13   ComboBox2.Items.Add("Pan Pizza")

14   ComboBox3.Items.Add("BBQ Turkey")
15   ComboBox3.Items.Add("Italian Sausage")
16   ComboBox3.Items.Add("Tuna Melt")

17   ComboBox4.Items.Add("Spring Water")
18   ComboBox4.Items.Add("Ice Tea")
19   ComboBox4.Items.Add("Soda")

20 End Sub
```

```
21   Private Sub Button1_Click(ByVal sender As System.Object, _
22           ByVal e As System.EventArgs) Handles Button1.Click ✶

23     ' Build references to use Form2
24     Dim Form2 As New Form2
25     ' Declare variables
26     Dim Hamburger As Double
27     Dim Pizza As Double
28     Dim Sandwich As Double
29     Dim Drink As Double
30     Dim Total As Double

31     ' Find prices
32     If ComboBox1.Text = "Choose Hamburger" Then
33        Hamburger = 0.0                              ✶
34     Else
35        If ComboBox1.Text = "Cheese Burger" Then
36           Hamburger = CheeseBurger
37        End If
38        If ComboBox1.Text = "Deeter Burger" Then
39           Hamburger = DeeterBurger
40        End If
41        If ComboBox1.Text = "Chicken Burger" Then
42           Hamburger = ChickenBurger
43        End If
44     End If

45     If ComboBox2.Text = "Choose Pizza" Then
46        Pizza = 0.0
47     Else
48        If ComboBox2.Text = "Pepperoni Pizza" Then
49           Pizza = PepperoniPizza
50        End If
51        If ComboBox2.Text = "Lowfat Pizza" Then
52           Pizza = LowfatPizza
53        End If
54        If ComboBox2.Text = "Pan Pizza" Then
55           Pizza = PanPizza
56        End If
57     End If

58     If ComboBox3.Text = "Choose Sandwich" Then
59        Sandwich = 0.0
```

```
60   Else
61   If ComboBox3.Text = "BBQ Turkey" Then
62      Sandwich = BBQTurkey
63   End If
64   If ComboBox3.Text = "Italian Sausage" Then
65      Sandwich = ItalianSausage
66   End If
67   If ComboBox3.Text = "Tuna Melt" Then
68      Sandwich = TunaMelt
69   End If
70   End If

71   If ComboBox4.Text = "Choose Drink" Then
72      Drink = 0.0
73   Else
74   If ComboBox4.Text = "Spring Water" Then
75      Drink = SpringWater
76   End If
77   If ComboBox4.Text = "Ice Tea" Then
78      Drink = IceTea
79   End If
80   If ComboBox4.Text = "Soda" Then
81      Drink = Soda
82   End If
83   End If

84   ' Calculate Total
85   Total = Hamburger * Val(TextBox1.Text) + _
86          Pizza * Val(TextBox2.Text) + _
87          Sandwich * Val(TextBox3.Text) + _
88          Drink * Val(TextBox4.Text)

89   'Fill Form2
90   If ComboBox1.Text = "Choose Hamburger" Then
91      Form2.Label5.Text = "No Hamburger"
92      Form2.Label6.Text = ""
93      Form2.Label7.Text = "0"
94   Else
95      Form2.Label5.Text = ComboBox1.Text
96      Form2.Label6.Text = Format(Hamburger, "Currency")
97      Form2.Label7.Text = TextBox1.Text
98   End If
99   If ComboBox2.Text = "Choose Pizza" Then
100     Form2.Label8.Text = "No Pizza"
101     Form2.Label9.Text = ""
102     Form2.Label10.Text = "0"
103  Else
104     Form2.Label8.Text = ComboBox2.Text
105     Form2.Label9.Text = Format(Pizza, "Currency")
106     Form2.Label10.Text = TextBox2.Text
107  End If
108  If ComboBox3.Text = "Choose Sandwich" Then
109     Form2.Label11.Text = "No Sandwich"
110     Form2.Label12.Text = ""
111     Form2.Label13.Text = "0"
112  Else
```

```
113        Form2.Label11.Text = ComboBox3.Text
114        Form2.Label12.Text = Format(Sandwich, "Currency")
115        Form2.Label13.Text = TextBox3.Text
116     End If
117     If ComboBox4.Text = "Choose Drink" Then
118        Form2.Label14.Text = "No Drink"
119        Form2.Label15.Text = ""
120        Form2.Label16.Text = "0"
121     Else
122        Form2.Label14.Text = ComboBox4.Text
123        Form2.Label15.Text = Format(Drink, "Currency")
124        Form2.Label16.Text = TextBox4.Text
125     End If

126     Form2.Label17.Text = _
127        "-----------------------------------------------------------"
128     Form2.Label19.Text = Format(Total, "Currency")

129     ' Use message box
130     If ComboBox1.Text = "Choose Hamburger" And _
131        ComboBox2.Text = "Choose Pizza" And _
132        ComboBox3.Text = "Choose Sandwich" And _
133        ComboBox4.Text = "Choose Drink" Then
134          MsgBox("You haven't chosen anything!", , "Choose Items")
135     End If

136     'Show Form2
137     Form2.Show()
138   End Sub
139 End Class
```

Listing 5.5   VB.NET code for Form1.vb.

We examine how the programs in Listing 5.5 for Form1 works. Lines **1–2** declare class Form1, and are paired with line **139** as the class template generated by the environment. Line **3** is a folder of generated code. It is not important for beginners. Lines **4–5** declare method Form1_Load, and are paired with line **20** as the method template. Line **6** allows Form1 to be accessible from the outside of the class. Lines **7–19** load the four combo boxes.

Lines **21–22** declare method Button1_Click for Button1, and are paired with line **138** as the method template. Line **24** declares Form2 as a shared form for this button. As will be shown later, Form2 is a summary of the order and allows the user to print a receipt. Lines **26–30** declare variables for this method.

Lines **32–44** are one If-Then-Else sentence which in turn has nested if statements to obtain prices for food items of Hamburger. Lines **45–57**, **58–70**, and **71–83** do the similar work for other types of food. Lines **85–88** calculate the total price of the chosen food items. In VB.NET, a space and underscore sign (_) must be used if one sentence is divided into more than one line.

Lines **90–98** are one If-Then-Else sentence that fills information of Hamburger order to the corresponding labels (Labels **5–7**) of Form2. Lines **99–107**, **108–116**, and **117–125** do the similar work for other labels of Form2.

Lines **126–127** fill a line to the label of Form2. Line **128** fills the total field on Form2. Lines **130–135** shows a **message box** for warning the user if no food item has been chosen for the order. Finally, line **137** brings Form2 up to the screen.

The next program is made for Form2. There are two buttons on Form2. One is to hide Form2 and allow the user to go back to Form1 to make changes to the order, and the other is to print the receipt. From the Windows operating system one can press the [PrintScrn] key and then paste it in Word to print a form window. However, this method is inefficient. First, a Form image is used for screen display, but is dark on paper and consumes much ink. Second, a Form image is small, and is unable to contain many lines for a large report. To print a good report for users, one needs to use a print method as shown in this example.

```
1 Imports System.Drawing.Printing
```

```
2 Public Class Form2
3 Inherits System.Windows.Forms.Form
```

```
4 [Windows Forms Designer Generated Code]
```

```
5 ' Declare an array of labels to make printing code shorter
6 Dim LabelArray(4, 3) As Label
```

```
 7 Private Sub Form2_Load(ByVal sender As System.Object, _
 8         ByVal e As System.EventArgs) Handles MyBase.Load

 9  ' To make Form2 a shared by other forms to show/hide it
10    Class1.Form2 = Me
11 End Sub
```

```
12 Private Sub Button1_Click(ByVal sender As System.Object, _
13         ByVal e As System.EventArgs) Handles Button1.Click

14    Class1.Form2.Hide()
15 End Sub
```

```
16 ' Declare a print document as an object
17 Private WithEvents myDocument As PrintDocument
```

```
18 ' To print a document
19 Private Sub Button2_Click(ByVal sender As System.Object, _
20         ByVal e As System.EventArgs) Handles Button2.Click

21    ' Retrieve data in all labels into LabelArray
22    LabelArray(1, 1) = Label5
```

```
23      LabelArray(1, 2) = Label6
24      LabelArray(1, 3) = Label7
25      LabelArray(2, 1) = Label8
26      LabelArray(2, 2) = Label9
27      LabelArray(2, 3) = Label10
28      LabelArray(3, 1) = Label11
29      LabelArray(3, 2) = Label12
30      LabelArray(3, 3) = Label13
31      LabelArray(4, 1) = Label14
32      LabelArray(4, 2) = Label15
33      LabelArray(4, 3) = Label16

34      ' Initialize the print document
35      myDocument = New PrintDocument

36      ' Use the Print method (_PrintPage) to print the document
37      myDocument.Print()
38 End Sub
```

```
39 ' Specific methods for printing the document
40 Private Sub myDocument_PrintPage(ByVal sender As Object, _
41          ByVal e As System.Drawing.Printing.PrintPageEventArgs) _
42          Handles myDocument.PrintPage

43      ' Declare a string line
44      Dim myText As String
45      ' Declare number of lines
46      Dim N As Integer = 1
47      ' Declare counters
48      Dim I, J As Integer
49      ' Declare date and time
50      Dim T As New Date

51      ' Declare font for the print document
52      Dim myFont As New Font("Courier New", 12, FontStyle.Regular,
53                        GraphicsUnit.Point)

54      ' Print the heading with margin starting at (50, 50) point
55      e.Graphics.DrawString(Label1.Text, myFont, _
56                        Brushes.Black, (50 + 50), 50)

57      ' Print Date starting at (150, 74) point
58      e.Graphics.DrawString(T.Today(), myFont, _
59                        Brushes.Black, (50 + 100), (50 + 24))

60      ' Use for-loops to print all items
61      For I = 1 To 4

62        ' Screen out non-selected items (0 Quantity)
63        If Val(LabelArray(I, 3).Text) <> 0 Then

64          N = N + 1      'Next line

65            ' Print three fields at the corresponding location
```

```
66        For J = 1 To 3
67            e.Graphics.DrawString(LabelArray(I, J).Text, myFont, _
68            Brushes.Black, (50 + (J - 1) * 480 / J), (50 + N * 24))
69          Next
70       End If
71     Next

72     ' Print a line
73     myText = "---------------------------------"
74     N = N + 1
75     e.Graphics.DrawString(myText, myFont, _
76                         Brushes.Black, 50, (50 + N * 24))

77     ' Print the Total. Note the space
78     myText = Label18.Text + "            " + Label19.Text
79     N = N + 1
80     e.Graphics.DrawString(myText, myFont, _
81                         Brushes.Black, 50, (50 + N * 24))
82   End Sub
```

```
83   ' You can make page setting
84   Private Sub PrintDocument1_QueryPageSettings(ByVal sender _
85          As Object, ByVal e As _
86          System.Drawing.Printing.QueryPageSettingsEventArgs) _
87          Handles myDocument.QueryPageSettings
88          e.PageSettings.Landscape = False
89   End Sub
90   End Class
```

Listing 5.6   VB.NET code for Form2.vb.

We examine how the programs in Listing 5.6 for Form2 works. Line **1** imports the library for printing. Programming manual is needed to determine what library is needed for a particular task. Lines **2–3** declare class Form1, and are paired with line **90** as the class template generated by the environment. Line **4** is a folder of generated code. It is not important for beginners. Line **6** declares an array to hold information in all labels of Form2. This makes the code for printing concise.

Lines **7–11** define the task for loading Form2. In this case, line **10** makes Form2 accessible from the outside of the class.

Lines **12–15** define the task for Button1. Note that in line **14** Class1 is used as a super class to hide Form2.

Line **17** declares myDocument as a PrintDocument object for printing

Lines **18–38** define the task for Button2. Lines **22–33** retrieve information from the labels to the array to use one for-loop to print all food items. Line **35** initializes the PrintDocument object (myDocument) and makes it ready to use. Line **37** applies the Print method to print the document. This method is specified in subroutine myDocument_PrintPage, as described in the following.

Lines **40–82** specify the task of printing for Button2. Note that in lines **40** and **42** the subroutine name must be the document object name followed by

_PrintPage, and the handled event is the document object name followed by .PrintPage.

Lines **43–50** declare variables for printing. Note line **50** that declare a variable for date. Line 52 declares the font used for printing. Courier font is easy for lining up.

Lines **55–56** draw a line for the heading, which is stored in Label1. Note that the margin is defined by the start position of the line (x–y coordinates). Lines **58–59** draw a line for the current date. Lines **60–71** are nested for-loops that print all data from the two-dimensional array. Line **63** screens out all items with no quantity. In line **68**, uneven field lengths are defined by the unfamiliar x-y coordinates. Lines **73–81** print a line and total for the receipt.

Lines **84–89** shows how one can set page orientation to landscape or portrait.

5.6 Programming with VB.NET

More detailed explanations for essential VB.NET programming techniques are provided as follows.

5.6.1 General Format of Code, Comments, and Keywords

The VB.NET coding environment automatically provides formats and pull-down lists of available attributes and methods for coding. In the editor window, if a line is too long to be displayed, the window rolls automatically. For printing the source code, one can use the line divider sign _ to divide a code line. Programmers insert comments to document programs and make the programs readable. A comment line begins with single quotation (') sign.

VB.NET has its **keywords**, such as Public, Private, Sub, End, Button1_Click, Me, ByVal, Dim, As, etc. Each keyword represents its specific meaning and cannot be used for user-defined words. The keyword **Me** is difficult for beginners to understand. Generally speaking, the keyword Me refers to the current instance of an object. We will explain most commonly used keywords in the following subsections.

5.6.2 Class and Object

VB.NET is an object-oriented language. A form is a class, a module is a class, a data type is class, etc. Many classes (e.g., data types) have been built in VB.NET. The programmer can use the following syntax to define a user-defined class.

```
[access-modifier] Class [class identifier]
[Inherits class-name]
      [class body]
End Class
```

Listings 5.3 and 5.4 are examples for class. The **access modifier** is typically the keyword Public that means the class can be accessed globally. The inheritance part is optional.

To make an actual class instance, or object, the programmer must declare the object. Two steps are needed to instantiate an object.

Step 1: Declare the object by writing an access modifier and an instance of the class, for example,

```
Private WithEvents myDocument As PrintDocument
```

and

```
Dim myText As String
```

Step 2: Allocate memory for the object using the keyword New, for example,

```
myDocument = New PrintDocument
```

The two steps can be combined into a single line, for example,

```
Dim T As New Date
```

5.6.3   Methods

VB.NET code for a method is written within the **procedure definition header** and the **end** of the method (subroutine or function) (e.g., Listing 5.6, lines 19–20). The environment generates pre-displayed template with the header and end for event handlers such as Button_Click and Form_Load.

```
Private Sub [sub_name](ByVal sender As System.Object, _
     ByVal e As System.EventArgs) Handles [event_name]
```

The procedure definition header defines parameters for the method. An event handler has two parameters. The first parameter is of type object and is called sender. It controls the event. The second parameter is of type Event Args class, and passes information about the event. The method is appended with the keyword Handles followed by the event name. VB.NET differentiates between passing parameters by value (ByVal) and passing parameters by reference (ByRef). ByVal is commonly considered by beginners.

5.6.4   Constant Variables

Programmers can create variables whose values do not change during the program execution. These variables, called **constant variables**, are defined by the keyword const. The use of constant variables makes the program easier to maintain.

5.6.5   Data Types

VB.NET provides many **data types**. Major data types include:

Boolean	True or False
Char	Unicode character
DateTime	e.g., 12/31/2099
Decimal	Fixed-precision and the position of the decimal point for business
Double	Double-precision floating point

```
Integer      Integer
String       A sequences of characters
```

The keywords **Dim** (stands for dimension) and **As** are used to define the data type for a user-defined class, variable, or **array**. One can also assign the initial value to a variable. In VB.NET the default value of a numerical variable is zero.

We often use textbox to receive numerical data from the user. In principle, the data type of text string is different from that of numeric data. `Val()` function converts a string in the textbox to a number (e.g., Listing 5.6, line 63).

5.6.6　Arithmetic Operations

The arithmetic operations of VB.NET are similar to C. For instance:

```
AssignValue = 50
TotalAmount = Amount1 + Amount2
DifferenceAmount = Amount1 - Amount2
MultiplyAmount = Amount1 * Amount2
DivideAmount = Amount1 / Amount2
```

5.6.7　If-Then-Else Statement

The **If-Then-Else** statement has the following syntax.

```
If [condition] Then
[action block 1]
Else
[action block 2]
End If
```

The condition is a logical expression. Note that the format is rigidly defined; that is, these subsentences (If ... Else ... End If) must not be written in the same line. In VB.NET there are **If-Then-ElseIf-Then** and **IIF** (if and only if) statement. They may not be easy to use by beginners.

5.6.8　For-Loop

For-loop is used when the times of iteration are pre-determined. The syntax of for-loop is

```
For [counter] = [start] To [end] [step]
[action block]
Next [counter]
```

In the Next phrase [counter] can be omitted. If [step] is omitted, the counter increases by 1 on each iteration.

5.6.9　String Processing and Format Statement

In VB.NET there are many methods for string manipulation, such as concatenating, testing, finding substrings, etc. In our examples, we use plus sign (+)

for concatenating strings. In many cases, the programmer wants to control the appearance of string that are displayed or printed. The format function Format( ) specifies exactly how the string should appear.

5.6.10 Print a Document

Printing a document in VB.NET is not as easy as in VB6.0. The syntax used for statement for printing a document is not straightforward. As shown in Listing 5.6, three basic steps are involved in printing a document.

Step 1. Declare a PrintDocument object, using the syntax as follows.

```
Private WithEvents [document_name] As PrintDocument
```

Step 2. In the subroutine of the button that is to print the document, initialize the PrintDocument object, and trigger the Print() method. The syntax is shown below.

```
    Private Sub [button]_Click(ByVal sender As System.Object, _
    ByVal e As System.EventArgs) Handles [button].Click
. . . .
[document_name] = New PrintDocument
        [document_name].Print()
 End Sub
```

Step 3. Write a subroutine to print the document. The general structure is shown below.

```
Private Sub [document_name]_PrintPage(ByVal _
    sender As Object, _
    ByVal e As System.Drawing.Printing.PrintPageEventArgs) _
    Handles myDocument.PrintPage
 . . . .
    Dim [string_name] As String
 . . . .
    Dim [font_name] As New Font("[font_type]", [font_size], _
        FontStyle.Regular, GraphicsUnit.Point)
 . . . .
    e.Graphics.DrawString([string_name], [font_name], _
                    Brushes.[color], _
                    [x-coordinate], [y-coordinate])
 . . . . .
End Sub
```

Note that in these methods we use e as a print event argument to pass parameters.

5.6.11 Message Box

The MsgBox statement displays a **message window** to the user when it is executed. Its syntax is as follows:

```
MsgBox [message body], [message box type], [message title]
```

5.7 Debugging

Traditionally, Visual Basic programs are easy to debug. However, since VB6.0 migrated to VB.NET, debugging VB.NET programs becomes difficult. First, unlike other object-oriented languages such as C++ and Java, the structure of VB.NET is rather disjointed. In the current version, although the VB.NET environment can help one to avoid syntax errors by showing available properties and methods for a class, and automatically place the cursor to the location where the error is actually caused, it does not provide much help for debugging. Common bugs include a misuse of user-defined variable, mismatching between the class name defined in the program and the actual element on the GUI, and references among the classes.

5.8 Self-Review Exercise

1. Given the VB.NET window in the "run mode," describe how you would design this GUI (Form1) by filling the table.

Name of the GUI Object	Properties: (Indicate "Text" only)
Label1	ONLINE AUCTION
Label 2	Merchandise
Combo Box 1	Choose Merchandise
Label 3	My Bid $
Text Box 1	"
Button 1	BID
Button 2	Find Bidding Result

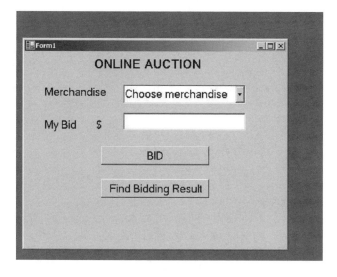

2. Read the following Visual Basic program for the above GUI, and fill in the blanks. Note that your answers must be consistent with your table in Question 1.

P. 206

```
1 Public Class Form1
2 Inherits System.Windows.  Forms  .Form
3 [Windows Forms Designer generated code]
```

P. 202

```
4 Private Sub Form1_Load(ByVal sender As System.Object, _
5       ByVal e As System.EventArgs) Handles MyBase.Load
6   ComboBox1. Items.Add ("Pentium X Computer")
7   ComboBox1. Items.Add ("Kodak Digital Camera")
8   ComboBox1. Items.Add ("Intel PC Camera")
9   ComboBox1. Items.Add ("HP LaserJet 9999")
10 End Sub
```

P. 203

```
11 Private Sub Button1_Click(ByVal sender As System.Object, _
12     ByVal  e As System.EventArgs) Handles Button1.Click
13   If (Val(TextBox1.Text) = 0) _
14     Or (ComboBox1.Text = "Choose merchandise") Then
15     MsgBox("Please Input your bid!", , "Missing input data")
16   Else
17       MsgBox("Offer is accepted. Please find the result!")
18   End If
19 End Sub
```

P. 203

205

```
20 Private Sub Button2_Click(ByVal sender As System.Object, _
21       ByVal e As System.EventArgs) Handles Button2.Click
22   Dim CurrentHighestBid As  integer
23   If ComboBox1.Text = "Pentium X Computer" Then
24       CurrentHighestBid = 1000
25   End if
26   If ComboBox1.Text = "Kodak Digital Camera" Then
27       CurrentHighestBid = 200
28   End If
29   If ComboBox1.Text = "Intel PC Camera" Then
30       CurrentHighestBid = 100
31   End If
32   If ComboBox1.Text = "HP LaserJet 9999" Then
33       CurrentHighestBid = 400
34   End If
35   If  Val  (TextBox1.Text) > CurrentHighestBid Then
36       MsgBox("You win!", , "You win!")
37   Else
38       MsgBox("Sorry, your bid is not high enough. Bid again!")
39   End If
40 End Sub
41  End class
```

Offer is accepted. Please find the result!.

3. In the "run mode" of the above VB.NET program, if the user selects "Pentium X Computer" using the combos, inputs 900 in the text box, and

Sorry, your bid is not high enough. Bid again!

then clicks the "Bid" and "Find Bidding Result" buttons, **what** and **where** is the expected result that appears?

4. In the "run mode" of the above VB.NET program, if the user selects "Pentium X Computer" using the combos, inputs nothing in the text box, and then clicks the "Bid," **what** and **where** is the expected result that appears?

5. In the "run mode" of the above VB.NET program, if the user selects "Intel PC Camera" using the combos, inputs 200 in the text box, and then clicks the "Bid" and "Find Bidding Result" buttons, **what** and **where** is the expected result that appears?

6. Develop a VB.NET project that produces a GUI with 1 form, 1 combo box, 3 to 5 label boxes or text boxes, 2 to 4 buttons.

7. Sketch the appearance of reports printed by the program in Listing 5.6.

8. Develop a VB.NET project that produces a GUI with 2 forms, images, several (at least 3) buttons, several label boxes or text boxes, at least 2 combo boxes, 1 module, 1 class, and message boxes. One of the buttons is to print a report on the default printer.

9. Learn more features of VB.NET from the online help. Create a VN.NET project that uses features (e.g., Checkbox and RadioButton) which are not fully explained in this book.

Appendix 5.1   Guideline for VB.NET Project Report

1. Front page
   Course name
   Title of the project
   Group members
   Date
2. Text
   Introduction and the purpose of the VB.NET project
   Application of VB.NET (forms, buttons, labels, message boxes, text boxes, combos ...)
   Discussion of the advantages and the disadvantages of VB.NET
3. Source code of the VB.NET programs
4. Examples of the GUI screen shots and the print results.

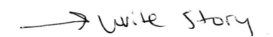

Chapter 6

Visual Basic for Applications and Decision Support Systems

6.1 Concepts of Decision Support Systems

Generally, three types of management information systems are encountered in the day-to-day business life: transaction processing systems, management report systems, and decision support systems (DSS).

1. **Transaction processing systems:** Transaction processing systems deal with well-structured routine data processing, such as payroll and order processing. In these systems, little decision making is involved. Efficiency and accuracy are the major concerns in these systems.

2. **Management report systems:** Management report systems (or management information systems in the narrow sense) provide information directly for decision processes, yet these decisions are usually structured, are routine and can be anticipated. Income statements, inventory control, and sales analysis systems are examples of this type of information system.

3. **Decision support systems:** DSS provide information to decision makers in situations where the decisions are not well structured or are unanticipated. One of the important characteristics of DSS is user–computer interaction. In other words, the user (decision maker) uses the computerized information system to add structure to the situation and convert the unstructured problem into a set of structured problems to solve the problem. As such, a combination of management judgment, paths of problem solving, decision

models, and data analysis is required in a DSS. **User–computer interface** and **model management** are the major concerns in DSS. Visual computer languages such as Visual Basic and Visual Basic for Applications (VBA) are best suitable for the development of DSS.

Decision support systems consist of three major components: **interface**, **database**, and **model base**. The interface of a DSS provides means for a user to interact with the DSS. It should allow a user to dialogue with the computer conveniently. It also should provide various output formats including text, tabular, and graphics. The database subsystem provides the means for retrieval and processing of data. The model base subsystem manages the storage and retrieval of the models. It also aids users in model building. A great deal of research is being conducted in model management. At this time, there is no commonly accepted scheme of model management. Generally speaking, there are two major components in a model base, although the boundary between them is not clear cut. One is a set of models that are shared by all decision makers for a variety of decisions. Examples of these models are linear programming and regression for forecasting. Another is a set of problem solvers or decision paths. Each of these problem solvers is designed for a specific situation of decision.

A sophisticated DSS is really complicated. To better understand the general concepts of DSS, we take a very simple example. This example will also give you some experience with spreadsheet **macro**. In our example, we suppose that the model base only consists of a couple of spreadsheets. Each spreadsheet represents one model. For instance, a production spreadsheet represents a production cost accounting model, and a marketing spreadsheet represents a marketing cost accounting model. A computer program coordinates these models, specifying a decision path and acting as a problem solver, and allows the user to make trials (e.g., "**what-if**" trials) through the user–computer interface to reach a decision. The system developer needs to design a user–computer interface and write programs for the interface and problem solvers. The framework of this simple DSS example is expressed in Figure 6.1.

Before developing a simple DSS by using VBA, we learn the basic concepts of **macro** first.

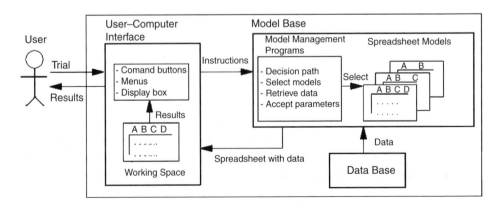

Figure 6.1   Framework of a DSS in the spreadsheet environment.

6.2 Macro

A **macro** is a series of commands and functions that are stored in a module and can be run whenever the user needs to repeat the task. A macro is actually a written or recorded program that stores a series of commands as a single command. In spreadsheet and database software, the macro approach is commonly used to automate complex tasks and reduce the number of steps required to complete tasks that one performs frequently. One can record a macro just as one records a "speech," and then run the macro to repeat, or "play back" the "speech." In Microsoft Excel and Access, a macro program is written in **VBA** programming.

To know what macro means, we practice a toy example of recording macro. Open Excel. Click [Tools], [Macro], and then [Record New Macro]. You will see the Record Macro Window. The default name of your macro is macro1. Click the [OK] button in the Record Macro Window. You will see a small window called Stop Rec shows up in the spreadsheet. Now you are in the recording mode, and the computer will record every step you make in the spreadsheet until you click [Stop] in the Stop Rec Window.

As an example, locate the cursor to the cell A1, and type in the following spreadsheet:

```
      A        B
1   Sales    50
2   Price    100
3   Tax      =B1*B2*0.05
--------------------------------
5   Total    =B1*B2+B3
```

Cut this spreadsheet and paste it to the cell C1. After you finish the operation, click the [Stop] button in the little Stop Rec Window.

After you stop the recording, the computer stops recording and saves all macro code in the program named macro1. To view how macro works, you may delete the spreadsheet you have done when recording the macro first, then click [Tools], [Macro], [Macros ...] to bring the Macro Window up, and then click the [Run] button in the Macro Window. You will see that the computer performs exactly the same steps as what you have performed during the recording process.

To bring the macro program up, click [Tools], [Macro], [Macros ...] to bring the Macro Window up, and then click the [Edit] button in the Macro Window. You will see the code window as shown in Figure 6.2. We will explain details of macro later in this chapter. At this point, you can figure out the meaning of this macro code by recalling what you have done during the recording process.

You might have noticed in practicing the example given that before you record a macro, it is important to plan the steps and commands you want the macro to perform. During the recording course, the macro will keep all mistakes you make and all corrections you make as well. Each time you record a macro, the macro is stored in a new module with a user-defined name.

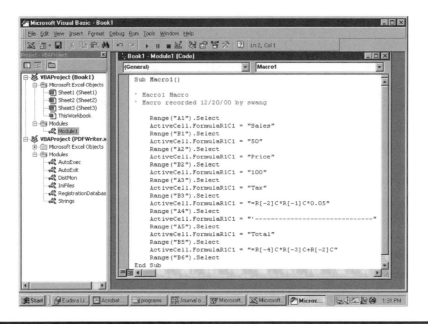

Figure 6.2   Recorded Macro.

To clean-up mistakes recorded, you need to use **macro editor** to edit the macro. For sophisticated users, recording macro is often inefficient. More importantly, the macro recorder system is not perfect. It is not unusual to have error messages when you run a recorded macro. Also, some instructions (e.g., IF statement) cannot be generated by recording macro. After you learn how to record a macro, you need to learn how to edit a macro and write macro programs using the VBA environment in an efficient way. Next, we develop a simple DSS by using VBA.

6.3   DSS Example of VBA

As discussed in the previous section, in Microsoft software products (e.g., Excel and Access) macros are recorded in the **VBA** programming language. One can also write macros directly by using **Visual Basic Editor** in these software environments.

Visual Basic for Applications programming language has specific functions for the particular software product (i.e., spreadsheet or database). Strictly speaking, VBA program language is not **Visual Basic** language, but they share common features.

To learn more about, VBA we use an example to show how to write macros in VBA of Microsoft Excel.

1. Log in Microsoft Excel.
2. Generate a spreadsheet in Sheet 1, as shown in Figure 6.3.

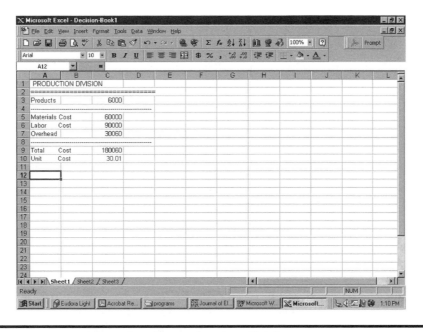

Figure 6.3   Spreadsheet for the production division.

The spreadsheet is designed for the cost accounting of the Production Division. The formula include:

```
C5   =10*C3
C6   =15*C3
C7   =30000+0.01*C3
C9   =SUM(C5:C7)
C10  =(C9/C3)
```

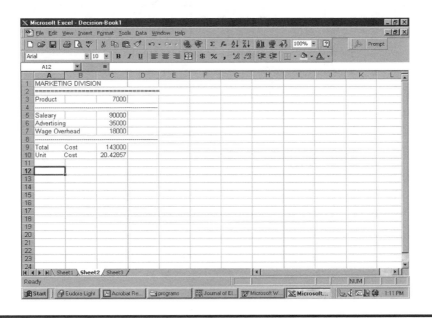

Figure 6.4   Spreadsheet for the marketing division.

3. Click Sheet 2, and create a spreadsheet for the Marketing Division, as shown in Figure 6.4.

The formula used in the Marketing Division for cost accounting include:

```
C5  =IF(C3<4000, 30000, 30000+(C3-4000)*20)
C6  =IF(C3<5000, 20000, 35000)
C7  =IF(C5<3500, 0.1*C5, 0.2*C5)
C9  =SUM(C5:C7)
C10 =(C9/C3)
```

4. Click Sheet 3, and create a spreadsheet for the Vice-President (VP)-planning, as shown in the range (A10:G18) in Figure 6.5. Reserve the other parts of the sheet for the next step.

The formula for the VP's spreadsheet include:

```
C14  =(C12*F12)
C18  =(C14-C15-C16)
G18  =(C18/F12)
```

5. The VP-planning wants to do "**what-if**" trials to determine the optimal production level for the company. To manage the models and assist the VP in performing a proper sensitivity analysis in the central planning spreadsheet, macro programs are developed for the problem solver.

To bring up the tool bars for macro programming, click [View], [Toolbars], and then [Visual Basic Editor]. You can see the "Visual Basic Tool Bar." Then go back to click [View], [Toolbars], and [Control] to bring up the "Control Tool Bar," as shown in Figure 6.5. Now you are in

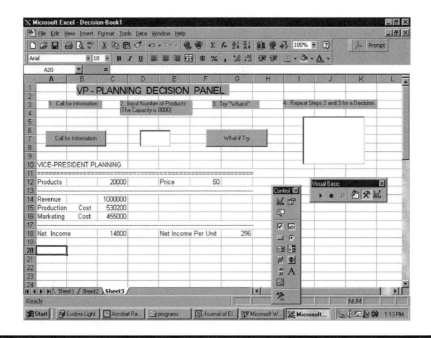

Figure 6.5   Spreadsheet for the VP-planning.

the "**Design Mode**." You can find user-computer interface widget icons on the Control Tool Bar, such as Label, Command Button, List Box, Text Box, Combo Box, etc. You can switch "**Design Mode**" and "**Run Mode**" by clicking the Design Mode icon. Note the difference between the two modes. The Design Mode allows you to develop macro, and the Run Mode allows you to run the macro.

6. You can create a widget object by clicking an icon on the Tool Bar, and drag it on the spreadsheet. Then, right click the widget object to edit the object. You can change the **properties** of the object such as object name, caption, color, font, etc. In this example, you create five Labels, two Command Buttons, one TextBox, and one ListBox, as shown in Figure 6.5.

7. In the design mode of VBA, double click the first command button, you are allowed to create programs for the command button, as shown in Figure 6.6.

8. Create macro code for the second Command Button for "What-if" trials as shown in Figure 6.7.

9. To run the user-computer interface in Figure 6.5, you must quite the design mode by clicking the icon [Design Mode] on the Visual Basic Toolbar. Now you can run the DSS.

For an exercise, first click the "Call for Information" button, and notice the actions of the spreadsheets. Then type a number in the textbox, say 2000. Then, click the "What-if" button, and see the result in the ListBox [3000 −11030], which means that if you produce 3000 units, the net income would be −11030. You input 4000 into the TextBox and click the "What-if" button again, the ListBox shows [4000 13960], which means that the net income becomes 13960

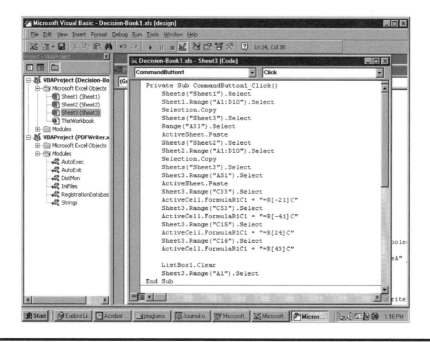

Figure 6.6 VBA code for the call-for-information button.

Figure 6.7 VBA code for the "What-If" trial button.

if you produce 4000 units. Finally, you will find that the optimal production level is just below 5000 in this case.

6.4 Macro Code of the Example

In the example provided, the macro code is to copy the two spreadsheets of Production and Marketing into the VP's spreadsheet, and build communication linkages among them. The first command button is to call individual spreadsheets. Its macro program is as listed in the following. The line numbers are used for the explanation purpose, and should not be typed in the program.

```
1  Private Sub CommandButton1_Click()
2      Sheets("Sheet1").Select
3      Sheet1.Range("A1:D10").Select
4      Selection.Copy
5      Sheets("Sheet3").Select
6      Range("A31").Select
7      ActiveSheet.Paste
8      Sheets("Sheet2").Select
9      Sheet2.Range("A1:D10").Select
10     Selection.Copy
11     Sheets("Sheet3").Select
12     Sheet3.Range("A51").Select
13     ActiveSheet.Paste
14     Sheet3.Range("C33").Select
15     ActiveCell.FormulaR1C1 = "=R[-21]C"
16     Sheet3.Range("C53").Select
17     ActiveCell.FormulaR1C1 = "=R[-41]C"
18     Sheet3.Range("C15").Select
```

```
19    ActiveCell.FormulaR1C1 = "=R[24]C"
20    Sheet3.Range("C16").Select
21    ActiveCell.FormulaR1C1 = "=R[43]C"

22    ListBox1.Clear
23    Sheet3.Range("A1").Select

24 End Sub
```

Listing 6.1   Macro Code for calling several spreadsheets.

Most of the instructions of the macro program emulate the human repeated work. For example, the first three sentences

```
Sheets("Sheet1").Select
Sheet1.Range("A1:D10").Select
Selection.Copy
```

mean "click Sheet 1, and click cell [A1] and drag a range from A1 to D10, and then click [Edit] and [Copy] on the menu bar."

You can see that macro code keeps the procedures of human manipulation. For example, when operating the spreadsheet, if you want to put 100 into cell A1, you must click cell A1 and type 100. This is exactly how macro should be written:

```
Range("A1").Select
ActiveCell.FormulaR1C1 = 100
```

A common sense sentence such as Cell("A1")=100 does not work.

Generally, macro are easy to understand, except for a few sentences like the following.

```
ActiveCell.FormulaR1C1 = "=R[-21]C"
```

This sentence means to create a formula for the currently active cell, and this formula brings in the component from the cell which is located at 21 rows back and the same column relating to the current cell. For example, suppose the current active cell is [C33]. After the execution of the above macro instruction, the component in the cell [C33] is equal to the component in [C12]; that is, the cell of column C and row 12 (i.e., 33–21).

We examine how the above program works. Lines **1** and **26** are displayed automatically by the editor environment. Line **2** selects Sheet1. Line **3** selects the range for the spreadsheet in Sheet1. Line **4** copies this part. Line **5** lets the computer turn to Sheet3. Line **6** selects the location on Sheet3, and line **7** pastes the current part copied in line 4 to the selected location. Lines **8–13** do the similar job for Sheet2.

Line **14** focuses on cell C33 on Sheet3. Line **15** gets the formula for C33 from C12. From Figures 6.3 and 6.5, you should figure out that this is to put the production level in C12 to the place of production level in the Production spreadsheet copied from Sheet1. Lines **16–17** do the similar job for the Marketing spreadsheet copied from Sheet2.

Lines **18–19** focus C15, and acquire its formula from C39. You should figure out that this is to find the production cost for C15 from the Production spreadsheet from Sheet1. Lines **20–21** do the similar job for the marketing cost in C16.

Note that lines **8** through **21** build the connections between the related cells on Sheet3.

Finally, line **22** clears the list box to be ready to show the "What-If" trial results, and return the cursor to A1.

You may have a question: Why do we need to copy these spreadsheets? Remember, when we use macro to manipulate multiple spreadsheets, the macro program might damage the original spreadsheets. To prevent such damages, we often copy them into a work space. Clearly, the work space shall not invade the space reserved for the user-computer interface.

The second command button is to perform "What-If" trials.

```
1 Private Sub CommandButton2_Click()
2    Dim S As String

3    Sheets("Sheet3").Select
4    Sheet3.Range("C12").Select
5    ActiveCell.Value = TextBox1.Text
6    Sheet3.Range("C18").Select
7    S = TextBox1.Text & "      " & ActiveCell.Value
8    ListBox1.AddItem (S)

9 End Sub
```

Listing 6.2   Macro Code for "What-If" trials.

We examine how the above code works. Line **2** defines a variable. Lines **3** and **4** let the computer focus on C12. Line **5** accepts the trial input data from the TextBox, and sign this value to the currently active cell (C12). Note that this is the production level.

Remember that the relations between the copied Sheet1 and Sheet2, and Sheet3 have been built up (lines **14** through **21** in Listing 6.1). Once the number in C12 is changed, all values in C14, C15, C16, and C18 will be changed automatically. Line **6** focuses on C18 (the net income generated based on the production level). Line **7** prepares a line for output. Finally, line **8** adds the trial result to the ListBox. Now, you can try this small decision support system as the user of the system.

6.5   Analyzing Code of VBA and Other Features of VBA

You can learn VBA programming by analyzing the code generated by the Macro Recorder. If you are not sure about how to write a macro, you may record a macro first, and then view the macro code. When copying the recorded macro code for VBA programming, you need to pay attentions to the entire active object path. For example, recorded macro code,

```
Range("A1").Select
```

assumes that the default sheet is Sheet1. It must be change to

```
Sheet1.Range("A1").Select
```

if the VBA interface is not on Sheet1, as the default active object is changed.

You can also learn more about VBA by using online help. To do so, click [View], [Tool Bars], [Visual Basic] to bring the VB tool bar up, click the [Editor] icon to bring the editor pane up, and click [Help]on the top menu bar. You can find many examples of VBA programs.

6.5.1 Syntax of VBA Statements

Generally, the syntax of a VBA statement is:

```
Object.{Sub-object}.Method
```

For example,

```
Sheet3.Range("C12").Select
```

or

```
Object.{Sub-object}.Property = value
```

For example,

```
ActiveCell.Value = TextBox1.Text
```

An **Object** is an element of Excel. A sheet, a cell, a range, a selection are all objects. A **sub-object** is the sub-element of the object. For instance, a cell is a sub-element of a sheet. A VBA statement may not have a sub-object, or can have a chain of sub-objects. A **method** is an action the computer is supposed to take. A **property** is the attribute of the object that is going to be set by the computer.

A VBA program is placed into a procedure template with head Sub and footer End Sub generated by the editor. If a statement is too long for print, you can use underscore sign _ to divide the statement into multiple lines. See an example in Listing 6.6.

Next, we learn several statements of VBA that cannot be generated by the Macro Recorder, but are important for programming.

6.5.2 Comments

A good programmer always inserts comments into the program to explain the program clearly for **self-documentation**. A comment statement starts with apostrophe sign ', and the computer simply ignores all comments.

For example,

```
' This macro implements what-if trial
```

6.5.3 Variable Setting

The programmer can set **variables** to hold data internally (i.e., without showing it on the spreadsheet) for further process. The syntax of **variable declares** is

```
Dim [variable-name] As [data-type]
```

For example,

```
Dim RowCount As Integer
```

A data type could be string, integer, or any type of number.

6.5.4 Combo Box

In the DSS example, commonly used widget objects such as Label, Textbox, Command Button, and List are used. Another commonly used widget object is Combo Box. You can use the Control Toolbar to create a Combo Box on your user–computer interface. To load a Combo Box, you need to add code in the VBA program of a command button, presumably the "Call for Information" button. Listing 6.3 shows an example of loading a Combo Box through click the button.

```
Private Sub CommandButton1_Click()
    ComboBox1.Clear
    ComboBox1.Text = "Choose a department"
    ComboBox1.AddItem ("Marketing")
    ComboBox1.AddItem ("Production")
    ComboBox1.AddItem ("Human Resource")
End Sub
```

Listing 6.3 Example of loading a Combo Box.

6.5.5 If-Then-Else Statement

More than often, one wants the computer to take an action based on conditions. If-Then-Else statements implement such function. The syntax of If-Then-Else statement is:

```
If [condition-1] Then
    [action-1]
Else
    [action-2]
End If
```

The format is rigid; that is, it is not allowed to mix the lines. An example that implements a simple ordering decision is shown in Listing 6.4.

```
' This macro tests whether A1 is lower than 100 for re-order
Sub OrderDecision()

  Range("A2").Select
  ActiveCell.Formula = "The re-order decision:"
  Range("A3").Select

  If Range("A1") <= 100 Then
    ActiveCell.Formula = "Re-order!"
  Else
    ActiveCell.Formula = "No re-order!"
  End If

End Sub
```

Listing 6.4 Use If-Then-Else to implement a conditional decision.

To practice, click [Tool], [Macro], [Macros], type the name Order Decision for the macro, and [Create]. Type the program in the editor pane, minimize the macro editor pane, and return to the spreadsheet. Type a number (around 100) that represents the inventory on hand. Click [Tools], [Macro], [Macros], choose the macro and [Run].

6.5.6 *Dialog Box*

In the example of Listing 6.4, the macro assumes the number for decision that has been there. If you want the computer to accept a number after running the macro, you use a dialog box implemented by InputBox. We change Listing 6.4 to Listing 6.5. Now you can run the macro before you input the number for the decision.

```
' This macro tests whether the number in A1 is lower than re-order

Sub Dialog()

    Dim Inventory As Integer
    Inventory = InputBox("Enter the inventory on hand")
        Range("A1").Select
    ActiveCell.Formula = "The re-order decision:"
        Range("A2").Select

    If Inventory <= 100 Then
        ActiveCell.Formula = "Re-order!"
          Else
        ActiveCell.Formula = "No re-order!"
          End If

End Sub
```

Listing 6.5   Use Input Box to implement dialog.

6.5.7 *For Loop and Do Loop Statement*

To repeat an action(s), you can use For loop or Do loop. The For loop syntax is

```
For [counter] = [start] To [end] Step [step]
    [actions]
Next [counter]
```

where the counter is a variable to count the repeat times. Step is optional, and defaults to 1.

In the next example, we use a For statements to implement dynamic array process that is depending upon the user's selection of part of the spreadsheet. The macro of Listing 6.6 changes the interior color of this part to red. The program does not specify particular cell index, but allows the user to select the location of the matrix based on specific needs. This is implemented by Selection.Rows.Count and Selection.Column.Count.

```
Sub ChangeColor()

Dim RowCount As Integer
Dim ColumnCount As Integer
```

```
For RowCount = 1 To Selection.Rows.Count
  For ColumnCount = 1 To Selection.Columns.Count
     Selection.Interior.ColorIndex = 3
  Next ColumnCount
Next RowCount

End Sub
```

Listing 6.6   Use For-Loop to implement a dynamic array.

To practice, click [Tool], [Macro], [Macros], type the name Change-Color for the macro, and then click [Create]. Type the program in the editor pane, close the macro editor pane, and return to the spreadsheet. Drag a matrix on the spreadsheet. Click [Tools], [Macro], [Macros], choose the macro and [Run]. A red matrix will display in the selected part on the spreadsheet. In Listing 6.6, ColorIndex specifies the color of the selected cells, and 3 is the code of red color. Again, you can learn the minor things such as color code by recording macros.

Similar to For loop, there is Do loop statement. The syntax of Do loop is

```
Do [While condition]
      [actions]
Loop
```

6.6   Self-Review Exercise

1. Record a macro program (e.g., copy and paste a spreadsheet) and run it.
2. Follow the example of VBA presented in the textbook. Suppose the two departmental spreadsheets are changed as follows:

Sheet1

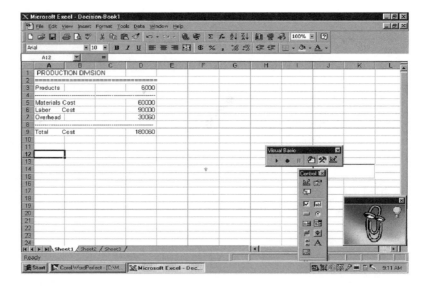

Sheet2

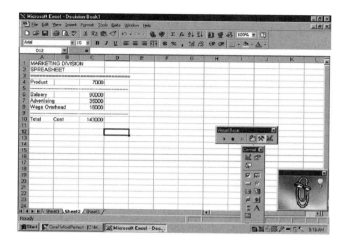

Sheet3 is the same as the one in the textbook.

Read the following two programs for the two Command Buttons, and fill in the blanks.

```
 1 Private Sub CommandButton1_Click()
 2   Sheets("Sheet1")._____
 3   Sheet1.Range("_____").Select
 4   Selection.Copy
 5   Sheets("Sheet3").Select
 6   Range("A31").Select
 7   _____.Paste
 8   Sheets("Sheet2").Select
 9   Sheet2.Range("_____").Select
10   _____.Copy
11   Sheets("Sheet3").Select
12   Sheet3.Range("A51").Select
13   ActiveSheet.Paste
14   Sheet3.Range("_____").Select
15   ActiveCell.FormulaR1C1 = "_____"
16   Sheet3.Range("_____").Select
17   ActiveCell.FormulaR1C1 = "_____"
18   Sheet3.Range("C15").Select
19   ActiveCell.FormulaR1C1 = "_____"
20   Sheet3.Range("C16").Select
21   ActiveCell.FormulaR1C1 = "_____"
22   ListBox1.Clear
23   Sheet3.Range("A1").Select
24 End Sub

25 Private Sub CommandButton2_Click()
26   Dim S As String
27   _____("Sheet3").Select
28   Sheet3.Range("C12").Select
29   ActiveCell._____ = TextBox1.Text
```

```
30   Sheet3.Range("C18").Select
31   S = TextBox1.Text & "      " & ActiveCell.Value
32   ListBox1._____ (S)
33 End Sub
```

3. Use Excel and create two spreadsheets. Record a macro program that copies and pastes the two spreadsheets to third spreadsheet. Create a command button that executes the recorded macro program. View the recorded macro program. Discuss the two approaches to create macros: recording and writing.

4. Develop a DSS project by using Excel and VBA language. The project has a GUI with two to three command buttons, two to four text boxes or list boxes.

5. Compare COBOL, C, C++, HTML, JavaScript, Java, VB.NET, and VBA by filling the following table.

	COBOL	C	C++	HTML	JavaScript	Java	VB.NET	VBA
Template for "Hello, World!"								
Computational Environment								
Function/Object Orientation								
Best Applications in Business Computing								

Chapter 7

Perl and CGI for Web-Based Applications

7.1 Web-Based Applications

Web-based applications are the important components of information systems based on Web technology and tightly integrated with conventional information systems such as databases and transaction processing systems. Web-based applications will become more pervasive than conventional computer applications and have high impact on business as well as people's lives in electronic commerce. Web-based applications enhance competitiveness of organizations by lowering transaction costs, focusing on groups of customers, or differentiating their products and services. Technically, Web-based applications share the common global information infrastructure and standardized communication protocols (**TCP/IP**) but allow the organizations to cordon off their private networks. Recently, common Web-based applications are based on the HTTP protocol to transfer hypertext documents and other resources. The **HTTP** protocol is built on a request–response paradigm and takes place over a TCP/IP connection on the Internet. Since they possess many features unique to the conventional computer applications, Web-based applications are considered to be the new generation of business data processing.

7.2 CGI and CGI Programming

The **CGI** is a mechanism (a combination of hardware and software) that allows Web clients to execute programs on the Web server and to receive the output from these programs. The CGI is implemented on the Web server, but is not mandatory for Web servers. However, in the early stage of e-commerce in the 1990s, CGI is one of the commonly adopted approaches in Web-based applications.

From the applications' view, CGI receives the input from the Internet and sends off the documents to the Internet. CGI regulates the environment in which some computer programs can execute to process and construct those dynamic documents. These computer programs installed on the server are written in special computer languages which can be handled by CGI. They are called **CGI programs** or **CGI scripts** (small pieces of programs).

Common gateway interface programs can be written in many programming languages, including C and C++. However, **Perl** has its advantages over other CGI programming languages in many aspects. Specifically, Perl has convenient syntax and powerful capabilities in text processing. Also, Perl is available by free downloading from <http://www.ActiveState.com> and is widespread in the CGI programming community.

To execute a CGI program, one makes a request (usually a Web page) to the server to run the program. One way of running a simple CGI program is to find the program in the folder specified by the URL using the Web browser (e.g., Netscape) and click on the program file name. More commonly, we use a **method** to trigger a CGI program from a FORM in the Web page. Methods are one of the underlying components of HTTP. The method defines how the program receives the data.

The method to trigger a CGI program is defined in the FORM submitted to the server. As learned from HTML, there are several methods that can be defined in FORM, including GET and POST. We recommend using POST only for CGI.

Common gateway interface may not be the perfect approach to Internet computing and Web-based business applications, as we pointed out in the chapters of Java servlet and ASP.NET. Many server products offer product-specific **application programming interfaces (API)** to improve the performance of the system. Most of these products are designed specifically to a particular type of server. Historically, CGI has been in existence for many years as a standard. CGI programming is simple. It is also believed that CGI is unlikely to be outdated. Currently, CGI programs are still running as Internet legacy systems, although it is believed that CGI will eventually phase out.

7.3 Introduction to Perl

Practical extraction report language (Perl) was initially created as a tool to aid system administration tasks in 1987. Perl has been adopted into the Web-based applications as one of the most widely used languages for CGI. Perl is of the C-style, but is an interpreted language so that it does not need to be compiled to run. This property makes the execution of Perl programs slow.

Perl was originally used for platforms with the Unix operating system. It is now used for many other operating systems platforms including Windows and

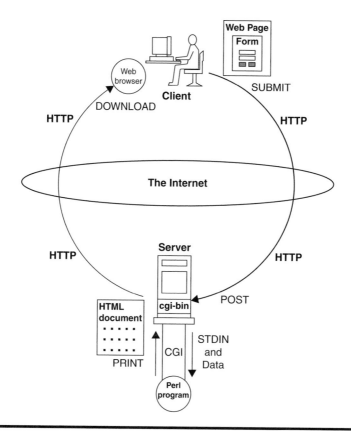

Figure 7.1   The information flows in an http transaction of Web-based applications.

Macintosh. For the examples of this chapter, the server operating system is Microsoft Windows 2000.

The cycle of the information flows in an HTTP transaction and the use of Perl programs accessed through CGI are shown in Figure 7.1. In this approach, the information flow cycle is actualized through the Perl programs on the server that handle the HTTP requests and writing HTML documents (dynamic Web pages).

7.4   Test Perl on the Server

Generally, Perl cannot be tested and run on a simple PC using just Web browser (e.g., Netscape). To run Perl, you must have a Web server. Perl is widely used on the Unix platform, and the installation procedure of Perl on the server with Windows platform has not been well documented in most books on Perl. Appendix 7.1 provides a general guideline for the installation of ActivePerl on the server with the Windows 2000 server operating system.

To test whether the Perl on the server works, you use Notepad to edit the simplest Perl program in Listing 7.1, and save to the cgi-bin folder on the server.

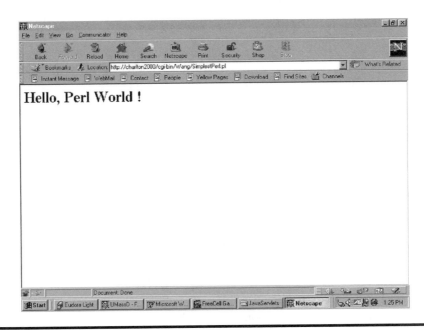

Figure 7.2   Expected result of the first Perl program.

Remember, you must save this program as a file with the extension name .pl (e.g., SimplestPerl.pl, not .txt file defaulted by Notepad).

```
#!C:/Perl-5.6/bin/perl.exe

print "Content-type: text/html\n\n";

print "<body>\n";
print "<h1>Hello, CGI Perl World !</h1>\n";
print "</body>\n";
```

Listing 7.1   Simplest Perl program (SimplestPerl.pl) for testing the installation.

Open a Web browser (e.g., Netscape) on a client PC, and type the URL of the Perl program. The URL of the Perl programs depend on the installation settings (see Appendix 7.1, e.g., http://Charlton2000/cgi-bin/ SimplestPerl.pl when the server is named as Charlton2000). If Perl has been successfully installed, you should have the result like Figure 7.2.

7.5   Perl Programming

In this section, we will learn essentials of Perl programming. Unlike programs in other languages we learned before, Perl programs are stored on server sides and must be tested on the client side. To run Perl programs on the server and present the results on the client side, we create a Web page that allows the user to trigger the Perl programs and view the execution results on the client side.

7.5.1 Web Page to Trigger Perl Programs

We create a simple Web page as a client-server interface to learn more about major functions of Perl. Through this interface, the user on the client side is able to trigger Perl programs by filling text boxes and clicking submit buttons.

```
 1 <HTML>
 2 <HEAD>
 3 <TITLE> Work on CGI - Perl </TITLE>
 4 </HEAD>

 5 <BODY>
 6 <H2> Panel to Trigger Perl Programs on the Server </H2>
 7 <BR>
 8 <H3> Command to trigger Perl program "HelloWorld.pl" </H3>
 9 <FORM ACTION="HelloWorld.pl" METHOD=POST>
10 <INPUT TYPE=SUBMIT VALUE="Hello, World!">
11 </FORM>

12 <BR><HR>
13 <H3> Learn ENVIRONMENT variables in Perl </H3>
14 <FORM ACTION="DisplayEnvVar.pl" METHOD=POST>
15 Your Name: <BR>
16 <INPUT TYPE=TEXT NAME="name" SIZE=50> <BR>
17 Your Brief Comments: <BR>
18 <TEXTAREA NAME="comments" ROWS="2" COLS="50"></TEXTAREA> <BR>
19 <BR>
20 <INPUT TYPE=SUBMIT VALUE="Look Environment Variables">
21 <INPUT TYPE=RESET VALUE="Start Over Again">
22 </FORM>

23 <BR><HR>
24 <H3> Command to trigger Perl program "CheckIP.pl" </H3>
25 <FORM ACTION="CheckIP.pl" METHOD=POST>
26 <INPUT TYPE=SUBMIT VALUE="Check in the server">
27 </FORM>

28 <BR><HR>
29 <H3> Display data submitted from FORM to the server </H3>
30 <FORM ACTION="DisplayFormData.pl" METHOD=POST>
31 Your Name: <BR>
32 <INPUT TYPE=TEXT NAME="name" SIZE=50> <BR>
33 Your Email Address: <BR>
34 <INPUT TYPE=TEXT NAME="email" SIZE=50> <BR>
35 Your Brief Comments: <BR>
36 <TEXTAREA NAME="comments" ROWS="2" COLS="50"></TEXTAREA> <BR>
37 <BR>
38 <INPUT TYPE=SUBMIT VALUE="Look the data sent to server">
39 <INPUT TYPE=RESET VALUE="Start Over Again">
40 </FORM>

41 <BR><HR>
42 <H3> Perl program saves data of FORM, and write them to a file
43 </H3>
44 <FORM ACTION="SaveForm.pl" METHOD=POST>
```

```
45 Your Last Name: <BR>
46 <INPUT TYPE=TEXT NAME="lname" SIZE=50> <BR>
47 Your First Name: <BR>
48 <INPUT TYPE=TEXT NAME="fname" SIZE=50> <BR>
49 Your Email Address: <BR>
50 <INPUT TYPE=TEXT NAME="email" SIZE=50> <BR><BR>
51 Your Orders: <BR>
52 Item:     <INPUT TYPE=TEXT NAME="item1" SIZE=10>
53 Quantity: <INPUT TYPE=TEXT NAME="Q1" SIZE=5> <BR>
54 Item:     <INPUT TYPE=TEXT NAME="item2" SIZE=10>
55 Quantity: <INPUT TYPE=TEXT NAME="Q2" SIZE=5> <BR>
56 Item:     <INPUT TYPE=TEXT NAME="item3" SIZE=10>
57 Quantity: <INPUT TYPE=TEXT NAME="Q3" SIZE=5> <BR>
58 <BR>
59 <INPUT TYPE=SUBMIT VALUE="Process the data">
60 <INPUT TYPE=RESET VALUE="Start Over Again">
61 </FORM>

62 <BR><HR>
63 <H3> Perl program posts users' comments to chat room </H3>
64 <FORM ACTION="ChatRoom.pl" METHOD=POST>
65 Your Name: <BR>
66 <INPUT TYPE=TEXT NAME="name" SIZE=50> <BR>
67 Your Email Address: <BR>
68 <INPUT TYPE=TEXT NAME="email" SIZE=50> <BR>
69 Your Brief Comments: <BR>
70 <TEXTAREA NAME="comments" ROWS="4" COLS="50"></TEXTAREA> <BR>
71 <BR>
72 <INPUT TYPE=SUBMIT VALUE="Chat Room">
73 <INPUT TYPE=RESET VALUE="Start Over Again">
74 </FORM>

75 </BODY>
76 </HTML>
```

Listing 7.2   Web page to trigger Perl programs on the server (Perl-Site.html).

In our case, the above HTML Web page is placed in the `cgi-bin` folder together with the Perl programs, for example, `c:/Inetpub/wwwroot/cgi-bin/Perl-Site.html`. These ACTION statements (lines 9, 14, etc.) indicate that the corresponding Perl programs are also placed in the `cgi-bin` folder.

Next, we explain the design of the above Web page.

7.5.1.1   Test Perl Program

In Listing 7.2, lines **6–11** build a Form that contains a button to trigger the simple Perl program named `HelloWorld.pl`. Note line **9**. `Action` defines the URL of the Perl program. `Method` must be `POST` to trigger a Perl program. The command button is defined by line **10**.

7.5.1.2 Learn ENVIRONMENT Variables

In Listing 7.2, lines **13–22** define a Form that accepts the input from the user, and sends these input data back to the server while the command button triggers the Perl program to show the values of the ENVIRONMENT variables for this Form. In this example, we use TEXTAREA to hold more input data. This part is designed merely for learning ENVIRONMENT variables. We seldom use this type of Form for any practical Web pages.

7.5.1.3 Check Your IP Address

In Listing 7.2, lines **24–27** build a Form that contains a button to trigger the Perl program named CheckIP.pl. As shown later, this program will check the remote client IP address. It might be used further to accept or deny the access from the client computer.

7.5.1.4 Learn CGI Data Strings

In Listing 7.2, lines **29–40** define a Form that accepts the input from the user, and sends these input data back to the server while the command button triggers the Perl program to show the exact text string received by the CGI. Again, this part is also designed merely for learning CGI and Perl.

7.5.1.5 Data Processing Using Perl Programs

In Listing 7.2, lines **42–61** define a Form that accepts the input from the user, and sends these input data back to the server while the command button triggers the Perl program to process these data. In this example, the user can input a commercial order to the server for processing. Later we will explain the Perl program SaveForm.pl and show how the Perl program processes these data and saves them on the disk. These data are accessible for Excel or other applications programs on the server for further business processes. Note that this example demonstrates the central concept of Perl-based Web applications.

7.5.1.6 Communication Interaction between the Client and the Server

In Listing 7.2, lines **63–74** are an extension of the above example. In this example, the user is allowed to input comments. When the user click the submit button, the comments are sent back to the server and the Perl program ChatRoom.pl is triggered to process your comments. After the process, your comments and all comments sent by previous users are summarized and are sent back to your spot and displayed on your screen.

After you save the above program, you test to see if the Web page works. Next, we learn Perl programming.

7.5.2 Simple Perl Program

We have demonstrated the "Hello, World!" Perl program in Listing 7.1 to test if Perl works on your server. We take a look at this example again, with slight changes, and walk through it line by line.

```
1 #!C:/Perl-5.6/bin/perl.exe

2 # This is a simple Perl example to check if Perl works with CGI

3 print "Content-type: text/html\n\n";

4 print "<head>\n";
5 print "<title>Hello, World - CGI Perl Test !</title>\n";
6 print "</head>\n";
7 print "<body>\n";
8 print "<h1>Hello, CGI Perl World !</h1>\n";
9 print "</body>\n";
```

Listing 7.3 Simple Perl program (HelloWorld.pl).

The first line of the program instructs the Windows operating system to run the program with a Perl interpreter defined by the path. In general, # sign in Perl indicates a comment line, as shown in line **2**, but line **1** is the only exceptional case where the portion after # is not a comment. Note that you must make sure there are no spaces or any blank lines before the first line of a Perl program. Line **2** is a notation for the documentation purpose.

Line **3** tells the Perl interpreter to output the content type. This Content-type line indicates to the Web browser that the document to follow will be an HTML document. This line is called header of the Perl program. \n means new line. Note that this is a standard line for any text HTML documents, and you must put two \n to signal to the Web browser that the header is complete and the actual HTML document is about to begin.

Lines **4–9** output the HTML document. The server passes this information on to the Web browser on the client side. The browser will display the Web page to the user. The HTML document printed by the Perl program is as follows:

```
<head>
<title>Hello, World - CGI Perl Test !</title>
</head>
<body>
<h1>Hello, CGI Perl World !</h1>
</body>
```

Listing 7.4 Output of the Perl program in Listing 7.3.

In this simple example, the Perl program prints an HTML program for the remote client user.

7.5.3 General Format of Perl

Generally, Perl is very like C. The syntax of Perl is similar to that of C. The structure of a Perl program is structural. You may not define the main program explicitly, but a single Perl program has one and only one main program.

The format of the first line of a Perl program is:

```
#![the path of the Perl interpreter]
```

Again, no spaces and blank lines are allowed before this line.

After the first line, any # indicates a comment line. If the Perl program outputs an HTML document, it must have a header line. The format of the header line is:

```
print "Content-type: text/html\n\n";
```

If the Perl program is to print plain text without HTML tags, the content type is text/plain. For a GIF image, the content type is image/gif.

Like C, the main program of a Perl program can call functions so-called subroutines in Perl, and a subroutine can in turn call other subroutines.

At the end of a Perl program, you may or may not use exit; to end the program.

7.5.4   *print Statement, Quotes, and Character* \n

print is to print information to standard output (STDOUT for CGI). This can be what is printed to the screen, a disk file, or another program document. The syntax of the print statement for printing a string to the screen and a program document is:

```
print [string];
```

The syntax of the print statement for printing a string to a disk file on the server is:

```
print [file name] [string];
```

If double quotes (" ") are used in a print statement, it prints the string within the quotes and the real value of the variable if any. Double quotes allow you to use \n to start a new line.

If single quotes (' ') are used, it prints exactly what is within the quotes. In this case, \n does not start a new line.

7.5.5   *Variables and Environment Variables*

Unlike in C, no explicit data type declaration is needed in Perl. The data type for a variable is determined by the program depending on the component in this variable.

7.5.5.1   Scalar Variable

A **scalar variable** (single value) variable starts with $. For example,

```
$NumVar = 7;
$CharVar = "This is a text string";
```

There is a special variable $_. Perl automatically copies the current line being read into $_.

7.5.5.2 Array

An array variable starts with @. Each array can have any number of elements. For example,

```
@NewArray = ("a", "1", 4);
```

means the array named NewArray has three elements: character "a," character "1," and number 4.

7.5.5.3 Associative Arrays

In Perl there are associative arrays. The difference between the ordinary arrays and associative arrays is that ordinary arrays are indexed by numbers but associative arrays are indexed by string or a variable. We refer to an associate array with %. However, when accessing individual elements we use $, and use { } for enclosing the index (also called key). For example,

```
$FORM{ $name } = "My name";
```

where $FORM is to access individual element of the associative array %FORM, $name is the index, and "My name" is the value of $name.

7.5.5.4 Global and Local Variables

A variable could be global or local. A local variable is only valid in the subroutine it is defined. This can avoid name conflict with other subroutines or the main program. The syntax of defining a local variable is:

```
local($LocalVar);
```

7.5.5.5 Environment Variables

The HTTP server shares information about the URL being requested and the properties of the client with the CGI. This information is communicated in the form of environment variables to the Perl program. Environment variables are associative arrays. Environment variables' format is:

```
$ENV{'[environment variable name]'}
```

Commonly used environment variables and information held by each of them are as listed in the following.

$ENV{'CONTENT_LENGTH'} The number of bytes of data received.
$ENV{'CONTENT_TYPE'} The content type of the data submitted by the
                        user.
$ENV{'GATEWAY_INTERFACE'} The name of the gateway interface.
$ENV{'REMOTE_ADDR'} The IP address of the client.

$ENV{'SERVER_NAME'}   The name of the server.
$ENV{'SERVER_PROTOCOL'}   The protocol in use.

The following Perl program will display the values of some important environment variables for the user in response to the form input specified by Listing 7.2, lines **13** through **22**.

```
1 #!C:/Perl-5.6/bin/perl.exe

2 # This is an example of learning Environment Variables

3 print "Content-type: text/html\n\n";

4 print "<html><body>\n";

5 $var = $ENV{'CONTENT_LENGTH'};
6 print "Value of CONTENT_LENGTH: ";
7 print $var;
8 print "\n<BR><BR>";

9 $var = $ENV{'CONTENT_TYPE'};
10 print "Value of CONTENT_TYPE: ";
11 print $var;
12 print "\n<BR><BR>";

13 $var = $ENV{'REMOTE_ADDR'};
14 print "Value of REMOTE_ADDR: ";
15 print $var;
16 print "\n<BR><BR>";

17 $var = $ENV{'REMOTE_HOST'};
18 print "Value of REMOTE_HOST: ";
19 print $var;
20 print "\n<BR><BR>";
21 print "</body></html>\n";
```

Listing 7.5   Print the values of environment variables to learn environment variables (DisplayEnvVar.pl).

The logic of the program in Listing 7.5 is very simple. After you use the Web page created by Listing 7.2 to submit the form to the server, you will see the values of these environment variables. Note that some values depend upon the contents typed in the form, and others depend upon the client PC you are using.

7.5.6   *Read Data from a File on the Server*

In this section, we will learn how a Perl program can read a disk file. The following Perl program is to response the command button on the form specified by Listing 7.2, lines **24** through **27**. The server will check the IP address of your computer against a disk file on the server. If your IP address is listed in the file, you will receive a greeting message; otherwise, you will receive a rejection message. The major part of this program is actually a subroutine. This subroutine can be used for other programs for security checking.

```perl
1 #!C:/Perl-5.6/bin/perl.exe

2 # This is an example of checking user list

3 print "Content-type: text/html\n\n";

4 print "<html><body>\n";

5 &CheckSecurity();

6 print "</body></html>\n";

7 sub CheckSecurity {
8   local($RemoteIPAddress, $LegalUser, $Flag);
9   $Flag = 0;
10  $RemoteIPAddress = $ENV{ 'REMOTE_ADDR' };
11  if (!$RemoteIPAddress) {
12    # Can't get the address
13    print "<p>We can not get your IP number ...</p>\n";
14  }

15 print "<p>Your IP Address is: $ENV{ 'REMOTE_ADDR' }</p>\n";

16 open(FILE1, "c:/Inetpub/wwwroot/cgi-bin/datafiles/uslist.txt");

17 if(!open(FILE1, "c:/Inetpub/wwwroot/cgi-bin/datafiles/uslist.txt"))
18 {
19 print "<h2> The server has a problem with data file ... </h2>\n";
20 }

21 while ($LegalUser = <FILE1>)
22 {
23   chop $LegalUser;
24
25 if ($RemoteIPAddress eq $LegalUser)
26   {
27     print "<h1>Hello, Welcome to ABC.com!</h1>\n";
28     $Flag = 1;
29   }
30 }
31 close (FILE1);

32 if ($Flag == 0)
33  {
34 print "<h1>Sorry! Your IP address is no good for this server.</h1>\n";
35  }
36 }
```

Listing 7.6   Read disk file though a subroutine (CheckIP.pl).

We examine how the program in Listing 7.6 works. Lines **1–4** are standard statements. Line **5** calls a subroutine, named CheckSecurity. The execution sequence turns to line **7** and goes through line **36**. After the subroutine, the computer returns to line **6** which is the end of this program.

Line **7** is the title of the subroutine. Line **8** defines three local variables. Line **9** assigns an initial value to $Flag. Line **10** obtains the IP address from the environment variable.

Lines **11–14** are an if statement. Line **11** means "if the variable $RemoteIPAddress is empty," and line **13** means "then print an error message to the HTML document." If this happens during the execution of the program, the system goes very wrong.

Line **15** prints the IP address to the HTML document.

Line **16** opens a disk data file on the server. In this case, the file is named uslist.txt on the server. It contains all legal users' IP address. Note that the disk file must be a text file in the ASCII format. You may use Notepad or Disk Operating System (DOS) editor to compose a disk file for Perl programs, and type one record each line. When you open a data file, you must define the path to locate the file (c:/Inetpub/wwwroot/cgi-bin/datafiles/uslist. txt in this case). You must also define an internal file name for it. In this case, FILE1 is the internal name of uslist.txt.

Lines **17–20** are another if statement. It means that if the computer cannot open the file then it outputs an error message. This error could occur when the server has problems in retrieving the data file.

Lines **21–30** are a while-loop. The instructions within the loop are repeatedly executed while the condition specified in the parenthesis is true. Line **21** means that while read FILE1 into $LegalUser as long as FILE1 still has content. Note that the FILE1 is an ASCII file. Each ASCII string is a length-varying record. Records are separated by **carriage return** (return key). For each time of the execution of the while-loop, $LegalUser gets one legal user's IP address stored in the disk data file.

In line **23**, the chop statement removes the last character of the string. In this case, it removes the new-line character from the end of the string in $LegalUser.

Lines **25–29** check if the remote IP address is equal to the string $LegalUser, then print a greeting message to the HTML document and set the flag to 1. Remember that this if statement is within the while-loop.

After the while-loop, line **31** closes the file. Lines **32–35** check whether the flag has been changed. If the value of the flag remains to be 0, then the program prints a warning message indicating that the current client user's IP address is not stored on the server. This program does not do anything further. However, this subroutine can be further used to deny illegal access.

More details about Perl are explained as follows.

7.5.7 Subroutines

Subroutines can be placed in the same program file together with the main program, or placed in separate program files. If a subroutine is placed in a separate program file, you must use the require statement to include the subroutine before the header of the Perl program. For example, suppose you have a subroutine named "sub1.pl" in the separate program file. If you want to use it, you must insert the following line before the executable statement of the program:

```
require "sub1.pl";
```

In our example, the subroutine is placed with the main program together. The concept of subroutines, including arguments and parameter passing, is exactly the same of that of functions we learned from C. Specifically, in Perl, use

```
&[called subroutine name]();
```

to call a subroutine.

7.5.8 *open–close Statements*

The open command opens a disk file to read, write, or append. The syntax of the open statement to read a disk file is:

```
open([internal file name],"[path and the disk file name on the server]");
```

The internal file name defined here will be used for the Perl program.

The syntax of the open statement to overwrite a disk file is:

```
open([internal file name], ">[path and the disk file name on the server]");
```

Note the ">" character in this syntax.

The syntax of the open statement to append a disk file is:

```
open([internal file name], ">>[path and the disk file name on the server]");
```

Note the ">>" characters in this syntax.

After the use of the data file, you must close the file. The syntax of the close statement is:

```
close([internal file name]);
```

7.5.9 *while Loop*

The while statement implements a loop. The syntax of while loop is:

```
while([condition])
{ [actions]; }
```

When the condition is true, the computer takes actions repeatedly until the condition becomes false. In Perl, the condition defined in the while statement might be not as straightforward as perceived. For example,

```
while(<FILE1>)
{ print; }
```

is equivalent to

```
while($_ = <FILE1>)
{ print($_); }
```

that means, read each record of FILE1, and while it has not finished, print the record.

7.5.10 *if-elseif-else Statement*

if statement in Perl is a little unique to other languages in including more test functions. A complete Perl if-statement is as follows:

```
if ([condition 1])
    { [action 1]; }
elsif ([condition 2])
    { [action 2]; }
elsif . . . . .
else
    { [final action]; }
```

In the given format, if condition 1 is true, then computer takes action 1. Once the if-sub-statement has been executed, the elsif-sub-statement is used to test if another condition is true. One if-statement can have many elsif-sub-statements, but can have only one else-sub-statement to handle anything that was not in the previous conditions. For beginners, it might be a good idea to avoid a complicated if statement.

7.5.11 *for Loop and foreach Loop*

The for-loop statement in Perl is similar to that in C. This syntax is:

```
for([set controller]; [condition]; [increment of the controller] )
{ [actions]; }
```

The foreach loop is used to process each of the variables within an array. Its syntax is:

```
foreach [variable name] (array name)
{ [actions on the defined variable] }
```

For example,

```
foreach $NameString (@NameArray)
{ print $NameString, "\n"; }
```

prints out each of the strings stored in the @NameArray array, line by line.

7.5.12 *String Processing*

As discussed earlier, the major purpose of Perl is to process the Form data inputted by the client user and outputs HTML documents. As most Form data and HTML documents are of the text type, Perl provides diversified functions of string processing. Here we introduce a few commonly used methods of string processing.

7.5.12.1 *chop Statement*

A record in the txt format contains a character of [new line] which is invisible (see an example in Listing 7.12). The chop statement removes such a last character of the string in the defined variable. Its syntax is:

```
chop [variable];
```

7.5.12.2 *split Statement*

The split statement splits the string into small strings based on the position of a particular character within the string and places each segment into an array or specified variables. Its syntax is:

```
[array] = split (/[character]/, [string]);
```

For example, the instruction

```
@pairs = split(/&/, $buffer);
```

splits the string in $buffer into small strings based on the & character, and assigns each of them to the element of the @pairs array.

7.5.12.3 *push and pop Statements*

The push statement adds a scalar value to the end of an array. Its syntax is:

```
push ([array], [scalar variable]);
```

The pop statement removes the last element of the array and returns it to a variable.

```
[scalar variable] = pop ([array]);
```

7.5.12.4 *String Appending*

We can use .= to append a string. For example,

```
$textString .= ".html";
```

means append ".html" to the current string in $textString.

7.5.12.5 *Translate*

Perl can translate each individual character in the string. Its syntax is:

```
[string variable] =~ tr/[from-characters]/[to-characters]/;
```

The =~ symbol is not really an assignment operator. It is used for "pattern matching." For example,

```
$value =~ tr/A-Z/a-z/
```

makes an uppercase to lowercase conversion in the string $value.

7.5.12.6   Substitution

Perl can also make substitutions; that is, replace a sub-string within the string. Its syntax is:

```
[string variable] =~ s/[from-substring]/[to-substring]/g;
```

The last character g means a "global" search to replace all specified sub-strings. Without the g option, only the first sub-string is replaced. For example,

```
$text =~ s/Pearl/Perl/g;
```

replaces all "Pearl" with "Perl" in the $text string.

7.5.13   Arithmetic Operations

In general, the arithmetic operations of addition (+), subtraction (−), multiplication (∗), and division (/) in Perl are of the same syntax as that we learned from C.

Next we learn more about the string processing from a Perl program example.

7.5.14   Read Standard Input Data Submitted by the Client through FORM

In this example we show how Perl can gather the inputted data from the client through Form, and what the text string as the standard input looks like before any processing. The following Perl program corresponds to the part of lines **29–40** of the Web page created by Listing 7.2. After you fill the Form on the Web page of Listing 7.2, click the submit button, and trigger the following Perl program. The Perl program gathers the inputted data and prints them to the HTML document without any further processing, and them sends back to you. You will see that the data string sent though the Form contains odd characters such as &, +, %, and hexadecimal numbers. The data is of the STDIN format.

```
1 #!C:/Perl-5.6/bin/perl.exe
2 # Read the input form
3 print "Content-type: text/html\n\n";

4 print "<html><body>\n";

5 read (STDIN, $buffer, $ENV{ 'CONTENT_LENGTH' } );
6 print $buffer;
7 print "</body></html>\n";
```

Listing 7.7   Gather and display the form data (DisplayFormData.pl).

The Perl program in Listing 7.7 reads the input data from the client through the POST method of the Form. Line **5** reads the Form data from standard input into the variable $buffer. The environment variable CONTENT_LENGTH specifies the read operator to read the exact number of characters. The syntax of read operator is:

```
read (STDIN, [string variable], $ENV{ 'CONTENT_LENGTH' } );
```

After the client user uses the POST method to submit Form data to the server, the server CGI sends these URL-encoded data to the triggered Perl program. In URL encoding, each name-value pair is separated by the character &, spaces in values are replaced with +, any non-alphanumeric character is replaced with corresponding hexadecimal value and escaped with %, and so on. The server will also send the CONTENT_LENGTH environment variable to the Perl program.

As seen in the following examples, one of the tasks of CGI programs is to parse the STDIN texts inputted by the Forms, and convert them to the desired format.

7.5.15   Write Data to a File on the Server

In this subsection, we will learn how a Perl program can parse the Form data and store the data in the ASCII format on disk on the server side. These ASCII data files on the server can be processed by other business application software including database management systems, spreadsheet, or any other computer languages (e.g., C, C++, Java, and COBOL).

```
 1 #!C:/Perl-5.6/bin/perl.exe

 2 # This is an example of saving data from a submitted form

 3 &ParseForm();

 4 print "Content-type: text/html\n\n";

 5 print "<HTML>\n<BODY>\n\n";

 6 if (!open(FILE1, ">c:/Inetpub/wwwroot/cgi-bin/datafiles/formdata1.txt"))
 7 {
 8 print "<H2>A new file cannot open on the server ... </H2>\n";
 9 }
10 else
11 {
12 &WriteRecord();
13 }

14 if (!open(FILE2, ">>c:/Inetpub/wwwroot/cgi-bin/datafiles/formdata2.txt"))
15 {
16 print "<H2>The file cannot open on the server ... </H2>\n";
17 }
18 else
19 {
20 &AddRecord();
21 }

22 print "<H3>Your order is being processed.</H3>\n";
23 print "<H4>(See data in formdata1.txt and formdata2.txt)</H4>\n";
```

```
24 print "<H3>Thank you for ordering from ABC.COM ! </H3>\n";
25 print "</BODY></HTML>\n";
26 exit;

27 sub WriteRecord
28 {
29 open(FILE1, ">c:/Inetpub/wwwroot/cgi-bin/datafiles/formdata1.txt");
30 $Order = "";
31 $Order .= "$FORM{ 'lname' }";
32 $Order .= " ";
33 $Order .= "$FORM{ 'fname' }";
34 $Order .= " ";
35 $Order .= "$FORM{ 'email' }";
36 $Order .= " ";
37 $Order .= "$FORM{ 'item1' }";
38 $Order .= " ";
39 $Order .= "$FORM{ 'Q1' }";
40 $Order .= " ";
41 $Order .= "$FORM{ 'item2' }";
42 $Order .= " ";
43 $Order .= "$FORM{ 'Q2' }";
44 $Order .= " ";
45 $Order .= "$FORM{ 'item3' }";
46 $Order .= " ";
47 $Order .= "$FORM{ 'Q3' }";

48 print FILE1 $Order;

49 close (FILE1);
50 }

51 sub AddRecord
52 {
53 open(FILE2, ">>c:/Inetpub/wwwroot/cgi-bin/datafiles/formdata2.txt");
54 $Order = "";
55 $Order .= "$FORM{ 'lname' }";
56 $Order .= " ";
57 $Order .= "$FORM{ 'fname' }";
58 $Order .= " ";
59 $Order .= "$FORM{ 'email' }";
60 $Order .= " ";
61 $Order .= "$FORM{ 'item1' }";
62 $Order .= " ";
63 $Order .= "$FORM{ 'Q1' }";
64 $Order .= " ";
65 $Order .= "$FORM{ 'item2' }";
66 $Order .= " ";
67 $Order .= "$FORM{ 'Q2' }";
68 $Order .= " ";
69 $Order .= "$FORM{ 'item3' }";
70 $Order .= " ";
71 $Order .= "$FORM{ 'Q3' }";
72 $Order .= "\n";

73 print FILE2 $Order;
```

```
74 close (FILE2);
75 }
76 sub ParseForm
77 {
78 # Read the input form to a buffer
79 read (STDIN, $buffer, $ENV{ 'CONTENT_LENGTH' } );

80 # Split the buffer into pairs
81 @pairs = split(/&/, $buffer);

82 # For each pair in the pair array, split it into name and value
83 foreach $pair (@pairs)
84 {
85  ($name, $value) =
86     split(/=/, $pair);

87  # Translate plus and percentage signs
88  $value =~ tr/+/ /;
89  $value =~ s/%([a-fA-F0-9][a-fA-F0-9])/pack("C", hex($1))/eg;

90  # Add the value under the corresponding name
91  $FORM{ $name } .= $value;
92  }
93 }
```

Listing 7.8   Parse the form data and write the data to disk (SaveForm.pl).

We examine how the above program works. We first take a look of the main program.

Line **3** calls the subroutine `ParseForm`. This subroutine reads the Form data from CGI and parses the data. Later we explain this subroutine in lines **76** through **93**.

Lines **6–13** are an if-else statement. It states that if the server cannot open the disk data file for overwriting, then it displays an error message; otherwise calls the `WriteRecord` subroutine. The `WriteRecord` subroutine overwrites a disk file with the current record. It is programmed in lines **27** through **50**.

Lines **14–21** are another if-else statement. It states that if the server cannot open the disk data file for appending a record then it displays an error message; otherwise calls the `AddRecord` subroutine. The `AddRecord` subroutine appends the current record to the existing file. It is programmed in lines **51–75**.

The rest of the main program is straightforward. Now we examine the three subroutines one by one.

We first take a look at the `ParseForm` subroutine. Line **79** reads the STDIN data from CGI to `$buffer` with the length specified in the environment variable `$ENV{'CONTENT_LENGTH'}`.

Line **81** splits the text string into small string pieces and put these string pieces into the array `@pairs`. Note that each name-value pair in the text box of the Form are separated by character & as you can see from the operation on the Web page specified in lines **29–40** of Listing 7.2.

Lines **83–92** are a **foreach-loop**. This loop processes each small string pieces, which is placed in $pair. Lines **85–86** split the string piece in $pair into a pair, and put the two parts of the pair into $name and $value, respectively. Remember that the text box name and the component of the text box of the Form are separated by character "=".

Line **88** restores spaces for the string which is the component of the text box. Remember, all spaces are represented by + in the STDIN format.

Line **89** accomplishes the other part of the decoding by substituting all hexadecimal values with corresponding characters. The sentence,

```
$value=~ s/%[a-fA-F0-9][a-fA-F0-9]/pack("C", hex($1))/eg;
```

converts %xx from hex numbers to alphanumeric characters, and uses Perl's pack function to convert this array into a character string. An in-depth technical explanation of any type of encoding is beyond the scope of this book. You may use these translation and substitute statements in Perl to parse any Forms sent through HTTP.

Line **91** adds the string in $value to the associative array FORM indexed by $name. After this subroutine, the associative array FORM contains the data in the ASCII format. These data are stored in the name-value pair.

Now we take a look at the subroutine WriteRecord in lines **27–50**. Line **29** opens the text data file. Note that this file is to be overwritten. Line **30** defines a variable to hold data.

Line **31** adds the string associated to $FORM{ 'lname' }. Remember that the name (lname) of the text box in the Form is specified in line **46** of Listing 7.2. Also, the value of this text box has been extracted by the subroutine ParseForm (line 91). Line **32** adds a space. At this point, the Perl program has created a field for the entire record to be written to the disk file. Note that, in this case, this space can be used for other software to separate fields after retrieving the disk file.

Lines **33–47** perform the similar task to create all the fields for the record. Line 48 writes the entire record to the disk file. Finally, line **49** closes this file.

The subroutine AddRecord in lines **51–75** performs the similar task as the subroutine WriteRecord does, except for appending the record to the existing records in the file. Note that line **53** opens the file for appending, and line **72** adds a new line character, indicating the end of this new record.

After the execution of the given Perl program several times, you may check the execution result by performing two steps.

1. Download the two files.

   ```
   c:/Inetpub/wwwroot/cgi-bin/datafiles/formdata1.txt and
   c:/Inetpub/wwwroot/cgi-bin/datafiles/formdata2.txt
   ```

   Using Notepad to open the two data files, you can see only one record in the formdata1.txt file which is what you have inputted last time, but you can see many records in the formdata2.txt file which are accumulated by the program.

2. Use Excel to open these ASCII data files. Since the Perl program has assembled the records on the disk using spaces and new lines, Excel can

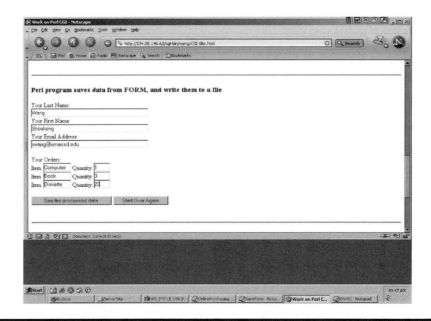

Figure 7.3   Web page triggers the Perl program in Listing 7.8.

"understand" these records and read them into the spreadsheet. You can find that each of the fields occupies a cell, and each of the records occupies a row. Actually, almost any business application software can "understand" these ASCII files. This demonstrates that these ASCII data files can be processed further through other business applications software, for example, database management systems, spreadsheet, and legacy systems.

Figure 7.3 shows the Web page that triggers the Perl program in Listing 7.8. Figure 7.4 shows the data submitted by the Web page retrieved by Microsoft Excel. Note that you need to select [Delimited] option and use [Space] as the delimiter (see Listing 7.8, Lines 56, 58 and so on) in Microsoft Excel.

7.5.16   Interaction between the User of the Client and the Server

In this example, we will learn how Perl can implement a direct communication between the client user and the server. By triggering the following Perl program, the user is allowed to send comments through the Form, and receive the post that contains all the comments the server has received thus far, including the present user's comments. The following program performs multiple tasks:

1. It receives and parses the comments from the user.
2. Retrieves the chat room Web page that contains comments received thus far.
3. Cumulates the comments on the server's disk in the chat room HTML document.
4. Sends all the summarized comments in HTML back to the user.

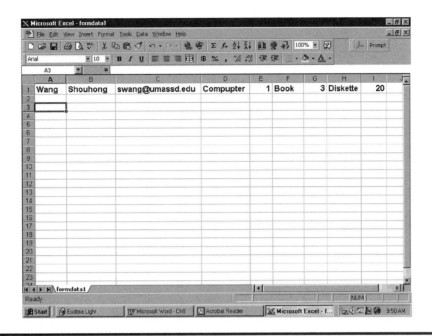

Figure 7.4   Using Microsoft Excel to view the data submitted by the client.

Listing 7.9a is the Perl program, and Listing 7.9b is the HTML program (chat. html) for the chat room Web page.

```perl
1 #!C:/Perl-5.6/bin/perl.exe

2 # This is an example of chat room

3 &ParseForm();

4 print "Content-type: text/html\n\n";

5 open(CHAT, "c:/Inetpub/wwwroot/cgi-bin/datafiles/chat.html");

6 while(<CHAT>)
7 {
8 push(@chat, $_);
9 }
10 close(CHAT);

11 open(CHAT, ">c:/Inetpub/wwwroot/cgi-bin/datafiles/chat.html");
12 $item = "";

13 foreach $line (@chat)
14 {
15  if ($line ne "<!-- special comment line -->\n")
16  {
17    print CHAT $line;
18  }
19  else
20  {
21    print CHAT $line;
```

```
22     $item .= "\n\n";
23     $item .= "Name: $FORM{ 'name' }\n";
24  $item .= "<A HREF=\"mailto:$FORM{ 'email' }\">  $FORM{ 'email' }</A>\n";
25     $item .= "<BR>\n";
26     $item .= "Comments:\n";
27     $item .= "<BR>\n";

28     while (<$FORM{ 'comments' }>)
29     {
30     $FORM{ 'comments' } =~ s/\r/\n<BR>/;
31     }

32     $item .= $FORM{ 'comments' };
33     $item .= "\n\n<HR>\n";

34     print CHAT $item;
35   }
36 }
37 close (CHAT);

38 open (CHAT, "c:/Inetpub/wwwroot/cgi-bin/datafiles/chat.html");
39 while (<CHAT>)
40 {
41  print $_;
42 }

43 close (CHAT);
44 exit;

45 sub ParseForm
46 {
47 # Read the input form to a buffer
48 read (STDIN, $buffer, $ENV{ 'CONTENT_LENGTH' } );

49 # Split the buffer into pairs
50 @pairs = split(/&/, $buffer);
51 # For each pair in the pair array, split it into name and value
52 foreach $pair (@pairs)
53 {
54  ($name, $value) = split(/=/, $pair);
55
56 # Translate plus and percentage signs
57  $value =~ tr/+/ /;
58  $value =~ s/%([a-fA-F0-9][a-fA-F0-9])/pack("C", hex($1))/eg;

59 # Screen out comment lines by substituting with spaces
60  $value =~ s/<!--(.|\n)*-->//g;

61 # Add the value under the corresponding name
62  $FORM{ $name } .= $value;
63 }
64 }
```

Listing 7.9a   Perl program of dialogue between the client user and server (ChatRoom.pl).

```
 1 <HTML>
 2 <HEAD>
 3 <TITLE>Chat Room</TITLE>
 4 <BODY BGCOLOR="Leaden">

 5 <H2>View the Summarized Comments </H2>

 6 <!-- special comment line -->
 7 <P>
 8 <A HREF="Perl-Site.html">Back to submit data</A>
 9 <P>
10 </BODY>
11 </HTML>
```

Listing 7.9b HTML program (chat.html). Used by the Perl program in Listing 7.9a.

We examine how the programs in Listing 7.9a and Listing 7.9b work. We first take a look at the Perl program in Listing 7.9a. Line **3** calls the subroutine `ParseForm` which is specified from line **45** to line **64**. This subroutine is exactly the same as that we have learned in Listing 7.8, except for line **60** which is to screen out the comment lines in the HTML document. The reason of line 60 is because this program uses a specific HTML comment line for a special purpose, as will be discussed later.

Line **5** opens the disk file of the HTML program. The original HTML program is shown in Listing 7.9b. When the HTML program is read by a Web browser, a Web page will display all comments for the user. As shown in Listing 7.9b, originally, this Web page contains no comments. However, once a user sends comment notes through a Form to the server and triggers the Perl program in Listing 7.9a, the Perl program will add the comment note to the HTML program. As a result, the updated Web page will contain the user's comment note. Note line 6 in Listing 7.9b.

Return to Listing 7.9a. Lines **6–9** are the while-loop to read the HTML program and add every line of the document to the array `@chat`. Line **10** closes the disk file.

Line **11** opens this disk file again, but this time it is for writing.

Line **12** defines a working storage to hold a string.

Lines **13–36** are a foreach-loop to process each line of the HTML document. For each line, there is an if-else statement to process it. Lines **15–18** checks if the current line is an HTML comment line in the HTML document, then copies it and writes it to the updated HTML document. Lines **19–35** are the else-sub-statement which is executed when a special HTML comment line is encountered. Now we turn to Listing 7.9b. Line **6** is the only comment line in this HTML program. It indicates the start of summarized comments. This tells the Perl program that new comments should be added right after this line.

We return to Listing 7.9a. Line **21** writes the HTML comment line to the updated HTML document. Lines **22–35** add new comments to the current HTML document. Line **23** adds new user's name. Remember that this user's name is obtained through the `ParseForm` subroutine from the submitted Form.

Line **24** adds a new "`mailto`" line to the HTML document. Line **24** shows that To print a quotation mark " to the dynamic Web page, you must use \" in the print sentence since quotation marks are used to quote the entire print sentence.

Lines **26–32** add new user's comment notes to the HTML document. Note that lines **28–31** replace the carriage return character \r with a new line. This is because the Web browser does not recognize \r which is used in typing for a new line.

Line **34** writes the new comment notes to the HTML document. The foreach-loop is still continuing if there are old comment notes in the HTML document.

Line **38** opens the HTML document again. This time it is for reading. Lines **39–42** implement the standard output and print the HTML document to CGI. The CGI then transmitted HTML document to the client user who requests the Perl program. As a result, the summarized comments including the new one are displayed on the user's screen.

7.5.17   Example of Web-Based Business Application Using Perl

In this subsection, we present an example of Web-based business application. The following four programs or data files implement the application. The first HTML document (Listing 7.10) is the home page. It allows the client to input a password to get into the system. It triggers the first Perl program (see Welcome.pl in Listing 7.11) to check the password against the data file which holds the valid passwords (see passwords.txt in Listing 7.12). If the password is valid, then the Perl program sends the second HTML document to the client (see Order.html in Listing 7.13). Note the difference between the two HTML documents. The first one can be accessed openly through the URL, and the second one is generated by the Perl program depending upon a certain condition.

The client can interact with the second HTML document, and place an order. This HTML document in turn triggers a Perl program, called OrderProcess.pl which is almost the same as the Perl program in Listing 7.8. The reader can write it readily to complete the application.

```
<HTML>
<HEAD>
<TITLE> Welcome Page </TITLE>
</HEAD>
<BODY>
<FORM ACTION="Welcome.pl" METHOD=POST>
Your Password: <BR>
<INPUT TYPE=TEXT NAME="pw" SIZE=10> <BR>
<INPUT TYPE=SUBMIT VALUE="Submit Password">
<INPUT TYPE=RESET VALUE="Reset">
</FORM></BODY></HTML>
```

Listing 7.10   Home Page of the application example (Home.html).

```
#!C:/Perl-5.6/bin/perl.exe
print "Content-type: text/html\n\n";

&ReadForm();
&PasswordChecking();
if ($Failure==0)
 {&PullOrderForm};
exit;

sub PullOrderForm {
open(OrderForm,
 "c:/Inetpub/wwwroot/cgi-bin/datafiles/Order.html");
while (<OrderForm>)
 { print $_; }
close (OrderForm);
}

sub PasswordChecking {

 print "<html><body>\n";
   $Failure = 1;
   $Password = $FORM{ 'pw' };
    if (!$Password) {
    print "<h1>Please enter your password ...</h1>\n";
 }

 open(FILE1,
 "c:/Inetpub/wwwroot/cgi-bin/datafiles/passwords.txt");

  if(!open(FILE1,
"c:/Inetpub/wwwroot/cgi-bin/datafiles/passwords.txt"))
 {
print "<h2> The server has a problem. Please try later ... </h2>\n";
 }

 while ($LegalUser = <FILE1>)
 {
 chop $LegalUser;
 if ($Password eq $LegalUser)
   { $Failure = 0; }
 }
 close (FILE1);

 if ($Failure == 1)
  { print "<h1>Sorry! Your Password is invalid.</h1>\n";
  }
 print "</html></body>\n";
}

sub ReadForm
{
 read (STDIN, $memory, $ENV{ 'CONTENT_LENGTH' } );
 @pairs = split(/&/, $memory);
 foreach $pair (@pairs)
 {
```

```
   ($name, $value) = split(/=/, $pair);
   $value =~ tr/+/ /;
   $value =~ s/%([a-fA-F0-9][a-fA-F0-9])/pack("C", hex($1))/eg;
   $FORM{ $name } .= $value;
  }
}
```

Listing 7.11   Perl program to check password (Welcome.pl).

```
12345
23456
34567
45678
```

Listing 7.12   Data file that holds valid passwords (passwords.txt).

```
<HTML>
<HEAD>
<TITLE> Order Form </TITLE>
</HEAD>
<BODY>
<H2>Welcome to ABC Company! Please Place Your Order</H2>
<FORM ACTION="OrderProcess.pl" METHOD=POST>
Your Name: <BR>
<INPUT TYPE=TEXT NAME="lname" SIZE=50> <BR>
Your Email Address: <BR>
<INPUT TYPE=TEXT NAME="email" SIZE=50> <BR><BR>
Your Orders: <BR>
Item:    <INPUT TYPE=TEXT NAME="Item" SIZE=10>
Quantity:  <INPUT TYPE=TEXT NAME="Quantity" SIZE=5> <BR>
<INPUT TYPE=SUBMIT VALUE="Order">
<INPUT TYPE=RESET VALUE="Reset">
</FORM></BODY></HTML>
```

Listing 7.13   Dynamic HTML document (Order.html) sent by Welcome.pl.

7.6   Debugging

Debugging Perl programs is a little different from that for other languages as both client and server are involved. Since Perl is interpreter, the debugging task is not difficult. When you run a Perl program from the client PC, you will see the CGI running error messages on the screen if the program has errors.

Common syntax errors are:

- Typos of misspelling a word.
- Omitting a symbol (e.g., missing one side of parenthesis).
- Violating format.
- Using an undefined user-defined variable.

Logical errors or runtime errors often occur when the computer performs wrong operations or not as directed by the user. To debug logical errors, you should use data samples to test the program based on the output of the program.

1. Exercise every possible option to check the computer outputs to see if the program does only as you direct it. if-statements are commonly examined to find possible options.
2. If a program is "dead," you must terminate it by closing the Web page. This is more likely caused by a "dead" loop. You should check while loop and if statements.
3. When you debug Perl as server-side programs, you need to re-upload your programs to the server. If you use your personal server on PC, you need to re-start the server once you make changes to the program.

7.7 Framework of CGI Implemented Web-Based Applications for Electronic Commerce

In this section, we study the essentials of Perl for Web-based applications. We have learned that Perl programs can play significant role in processing and storing the data submitted from the client user and printing a HTML document for the user. The framework for this approach is depicted in Figure 7.5.

As shown in Figure 7.5, the user on the client side sends a Form through the SUBMIT type, POST method and ACTION to trigger a Perl program on the server. The data contained in the Form are then transmitted by the Internet through HTTP, and received by the server. In the Windows platforms, Internet information service (IIS) implements the CGI. The CGI then triggers the Perl program specified in ACTION of the Form. The Perl program processes these data. Usually, a Perl program for the data processing reads or writes disk files on the server. These data files must be in the ASCII format.

According to this framework, the disk files in the ASCII format is the interface between Perl programs and other business application software on the

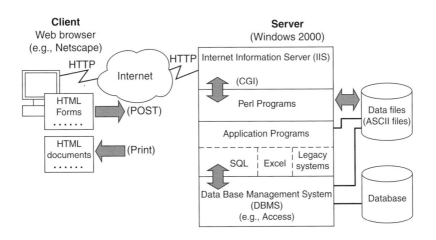

Figure 7.5   Framework of CGI implemented Web-based applications.

server. Business application software includes database manipulations (SQL), spreadsheet data processing (e.g., Excel), legacy systems (e.g., COBOL), and so on. However, these business applications exchange information with the Perl programs through the intermediate disk data files, instead of communicating with the Perl programs directly. Apparently, this framework is simple, but not efficient for real-time online processing (e.g., online database query).

To overcome the disadvantages of this simple model, some versions of Perl have database interface (**DBI**) or database driver (**DBD**) to interact with relational databases directly. On the database side, the database management system must have its part for the interface. For example, Microsoft Access can have an interface with Perl if it comes with **Win32::ODBC** driver. Since there are many different platforms for databases, it is hard to find a single driver on the Perl side that can fit all kinds of databases. Nowadays, new server-side technologies such as Java and .NET for Web-based business applications have become popular, while many CGI programs are still running as e-commerce legacy systems.

7.8   Self-Review Exercise

1.   Check the settings of a server with the Windows platform for Perl programming.
2.   Download Perl from ActivePerl. Make sure you read the copyright agreements before downloading.
3.   Read the following Perl program, and fill in the blanks.

```
 1 #!C:/Perl-5.6/bin/_____
 2 # This is an example of saving comments from a submitted form
 3 &ParseForm()_____
 4 print "Content-type: _____/html_____";
 5 _____ "<HTML>\n<BODY>\n\n";
 6 if (!open(FILE1, ">c:/Inetpub/wwwroot/cgi-bin/ _____"))
 7 {
 8 print "<H2>A new file cannot open on the server ... </H2>\n";
 9 }
10 else
11 {
12 &KeepRecord();
13 }
14 if (!open(FILE2, ">>c:/Inetpub/wwwroot/cgi-bin/_____"))
15 {
16 print "<H2>The file cannot open on the server ... </H2>\n";
17 }
18 else
19 {
20 &CumulRecord();
21 }
22 print "<H3>Your order is being processed.</H3>\n";
23 print "<H3>Thank you for ordering from ABC.COM ! </H3>\n";
24 _____ "</BODY></HTML>\n";
25 exit;
```

```
26 sub KeepRecord
27 {
28 open(FILE1, ">c:/Inetpub/wwwroot/cgi-bin/custform1.txt");
29 $Order = "";
30 $Order .= "$FORM{ 'lname' }";
31 $Order .= " ";
32 $Order .= "$FORM{ 'fname' }";
33 $Order .= " ";
34 $Order .= "$FORM{ 'email' }";
35 $Order .= " ";
36 $Order .= "$FORM{ 'item1' }";
37 $Order .= " ";
38 $Order .= "$FORM{ 'Q1' }";
39 $Order .= " ";
40 $Order .= "$FORM{ 'item2' }";
41 $Order .= " ";
42 $Order .= "_____";
43 $Order .= " ";
44 $Order .= "$FORM{ 'item3' }";
45 $Order .= " ";
46 $Order .= "$FORM{ 'Q3' }";
47 print FILE1 _____;
48 close (FILE1);
49 }

50 sub CumulRecord
51 {
52 open(FILE2, ">>c:/Inetpub/wwwroot/cgi-bin/custform2.txt");
53 $Order = "";
54 $Order .= "$FORM{ 'lname' }";
55 $Order .= " ";
56 $Order .= "$FORM{ 'fname' }";
57 $Order .= " ";
58 $Order .= "$FORM{ 'email' }";
59 $Order .= " ";
60 $Order .= "$FORM{ 'item1' }";
61 $Order .= " ";
62 $Order .= "_____";
63 $Order .= " ";
64 $Order .= "$FORM{ 'item2' }";
65 $Order .= " ";
66 $Order .= "$FORM{ 'Q2' }";
67 $Order .= " ";
68 $Order .= "$FORM{ 'item3' }";
69 $Order .= " ";
70 $Order .= "$FORM{ 'Q3' }";
71 $Order .= "\n";
72 print FILE2 $Order;
73 close (_____);
74 }
75 _____ ParseForm
76 {
77 # Read the input form to a buffer
78 read (_____, $buffer, $_____{ 'CONTENT_LENGTH' } );
79 # Split the buffer into pairs
```

```
80 @tuples = split(/_____/, $buffer);
81 # For each pair in the pair array, split it into name and value
82 foreach $tuple (@_____)
83 {
84  ($name, $value) =
85    split(/=/, $tuple);

86  # Translate plus and percentage signs
87  $value =~ tr/+/ /;
88  $value =~ s/____([a-fA-F0-9][a-fA-F0-9])/pack("C", _____)/eg;
89  # Substitute the comment lines with spaces
90  $value =~ s/<!--(.|\n)*-->//g;
91  # Add the value under the corresponding name
92  $FORM{ $name } .= $value;
93  }
94 }
```

4. Read the following Perl program that uses the ParseForm subroutine in the previous question, and fill in the blanks.

```
 1 #_____C:/Perl-5.6/bin/perl.exe
 2 # This is an example of saving data from a submitted form
 3 _____ParseForm();
 4 print "Content-type: text/_____\n\n";
 5 open(_____, "c:/Inetpub/_____ /cgi-bin/note.html");
 6 while(<FORUM>)
 7 {
 8 push(@forum, $_);
 9 }
10 close(FORUM);
11 open(FORUM, ">c:/Inetpub/wwwroot/cgi-bin/_____");
12 $item = "";
13 foreach $line (@forum)
14 {
15  if ($line ne "<!-- comments -->\n")
16  {
17    print FORUM $line;
18  }
19  else
20  {
21    print FORUM $line;
22    $item .= "\n\n";
23    $item .= "_____: $FORM{ 'name' }\n";
24 $item .= "<<A HREF=\"mailto:$FORM{ 'email' }\">$FORM{ 'email' }</A>>\n";
25    $item .= "<BR>\n";
26    $item .= "Comments:\n";
27    $item .= "<BR>\n";
28    while (<$FORM{ 'comments' }>)
29    {
30    $FORM{ '_____' } =~ s/\r/\n<BR>/;
31    }
32    $item .= $FORM{ 'comments' };
33    $item .= "\n\n<HR>\n";
34    print FORUM $item;
35  }
36 }
```

```
37 close (_____);
38 open (FORUM, "c:/Inetpub/wwwroot/cgi-bin/_____");

39 while (<FORUM>)
40 {
41  print $_;
42 }
43 _____ (FORUM);
44 exit;
```

5. Develop a Web-based application project by using Perl and Excel. The project has a Web page with a form. On the client side, the user can submit the form with inputted data. On the server side, the submitted data is stored and cumulated on a disk file. This disk file is further processed by Excel in batch.

6. Develop a Web-based application project by using Perl and Access. The project has a Web page with a form. On the client side, the user can submit the form with inputted data. On the server side, the submitted data (e.g., queries for the database) are stored and cumulated on a disk file. This disk file is further processed by Access in batch. The processing results (e.g., query results from the database) are stored on another disk file. The user on the server side can send the processing results through a Web page.

7. Using Perl, implement the following scenario.

   A. The company has its Web site (home page in HTML) on the server, and allows any clients to access the Web site using its URL.
   B. The home page is a log-in page that asks the client to enter user-ID (e-mail address) and password. After the client enters the user-ID and password and clicks the log-in button, the server will check the user-ID and password against a disk file to see whether the user is permitted to enter the system.
   C. The client will receive a sorry message if the user-ID and password do not match. Otherwise, the client will see an online auction window with a greeting message and the auction item image. The dynamic Web page is generated by Perl.
   D. After the client enters the online auction by clicking a button, a window that tells the current highest bid will show up. The client is allowed to enter his or her bid.
   E. After bidding, the server will record the bidding data on the disk.
   F. Upon the closing time, the server will send the auction winning result to all bidders.

8. Discuss the advantages and disadvantages of Perl.

Appendix 7.1   Installation of ActivePerl on the Server with the Windows Platform

The following install instructions are based on Windows 2000. For other Windows operating systems, the instructions could vary. Search the Internet to find out specific instructions for your operating system.

1. Download and install Perl.

    A. Use a Web browser (e.g., Netscape) to access the Web site of **Active-State** (<http://www.ActiveState.com> at the time of writing this chapter). Download the most recent version of ActivePerl. Before downloading, read the copyright agreement.
    B. If the downloading is successful, you should see an icon "ActivePerl-5...." on the desktop screen. The number appearing on the icon is the version of ActivePerl.
    C. Click the ActivePerl icon to install Perl on C drive. Follow the instructions displayed by the ActivePerl installation procedure.
    D. If the installation succeeds, you should have a folder of Perl on C drive, for example, `C:/Perl5.6`.

2. Create a folder for your CGI programs and define its properties.

    A. A Web server has its default folder for all the Web sites. In our case (Windows 2000), the default folder is named `C:/.../wwwroot` . For instance, the server we work on is named `Charlton2000`, and if you put a Web page `MyWeb.html` into this folder at `C:/Inetpub/wwwroot/MyWeb.html` then the URL of this Web page is <http://Charlton2000/MyWeb.html>. A server can be set in such a way that the home Web page is placed in a default folder and represents the Web site (e.g., `http://Charlton2000`), but the home page must be named `index.html` as the default name. The system manager of the server will tell you more about this.

Usually, CGI programs should be put into a single folder. By common practice, this folder is named `cgi-bin` . Accordingly, create a folder named `cgi-bin` within the Web server default folder for Web pages; that is, `C:/Inetpub/wwwroot/cgi-bin`.

    B. Define the cgi-bin folder's properties.

Click the cgi-bin folder using the right button of the mouse, and bring the Properties window up.

Click the "`Web Sharing`" tag and make sure "`Default Web Site`" in the text box is named "`Share on.`"

Click the "`Sharing`" tag in the Properties window, and click "`Permission`" button. You have "`Share Permission`" window now. Click the "`Add`" button to add any person and group who may share this folder. For learning and practicing, you may want to add as many persons and groups as you like to share this folder. Make sure you define the permissions such as "`Allow to Change,`" "`Allow to Read,`" "`Allow to Write,`" and so on, in the "`Permission`" sub-window.

Go back to the "`Properties`" window, click tag "`Security`" and define the security for the folder. You may want to add as many persons and groups for this category using the "`Add`" button. Then define permissions such as

"Allow Full Control," "Allow to Modify," "Allow to Read," "Allow to Write," and so on, in the "Permission" sub-window.

3. Configure Microsoft IIS to support Perl.

   A. Click Start, Programs, Administrative tools, and Computer management, and bring the Microsoft Management Console tree up.

   B. From the tree display on the left, click "Service and applications" to expand the leaf and find "Internet Information Services." Click it using the right button of the mouse, and bring IIS Properties window up.

   C. Click the "Internet Interface Service" tag, and click the "Edit" button under "Master Properties." This opens WWW Service Mater Properties window.

   D. Click the "Home Directory" tag, and click the "Configuration" button. This opens the Application Configuration window.

   E. Click the "App Mapping" tag, and click the "Add" button. This brings the "Add/Edit Application Extension Mapping" window up.

   F. To run Perl as a CGI application, type full path to Perl.exe followed by %s %s in the "Executable" text box, for example, C:/Perl5.6/bin/Perl.exe%s%s. When a Perl program is executed, the first %s will be replaced by the full path to the program, and the second %s will be replaced by the program parameters.

   G. In the "Extension" field, type .pl (or whatever extension you want to use).

   H. Check the "Script engine" box, and click the "OK" button. Now, in the "App Mapping" window, you can check if the extension and executable path have been set correctly.

   I. Click the "Apply" or "OK" button to dismiss all dialog windows and properties sheets, and close the IIS Internet service manager.

4. Test the installation.

To test whether the Perl on the server works, use Notepad to edit the simplest Perl program in Listing 7.1, and save to the cgi-bin folder on the server. Remember, you must save this program as a file with the extension name .pl (e.g., SimplestPerl.pl, not .txt file defaulted by Notepad). Open a Web browser (e.g., Netscape) on a client PC, and type the URL of the Perl program (e.g., http://Charlton2000/cgi-bin/SimplestPerl.pl). You should have the result like Figure 7.2, if Perl has been successfully installed.

Appendix 7.2 Guideline for Server-Side Programming (Perl) Project Report

1. Front page

   Course name
   Title of the project

Group members (names and ID)
Date

2. Text

    Introduction and the purposes of Perl
    Application of HTML and Perl

3. Source code of the HTML and Perl programs.
4. Screen shots of the home Web site and dynamic Web pages that demonstrate the interactions between the client and server.
5. Test data files that are used for the application, inputted by the client, and stored on the server.

Chapter 8

PHP for Web-Based Applications

8.1   Introduction to PHP

PHP script was developed in 1994. Originally it was called Personal home page, and now it is referred to as PHP Hypertext Preprocessor. At first sight, PHP seems like JavaScript and can be embedded in HTML. In fact, PHP script is very similar to Perl and can print dynamic HTML documents as a server-side programming tool. It has been popular for three major reasons: First, PHP is easy to use. Second, PHP is free software. Supported by The Apache Software Foundation <http://www.apache.org>, an open source software development community, PHP can be downloaded for free from The PHP Group at <http://www.php.net>. Third, PHP can be installed on different platforms, including UNIT, Windows, and others.

To build PHP web applications, you need a server to run PHP. You can install a PHP server by using free software packages provided by PHP <http://www.php.org> and Apache <http://www.apache.org>. With a PHP server, you can upload PHP programs to the server and run them though the Internet. However, for novice students, installation of a real server probably is not a pleasant job. Alternatively, it is suggested to download a free software package, called EasyPHP from <http://www.easyphp.org>, to install a personal server on your PC that emulates a real server to test your PHP programs. EasyPHP is easy to install, following the instructions provided by the Web site. After installing EasyPHP on your Windows PC, you can start emulating server on your PC by clicking [Start]-[Programs]-[EasyPHP]. Once EasyPHP

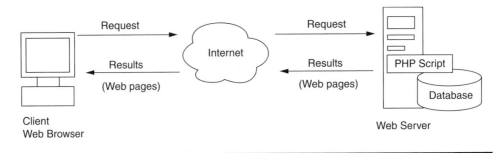

Figure 8.1   Execution cycle of a PHP program.

is launched, you can see the EasyPHP Window Pane. Click on the logo icon, and a menu allows you to start and stop the server and to pull up the local Web which is supposed to be <http://localhost/>. Three things you need to know to use EasyPHP for programming PHP on your PC. First, your PHP programs must be placed in a folder C:\ProgramFiles\EasyPHP\www. Second, your PHP program must have extension name [.php]. Third, to open the PHP program, you must use the EasyPHP menu to load the local Web and then type the URL in the Web browser window (such as http://localhost/ HelloWorld.php). The screenshots of the examples in this chapter are all created by EasyPHP.

In terms of the roles of Web applications, PHP is not very different from Java servlets, Perl, ASP.NET, and other server-side programs. A general process for a Web application supported by PHP is shown in Figure 8.1, and is described as follows: The user on the client side sends a request, which might include data, over the Internet to the server. The request and data received by the Web server are used as input for a PHP script. The PHP program processes the request and generates an HTML Web page. The Web server then sends the Web page back to the client side. This dynamic Web page is shown on the client computer by the Web browser.

8.2   Structure of a PHP Script

We present a simplest PHP script, called HelloWorld.php, in Listing 8.1. As usual, the line numbers are added for explanation, and should not be included in the program.

```
1    <html>
2    <body>
3    <?php print("Hello, PHP World!");
4    ?>
5    </body>
6    </html>
```

Listing 8.1   HelloWorld.php.

If you install the PHP system correctly, the execution result of Listing 8.1 is like Figure 8.2.

Figure 8.2   Execution result of Listing 8.1.

Instead of using `<?` and `?>`, you might use `<script>` tag for PHP script, as shown in Listing 8.2.

```
<html>
<body>
<script language="PHP">
    print("Hello again, PHP World!");
</script>
</body>
</html>
```

Listing 8.2   Use `<script>` tag for Listing 8.1.

As shown in Listing 8.1 and 8.2, PHP seems to be similar to JavaScript, but actually PHP may not be embedded within HTML. It can print HTML document as Perl, Java Servlets, and ASP.NET do, since it is a server-side programming tool. Listing 8.3 shows the PHP script that produces the same result as Listing 8.1 does. In the remaining part of this chapter, we use this format for all PHP programs.

```
<?php
    print("<html><body>");
    print("Again, hello, PHP World!");
    print("</body></html>");
?>
```

Listing 8.3   Alternative to Listing 8.1.

Listing 8.4 shows an example of PHP that displays the current date in several formats, as shown in Figure 8.3.

```
1 <?php
2     print("<html><body>");

3 // This is to show the day of month
4     $day=date("d");
5     print("Day=$day");
6     print("<br>");

7 // This is to show the current month of year
8     $month=date("M");
9     print("Month=$month");
10    print("<br>");
```

Figure 8.3   Execution result of Listing 8.4.

```
11 // This is to show today date
12    print(date("F d, Y"));
13    print("</body></html>");
14 ?>
```

Listing 8.4   PHP program displaying current date in several formats (date.php).

The format of a PHP program is quite similar to Perl. A PHP statement ends with a semicolon (;). // indicates a comment line. The first character of a variable name must be a dollar sign ($). In Listing 8.4, $day and $month are variables. PHP is a function-oriented language. The general syntax of a PHP built-in function is:

function_name(arguments).

In Listing 8.4, print() is a built-in function, and its argument is a string. date() is also a built-in function, and its argument is the format of the date, including many formats such as d for numerical day of month, D for day of week, M for current month in short form, F for current month in long form, m for current month in number, Y current year, etc.

Other commonly used PHP functions and their arguments include:

- rand (*low limit, high limit*) to generate random numbers in the defined range.
- substr (*string, start position, end position*) for extracting a portion of the characters from the defined string.
- trim (*string*) for removing blanks from the beginning and end of the defined string.

Later we will learn that the formats of arithmetic operations, if-statement, for-loop, and user-defined functions are all similar to that of JavaScript.

8.3   Web Page to Trigger PHP

In this section, we present an example to show how PHP program makes a response to a request sent by a Form. Listing 8.5 is HTML for a Web page. On the Web page, the user is allowed to input data, includeing delivery weight, days needed for transportation, and location, and send the Form to the server to find out the delivery charges. Listing 8.6 is a PHP program that makes a response to the Form input.

```
 1 <HTML>
 2 <HEAD>
 3 <TITLE> Delivery Charge Calculation </TITLE>

 4 </HEAD>

 5 <BODY>
 6 <H2>Find the delivery charge.</H2>
 7 <FORM ACTION="CalCharge.php" METHOD="POST">
 8 <P> Input the weight of package for the delivery:
 9 <INPUT TYPE=TEXT SIZE=10 NAME="Weight"> lb<BR>
10 </P>
11 <P>Input the days needed for transportation:
12 <INPUT TYPE=TEXT SIZE=10 NAME="Days"><BR>
13 </P>
14 <P>Choose the destination State:</P>
15 <INPUT TYPE=RADIO NAME="State"
16    VALUE="Yes" checked>In State<BR>
17 <INPUT TYPE=RADIO NAME="State" VALUE="No">Out State
18 <BR></P>
19 <INPUT TYPE="SUBMIT" VALUE="Find Out Delivery Charge">
20 <INPUT TYPE="RESET" VALUE="Reset">
21 </FORM>
22 </BODY>
23 </HTML>
```

Listing 8.5   Web page to trigger a PHP program (Request.html).

```
 1 <?php
 2 print("<html><body>");
 3 print("Thank you for your request!");

 4 $Weight=$_POST["Weight"];
 5 $Days=$_POST["Days"];
 6 $State=$_POST["State"];

 7 $Charge=CalculateCharge($State, $Weight, $Days);

 8 print("The delivery charge is: $ $Charge");
 9 print("</body></html>");

10 function CalculateCharge($ST, $WT, $DS) {
11  if ($ST=="Yes")
12   { $CH=$WT * $DS * 1; }
13  else
14   { $CH=$WT * $DS * 2; };
15  return($CH);
16  }
17 ?>
```

Listing 8.6   PHP program (CalCharge.php) triggered by the form in Listing 8.5.

This example is quite similar to the example of Listing 3.7 of JavaScript. The difference between JavaScript and PHP in this case is that JavaScript perform calculation on the client side, while the PHP script performs calculation on the server side.

In Listing 8.5, line **7** specifies the action when the user clicks the submit button on the Form. It instructs the server to trigger `CalCharge.php`. Note that, the PHP program and the HTML Web page should be placed in the same folder on the server. Otherwise, you must define the access path here. Line **7** also instructs the method used by the Web browser to send the data back to the server. In PHP `POST` is always used for the method attribute.

In Listing 8.6, lines **4–6** receive the values from the calling Form. Note that, to improve the PHP performance, the PHP version of EasyPHP uses `$_POST` [`"variable_name"`] to receive the input values from the corresponding variables in the Form through the POST method. This rule may not be applied in many other PHP versions where the global variable form `$variable_name` is used directly. Line **7** calls a function for calculation. Lines **10–16** are a user-defined function. The format of user-defined functions is similar to C. Within the function there is an if-else statement in lines **11–14**. We explain them in detail in the following section.

8.3.1   PHP Functions

As discussed   earlier in this chapter, the general syntax of a PHP built-in function is

```
function_name( arguments )
```

The syntax of user-defined function is

```
function function_name( arguments )
  { [actions] ;
    return( argument ); }
```

The location of the user-defined function is not important; in other words, the programmer can place a user-defined function anywhere in the PHP script.

8.3.2   *if-else* Statement

The syntax of if-else statement of PHP is similar to C, that is,

```
if ( [condition] ) { [action_1] ; }
else        { [action_2] ; };
```

Personal home page also provides `if-elseif` controlling which might be confusing for beginners.

8.4   Read Data Files from the Server

Listing 8.7 shows a brief HTML Web page for travelers to check air-ticket prices online.

```
<HTML><BODY>
<FORM ACTION="Airticket.php" METHOD=POST>
<H2>Welcome to Spring Travel Agency</H2>
<INPUT TYPE=SUBMIT VALUE="Check the Prices">
</FORM></BODY></HTML>
```

Listing 8.7   Web page to access air-ticket prices (Travel.html).

Suppose there has been an ASCII file, called air-ticket.txt, on the server disk, as shown in Listing 8.8. The PHP program is suppose to read the disk file and send the data back to the client.

```
New York - Boston
$99.90
Toronto - Las Vegas
$155.50
Halifax - Providence
$109.50
```

Listing 8.8   Text data file (air-tickets.txt) used for Listing 8.9.

The PHP program triggered by Listing 8.7 to access the air-ticket prices is listed in Listing 8.9.

```
 1  <?php
 2  print("<html><body>");
 3  print("<h3>Airticket Price Table</h3>");
 4  $FileName='air-tickets.txt';
 5  $File=fopen($FileName, 'r') or die("Cannot open file!");
 6  print("<table border=1>");

 7  while(!feof($File)) {
 8    $line1=fgets($File, 120);
 9    $line2=fgets($File, 120);
10    print("<tr><td>$line1</td><td>$line2</td></tr>");
11  };

12  fclose($File);
13  print("</table>");
14  print("</body></html>");
15  ?>
```

Listing 8.9   PHP program reads file for password validation (Airticket.php).

In Listing 8.9, line **4** maps the external data file name (on the disk) to the server data file name. Line **5** opens the data file for read-only. It uses the internal data file name for the program. Lines **6** and **13** define a table. Line **7** through **11** are a while-loop. Line **7** means that while the data file has not reached the end, execute the following instructions. For each time of the loop, lines **8–9** read two lines from the disk file, and line **10** prints them into the table. Once the process reaches the end of file, line **12** closes the file. Several important functions are described later in the chapter.

8.4.1 `fopen()` and `fclose()`

PHP uses `fopen()` to open a disk file on the server, and `fclose()` the opened file. The syntax of these functions are:

```
fopen($server data file name, 'open mode');
fclose($internal data file name);
```

Note that, in PHP the server data file name and the internal data file name are different, as shown in Listing 8.9. Where the file open mode could be 'r' for read-only, 'w' for over-write-only, 'r+' for read and write, 'a' for append, and 'a+' for read and append. Function `die()` often follows `fopen()` give instructions when the open process fails.

8.4.2 `feof()` and `fgets()`

Function `feof()` indicates the end of file. Its argument is internal data file name. Function_fget() reads one line from the disk file. Its syntax is:

```
fgets($internal data file name, maximum bytes);
```

8.4.3 `while` Loop

`while` loop implements a loop to execute a set of instructions repeatedly while the specified condition is true. The syntax of `while` loop is:

```
while( condition ) { actions; };
```

The condition could contain operators such as ! for NOT, && for AND, || for OR.

8.5 Write Data Files to the Server and `fputs()`

In this section we show how PHP saves the data sent by a Form and writes them to the server disk. Listing 8.10 is an HTML Web page that contains user's input and triggers a PHP program to save the data. Listing 8.11 is the PHP program that receives the data of the Form and appends them to the disk file.

```
 1 <HTML> <BODY>
 2 <H3> PHP saves data of FORM, and write them to a file </H3>
 3 <FORM ACTION="SaveForm.php" METHOD=POST>
 4 Your Last Name: <BR>
 5 <INPUT TYPE=TEXT NAME="lname" SIZE=50> <BR>
 6 Your First Name: <BR>
 7 <INPUT TYPE=TEXT NAME="fname" SIZE=50> <BR>
 8 Your Email Address: <BR>
 9 <INPUT TYPE=TEXT NAME="email" SIZE=50> <BR><BR>
10 Your Orders: <BR>
11 Item:    <INPUT TYPE=TEXT NAME="item" SIZE=10>
12 Quantity: <INPUT TYPE=TEXT NAME="Quantity" SIZE=5> <BR>
13 <BR>
14 <INPUT TYPE=SUBMIT VALUE="Process the data">
```

```
15 <INPUT TYPE=RESET VALUE="Start Over Again">
16 </FORM>
17 </BODY></HTML>
```

Listing 8.10   Web page for online order (Order.html).

```
 1 <?php
 2 print("<html><body>");
 3 $lname=$_POST["lname"];
 4 $fname=$_POST["fname"];
 5 $email=$_POST["email"];
 6 $item=$_POST["item"];
 7 $Q=$_POST["Quantity"];

 8 $FileName='form-data.txt';
 9 $File=fopen($FileName, 'a+') or die("Cannot open file!");
10 fputs($File, "$lname\n");
11 fputs($File, "$fname\n");
12 fputs($File, "$email\n");
13 fputs($File, "$item\n");
14 fputs($File, "$Q\n");
15 fclose($File);
16 print("<h2>Thank you for sending the order Form!</h2>");
17 print("</body></html>");
18 ?>
```

Listing 8.11   PHP program writes data to disk file (SaveForm.php).

In Listing 8.11, line **3** through line **7** receive the values of these variables from the Form. Line **8** maps the server file name to the external disk file name. After the execution of this program, you will find a disk file named `form-data.txt` in the www folder of the server. Line **9** opens the file in the append and read mode. Line **10** through line **14** write these data to the disk file. Note that \n indicates a new line to separate these date items. Notepad might show an unrecognized character, and Excel will show the new line clearly. `fputs()` writes a record to the file. Its syntax is:

```
fputs($internal file name, "string name");
```

Finally, line **15** closes the file.

8.6   Relay Data through Multiple Forms Using Hidden Fields

You might have noticed that when a PHP program sends a dynamic Web back to the client in response to a Form, the data of the Form might be lost if they are not stored in the server. In cases where several interactions are involved in a process, such as shopping cart, it is important to pass data from one Form to another. However, if the PHP program saves these data to the server every time, then the programming becomes complicated and the execution time becomes long. Here, we present a simple way to relay data through multiple Forms using hidden fields of Form. The user on the client side would not see the data in the hidden fields on the Web page unless its source code is viewed.

The following three programs show how one can relay data through three Forms using hidden fields without interrupting user's view. Listing 8.12 is a Web page Form that allows the user to input e-mail address. Note line **5** that catches the input. The submit button in Listing 8.12 triggers the PHP program in Listing 8.13. The PHP program in Listing 8.13 is similar to Listing 8.9, except for line **14** through line **18**. Line **14** receives the data (e-mail address) sent by the Form in Listing 8.12. Line **15** defines a new Form for sending back to the client. Line **16** defines a hidden field that contains the e-mail address. This e-mail address will not be displayed at this time, but is passed on to the next Form. Line **18** defines a button to trigger another PHP program in Listing 8.14. In Listing 8.14, line **3** receives the e-mail address from the hidden field of the second Form, and line **5** displays it to the client. Note that the hidden field name (`hiddenemail`) should be consistent in all programs; that is, line **5** in Listing 8.12, line **14** and line **16** in Listing 8.13, and line **3** in Listing 8.14 should all use the same hidden field name.

Figure 8.4 illustrates the data relay through Forms using hidden field.

```
1  <HTML><BODY>
2  <FORM ACTION="AirticketEmail.php" METHOD=POST>
3  <H2>Welcome to Spring Travel Agency</H2>
4  <H3>Please enter your email address</H3>
5  <INPUT TYPE=TEXT NAME=hiddenemail SIZE=20><BR><BR>
6  <INPUT TYPE=SUBMIT VALUE="Check the Prices">
7  </FORM></BODY></HTML>
```

Listing 8.12 Web page (Email.html) that triggers a PHP program (AirticketEmail.php).

```
1  <?php
2  print("<html><body>");
3  print("<h3>Airticket Price Table</h3>");
4  $FileName='air-tickets.txt';
5  $File=fopen($FileName, 'r') or die("Cannot open file!");
6  print("<table border=1>");
7  while(!feof($File)) {
8    $line1=fgets($File, 120);
9    $line2=fgets($File, 120);
10   print("<tr><td>$line1</td><td>$line2</td></tr>");
11 };
12 fclose($File);
13 print("</table>");
14 $e=$_POST["hiddenemail"];
15 print("<form action=AirticketConfirm.php method=post>");
16 print("<input type=hidden name=hiddenemail value=$e>");
17 print("Please confirm:<br><br>");
18 print('<input type="submit" value="OK">');
19 print("</form></body></html>");
20 ?>
```

Listing 8.13 PHP program (AirticketEmail.php) that uses hidden field to relay data.

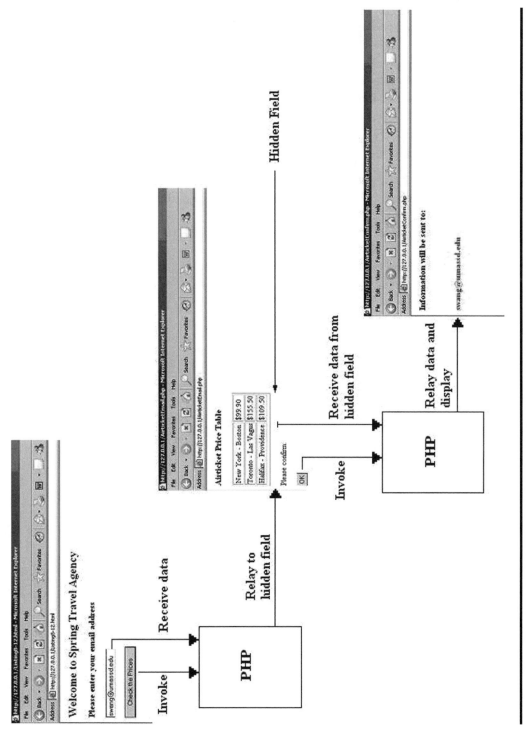

Figure 8.4 Example of data replay through forms using hidden field.

```
1 <?php
2 print("<html><body>");
3 $e=$_POST["hiddenemail"];
4 print("<h3>Information will be sent to:</h3><br><br>");
5 print("<h3><font color=red> $e</h3>");
6 print("</body></html>");
7 ?>
```

Listing 8.14   PHP program (AirticketConfirm.php) that receives and displays the data passed by the hidden field.

8.7   Debugging

Since PHP is simple script, the debugging task is not difficult. When you run a PHP program on your PC, you will see the PHP running error messages on the screen if the program has errors.

Common syntax errors are:

- Typos of misspelling a word.
- Omitting a symbol (e.g., missing one side of parenthesis).
- Violating format.
- Using an undefined user-defined variable.

Logical errors or runtime errors often occur when the computer performs wrong operations or not as you direct it. To debug logical errors, you should use data samples to test the program based on the output of the program.

1. Exercise every possible option to check the computer outputs to see if the program does only as you direct it. if-statements are commonly examined to find possible options.
2. If a program is "dead," you must terminate it by closing the Web page. This is more likely caused by a "dead" loop. You should check `while` loop and `if` statements.

8.8   Self-Review Exercise

1. Fill in the blanks in the following PHP program, and sketch the screen shot of its execution results.

```
1 <?php
2 _____("<html>_____");
3 print("Example");

4 $Weight=$_____["Weight"];
5 $Days=$_POST["Days"];
6 $State=$_POST["State"];

7 $_____=_____($State, $Weight, $Days);

8 print("The payment is: $ $Payment");
```

```
 9 print("</body></html>");

10 function CalPayment($ST, $WT, $DS) {
11  if ($ST=="Yes")
12   { $CH=$WT * $DS * 1; }
13  else
14   { $CH=$WT * $DS * 2; };
15  return($CH);
16  _____
17 _____>
```

2. Fill in the blanks in the following PHP programs, and sketch the screen shots of the page and its execution.

```
 1 <?php
 2 print("<html><body>");
 3 print("<h3>Airticket Price Table</h3>");
 4 $_____='air-tickets.txt';
 5 $File=_____($FileName, 'r') or die("Cannot open file!");
 6 print("<table border=1>");

 7 while(!feof($_____)) {
 8  $line1=fgets($_____, 120);
 9  $line2=_____($_____, 120);
10  print("<tr><td>$line1</td><td>$line2</td></tr>");
11 };
12 fclose($_____);
13 print("_____");
14 print("</body></html>");
15 ?>
```

3. Develop a Web-based application project by using PHP. The project has a Web page with a form. On the client side, the user can submit the form with inputted data. On the server side, the submitted data are stored and cumulated on a disk file. This disk file is further processed by Excel in batch.

4. Develop a Web-based application project by using PHP to pass data through 3 Forms using hidden fields.

5. Using PHP, implement the following scenario:

   A. The company has its Web site (home page in HTML) on the server, and allows any client to access the Web site using its URL.

   B. The home page is a log-in page that asks the client to enter user ID (e-mail address) and password. After the client enters the user ID and password and clicks the log-in button, the server will check the user ID and password against a disk file to see whether the user is permitted to enter the system.

   C. The client will receive a sorry message if the user ID and password do not match. Otherwise, the client will see an online auction window with a greeting message and the auction item image. The dynamic Web page is generated by PHP.

   D. After the client enters the online auction by clicking a button, a window that tells the current highest bid will show up. The client is allowed to enter his or her bid.

E. After bidding, the server will record the bidding data on the disk.

F. Upon the closing time, the server will send the auction winning result to all bidders.

6. Discuss the advantages and disadvantages of PHP, compared with Perl.

Appendix 8.1   Guideline for Server-Side Programming (PHP) Project Report

1. Front page

Course name
Title of the project
Group members (names and ID)
Date

2. Text

Introduction and the purposes of PHP
Application of HTML and PHP

3. Source code of the HTML and PHP programs.

4. Screen shots of the home Web site and dynamic Web pages that demonstrate the interactions between the client and server.

5. Test data files that are used for the application, inputted by the client, and stored on the server.

Chapter 9

ASP.NET for Web-Based Applications

9.1   Introduction to ASP.NET

ASP.NET is a framework for building web applications. Its predecessor is **ASP**. ASP.NET supports all .NET programming languages for web application development, including VB.NET and C#.NET.

To publish ASP.NET web applications on the web, an **IIS** server and **Microsoft .NET Framework** are required. IIS is a component in Windows XP Professional Edition and Windows Server 2003. The step-by-step instructions for installations of IIS are listed in Appendix 9.1. Microsoft .NET Framework is a separate component that is available for free download from the Microsoft ASP.NET site <http://asp.net>. To design and test ASP.NET web applications, **Microsoft Visual Studio 2005** is required. Alternatively, you can download for free from the Microsoft ASP.NET site <http://asp.net> and install **Microsoft Visual Web Developer 2005 Express Edition** on your PC to design and test ASP.NET programs. All ASP.NET programs in this chapter are ASP.NET 2.0 and run in the environment Microsoft Visual Studio 2005 or Microsoft Visual Web Developer 2005 Express Edition.

In terms of the roles of Web applications, ASP.NET does not have much difference from Java servlets, Perl, PHP, and other server-side programs. A general process for a Web application supported by ASP.NET is shown in Figure 9.1, and is described as follows. The user on the client side sends a request, which might includes data, over the Internet to the server. The request and data received by the Web server are used as input for an ASP.NET program. The ASP.NET program processes the request and generates an HTML Web page. The Web server then sends the Web page back to the client side. This dynamic Web page is shown on the client computer by the Web browser.

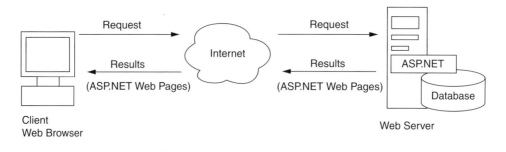

Figure 9.1 Execution cycle of an ASP.NET program.

ASP.NET program files have the extension name `.aspx`, and are called ASP. NET Web pages. Each ASP.NET Web page contains the user interface and the underlying code for the Web application. The user requests or navigates directly to an ASP.NET page to start a Web application. The code used for ASP.NET page can be VB.NET, C#, or others. In this book we assume students have learned HTML and VB.NET before studying this chapter. We use VB.NET for all ASP.NET applications in this book. VB.NET files have the extension name **.vb**, and are called **code-behind** files.

To test an ASP.NET Web application on your PC in the VS2005 (or VWD2005 Express) environment, [Open] the ASP.NET program file, and click [File] on the Menu Bar, and then click [View in Browser]. In case [View in Browser] is not in the [File] menu, it can be added to the menu by clicking [Tools] on the Menu Bar, clicking [Customize], clicking [Commands] tab, and then adding [View in Browser] to the [File] menu.

9.2 Structure of an ASP.NET Program

Generally speaking, an ASP.NET program includes two parts: the user interface logic and the Web form. In this book, we use VB.NET for user interface logics. We present a simplest ASP.NET Web page, called `HelloWorld.aspx`, in Listing 9.1. As usual, the line numbers are added for explanation, and should not be included in the program. Bold font is used for highlighting some important words that connect the two parts.

```
1 <%@ Page Language="VB" %>
2 <script runat="server">

3  Public Sub Page_Load()
4    label1.text="Hello, World!"
5  End Sub
6 </script>

7 <html>
8 <body>
9  <form id="form1" method="post" runat="server">
10    <asp:Label id="label1" runat="server"></asp:Label>
11  </form>
```

```
12 </body>
13 </html>
```

Listing 9.1 ASP.NET Web Page `HelloWorld.aspx`.

As shown in Listing 9.1, the ASP.NET Web page has one heading line (line **1**) and two parts. The heading line informs the Web browser that this is ASP.NET Web page and use VB.NET language. The first part (lines **2–6**) is a script block which contains VB.NET code, and the second part (lines **7–13**) is an HTML Web form that holds all ASP.NET server controls.

Line **2** and line **6** are the pair of tags of the script block. We always use the attribute `runat="server"` for the script tag. Lines **3–5** are the VB.NET code that instructs the Web browser to load the page and display the "Hello, World!" string in the label box named `label1`. We will explain the VB.NET code after having a look at the second part. Line **7** and line **13** are the pair of tags for the HTML block. `<html>` could be replaced by `<html xmlns="http://www.w3.org/1999/xhtml">`. The former makes the generated HTML Web page follow the HTML 4.01 standard while the latter makes the generated HTML Web page follow the XHTML standard. We use the former for all examples in this chapter. Lines **9–11** define the form. Line **9** uses several attributes. The attribute `id` specifies the name of the form. The other two attributes are quite standardized; that is, when creating a Web form, we always specify the `runat="server"` and `method="post"` for the attributes. Note that there are no `NAME` and `ACTION` attributes here which are normally used in the HTML FORM tag. Line **10** defines an ASP.NET control that outputs plain text (as Label). You can use/ in the open tag (i.e., `<asp:Label .../>`) to replace the closing tag `</asp:Label>` if there is nothing in the container. The entire line outputs plain text (Label). When creating an ASP.NET control, we always need the `id` attribute which assigns a unique name to the control. Again, we use the `runat="server"` attribute. This specifies that your control is based on the server, and allows your code to interact with the server directly.

Now we return to the first part and examine the VB.NET code in detail. Line **3** `Page_Load()` is a special subroutine defined by ASP.NET that will be executed when the ASP.NET Web page is requested (i.e., when the Web page is loaded into the web browser). In line **4** `label1` is bounded to the `<asp:Label>` control by the identical id name.

To edit the ASP.NET code of `HelloWorld.aspx`, you can use a plain text editor such as Notepad, and save it to a folder using the right extension name, and then open and run it in Visual Studio 2005 or Visual Web Developer 2005 Express Edition. Alternatively, you can design and edit the ASP.NET codes in the same fashion as VB.NET programs in Visual Studio 2005 or Visual Web Developer 2005 Express Edition.

The entire execution process can be described as follows. When a user requests `HelloWorld.aspx` through the browser, the server passes this request to ASP.NET. ASP.NET compiles the `HelloWorld.aspx` file, and run the `Page_Load()` subroutine. When the code is finished, ASP.NET transforms the control to the HTML tags and generates an HTML document as specified in the Web form block. The HTML document is sent back to the client side, and displayed by the Web browser.

9.3 HTML Controls vs. Web Controls

An ASP.NET Web page instructs the server to execute a certain sequence of actions. Those instructions are called **server controls**. Controls specified by the HTML form object tags are called **HTML controls**, and controls specified in the <asp> tag are called **Web controls**. For example, in Listing 9.1, line **10** is a Web server control. Next, we learn the two types of controls through typical examples.

9.4 HTML Controls

In this section we learn several typical HTML server control tools.

9.4.1 Submit Button

Listing 9.2 shows an ASP.NET Web page that generates a Submit Button through the HTML block. Running this ASP.NET program, the user can receive a message "Hello, World!" by clicking the Submit Button on the screen.

```
 1 <%@ Page Language="VB" %>
 2 <script runat="server">

 3   Public Sub Page_Load()

 4   End Sub
 5   Public Sub abc(sender As Object, e As EventArgs)
 6     label1.text="Hello, World!"
 7   End Sub

 8 </script>

 9 <html>
10 <body>
11 <form id="form1" method="post" runat="server">
12   <input id="submit1" type="submit" value="Submit"
13      runat="server" onserverclick="abc" />
14   <asp:Label id="label1" runat="server"></asp:Label>
15   </form>
16 </body>
17 </html>
```

Listing 9.2 ASP.NET Web page (HelloWorld2.aspx) with HTML Submit Button control.

We read the HTML part first. Line **11** defines a form, and lines **12–13** define the Submit Button in the form. Note line **13** where an HTML Submit Button control is implemented. It specifies the subroutine to be run through the use of the OnServerClick attribute of the server control. The button click will trigger the so-called **postback** process that the data contained in the form (in this case, nothing) is sent back to the server and run the VB.NET program of the ASP.NET file. Line **14**, again, defines an ASP.NET Web control that outputs plain text (as Label).

Now we examine the VB.NET block. It has a subroutine with the same name as the HTML control instructs to run. In this case, it is subroutine abc (see line **5** and line **13**). The subroutine must be declared as Public. The parameters of the subroutine must be (sender As Object, e As Event-Args). The Page_Load subroutine (lines **3–4**) is always included.

9.4.2   Textbox

The ASP.NET Web page in Listing 9.3 implements a postback process so that the user is allowed to type the user's name in the TextBox, and the server then posts a greeting in the Label back to the user's side.

```
 1 <%@ Page Language="vb" %>
 2 <script runat="server">

 3   Public Sub Page_Load()
 4   End Sub

 5   Public Sub abc(sender As Object, e As EventArgs)
 6       label1.text="Hello! " + textbox1.value
 7   End Sub

 8 </script>

 9 <html>
10 <body>
11  <form id="form1" method="post" runat="server">
12  Name:
13  <input type="text" id="textbox1" runat="server">
14 <br>
15 <input type="submit" id="submit1" value="Submit"
16       runat="server" onserverclick="abc">
17 <br>
18 <asp:Label id="label1" runat="server"></asp:Label>
19 </form>
20 </body>
21 </html>
```

Listing 9.3   ASP.NET Web page (Textbox.aspx) with HTML TextBox control.

In Listing 9.3, line **5** corresponds to lines **15–16** for the Submit Button control. Line **6** and line **13** correspond to the TextBox control. Since the Label is specified in line **18**, it should appear after the Submit Button which is specified in line **15**. When you run this ASP.NET Web page, you can see that the screen is updated after clicking the Submit Button without losing the original form on the screen.

9.4.3   Checkbox

Listing 9.4 lists the ASP.NET Web page with a Checkbox control. By activating this ASP.NET program, the user is allowed to choose merchandise by checking a checkbox(es) and then click the Submit Button to find the total price. The server then calculates the total price and posts it back to the client side.

```
1 <%@ Page Language="VB" %>
2 <script runat="server">

3  Public Sub Page_Load()
4  End Sub

5  Public Sub abc(sender As Object, e As EventArgs)
6     Dim TotalPrice As Integer
7     label1.text = ""
8     if (chk1.checked) then
9       TotalPrice = TotalPrice + 10
10    end if
11    if (chk2.checked) then
12      TotalPrice = TotalPrice + 20
13    end if
14    if (chk3.checked) then
15      TotalPrice = TotalPrice + 30
16    end if
17    label1.text="Total Price is: $" & TotalPrice
18  End Sub

19 </script>

20 <html>
21 <body>
22   <form id="form1" method="post" runat="server">
23     Select:
24     <input id="chk1" type="checkbox" name="checkbox1"
25        runat="server" />
26     CD
27     <input id="chk2" type="checkbox" name="checkbox1"
28        runat="server" />
29     DVD
30     <input id="chk3" type="checkbox" name="checkbox1"
31        runat="server" />
32     TV
33     <br>
34     <input id="submit1" type="submit"
35        value="Submit to view the total price"
36        runat="server" onserverclick="abc" />
37     <br>

38     <asp:Label id="label1" runat="server"></asp:Label>
39   </form>
40 </body>
41 </html>
```

Listing 9.4 ASP.NET Web page (Checkbox.aspx) with HTML Checkbox control.

9.4.4 Radio Button

Radio Button allows the user to make just one choice. An example of HTML Radio Button control is shown in Listing 9.5.

```
1 <%@ Page Language="VB" %>
2 <script runat="server">

3   Public Sub Page_Load()
4   End Sub

5   Public Sub abc(sender As Object, e As EventArgs)
6     Dim Price As Double
7     label1.text = ""
8     if (rad1.checked) then
9         Price = 20.50
10    end if
11    if (rad2.checked) then
12        Price = 30.50
13    end if
14    if (rad3.checked) then
15        Price = 100.50
16    end if
17    label1.text = "The Price is: $" & Price
18   End Sub
19 </script>

20 <html>
21 <body>
22 <form id="form1" method="post" runat="server">
23  Select:
24 <input id="rad1" type="radio" name="radio1" runat="server" />
25  CD
26 <input id="rad2" type="radio" name="radio1" runat="server" />
27  DVD
28 <input id="rad3" type="radio" name="radio1" runat="server" />
29  TV
30  <br>
31  <input id="submit1" type="submit" value="Submit"
32     runat="server" onserverclick="abc" />
33  <br>
34  <asp:Label id="label1" runat="server"></asp:Label>
35 </form>
36 </body>
37 </html>
```

Listing 9.5   ASP.NET Web page (Radio.aspx) with HTML Radio Button control.

9.4.5 Select

HTML Select control allows the user to view a dropdown (combo) menu and select a menu item for an action. An example of HTML Select control is shown in Listing 9.6.

```
1 <%@ Page Language="VB" %>
2 <script runat="server">

3   Public Sub Page_Load()
4   End Sub
```

```
 5   Public Sub abc(sender As Object, e As EventArgs)
 6     label1.text = "Thank you for purchasing " & list1.value
 7   End Sub

 8 </script>

 9 <html>
10 <body>
11 <form id="form1" method="post" runat="server">
12   Select:
13   <select id="list1" runat="server">
14     <option>CD</option>
15     <option>DVD</option>
16     <option>TV</option>
17   </select>
18   <br>
19   <input id="submit1" type="submit" value="Submit"
20     runat="server" onserverclick="abc" />
21   <br>
22   <asp:Label id="label1" runat="server"></asp:Label>
23 </form>
24 </body>
25 </html>
```

Listing 9.6   ASP.NET Web page (Select.aspx) with HTML Select control.

9.5   Web Controls

Web controls are specified in the <asp> tag. A Web control is a programmed object. As you can see in this section, Web controls can do similar jobs as HTML controls do, but support more features (attributes or properties) that HTML controls do not have. Listing 9.7 lists major Web controls of ASP.NET.

Label	<asp:Label>
Button	<asp:Button>
TextBox	<asp:TextBox>
CheckBox	<asp:CheckBox>
RadioButton	<asp:RadioButton>
ListBox	<asp:ListBox>
DropDownList	<asp:DropDownList>
CheckBoxList	<asp:CheckBoxList>
RadioButtonList	<asp:RadioButtonList>

Listing 9.7   List of Web controls.

A Web control can have several attributes depending on the needs. Only the attributes id and runat are required. All attributes of Web controls can be set and edited manually in Visual Studio 2005 or Visual Web Developer 2005 Express Edition. We do not go through every Web control tool, but give one example to explain the use of Web controls, as listed in Listing 9.8.

```
 1 <%@ Page Language="VB" %>
 2 <script runat="server">
```

```
3   Public Sub Page_Load()
4   End Sub

5   Public Sub abc(sender as Object, e as EventArgs)
6     DropDownList1.visible=false
7     RadioButtonList1.visible=false
8     Button1.visible=false
9     label1.text="Ship to " & _
10       DropDownList1.SelectedItem.text & _
11       " by " & RadioButtonList1.SelectedItem.text
12    label2.text="Shipping Cost is: $" & _
13          (Val(DropDownList1.SelectedItem.value) * _
14           Val(RadioButtonList1.SelectedItem.value))
15  End Sub

16 </script>

17 <html>
18 <body>
19 <form id="form1" method="post" runat="server">
20   <asp:DropDownList id="DropDownList1" runat="server">
21     <asp:ListItem Value="0" Selected="True">
22       Select Country</asp:ListItem>
23     <asp:ListItem Value="50">Canada</asp:ListItem>
24     <asp:ListItem Value="100">USA</asp:ListItem>
25   </asp:DropDownList>
26   <br>
27   <asp:RadioButtonList id="RadioButtonList1"
28           runat="server">
29     <asp:ListItem Value="2" Selected="True">
30       Express</asp:ListItem>
31     <asp:ListItem Value="1">Regular</asp:ListItem>
32   </asp:RadioButtonList>
33   <br>
34   <asp:Button id="Button1" onclick="abc" runat="server"
35        Text="Find Shipping Cost" />
36   <br>
37   <asp:Label id="label1" runat="server" />
38   <br>
39   <asp:Label id="label2" runat="server" />
40 </form>
41 </body>
42 </html>
```

Listing 9.8   Example of ASP.NET Web controls (ShippingCost.aspx).

The ASP.NET Web page in Listing 9.8 provides information for the consumer to find out shipping cost. The user is allowed to select a shipping destination and choose a shipping class, and click the button to get an answer. Lines **20–25** define a Dropdown list Web control. The attribute `Value` assigns a value to the selected item that will be used for processing. The attribute `Selected="True"` means the default choice. Lines **27–32** define a Radio Button list. Line **34** triggers the subroutine declared in line **5**. Lines **6–8** make all Dropdown list, Radio Button list, and the Command Button invisible when the calculated shipping cost is displayed.

9.6 Validation Controls

ASP.NET provides various **validation control** tools that validate the user's input. In ASP.NET all validations are performed on the server side. Listing 9.9 lists important Validation controls.

RequiredFieldValidator   Ensure that a field fills with data
CompareValidator   Compare the values of two entries
RangeValidator   Ensure an entry to fall within a defined range
RegularExpressionValidator   Ensure an entry to follow a particular pattern
CustomValidator   Validate user's input using a program subroutine

Listing 9.9   Important Validation controls.

Listing 9.10 is an example of Validation controls. In this example, the user is allowed to select a merchandise to buy, and input a number for the purchase quantity. The ASP.NET Web page makes validation so that the user has chosen an item and the number is an integer no greater than 10.

```
 1 <%@ Page Language="VB" %>
 2 <html>
 3 <body>
 4 <form id="form1" method="post" runat="server">
 5     Choose to buy:
 6 <asp:RequiredFieldValidator id="RequiredFieldValidator1"
 7       runat="server" ControlToValidate="RadioButtonList1"
 8       ErrorMessage="You must select one of the items!">
 9 </asp:RequiredFieldValidator>
10 <br>
11 <asp:RadioButtonList id="RadioButtonList1" runat="server"
12     RepeatDirection="Horizontal">
13  <asp:ListItem Value="CD">CD</asp:ListItem>
14  <asp:ListItem Value="DVD">DVD</asp:ListItem>
15  <asp:ListItem Value="TV">TV</asp:ListItem>
16 </asp:RadioButtonList>
17 <br>
18 Quantity to buy:
19 <asp:TextBox id="TextBox1" runat="server"></asp:TextBox>
20 <br>
21 <asp:CompareValidator id="CompareValidator2"
22       runat="server"
23       ErrorMessage="Value1 must be an integer"
24       ControlToValidate="TextBox1" Operator="DataTypeCheck"
25       Type="Integer"></asp:CompareValidator>
26 <br>
27 <asp:RangeValidator id="RangeValidator1" runat="server"
28       MinimumValue="0" MaximumValue="10"
29       ControlToValidate="TextBox1" Type="Integer"
30       ErrorMessage="Must be less than 10 inclusively">
31 </asp:RangeValidator>
32 <br>
33 <asp:Button id="Button" runat="server"
34       Text="Buy"></asp:Button>
35 </form>
```

```
36 </body>
37 </html>
```

Listing 9.10   Validation example (ValidationExample.aspx).

As shown in Listing 9.10, there are three Validation controls in this example: `RequiredFieldValidator` (line **6**), `CompareValidator` (line **21**), and `RangeValidator` (line **27**). Each Validation control must have required attributes including `id`, `ControlToValidate`, and `ErrorMessage`. Some attributes, such as `Operator` and `Type`, are only required for specific Validation controls. All attributes of Validation controls can be set and edited manually in Visual Studio 2005 or Visual Web Developer 2005 Express Edition.

You might remember JavaScript that is commonly used to validate user's input on the client side. Compared with JavaScript, ASP.NET Validation controls are slow since they are executed on the server side. However, ASP.NET Web pages are securer since the code is invisible on the client side.

9.7   Code-Behind Programming Framework

The ASP.NET framework supports OOP and **code-behind programming** that allows the programmer to re-use a separate code file. By doing so, the ASP.NET Web page contains the user interface implemented by a series of HTML and ASP.NET tags, and the so-called program contains VB.NET code only. Listing 9.11a is an example of code-behind programming ASP.NET Web page. It allows the user to input her or his name, and calls a VB.NET program named `Greeting.vb` to post a greeting message in green color to the client side.

```
 1 <%@ Page Language="VB" Inherits="DisplayMessage"
 2    CodeFile="Greeting.vb" %>
 3 <html>
 4 <body>
 5   <form runat="server">
 6     Name:
 7     <input id="textbox1" type="text" runat="server" />
 8     <br>
 9     <input id="submit1" type="submit" value="Submit"
10       runat="server" onserverclick="abc" />
11     <br>
12     <asp:Label id="Label1" runat="server"
13        forecolor="Green"></asp:Label>
14   </form>
15 </body>
16 </html>
```

Listing 9.11a   Code-behind programming ASP.NET Web page (Greeting.aspx).

The VB.NET code is listed in Listing 9.11b.

```
1 Imports System

2 Public Class DisplayMessage
```

```
3   Inherits System.Web.UI.Page

4   Public Sub abc (sender As Object, e As EventArgs)
5   Label1.Text = "Hello, " & textbox1.value & "!"
6 End Sub

7 End Class
```

Listing 9.11b   VB.NET code (Greeing.vb) called by Greeting.aspx in Listing 9.11a.

Compare Listings 9.11a and 9.11b by noting the words in bold. In the ASP.NET heading tag, the `Inherits` attribute specifies the class name (`DisplayMessage` in this case) that must also be used in the `Public Class` statement of the VB.NET program. The `CodeFile` attribute specifies the name of the .vb part. Even in this simple example, there are many parameters that connect the ASP.NET Web page and the VB.NET program, including abc (for the subroutine), Label1 (for the Label), textbox1 (for the Textbox), and submit1 (for the Submit Button).

An advantage of code-behind programming is that the user interface is separated from the codes. The programmer may change only the codes in the .vb part without touching the user interface in the .aspx part. In Listings 9.11a and 9.11b, if the programmer wants to change the subroutine name abc, then we have to make changes in both .aspx and .vb parts. As illustrated in the following example, ASP.NET support features to avoid such hassle.

```
 1 <%@ Page Language="VB" Inherits="DisplayMessage"
 2   CodeFile="Greeting2.vb" AutoEventWireup="False" %>
 3 <html>
 4 <body>
 5  <form runat="server">
 6    Name:
 7    <input id="textbox1" type="text" runat="server" />
 8    <br>
 9    <input id="submit1" type="submit" value="Submit"
10      runat="server" />
11    <br>
12    <asp:Label id="Label1" runat="server"
13       forecolor="Green"></asp:Label>
14  </form>
15 </body>
16 </html>
```

Listing 9.12a   Code-behind programming ASP.NET Web page using Auto-EventWireup (Greeting2.aspx).

The VB.NET code is listed in Listing 9.12b.

```
1 Imports System

2 Public Class DisplayMessage
3   Inherits System.Web.UI.Page
```

```
4   Public Sub abc (sender As Object, e As EventArgs)Handles
5        submit1.ServerClick
6      Label1.Text = "Hello, " & textbox1.value & "!"
7   End Sub

8 End Class
```

Listing 9.12b   VB.NET code (Greeing2.vb) called by Greeting2.aspx in Listing 9.12a.

In this example, the attribute `AutoEventWireup` is set to `False` in line **2** of the `.aspx` part. The default value of `AutoEventWireup` is `True`. When `AutoEventWireup` is set to `False`, ASP.NET will rely only on the `Handles` keyword in the `.vb` part to connect events to event handler subroutines, as shown in line **4** of Listing 9.12b. Line **5** is the continuation of line **4**, and it specifies that the `ServerClick` event of the `submit1` button will be handled by the subroutine `abc`. Correspondingly, we do not specify any subroutine name in the `.aspx` part.

9.8   ASP.NET Web Page Application Examples

In this section we introduce several useful ASP.NET Web page application examples.

9.8.1   Sending E-Mail Message

ASP.NET supports e-mail sending in a simple way. Listing 9.13 is an ASP.NET 2.0 Web page that allows the user to type an e-mail receiver's address and send a message. To make the program work, the e-mail server must be valid.

```
1 <%@ Page Language="VB" %>
2 <script runat="server">

3 Public Sub Page_Load()
4 End Sub

5 Public Sub abc(sender As Object, e As EventArgs)
6   'Textbox1.text must not be empty
7   'There are two parameters for MailMessage:
8   '      From address and To address
9   Dim myMsg As New _
10   System.Net.Mail.MailMessage("me@xyz.com", TextBox1.text)
11   Dim mySmtpClient As New System.Net.Mail.SmtpClient()
12   myMsg.Subject = "Hello"
13   myMsg.Body = "To be or not to be"
14   'set your own email smtp server here
15   mySmtpClient.Host = "smtp.smu.ca"
16   mySmtpClient.Send(myMsg)
17 End Sub

18 </script>
```

```
19 <html>
20 <body>
21 <form id="form1" method="post" runat="server">
22 <p>
23   Email Address:
24   <asp:TextBox id="TextBox1" runat="server"></asp:TextBox>
25 </p>
26 <p>
27   <asp:Button id="Button1" onclick="abc" runat="server"
28        Text="Send a Greeting Email"></asp:Button>
29 </p>
30 </form>
31 </body>
32 </html>
```

Listing 9.13   ASP.NET Web page (Email.aspx) for sending e-mail.

9.8.2   Calendar

ASP.NET has Calendar Web control that displays the calendar of the current month. The example in Listing 9.14 allows the user to click a date on the calendar and view the date in the long date string format, such like "Sunday, January 01, 2006."

```
1 <%@ Page Language="VB" %>
2 <script runat="server">

3   Public Sub Page_Load()
4   End Sub

5   Public Sub abc(sender As Object, e As EventArgs)
6    Label1.text = Calendar1.SelectedDate.ToLongDateString()
7   End Sub

8 </script>

 9 <html>
10 <body>
11  <form id="form1" method="post" runat="server">
12    <br>
13    <asp:Calendar id="Calendar1" runat="server"
14      forecolor="Blue" />
15    <br>
16    <asp:Button id="Button1" runat="server" onclick="abc"
17         text="Find Long Date String" />
18    <br>
19    <asp:Label id="Label1" runat="server" forecolor="Red" />
20  </form>
21 </body>
22 </html>
```

Listing 9.14   ASP.NET Web page (Calendar.aspx) for showing Calendar.

9.8.3 File Input/Output

In this subsection we give an example of ASP.NET Web page that allows the user to input his or her e-mail address to join a group. The e-mail address will be added to the e-mail list that is permanently stored on the disk. After the user adds the e-mail address, the group e-mail list is then displayed on the screen for the user to view. The ASP.NET Web page is shown in Listing 9.15.

```
 1 <%@ Page Language="VB" %>
 2 <%@ import Namespace="System" %>
 3 <%@ import Namespace="System.IO" %>
 4 <script runat="server">

 5 Public Sub Page_Load()
 6 End Sub

 7 Public Sub abc (sender As Object, e As EventArgs)
 8   WriteToFile()
 9   ReadFromFile()
10 End Sub

11 Public Sub WriteToFile()
12  Dim S As StreamWriter
13  Dim FileName As String = "..\ASP\InputOutput.txt"
14  Dim Fi As FileInfo = New FileInfo(FileName)
15  If Fi.Exists = False Then
16    S = File.CreateText(FileName)
17    S.WriteLine(Textbox1.Text)
18  Else
19    S = File.AppendText(FileName)
20    S.WriteLine(Textbox1.Text)
21  End If
22  S.Close()
23 End Sub

24 Public Sub ReadFromFile()
25   Dim S As StreamReader
26   Dim FileName As String = "..\ASP\InputOutput.txt"
27   Dim Fi As FileInfo = New FileInfo(FileName)
28   ListBox1.Items.Clear
29   If Fi.Exists = True Then
30    S = File.OpenText(FileName)
31    Do While S.Peek() > 0
32      ListBox1.Items.Add(S.ReadLine())
33    Loop
34  End If
35  S.Close()
36 End Sub

37 </script>

38 <html>
39 <body>
40  <form id="form1" method="post" runat="server">
```

```
41      Add you email address to join the group:
42      <br>
43      <asp:TextBox id="TextBox1" runat="server">
44      </asp:TextBox>
45      <br>
46      <asp:Button id="Button1" onclick="abc" runat="server"
47           text="View the email list of the group">
48      </asp:Button>
49      <br>
50      <asp:ListBox id="ListBox1" runat="server"
51             forecolor="Red">
52      </asp:ListBox>
53    </form>
54   </body>
55   </html>
```

Listing 9.15   ASP.NET Web page (FileProcess.aspx) for writing and reading disk file.

The ASP.NET Web page in Listing 9.15 displays one TextBox (lines **43–44**), one Button (lines **46–48**), and one ListBox (lines **50–52**). The TextBox accepts the user's input. The ListBox displays the e-mail list of the group. When the user clicks the button, it calls the subroutine abc which in turn calls two subroutines: WriteToFile() and ReadFromFile().

As shown in lines **12–14** and **25–27**, three variables are generally needed for a disk file processing subroutine. The first one is StreamWriter or StreamReader that represents the disk file. The second one defines the file name on the disk. In this case, the physical name of the file is InputOutpt. txt. Note that you'd better define the path of the data file (line 13 and line 26). Here ".." indicates the default server. The third one holds information about the file, such as whether it exists, to avoid errors. To create these three variables, the ASP.NET Web page need to import the namespaces System and System. IO, as shown in lines **2–3**.

Lines **15–21** are an If-Then-Else sentence, which means that if the file does not exist, then the program creates the file on the disk and writes the e-mail address passed on by the TextBox to the disk; otherwise, the program appends the e-mail address to the group list. After the process, the file must be closed (line **22**).

Line **28** clears anything in the ListBox that might be left from the previous operation. Line **30** opens the file. Lines **31–33** are a Do-loop that means as long as the file has not reached the end, the computer reads a record and adds it to the ListBox. Line **35** closes the file. If the InputOutput.txt contains the following e-mail list

```
who@abc.org
some@bcd.net
swang@umassd.edu
```

the execution result of this APS.NET Web page appears similar to that shown in Figure 9.2.

Flat data file is the simplest form of database. To deal with relational databases directly from a Web page, database connection software must be integrated

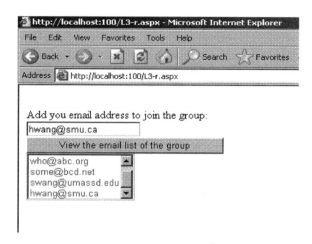

Figure 9.2　Result of the ASP.NET Web page in Listing 9.15.

into the Web application development tool. The .NET framework includes **ADO. NET**, a database connection that allows a Web page to access databases such as Access, SQL Server, and other databases from .NET applications. ADO.NET database connection and manipulation are introduced in Chapter 11—SQL for Database Query.

9.8.4　Security

Security is an important issue in Web applications. At the communication level, encryption technologies are used to encrypt communication between a Web client and a Web server. **Secure Sockets Layer (SSL)** is one of the popular encryption technologies to transmit private or sensitive information between an authenticated client and a Web server. Both the Web client and Web server must have certificates that are installed on the computers. To access a page through SSL, the user simply types the URL with a preceding "https" instead of "http."

At the application level, authentication and authorization ensures the application security. **Authentication** is the process that enables the determination of a user's identity by asking the user to prove. User's name and password and or IP address are commonly used in authentication. **Authorization** is the process that determines which resources an authenticated user can access and how those resources can be used. For example, the user must use password to access restricted files.

ASP.NET provides various approaches to security. ASP.NET supports three types of authentication: **Windows authentication, Passport authentication,** and **Forms authentication**.

When using Windows authentication, ASP.NET Web page calls IIS at the operating system level for authentication. The goal of Windows authentication is to verify the user against the accounts on the Web server. Passport authentication is carried out through Microsoft Passport that is maintained by Microsoft to authenticate registered users. Forms authentication is the commonly used approach for authentication that uses login forms in Web pages. ASP.NET has built-in utilities for Form authentication. To use these built-in utilities, you need to specify the requirements through the web.config files provided by the ASP. NET development environment. For the beginners, this may not be straightforward. Here, we provide a simple example that implements Form authentication within the ASP.NET Web page in Listing 9.16.

```
1  <%@ Page Language="VB" %>
2  <script runat="server">
3  Public Sub abc (sender As Object, e As EventArgs)
4   If (((TextBox1.text="wang") AND (TextBox2.text="12345")) OR _
5      ((TextBox1.text="john") AND (TextBox2.text="23456")) OR _
6      ((TextBox1.text="anna") AND (TextBox2.text="34567"))) Then

7    Response.Redirect("Authen-Redirect.aspx")

8   Else
9    Label1.Text = "Your ID and password do not match. Try again!"
10  End If
11  End Sub
12 </script>

13 <html>
14 <body>
15  <form id="form1" method="post" runat="server">
16   <h2>Please Log In</h2>
17   <hr><br>
18 <table>
19   <tr>
20    <td>User ID</td>
21    <td><asp:TextBox id="TextBox1" runat="server" /></td>
22   </tr>
23   <tr>
24    <td>Password</td>
25    <td><asp:TextBox id="TextBox2" runat="server" /></td>
26   </tr>
27   </table>

28   <br>
29   <asp:Button id="Button1" onclick="abc" runat="server"
30     Text="Login - Case sensitive!"></asp:Button>
31   <br><br>
32   <asp:Label id="Label1" runat="server" />
33  </form>
34 </body>
35 </html>
```

Listing 9.16   Example of Form authentication (Authentication.aspx).

The HTML part in Listing 9.16 includes two TextBox, one Button, and one Label. Use HTML table tags to make the two text boxes line up, as shown in Figure 9.3. The VB part performs the authentication work. Lines **4–6** contain a list of legal users and their passwords. Practically, this list can be stored on the server and maintained by the application system. The VB program makes the decision of whether the user's request is granted or rejected based on the

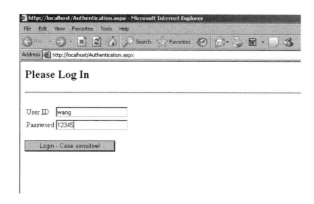

Figure 9.3 ASP.NET Web page of the Form authentication example of Listing 9.16.

inputted user ID and the password. If access is granted, line **7** redirects the response to the permitted Web page. In this example, the new ASP.NET Web page Authen-Redirect.aspx will be loaded on the screen, and thus the workflow of the Web application is continuous. As an example, you may use the following simple ASP.NET Web page as Authen-Redirect.aspx.

```
1 <%@ Page Language="VB" %>
2 <script runat="server">

3 Public Sub Page_Load()
4   label1.text="This is the follow-up Web page...."
5   label2.text="Welcome to the new world!"
6 End Sub

7 </script>

8 <html>
9 <head>
10 </head>
11 <body>
12  <form id="form1" method="post" runat="server">
13   <asp:Label id="label1" runat="server" />
14   <br>
15   <asp:Label id="label2" runat="server" />
16  </form>
17 </body>
18 </html>
```

Listing 9.17 Example of follow-up Web page (Authen-Redirect.aspx) for Listing 9.16.

9.9 Debugging

Debugging ASP.NET programs is a little different from that for other languages as both VB.NET and server control are involved.

Common syntax errors are:

- Typos of misspelling a word.
- Omitting a symbol (e.g., missing one side of parenthesis).
- Violating format.
- Using an undefined user-defined variable.

Logical errors or runtime errors often occur when the computer performs wrong operations or not as directed. To debug logical errors, you should use data samples to test the program based on the output of the program.

1. Exercise every possible option to check the computer outputs to see if the program does only as you direct it. if-statements are commonly examined to find possible options.
2. If a program is "dead," you must terminate it by closing the Web page. This is more likely caused by a "dead" loop. You should check `for` loop and `if` statements.
3. When you debug ASP.NET as server-side programs, you need to re-upload your programs to the server. If you use your personal server on PC, you need to re-start the server once you make changes to the program.

9.10   Self-Review Exercise

1. Fill in the blanks in the following ASP.NET Web page, and sketch the screen shots of the page and its execution.

```
 1 <%@ Page _____>
 2 <script _____="server">
 3  Public Sub Page_Load()
 4  End Sub

 5  Public Sub _____(sender As Object, e As EventArgs)
 6    Dim TotalPrice As Integer
 7    label1.text = ""
 8    if (_____.checked) then
 9      TotalPrice = TotalPrice + 10
10    end if
11    if (_____.checked) then
12      TotalPrice = TotalPrice + 20
13    end if
14    if (_____.checked) then
15      TotalPrice = TotalPrice + 30
16    end if
17    label1.text="Total Price is: $" & TotalPrice
18  End Sub
19 _____

20 <html>
21 <body>
22  <form id="form1" method="post" runat="server">
```

```
23    Select:
24    <input id="check1" type="checkbox" name="checkbox1"
25        runat="server" />
26    Computer
27    <input id="check2" type="checkbox" name="checkbox1"
28        runat="server" />
29    Printer
30    <input id="check3" type="checkbox" name="checkbox1"
31        runat="server" />
32    Laptop
33    <br>
34    <input id="submit1" type="submit"
35        value="Submit to view the total price"
36        runat="server" onserverclick="abc" />
37    <br>
38    <asp:Label id="_____" runat="server"></asp:Label>
39    _____
40 </body>
41 </html>
```

2. Fill in the blanks in the following ASP.NET Web page and the so-called VB.NET code, and sketch the screen shots of the page and its execution.

```
 1 <%@ Page Language="VB" Inherits="_____"
 2    CodeFile="_____" %>
 3 <html>
 4 <body>
 5    <form id="form1" method="post" runat="server">
 6    <br>
 7    Add you email address to join the group:
 8    <br>
 9    <_____ id="TextBox1" runat="server" />
10    <br>
11    <asp:Button id="Button1" onclick="joingroup"
12        runat="server"
13        text="Join the group" />
14    <br>
15    <asp:Label id="Label1" runat="server" forecolor="Red" />
16    </form>
17 </body>
18 </html>
```

```
 1 Imports System
 2 _____Class JoinGroup
 3 _____ System.Web.UI.Page
 4 Public Sub _____ (sender As Object, e As EventArgs)
 5    Textbox1.visible=false
 6    Button1._____=false
 7    Label1._____="The email address " & _
 8       Textbox1._____ & "has been added " & _
 9       "to the group"
10 End Sub

11 _____
```

Online Reservation

Reservation Information

Check-In Date: [(Should be the ASP.NET Calendar Control)]

Check-Out Date: [(Should be the ASP.NET Calendar Control)]

Number of Guests: [1 ▼]

Number of Rooms: [1 ▼]

Contact Information

Last Name: [＿＿＿＿＿＿]

First Name: [＿＿＿＿＿＿]

Street Number: [＿＿＿＿＿＿＿＿＿]

City: [＿＿＿＿＿]

Province/State: [＿＿]

Country: [Canada ▼]

Postal Code   [＿＿＿]

Phone Number: [＿＿＿＿＿＿]

E-mail Address: [＿＿＿＿＿＿＿＿＿]

Credit Card Information

Credit Card: ◯ Visa   ◯ MasterCard   ◯ American Express   ◯ Discover

Name on Credit Card: [＿＿＿＿＿＿＿＿＿]

Credit Card Number: [＿＿＿＿＿] (No spaces or dashes, please)

Expiration Date: [＿＿＿] (MM/YYYY)

[Submit Form]   [Clear Form]

---

3. Use ASP.NET to develop the following Web application project for hotel reservation.

    The following server-based validations will be performed on the user input of the form given when you click on the "Submit Form" button.

    All fields in the form must be entered (i.e., all fields are required).

    The check-out date should be greater than the check-in date.

    The last name, first name, city, province/state, and credit card holder's name should not contain the following characters:

    ; : ! @ # $ % ^ * + ?

    The country should be either Canada or US.

    If the country is Canada, then the postal code must be a valid Canadian postal code.

    If the country is USA, then the postal code must be a valid US zip code.

    The phone number is a valid US or Canadian phone number.

    The e-mail address is a valid Internet e-mail address.

    The type of the credit card must be selected.

The credit card number should consist of digits only, and must have the following properties:

Credit Card	Prefix	Length
MasterCard	51–55	16
Visa	4	16
American Express	34 or 37	15
Discover	6011	16

The format of the expiration date should be MM/YYYY, where MM means month and YYYY means year. Both M and Y represent a single digit. The range of MM is between 01 and 12, and YYYY is between 2007 and 2017 (inclusively).

All validations described should be server-based (i.e., these validations are performed on the server side). When the form is validated and submitted, a new Web page will be generated to display the customer's input, and ask for the customer's confirmation. Once the customer confirms, another new Web page will be generated to inform the customer that the reservation is being processed, and the reservation information will be recorded in a file on the server to allow the hotel manager to process the reservation.

Appendix 9.1   Install IIS for ASP.NET

1.   Install IIS on Windows XP Professional

   1.   Insert the Windows XP Professional CD into your CD Drive.
   2.   Click[Start] – [Settings] – [Control Panel].
   3.   In the Control Panel window select [Add/Remove Programs].
   4.   In the [Add/Remove] window select [Add/Remove Windows Components].
   5.   In the [Wizard] window check [Internet Information Services], click [OK].
   6.   An Inetpub folder will be created on your hard drive.
   7.   Open the Inetpub folder, and find a folder named wwwroot.
   8.   Create a new folder, such like "MyWeb", under wwwroot.
   9.   Use a text editor (Notepad) to write ASP.NET code, save the file as "test .aspx" in the "MyWeb" folder.
   10. Run your Web server. Go into the [Control Panel], then [Administrative Tools], and double-click the [IIS Manager] icon to run the server.
   11. Open your browser and type in "http://localhost/MyWeb/test .aspx", to view your first ASP.NET program.

2.   Install IIS on Windows Server 2003 (Windows .NET Server)

   1.   When you start the Windows Server 2003, you should see the [Manage Your Server] wizard. If the wizard is not displayed, go to [Administrative Tools], and select [Manage Your Server].

2. In the wizard, click [Add or Remove a Role], click [Next].
3. Select [Custom Configuration], click [Next].
4. Select [Application Server Role], click [Next].
5. Select [Enable ASP.NET], click [Next].
6. If the wizard asks for the Server 2003 CD, insert the CD and let it run until it is finished, then click the [Finish] button.
7. The wizard should show the Application Server has been installed.
8. Click on [Manage This Application Server] to bring up [Application Server Management Console (MMC)].
9. Expand the [Internet Information Services (IIS) Manager], then expand your server, and then the Web sites folder. You should see the default Web site.
10. In the [Internet Information Services (IIS) Manager] click on the Web Service Extensions folder.
11. You will see Active Server Pages are Prohibited which is the default configuration of IIS 6.
12. Highlight [ASP.NET], and click [Allow] button to activate ASP.NET.

Appendix 9.2   Guideline for Server-Side Programming (ASP.NET) Project Report

Please submit a short written report in hard copy as well as a floppy disk (or CD) that contains all relevant files (including the report). The report should be 3–5 pages long (excluding the title page and table of contents), and should include the following sections:

(1) Title Page
(2) Table of Contents
(3) Text

    1. Introduction

    (A brief description of the project.)

    2. Web Site Structure

    (High-level design of the web site, i.e., the structure of the web pages.)

    3. Features and Limitations

    (Details of design of the web site, such as the layout of each web page. The limitations/bugs should also be mentioned.)

    4. Future Improvement

    (Features that you would like to incorporate into the web site in the future.)

    5. Teamwork

    (Brief description of the roles and responsibilities of each group member.)

Chapter 10

XML and the Uniform Data Format for the Internet

10.1 Introduction to XML

Extensible Markup Language (XML) is a computer language designed to provide a standard information description framework used for Internet computing. XML and HTML are both derived from the **Standard Generalized Markup Language** (**SGML**) which was defined in 1986 as an international standard for document markup. XML was completed in early 1998 by **World Wide Web Consortium** (W3C). However, the implementation of the XML standard is far from over and depends upon the progress of the entire information technology industry. Also, the XML technology is more complicated than any other computer language.

Why do we need XML? Two major reasons of this are discussed here.

10.1.1 HTML Documents Are Difficult to Extract

HTML and Web pages have been discussed earlier. Web pages written in HTML can be presented by a Web browser for users. However, HTML documents are difficult to be used for data processing by computers. Specifically, information hiding in HTML documents is hard to extract by computers. We use an example to illustrate this.

Suppose we have the following HTML document for online auctions.

```
<HTML>
<HEAD>
<TITLE>Online Auction</TITLE>
</HEAD>
<BODY>
<H2>ABC Online Auction Web Page</H2>
<TABLE BORDER=1>
 <TR><TD>Merchandise on Auction</TD>
   <TD>Current Highest Bid</TD>
 </TR>
 <TR><TD>IBM ThinkPad</TD>
   <TD>$200</TD>
 </TR>
 <TR><TD>HP Laser Printer</TD>
   <TD>$100</TD>
 </TR>
 <TR><TD>Kodak Camera</TD>
      <TD>$50</TD>
 </TR>
</TABLE>
</BODY>
</HTML>
```

Listing 10.1   Example of HTML document.

Figure 10.1 shows the presentation of this HTML document. This presentation is perfect for reading for users.

Suppose many bidders want to use computer programs to extract the bidding information from the HTML documents every hour, and then store the

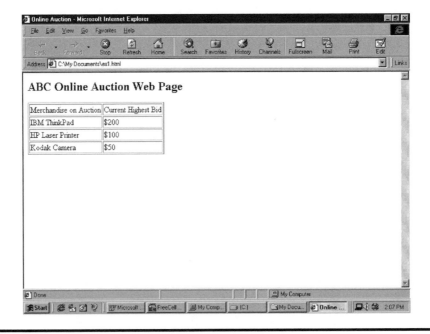

Figure 10.1   Presentation of the HTML document.

data on their computers without retyping, the extracting task for programmers is quite tedious and difficult. A programmer might consider that the bidding data start from line 11 in the HTML document. However, if the auctioneer's Web master changes the HTML document format, such an extracting method will not work. Another programmer might consider the tag <TABLE> is a reference point to find these bidding data. However, if another table is added to this HTML document, the programmer must re-do programming. The issue raised here is the so-called independence of data and presentation.

Later we will see that XML provides a uniform data format for Web documents so that the Web documents circulated on the Internet can be searched and processed by computers easily and accurately. The price for achieving this objective is that the data documents must be formatted in XML, and additional documentation for presentations is needed.

10.1.2 Databases Need Common Data Format to Make Data Exchange

The second major reason why we need XML is the requirement for uniform data format for databases for Internet computing. There have been many database systems commonly used in the information industry. Although SQL is a standard language for databases, the data formats are all platform-dependent. To transfer data from one database to another, usually one needs an interface implemented by programming to describe the data format (see Figure 10.2).

To make data transfers on the Internet efficient, we need a common data format description framework so that each database can understand exactly what is requested or what is received. The price for this is that each database must support the XML standard (so-called XML-enabled database) to exchange data in the common XML format (see Figure 10.3).

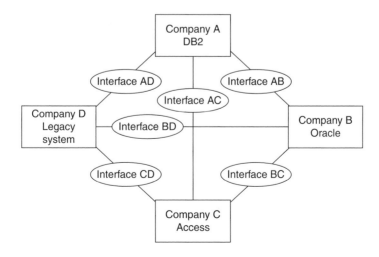

Figure 10.2   Without a common interface data transfer on the Internet is difficult.

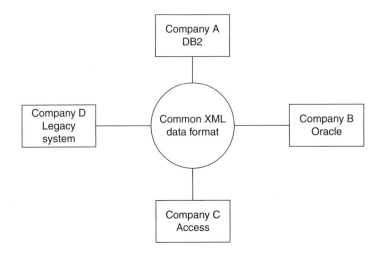

Figure 10.3   Common XML data format makes data transfer efficient.

Furthermore, traditional relational databases are typically used for processing numerical data and character data. However, the formats of data available
on the Internet are rich, including audio, video, complex documents, and international characters. Using XML data, these rich data formats can be easily
handled.

Since the XML standard has not been universally implemented at this point,
to use the XML technology to implement a complete end-to-end business application which involves client-side computing and server-side relational database
processing, one usually needs particular XML-enabled databases which are
usually not commonly available. For this reason, it is difficult to demonstrate a
comprehensive business application example that can be done by XML and
Internet browser (e.g., Microsoft Internet Explorer) without additional expensive
software. On the other hand, if we are working on a single specific e-business
application, one may find that simple traditional computer languages such as
HTML, Perl, Java servlets, and SQL can do the job without the use of XML, in
a less complicated manner. In this chapter we discuss the essentials of XML.
However, simple examples might not be adequate for learners to perceive the
advantages of XML. Overall, the XML technology may or may not be "a must"
for Internet computing at this time, but we need to learn it and be prepared for
the future when it becomes a universally implemented standard for the information technology field.

Microsoft Internet Explorer and Notepad are the only software we need for
practicing XML examples. If you want to develop a business application project
to handle a relational database, you must use the XML-enabled database.

10.2   Simplest Examples of XML

For simplicity, we use Notepad for editing XML programs. However, there are
many XML editors (e.g., XML Spy <http://www.xmlspy.com>) with more functions. These editors can help programmers to format and validate the programs.

10.2.1   Feature of XML Instance Documents

Use Notepad to edit the following XML document.

```
<?xml version="1.0" standalone="yes"?>
<GREETING>
Hello, XML World!
</GREETING>
```

Listing 10.2   First XML example (greetingxml.xml).

In Notepad, click [File], [Save As], and choose file type [All files], and save the document of Listing 10.2 as *file-name*.**xml**, say,

```
C:\Myfolder\greetingxml.xml
```

Using Microsoft Internet Explorer, open the XML document file to view it (Figure 10.4). You will find that the browser simply displays the document, but does not show the presentation. This means that XML makes data and presentation independent. An XML document containing data is called **instance document** which is stored on computer with extension name **.xml**. The document used for the presentation of an instance document is called **style sheet** that can be implemented by various languages as discussed later.

10.2.1.1   Declaration

The first line of an XML instance document is a **processing instruction**, enclosed by pair <? and ?>. The first word xml after <? is the **name of instruction**. In this case, the first line of the document is **XML declaration**.

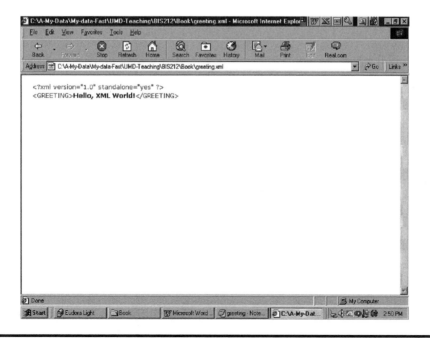

Figure 10.4   XML document is viewed in the Web browser.

10.2.1.2   Tags and Element

XML uses **tags**. For example, <GREETING> is a **start tag**, and </GREETING> is the **end tag**. Unlike HTML, XML tags can be named by the programmer. A pair of tags defines an **element**. In this example, lines 2–4 define the GREET-ING element, and Hello, XML World! is the **content** of this element. Every well-formed XML document must have a **root element**. The root element con-tains every other element in the document. Later we will learn more about how XML tags are used to designate data structure.

10.2.1.3   Attribute

An XML element can have attributes and their values. For example:

```
<CAR COLOR="Red">
</CAR>
```

COLOR is the attribute of element CAR, and "Red" is the **value** of attribute COLOR. In many cases, one can use either an attribute or a content (e.g., <CAR>Red</CAR>) to represent a piece of data. However, using multiple attri-butes, one can describe the elements in a concise way, as seen in the examples later in this chapter.

10.2.1.4   Comment Line and Editorial Style

Like HTML, comments for the XML program can be contained in pair <!-- and -->. XML is case sensitive. A good programmer applies a consistent program-ming style of uppercase and lowercase for the XML document.

10.2.1.5   Empty Tag

If an element has no content, one can use empty tag as short cut. An empty tag does not have corresponding end tag, but ends with /> instead of just >. For example:

```
<xsl:value-of/>
```

is an empty tag. This will be discussed later in the chapter.

10.2.2   Cascading Style Sheets (CSS)

To instruct the Web browser on how the contents of XML tags are displayed, one may use **Cascading Style Sheets** (**CSS**). CSS is well supported by many Web browsers.

As an exercise of CSS, open Notepad, and type the following CSS document.

```
GREETING {display: block; font-size: 50pt; font-weight: bold;}
```

Listing 10.3   Example of CSS (greetingcss.css) for the XML document in Listing 10.2.

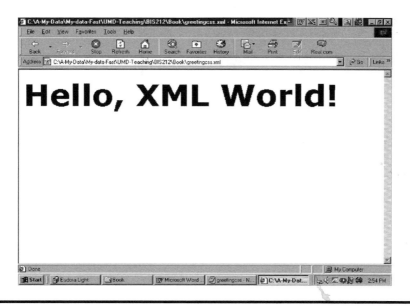

Figure 10.5   Present the XML document.

Save this CSS as *file-name*.**css**, say,

```
C:\Myfolder\greetingcss.css
```

Open `C:\Myfolder\greetingxml.xml`, and re-edit it as follows. Note the bold lines for processing instructions that associate the XML document with the CSS document.

```
<?xml version="1.0" standalone="yes"?>
<?xml-stylesheet type="text/css"
   href="greetingcss.css"?>
<GREETING>
Hello, XML World!
</GREETING>
```

Listing 10.4   XML document (greetingcss.xml) associated to the CSS.

Save the XML instance document given in Listing 10.4 as, say,

```
C:\Myfolder\greetingcss.xml
```

Open this XML document in Internet Explorer. You can view it as shown in Figure 10.5.

10.2.3   Extensible Style Language

One can also use **Extensible Style Language** (**XSL**) to detail instructions on how to display the contents of XML tags. XSL has two specific technologies: **XSL formatting objects** (**XSL-FO**) and **XSL transformation** (**XSLT**). XSLT enables the programmer to replace XML tags with standard HTML tags, reorder elements in document, and add additional contents. XSL-FO enables the programmer to define a powerful view of the document as pages by specifying appearance and layout of the page. XSLT is W3C recommendation, and XSL-FO has not been well supported as yet.

As an exercise, edit the following XSLT document in Notepad. The line numbers are used for explanation only, and must not be typed in the program.

```
1   <?xml version="1.0"?>
2   <xsl:stylesheet
3    xmlns:xsl="http://www.w3.org/TR/WD-xsl">
4     <xsl:template match="/">
5      <HTML>
6       <BODY>
7        <xsl:for-each select="GREETING">
8         <H2>
9          <xsl:value-of/>
10        </H2>
11       </xsl:for-each>
12      </BODY>
13     </HTML>
14    </xsl:template>
15  </xsl:stylesheet>
```

Listing 10.5 XSLT document (greetingxsl.xsl) for the XML document in Listing 10.2.

Save the XSLT document in Listing 10.2 as *file-name*.xsl, say,

`C:\Myfolder\greetingxsl.xsl`

Open the XML document of `C:\Myfolder\greetingxml.xml` and re-edit it as follows:

```
<?xml version="1.0" standalone="yes"?>
<?xml-stylesheet type="text/xsl"
  href="greetingxsl.xsl"?>
<GREETING>
Hello, XML World!
</GREETING>
```

Listing 10.6 XML document (greetingxsl.xml) associated to the XSLT program.

Save this XML document as, say,

`C:\Myfolder\greetingxsl.xml`

Open this XML document in Internet Explorer. You will view the similar presentation as shown in Figure 10.5.

Now, we examine the XSLT program in Listing 10.5.

10.2.3.1   <xsl:stylesheet>

Extensible Style Language transformation performs its tasks with 37 **elements** and their **attributes**. The syntax of XSLT element is <xsl: *[element-name]* *[attribute]*=value>. We learn a few of these elements in this chapter.

The very first element in an XSLT document is `<xsl:stylesheet>` (see lines **2** and **15** in Listing 10.5). It indicates that the document is an XSLT style sheet. The element has a mandatory attribute: a **namespace declaration** for the XSLT **namespace** (see line **3** in Listing 10.5). Namespace is a technique that ensures that the element names are unique and will not lead to confusion. In this example, we use the Microsoft's technology preview implementation based on working draft (WD).

10.2.3.2   `<xsl:template>`

The data contained in the XML document are organized into a **tree**. The data tree has a **root** and many **nodes**. To match the data tree, we need a template. Every style sheet must contain a template which is declared with the `<xsl:template>` element (see lines **4** and **14** in Listing 10.5). This element has attributes, and the `match` attribute is almost always necessary. As will be learned later, XML data is organized into a tree. The / character is shorthand for the root of the tree. Thus, the **value** of the `match` attributes is "`/`".

10.2.3.3   HTML Presentation

When transforming an XML document for presentation, you can use HTML's features to control the appearance of the data on the screen. See lines **5** and **13**, lines **6** and **12**, and lines **8** and **10** for the HTML tag pairs in Listing 10.5.

10.2.3.4   `<xsl:for-each>`

This element implements a loop. It operates on a collection of nodes designated by the value of its `select` attribute. The selected node becomes the **current** node. In the example in Listing 10.5, the `<xsl:for-each>` element (lines **7** and **11**) selects the source `<GREETING>` element in the XML document.

10.2.3.5   `<xsl:value-of>`

If we want to display the value of a data node as a string, we may use the element `<xsl:value-of>`. In the example of Listing 10.5, the element `<xsl:value-of>` does not have the `select` attribute, and the current data node (i.e., `<GREETING>` element) is to be displayed. The slash character in the tag (Line **9** in Listing 10.5) is used for the empty tag.

10.2.4   CSS vs. XSL

Cascading style sheets can only change the format of a particular element based on the chosen tag. In other words, CSS implements styles on an element-wide basis, but does not change these elements. On the other hand, XSL can choose style based on tag, contents and attributes of tag, position of tag in the document relative to other elements, and so on. XSL style sheet can re-arrange and re-order the elements. Obviously, XSL is more flexible in defining presentation style.

10.2.5 More Simple Examples of XML with CSS and XSLT

To learn more about CSS and XSLT for XML documents, we take more simple examples. Open `C:\Myfolder\greetingcss.xml` in Notepad, re-edit as follows, and save it.

```
<?xml version="1.0" standalone="yes"?>
<?xml-stylesheet type="text/css" href="greetingcss.css"?>
<MESSAGE>
 <GREETING>
 Hello, XML World!
 </GREETING>
 <GREETINGAGAIN>
 Hello Again!
 </GREETINGAGAIN>
</MESSAGE>
```

Listing 10.7   XML document (greetingcss.xml) with more elements associated to CSS.

In the XML document in Listing 10.7, we have more elements. In this example, MESSAGE is the root element, and it contains two elements: GREETING and GREETINGAGAIN. Figure 10.6 shows this simple tree.

To present the given XML document using CSS, open `C:\Myfolder\greetingcss.css` in Notepad, re-edit it as follows, and save it.

```
GREETING {display: block; font-size: 50pt;
     background: green; color: yellow; font-weight: bold;}

GREETINGAGAIN {display: block; font-size: 50pt;
     background: blue; color: red; font-weight: bold;}
```

Listing 10.8   CSS (greetingcss.css) for the XML document in Listing 10.7.

The CSS stated earlier shows how to describe the presentation style for each element. To view the presentation of the XML document in Listing 10.7, open the XML document in Internet Explorer.

Next, open `C:\Myfolder\greetingxsl.xml` in Notepad, re-edit it as follows, and save it.

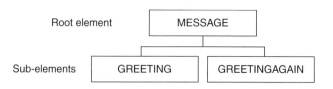

Figure 10.6   Element tree for the XML document in Listing 10.7.

```
<?xml version="1.0" standalone="yes"?>
<?xml-stylesheet type="text/xsl" href="greetingxsl.xsl"?>
<MESSAGE>
 <GREETING>
 Hello, XML World!
 </GREETING>
 <GREETINGAGAIN>
 Hello Again!
 </GREETINGAGAIN>
</MESSAGE>
```

Listing 10.9 XML document (greetingxsl.xml) with more elements associated to XSLT.

Open C:\Myfolder\greetingxsl.xsl in Notepad, re-edit it as follows, and save it.

```
<?xml version="1.0" ?>
<xsl:stylesheet
 xmlns:xsl="http://www.w3.org/TR/WD-xsl">
 <xsl:template match="/">
  <HTML>
    <BODY>
    We are learning XML!
     <xsl:for-each select="MESSAGE/GREETING">
      <H1>
       <xsl:value-of/>
      </H1>
     </xsl:for-each>
     <xsl:for-each select="MESSAGE/GREETINGAGAIN">
      <H2>
       <xsl:value-of/>
      </H2>
     </xsl:for-each>
    </BODY>
   </HTML>
  </xsl:template>
 </xsl:stylesheet>
```

Listing 10.10 XSLT (greetingxsl.xsl) for the XML document in Listing 10.9.

To view the XML document in Listing 10.9, open it in Internet Explorer.

In summary, an XML document contains data that is organized into a tree. The XML document can be used to transmit data, but is not used for presentation directly. To display these data, CSS or XSLT must be used. XSLT is flexible and incorporates HTML tags to control the presentation. The relationships between XML, XSLT, HTML, and presentations are summarized in Figure 10.7.

10.3 Document Type Definition and Validation

In XML, the set of tags and the tree structure of the element are defined with a **document type definition (DTD)**. A DTD document provides a list of elements, attributes, notations, and entities contained in the XML document as well as

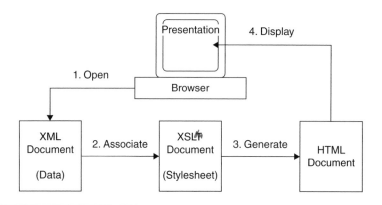

Figure 10.7   XML, XSLT, HTML, and data presentation.

their hierarchical relationships. DTD ensures that people can share the data in the XML document correctly and accurately.

A DTD document can be embedded in the corresponding XML document (called **internal DTD**), or an independent file stored at an external URL (called **external DTD**).

To ensure that an XML document meets the specification defined by the DTD, one must **validate** the XML document against the DTD. The validation of the XML document includes two aspects: formats and semantics. There have been many validating parsers available in the software market. Microsoft Internet Explorer has a validation parser. Generally, validation in Internet Explorer is easier than using a special validation parser. One can download the **validation parser** from Microsoft Web site:

http://msdn.microsoft.com/archive/default.asp?url=/archive/en-us/samples/internet/xml/xml_validator/default.asp

and use [Demo] to validate your XML document against internal DTD.

Note that Web browsers do not check XML documents for validity automatically. An invalidated XML document could cause unpredictable and serious errors, especially if the data is going to be used for updating a database. It is ultimately the responsibility of the user of the XML document to validate the XML document with the DTD.

10.3.1   Simple Example of Internal DTD

To learn how to use internal DTD for an XML document, we return to C:\ Myfolder\greetingxsl.xml. Using Notepad, re-edit the XML document as follows, and save it as, say, C:\Myfolder\greetingxsl-idtd.xml. Note the DTD part in bold.

```
<?xml version="1.0" standalone="yes"?>
<?xml-stylesheet type="text/xsl" href="greetingxsl.xsl"?>

<!DOCTYPE MESSAGE [
   <!ELEMENT MESSAGE (GREETING+, GREETINGAGAIN+)>
```

```
   <!ELEMENT GREETING (#PCDATA)>
     <!ELEMENT GREETINGAGAIN (#PCDATA)>
]>
<MESSAGE>
  <GREETING>
  Hello, XML World!
  </GREETING>
  <GREETINGAGAIN>
  Hello Again!
  </GREETINGAGAIN>
</MESSAGE>
```

Listing 10.11   Example of XML document (greetingxsl-idtd.xml) with internal DTD.

A DTD document begins with **document type declaration**. It declares the root element of the XML document, and includes the DTD declarations. The syntax of document type declaration for internal DTD is

```
<!DOCTYPE root-element [ DTD declarations  ]>
```

Before we learn DTD declarations, we present an example of external DTD.

10.3.2   Simple Example of External DTD

To learn how to use external DTD for an XML document, we return to C:\ Myfolder\greetingxsl.xml. Using Notepad, re-edit the XML document as follows, and save it as, say, C:\Myfolder\greetingxsl-edtd.xml. Note the part related to external DTD in bold.

```
<?xml version="1.0" standalone="no"?>
<?xml-stylesheet type="text/xsl" href="greetingxsl.xsl"?>
<!DOCTYPE MESSAGE SYSTEM "greeting.dtd">

<MESSAGE>
 <GREETING>
 Hello, XML World!
 </GREETING>
 <GREETINGAGAIN>
 Hello Again!
 </GREETINGAGAIN>
</MESSAGE>
```

Listing 10.12   XML document (greetingxsl-edtd.xml) associated to external DTD.

As seen in Listing 10.12, the value of standalone is "no" indicating this XML document must have an external DTD. The syntax of document type declaration for external DTD is

```
<!DOCTYPE root-element SYSTEM "DTD-URL">
```

The "DTD-URL" declares the location of the DTD document which is separated from the XML document.

Using Notepad, edit the following DTD document, and save it as `C:\ Myfolder\greeting.dtd`. Note that some computers may not have set file type of DTD for the Windows operating system, and you are unable to save as a DTD file in Notepad. If so, you need to set file type of DTD to use Notepad to save it as a file with the extension name `.dtd`. To do this, click `[Start]`, `[Settings]`, `[Folder Options]`, select the folder `[File Types]`, and click the `[New Type]` button to edit the file type. You may choose an icon for DTD files. In the `[Description of type]` textbox, type `DTD` and in the `[Associated extension]` type `.dtd` to assign the extension name for DTD files. In the `[Default extension for Content Type]` choose `.dtd`. Click `[New]` for `Actions`. In the `Action` box type `open`. In the `[Application used to perform action]` textbox, click `[Browse]` and select `C:\WINDOWS\Notepad.exe` for the default action. Then click [OK] or [Close] to quit. The setting approach can be used for other file types such as XML Schema files with extension name `.xsd` if they have not been set.

```
<!ELEMENT MESSAGE (GREETING+, GREETINGAGAIN+)>
  <!ELEMENT GREETING (#PCDATA)>
  <!ELEMENT GREETINGAGAIN (#PCDATA)>
```

Listing 10.13   External DTD (greeting.dtd) for the XML document in Listing 10.12.

Apparently, the external DTD document is exactly the same as the part `[DTD declaration]` in the internal DTD document in Listing 10.11.

10.3.3   Features of DTD

A DTD document shows three major declarations: `<!ELEMENT>`, `<!ENTITY>`, and `<!ATTLIST>`. It declares all necessary elements and their attributes, and the structure of the hierarchical tree of elements in the corresponding XML document.

10.3.3.1   <!ELEMENT>

`<!ELEMENT>` declaration declares an XML element type name and its permissible sub-elements ("**children**"). For example:

```
<!ELEMENT MESSAGE (GREETING+, GREETINGAGAIN+)>
```

means that `MESSAGE` is the root element, and has two children: `GREETING` and `GREETINGAGAIN`. The plus sign (+), called **cardinality operator**, means that the sub-element can have one or more instances. If one uses `*` as the cardinality operator, it means that the sub-element can have one, more than one, or not at all instances. Next,

```
<!ELEMENT GREETING (#PCDATA)>
```

means that GREETING is a leaf of the data tree. #PCDATA stands for "Parsed Character Data." It defines that GREETING can have only textual data.

10.3.3.2 <!ATTLIST>

<!ATTLIST> declaration declares element attributes and their permissible values. Examples of this declaration will be discussed. For example:

```
<!ATTLIST CAR
owner   CDATA #IMPLIED
VID     CDATA #REQUIRED
maker   CDATA #REQUIRED>
```

means that CAR is the element concerned, and owner, VID, and maker are its attributes. CDATA means the attribute can have character data. The keyword #IMPLIED means optional, and #REQUIRED means this attribute must appear. <!ATTLIST> declarations are usually placed after all <!ELEMENT> declarations.

10.3.3.3 <!ENTITY>

<!ENTITY> declaration declares special character references, text macros (similar to C/C++ #define), and other content from external sources (similar to C/C++ #include). Entity declaration provides reference mechanisms for any non-ASCII characters (including international characters) that do not have a direct input method on keyboard. It can also provide references to pre-stored texts or image files. Listing 10.14 is a simple XML document with DTD entity declarations.

```
<?xml version="1.0" standalone="yes"?>

<!DOCTYPE MESSAGE [
    <!ENTITY copy "&#x00A9;">
    <!ENTITY author "Shouhong Wang">
    <!ENTITY copyright "&copy; 2002 &author;">
<!ELEMENT MESSAGE (#PCDATA)>
]>
<MESSAGE>
 &copyright;
</MESSAGE>
```

Listing 10.14   Example of XML document with DTD entity declarations.

This XML document can be viewed in Internet Explorer as in Figure 10.8.

In Listing 10.14, the first entity declaration defines the reference to a special character © using the **Unicode** standard hex value. The general entity references begin with ampersand (&) and end with semicolon (;), with entity's name between these two characters. The second entity declaration defines the pre-stored text. The third entity declaration defines the text macro named copyright that in turn cites the two declared entities. In the XML document, the copyright entity is cited.

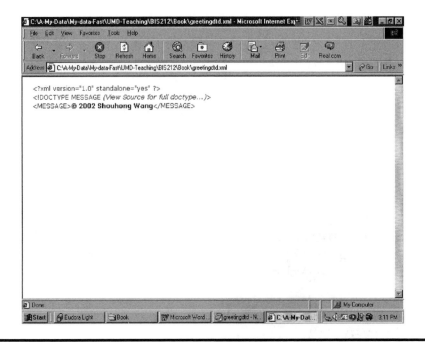

Figure 10.8　Entity references are expanded.

10.4　XML Schemas

There have been critiques of DTD, although DTD is still popular and easy to use. DTD has its unique syntax. It has limited functionality. A number of alternatives to DTD have arisen. **XML Schemas** is one of these alternatives. XML Schemas standard was released by W3C in 2001.

　　Several points are worth noting.

1. An XML Schemas document is an XML document, and is normally saved with the extension name **.xsd**.
2. For an XML document, the way to describing the data tree using XML Schema may not be unique.
3. In the XML document, one can declare the association with the XML Schema; however, such an association is not mandatory. More often, other indications for the association, which is specified by the validation parser, can be provided at the validation time.

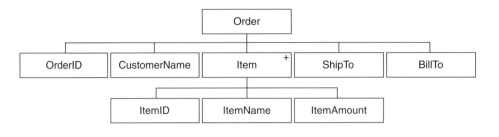

Figure 10.9　Data tree of order.

We use an example to explain the major features of XML Schemas. Suppose we have the data tree shown in Figure 10.9.

The XML document for this example is listed in Listing 10.15.

```
1  <?xml version="1.0"?>
2  <Order OrderID="A4567">
3        <CustomerName>
4        John Smith
5        </CustomerName>
6        <ShipTo>
7        285 Dartmouth
8        </ShipTo>
9        <Item>
10             <ItemID>
11             C-105
12             </ItemID>
13             <ItemName>
14             Computer
15             </ItemName>
16             <ItemAmount>
17             30
18             </ItemAmount>
19        </Item>
20        <Item>
21             <ItemID>
22             T-298
23             </ItemID>
24             <ItemName>
25             Television
26             </ItemName>
27             <ItemAmount>
28             50
29             </ItemAmount>
30        </Item>
31  </Order>
```

Listing 10.15   XML document for the data tree in Figure 10.9.

One can have several approaches to describe the data tree in XML Schemas. Here, we demonstrate a straightforward design that defines each element and attribute in order and multiple occurrences. The XML Schemas is shown in Listing 10.16. Note that the line numbers are used merely for the convenience of explanation, and are not a part of the document.

```
1  <?xml version="1.0"?>
2  <xs:schema xmlns:xs="http://www.w3.org/2001/XMLSchema">
3  <xs:element name="Order">
4   <xs:complexType>
5     <xs:sequence>
6     <xs:element name="CustomerName" type="xs:string"/>
7     <xs:element name="ShipTo" type="xs:string"/>
8     <xs:element name="Item" minOccurs="0" maxOccurs="unbounded">
9     <xs:complexType>
10     <xs:sequence>
11      <xs:element name="ItemID" type="xs:string"/>
```

```
12        <xs:element name="ItemName" type="xs:string"/>
13        <xs:element name="ItemAmount" type="xs:string"/>
-10      </xs:sequence>
-9      </xs:complexType>
-6      </xs:element>
-5      </xs:sequence>
14       <xs:attribute name="OrderID" type="xs:string"/>
-4   </xs:complexType>
-3 </xs:element>
-2 </xs:schema>
```

Listing 10.16 XML Schemas document for the XML document in Listing 10.15.

Next, we explain the main features of XML Schemas using the example given earlier.

10.4.1   Schema Element

Line **2** is the **schema element**. It defines the target namespace. The **prefix** xs: indicates that association with XML Schemas. Line **−2** is the end tag.

10.4.2   Data Element, Element Name, and Element Type

The element tag is used to define a data element of the data tree (line **3**). The name attribute defines the name of the element. If the data element has its sub-elements, complexType is used to define the sub-elements, as discussed shortly. If the data element has simple data type, it is defined by type in the element tag (e.g., line **6**). In fact, one can use XML Schemas to define specific type, such as date, zip, etc.

10.4.3   `complexType`

If the element has its attributes and its children, then the data type is complex. We need to use complexType to describe these sub-elements that are included within the tag pair (e.g., line **4** and line **−4**).

10.4.4   `sequence`

The sequence tag is a compositor that defines the ordered sequence of the sub-elements of the present element. Line **5** and line **−5** shows an example.

10.4.5   Cardinality

In the example of Listing 10.16, the Item element can repeat. We use minOccurs and maxOccurs to define its **cardinality**. In this example, the number of Item can range from 0 to infinite.

10.4.6 Attribute

The declaration of the attributes (`OrderID` in this case) of the document element (`Order` in this case) always come right before the end tag `</xs:complexType>` (see line **14** and line **−4**). This rule of XML Schemas seems to be abnormal.

10.5 Business Applications of XML

In this section we present an illustrative example of the use of XML documents for business applications to share the data with the uniform format. Suppose we have an XML document, with the internal DTD, that records all current highest bids in an online auction session as follows:

```
<?xml version="1.0" standalone="yes"?>
<!DOCTYPE Auction [
    <!ELEMENT Auction (Item+)>
    <!ELEMENT Item (#PCDATA)>
      <!ATTLIST Item
              ItemName        CDATA #REQUIRED
              Seller          CDATA #REQUIRED
              ClosingTime     CDATA #REQUIRED
              ReservedPrice   CDATA #IMPLIED
      CurrentBid      CDATA #IMPLIED >
  ]>
  <Auction>
      <Item
            ItemName="IBM Computer"
            Seller="Office Equipment"
            ClosingTime="8:00pm 02/05"
            ReservedPrice="$400"
            CurrentBid="$300">
      </Item>
      <Item
            ItemName="Honda Motorcycle"
            Seller="Motor Dealer"
            ClosingTime="4:00pm 02/12"
            ReservedPrice="$4000"
            CurrentBid="$4500">
      </Item>
      <Item
            ItemName="Sony DVD Player"
            Seller="Best Purchase"
            ClosingTime="10:00am 02/08"
            ReservedPrice="$150"
            CurrentBid="$200">
      </Item>
      <Item
            ItemName="Dartmouth Concert Ticket"
            Seller="U Mass D"
            ClosingTime="8:00pm 02/10"
            ReservedPrice="$25"
            CurrentBid="$32">
      </Item>
  </Auction>
```

Listing 10.17 Example of XML document.

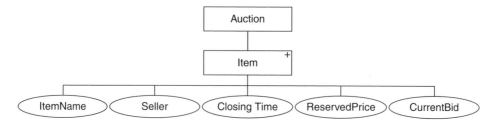

Figure 10.10   Data structure tree for the XML document.

Figure 10.10 shows the tree for the auction data structure presented by the DTD in the XML document in Listing 10.17. Note that, in this case, we use many attributes for the `Item` element. One can also use elements to model the structure. For example, `Seller` could be modeled as a sub-node of `Item`.

Using Microsoft validation software online, the XML document is validated against the DTD, as shown in Figure 10.11.

Suppose the Auction Manager is interested in all attributes but `Seller`. The following XSLT style sheet is used for the Manager.

```
<xsl:stylesheet
    xmlns:xsl="http://www.w3.org/TR/WD-xsl">
    <xsl:template match="/">
      <HTML>
      <BODY>
      <H2>Auction Items Listed for the Manager</H2>
```

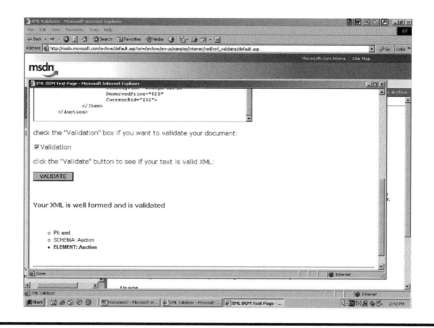

Figure 10.11   Use Microsoft validation software (Demo) to validate the XML document.

```
    <TABLE BORDER="1">
    <THEAD>
    <TR BGCOLOR="PINK">
    <TH>Item Name</TH>
    <TH>Closing Time</TH>
    <TH>Reserved Price</TH>
    <TH>Current Highest Bid</TH>
    </TR>
    </THEAD>

    <TBODY>
     <xsl:for-each select="Auction/Item">
      <TR>
      <TD><xsl:value-of select="@ItemName"/></TD>
      <TD ALIGN="RIGHT">
         <xsl:value-of select="@ClosingTime"/></TD>
      <TD ALIGN="RIGHT">
         <xsl:value-of select="@ReservedPrice"/></TD>
      <TD ALIGN="RIGHT"><xsl:value-of select="@CurrentBid"/></TD>
      </TR>
     </xsl:for-each>
    </TBODY>
   </TABLE>

   </BODY>
   </HTML>
  </xsl:template>
</xsl:stylesheet>
```

Listing 10.18   XSLT document (manager.xsl) for the XML document in Listing 10.17 for Manager.

Clearly, to associate the XSLT document to the XML document, a line like `<?xml-stylesheet type="text/xsl" href="manager.xsl"?>` needs to be added to the XML document after the first line in Listing 10.17.

Figure 10.12 shows the data presentation for Managers.

In another application, bidders are not supposed to view any values of the attribute `ReservedPrice`. Accordingly, the following XSLT style sheet is applied to all bidders.

```
<xsl:stylesheet
    xmlns:xsl="http://www.w3.org/TR/WD-xsl">
  <xsl:template match="/">
   <HTML>
   <BODY>
   <H2>Auction Items Listed for Bidders</H2>

   <TABLE BORDER="1">
   <THEAD>
   <TR BGCOLOR="#9acd32">
   <TH>Item Name</TH>
   <TH>Seller</TH>
   <TH>Closing Time</TH>
   <TH>Current Highest Bid</TH>
```

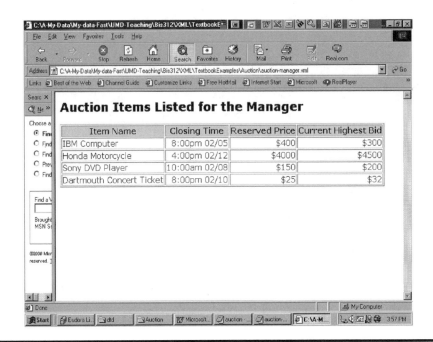

Figure 10.12   Auction data is presented for managers.

```
  </TR>
  </THEAD>

  <TBODY>
 <xsl:for-each select="Auction/Item">.
  <TR>
  <TD><xsl:value-of select="@ItemName"/></TD>
  <TD><xsl:value-of select="@Seller"/></TD>
  <TD ALIGN="RIGHT">
      <xsl:value-of select="@ClosingTime"/></TD>
  <TD ALIGN="RIGHT"><xsl:value-of select="@CurrentBid"/></TD>
  </TR>
  </xsl:for-each>
 </TBODY>
  </TABLE>

  </BODY>
  </HTML>
 </xsl:template>
</xsl:stylesheet>
```

Listing 10.19 XSLT document (bidder.xsl) for the XML document in Listing 10.17 for bidders.

Again, to associate the XSLT document to the XML document, a line like `<?xml-stylesheet type="text/xsl" href="bidder.xsl"?>` needs to be added to the XML document after the first line in Listing 10.17.

Figure 10.13 shows the data presentation for bidders.

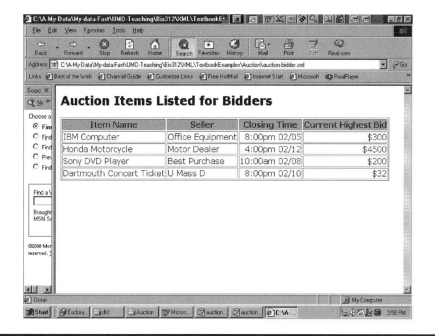

Figure 10.13 Auction data is presentated for bidders.

XSLT condition tags can vary the output. For instance, making changes to Listing 10.19 by including tag `<xsl:if>`, one can select the auction items with the seller "`Best Purchase`" for bidders. However, XSLT condition tags may not be supported by Internet Explorer.

```
......
<xsl:if test="@Seller='Best Purchase'">
        <TR>
        <TD><xsl:value-of select="@ItemName"/></TD>
        <TD><xsl:value-of select="@Seller"/></TD>
        <TD ALIGN="RIGHT">
        <xsl:value-of select="@ClosingTime"/></TD>
        <TD  ALIGN="RIGHT">
        <xsl:value-of select="@CurrentBid"/></TD>
        </TR>
</xsl:if>
......
```

Listing 10.20   XSLT condition tags.

From the illustrative examples stated earlier, we can see that a single XML document can be easily used dynamically for a variety of clients. An XML document can be viewed as a database that contains numerical numbers, texts, images, sound clips to be shared by all clients on the Internet. More advantages of XML can be observed if one incorporates XML with Java and database technologies.

10.6 XHTML

As shown in this chapter, HTML and XML are not compatible. Apparently, it is straightforward to convert an HTML document to an XML document, since the tags in HTML can be defined as elements in XML and the structure can further be defined by DTD. XHTML is such a language that keeps the feature of HTML, and makes the markup document compatible with XML. There have been three DTDs for three versions of XHTML that define the rules for the language, and available on the W3C Web site for every one to use.

Transitional: `http://www.w3.org/TR/xhtml1/DTD/xhtml1-transitional.dtd`
Frameset: http://www.w3.org/TR/xhtml1/DTD/xhtml1-frameset.dtd
Strict: http://www.w3.org/TR/xhtml1/DTD/xhtml1-strict.dtd

Each version of XHTML supports its unique features.

One can follow structured steps to convert a not well formed HTML document to XHTML document. For example, suppose we have an HTML document as follows:

```
<HTML>
<HEAD>
<TITLE>Convert HTML to XHTML</TITLE>
</HEAD>
<BODY>
<P>
<H2>Hello, XHTML!</H2>
<BR>
<IMG SRC=Book.jpg ALT="Book">
</BODY>
</HTML>
```

Listing 10.21   Example of HTML document.

To convert the HTML document to XHTML document, one performs the following steps.

Step 1. Add DOCTYPE declaration:

```
<?xml version="1.0"?>
<!DOCTYPE html PUBLIC "-//W3C//DTD XHTML 1.0 Transitional//EN"
    "http://www.w3.org/TR/xhtml1/DTD/xhtml1-transitional.dtd">
```

Step 2. Add the XHTML namespace to the root element:

```
<html xmlns="http://www.w3.org/1999/xhtml">
```

Step 3. Follow the following rules to create a well-formed document:

   (1)   Change tags to lowercase.
   (2)   No missing close tag.
   (3)   Make up proper syntax for empty elements.
   (4)   No missing values and quotation marks in all attributes.

The XHTML document for Listing 10.21 is listed in Listing 10.22. You can practice the steps given earlier and check the conversion result.

```
<?xml version="1.0"?>
<!DOCTYPE html PUBLIC "-//W3C//DTD XHTML 1.0 Transitional//EN"
    "http://www.w3.org/TR/xhtml1/DTD/xhtml1-transitional.dtd">
<html xmlns="http://www.w3.org/1999/xhtml">

<html>
<head>
<title>Convert HTML to XHTML</title>
</head>
<body>
<p>
<h2>Hello, XHTML!</h2>
</p>
<br />
<img src="Book.jpg" alt="Book">
</body>
</html>
```

Listing 10.22   XHTML for the HTML document in Listing 10.21.

You may use Notepad to edit the XHML document and save it as a file with the extension name `.html`, and then open it in the Web browser to view the presentation. As shown in this example, XHTML is merely to make an HTML document well formed and compatible with XML.

Note that some HTML tags may not be supported by a particular version of XHTML (e.g., FRAME), or must be replaced by their equivalent XHTML tags (e.g., FONT). There have been software tools for converting an HTML document to XHTML, such as W3C's Tidy (`http://www.w3.org/People/Raggett/tidy/`).

10.7   eXtensible Business Reporting Language

eXtensible Business Reporting Language (**XBRL**), is an extension of XML which has been defined specifically for business accounting and financial reports. Under XML, tags are applied to items of business accounting and financial data so that they can be read and processed by computers.

It enables unique identifying tags to be applied to items of business data. For example, a tag `<tax>` would identify the data of tax in a business document. The true power of XBRL is more than simple identifiers. The XML language can provide links to relative information about the data item. For example, the XBRL can link the tax data item to various sources of the tax. More importantly, XBRL can be easily extended to meet a variety of special needs in business document processes. XBRL has been in practical use internationally, and is still under development. The use of XBRL is to support all aspects of reporting in different countries and industries.

10.7.1   Comparison of XBRL with XML

Similar to XML, XBRL has three basic concepts: schema (**taxonomy** in XBRL term), instant document of the data, and style sheets for presentation.

Compared with XML, XBRL has the following major extensions to XML.

1. XBRL provides a framework for defining and extending business data dictionaries that make business report process and exchange more efficiently.
2. XBRL provides the ability to define and validate specific **semantics** (or **business rules**) for the business reporting domain. For instance, for numeric accounting data set {Assets, Liability, Equity}, XBRL can validate whether "Assets = Liability + Equity." Such business domain-based semantics are beyond XML Schema.
3. XBRL provides application features such as comparison and extension. For example, a financial report from company A "Assets of Fiscal Year 2006 of Company A" can be directly compared with a financial report from company B "Assets of Fiscal Year 2006 of Company B."
4. XBRL supports multiple hierarchies such as content, calculation, definition, while XML supports one hierarchy of content.

Because of the extensions of XBRL, XML parser or other XML software are unable to handle XBRL. One must use XBRL software to convert business reports into XBRL documents through computerized mapping processes. However, XBRL does not address formatting for presentation. The existing tools and standards for presenting data (e.g., XSLT) are intended to be used for XBRL document presentation.

10.7.2 Taxonomy

Taxonomy is an important concept of XBRL. XBRL taxonomies are the dictionaries that XBRL uses. These dictionaries define the specific tags for individual items of data (e.g., net income). Since countries have different accounting documentation regulations, each country may have its own taxonomy for business reporting. Many governments, industries, or even companies, may also have taxonomies to meet their own business needs.

Taxonomies enforce standardization of terminologies used in business reports. For instance:

```
<element name="NetIncome" />
<element name="netprofit" />
<element name="netProfit" />
```

describe the same figure of net income, but use different element names. Taxonomy is to make the meaning of data less ambiguous for processing.

10.7.3 Prepare XBRL-Based Reports

The following steps are needed to create an XBRL-based business report:

1. Select, or create, or extend a taxonomy for the report.
2. Using specific software, translate the data from its current form or application to an XBRL instance document that complies the XBRL taxonomy.
3. Validate the taxonomy and instance document against external or internal measures.

4. Create style sheets for document presentation.
5. Publish the three components (taxonomy, instance document, and style sheets) on the Internet.

To provide technical support of XBRL, many countries have established XBRL organizations. You may check the Web site <http://www.xbrl.org/> and its links to find technical details of XBRL.

10.8   Self-Review Exercise

1. Fill in the blanks in the following XML document.

```
 1 <?xml version="1.0" standalone=_____ ____>
 2 <?xml-stylesheet _____="text/xsl" _____="cd.xsl"?>
 3 <_____>
 4 <_____>
 5 <Title>Soulsville<_____>
 6 <Artist>Jorn Hoel<_____>
 7 <Country>Norway<_____>
 8 <Publisher>WEA<_____>
 9 <RegularPrice>8.90<_____>
10 <SalePrice>7.85</_____>
11 <Year>1996<_____>
12 </CD>
13 <CD>
14 <_____>Empire Burlesque</Title>
15 <_____>Bob Dylan</Artist>
16 <_____>USA</Country>
17 <_____>Columbia</Publisher>
18 <_____>11.90</RegularPrice>
19 <_____>9.99</SalePrice>
20 <_____>1985</Year>
21 <_____>
22 <CD>
23 <Title>Hide your heart</Title>
24 <Artist>Bonnie Tyler</Artist>
25 <Country>UK</Country>
26 <Publisher>CBS Records</Publisher>
27 <RegularPrice>10.90</RegularPrice>
28 <SalePrice>8.95</SalePrice>
29 <Year>1988</Year>
30 <_____>
31 </CATALOG>
```

2. Draw the data tree for the XML document in Question (1).
3. Write the DTD for the XML document in Question (1), and validate it.
4. Write the XML Schema for the XML document in Question (1), and validate it using a validation parser.
5. Fill in the blanks in the following XSLT document that is applied to the XML document in Question (1). Applying this XSLT, what is the expected presentation output of the XML document in Question (1)?

```
 1 <xsl:stylesheet
 2     _____:xsl="http://www.w3.org/TR/WD-xsl">
 3 <xsl:template _____="/">
 4 <_____>
 5 <BODY>
 6 <H2>Online CD Catalog</H2>
 7    <TABLE BORDER="1">
 8    <TR>
 9    <TH>Title<_____>
10    <TH>Artist<_____>
11     <TH>Price<_____>
12    </TR>
13    <xsl:for-each select="CATALOG/CD">
14    <TR>
15    <TD><xsl:_____ select="_____"/></TD>
16    <TD><xsl:_____ select="Artist"/></TD>
17    <TD><xsl:_____ select="RegularPrice"/></TD>
18    </TR>
19    <_____>
20    </TABLE>
21 </BODY>
22 </HTML>
23 <_____>
24 </xsl:stylesheet>
```

6. Change the XSLT document in Question (5) so that the data of Regular-Price are not displayed, but the data of SalePrice are displayed.
7. Develop an XML document and a CSS for it.
8. Develop an XML document and an XSLT for it.
9. Develop an XML document and its internal and external DTD documents with !ELEMENT, !ATTLIST, and !ENTITY.
10. Develop an XML document and its XML Schemas.
11. Develop an XML project for electronic commerce.
12. Check the Web site <http://www.xbrl.org/> to write a short essay about XBRL.
13. Convert an HTML document to XHTML document.

Appendix 10.1 Guideline for XML Project Report

1. Front page

   Course name
   Title of the project
   Group members (names and ID)
   Date

2. Text

   Introduction and the purposes of XML
   Application of XML, CSS, XSLT, DTD, Schema

3. Data structure diagram for your application
4. Source code of the XML, CSS, XSLT, DTD, and Schema
5. Screen shots of several data presentations on the same XML data set
6. Screen shots of the validation.

Chapter 11

SQL for Database Query

11.1 Introduction to SQL

Structured Query Language (**SQL**) is a universal language for querying and updating databases. It can be used for all database management systems (DB2, Access, Oracle, etc.) as well as computer language platforms (Java, .NET C#, etc.). SQL was developed under the name SEQUEL by IBM in the mid-1970s. This is the reason why people pronounce SQL as (sequel) more often than (ess-que-ell). SQL has been standardized by ANSI.

When using a particular database management system, such as Access, we can use the query development environment to create queries. Internally, the database management system generates the query code in SQL, as seen in the following section. In principle, we do not need to write SQL code if we use a single database management system. However, when using Java or .NET to develop a Web application that is connected to databases (Oracle, DB2, Access, etc.) one must write SQL code that is embedded in the programs to querying and updating the databases. This is the major motivation for use to learn SQL in this course.

11.2 View SQL of a Query Created in Access

To write and run a SQL program, we must have a database management system. Access is the most available database management system. The first step of learning SQL is to get familiar with the Access database management system environment, and develop several tables and queries. We assume that students have learned basic features of Access in a freshman computer literacy course.

Suppose we have a table, called `tblStudent`, and a query called `qry-Student`, that have been created in Access. Click the query `qryStudent`, you can view the query result. Click [View] on the top menu, and choose [SQL View], you can view the SQL code generated by the Access database management system when the `qryStudent` was created (see Listing 11.1 and Figure 11.1).

```
SELECT tblStudent.StudentID, tblStudent.StudentName,
    tblStudent.StudentAddress
FROM tblStudent;
```

Listing 11.1   Example SQL code generated by Access for query.

The SQL in Listing 11.1 means: select the data of `StudentID`, `Student Name`, and `StudentAddress` from table `tblStudent`. We will describe SQL syntax later in this part. Here, we show that one can learn SQL through those queries created by the Access database management system.

11.3   Write and Run SQL in Access

To edit SQL in Access,

- Open the database.
- In the Database Window click object [Queries], and choose [New] on the menu.
- You will see "New Query" pane. Select [Design View], and click [OK].

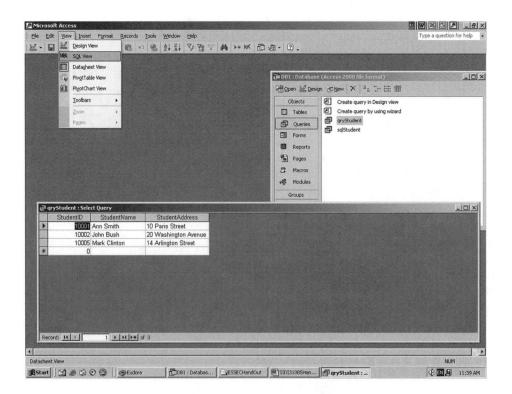

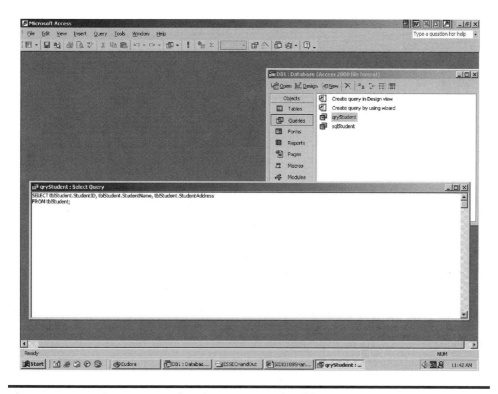

Figure 11.1   View SQL code of a query created in Access.

- Close the table Dialog Box.
- Maximize the "Query1: Select Query" window.
- Click [View] on the top menu, and then choose [SQL View]. Now you have the SQL edit window which has word "SELECT;" already, and you are ready to write SQL code here.

After editing SQL, you can save it as a query. To differentiate query generated by Access or written in SQL, you may use different file name. For example, you can name the SQL in Listing 11.1 as sqlStudent, which is equivalent to SQL in Listing 11.1.

```
SELECT StudentID, StudentName, StudentAddress
FROM tblStudent;
```

Listing 11.2   SQL code example (sqlStudent).

To run the SQL, you click the button marked with ! on the top menu.

11.4   Major Features of SQL—SELECT

The general structure that includes the major features of SQL is

```
SELECT            [fields] [built-in functions]
FROM              [tables]
GROUP BY          [fields]
```

```
ORDER BY          [fields]
WHERE             [conditions]
AND               [conditions];
```

A SQL query starts with "SELECT" and ends with ";".

To demonstrate SQL examples, we assume the database has three tables and their fields as follows:

Table `tblStudent` has fields
`StudentID, StudentName, StudentAddress, StudentBirthDate, StudentEnrolYear`

Table `tblCourse` has fields
`CourseNumber, CourseName, CourseDescription`

Table `tblStudentCourseGrade` has fields
`StudentID, CourseNumber, StudentCourseGrade`

These three tables are normalized 3NF.

11.4.1   Including Fields

The syntax of SQL to include certain fields from a table is:

```
SELECT [fields name], ..., [fields name]
FROM [table name];
```

For example,

```
SELECT StudentID, StudentName, StudentAddress
FROM tblStudent;
```

is to select the data from the named three fields from `tblStudent` table. You can select all fields from a table using asterisk (*), for example:

```
SELECT *
FROM tblStudent;
```

11.4.2   Conditions

To include conditions, you add WHERE statement in the third line.

```
SELECT [fields name], ..., [fields name]
FROM [table name]
WHERE [condition];
```

For example, the following SQL query is to find student data under the condition that the student name is "Ann Smith."

```
SELECT StudentID, StudentName, StudentAddress
FROM tblStudent
WHERE StudentName="Ann Smith";
```

11.4.3   Grouping and Sorting

To group and sort the query results, you use GROUP BY and ORDER BY. For instance,

```
SELECT *
FROM tblStudent
GROUP BY StudentEnrolYear
ORDER BY StudentID;
```

will group the student records based on the enrollment year, and order them by the ID numbers.

11.4.4   Built-In Functions

Structured Query Language has built-in functions, such as COUNT, SUM, AVG, MAX, MIN. For instance,

```
SELECT COUNT(*)
FROM tblStudent
WHERE StudentEnrolYear="2004";
```

is to count students who enrolled in the year 2004.

11.4.5   Joining Tables

Suppose we have another table named tblStudentCourse which has StudenID, CourseNumber, and StudentCourseGrade. The SQL in Listing 11.3 can join the two normalized tables tblStudent and tblStudent Course to show the denormalized data for users.

```
SELECT tblStudent.StudentID,
         StudentName, CourseNumber, StudentCourseGrade
FROM tblStudent, tblStudentCourse
WHERE tblStudent.StudentID = tblStudentCourse.StudentID;
```

Listing 11.3   Join tables to show the denormalized data.

The SQL query will display all students' number, names, the numbers of the courses they have taken, and their grades, as shown in Figure 11.2. Note that, since the same field name StudentID are used in the two different tables, you must quote the table name to specify what table StudentID refers to.

The SQL query in Listing 11.4 lists all students with "A" grades.

```
SELECT tblStudent.StudentID, StudentName,
     CourseNumber, StudentCourseGrade
FROM tblStudent, tblStudentCourse
WHERE tblStudent.StudentID = tblStudentCourse.StudentID
AND StudentCourseGrade="A";
```

Listing 11.4   SQL with joint and conditions.

11.5   Sub-Query

One difficult concept of SQL is sub-query, which the textbook does not include. Here is an example. Suppose we have an Access database which has table

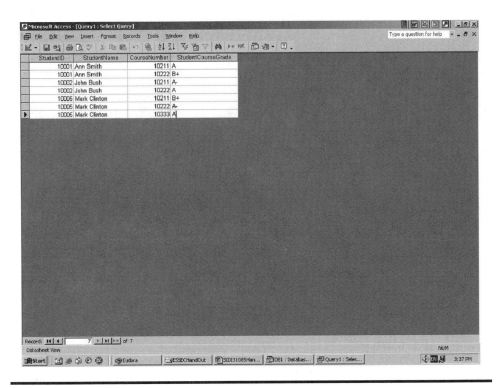

Figure 11.2   Joining tables.

`tblStudent` which is the same as the example in the textbook. We want to find the names of students who have the earliest graduation year. Students often have the following wrong answer.

```
SELECT StudentName
FROM tblStudent
WHERE StudentYear=MIN(StudentYear);
```

This query does not work, because SQL does not allow an uncertain term on the right side of a `WHERE` clause, because the value is actually unknown for the current query. This is equivalent to

```
WHERE StudentYear=?
```

To make a right `WHERE` clause, you need to put either a certain value or a sub-query for the right side. Thus, the right SQL for the above query should be as follows.

```
SELECT StudentName
FROM tblStudent
WHERE StudentYear=
      (SELECT MIN(StudentYear)
      FROM tblStudent);
```

A sub-query can have its sub-query and go on.

In many cases sub-queries that involve multiple tables can avoid join operations to improve the query performance in time.

11.6 Other SQL Features

There are other SQL functions including CREATE, INSERT, UPDATE, DELETE, etc. They are not typical queries but are used for database maintenance.

```
INSERT INTO tblStudent ( StudentID, StudentName,
   StudentAddress, StudentBirthDate, StudentEnrolYear )
VALUES (10003, "Ron McNeil",
   "32 Eastport", "02-Jul-89", "2008");

UPDATE tblStudent SET StudentName = "Anne Smith"
WHERE StudentID=10001;

DELETE FROM tblStudent
WHERE StudentID=10003;
```

Listing 11.5   Examples of SQL other than SELECT.

11.7 SQL in Web Applications

Practical Web applications deal with relational databases directly from a Web page. To make a connection to databases, database connection software must be integrated into the Web application development tool. In the Microsoft .NET framework, **ADO.NET** (ADO stands for ActiveX Data Objects) provides such a database connection that allows a Web page to access databases such as Access, SQL Server, and other databases from .NET applications. We assume students have studied Chapter 9 for ASP.NET before reading this section.

Listing 11.6 (ADOAccess.aspx) is an example of Web application that uses SQL to access Access database in the ADO.NET environment. In this example, the Access database is named `student.mdb` that is stored in the same folder as this ASP.NET Web page. As we learned from Chapter 9, an ASP.NET Web page has heading lines and two parts. The first part is VB.NET that process the database, and the second parts is Web page that calls the VB.NET and present the data to the client. In Listing 11.6 particular lines that is relevant to SQL is highlighted in bold.

```
1 <%@ Page Language="VB" %>
2 <%@ import Namespace="System.Data.OleDb" %>
3 <script runat="server">

4 Public Sub Page_Load()
5 dim dbconn,sql,dbcomm,dbread

6 dbconn=New OleDbConnection("Provider=Microsoft.Jet.OLEDB.4.0; data source=" _

7          & server.mappath("Student.mdb"))

8 dbconn.Open()

9 sql="SELECT * FROM tblStudent"

10 dbcomm=New OleDbCommand(sql,dbconn)
11 dbread=dbcomm.ExecuteReader()
12 tblStudent.DataSource=dbread
```

```
13 tblStudent.DataBind()
14 dbread.Close()
15 dbconn.Close()
16 End Sub

17 </script>

18 <html>
19 <head>
20 </head>
21 <body>
22 <form runat="server">
23  <asp:Repeater id="tblStudent" runat="server">
24   <HeaderTemplate>
25   <table border="1" width="100%">
26   <tr>
27   <th>StudentID</th>
28   <th>StudentName</th>
29   <th>StudentAddress</th>
30   <th>StudentEnrolYear</th>
31   </tr>
32  </HeaderTemplate>
33  <ItemTemplate>
34   <tr>
35   <td><%#Container.DataItem("StudentID")%></td>
36   <td><%#Container.DataItem("StudentName")%></td>
37   <td><%#Container.DataItem("StudentAddress")%></td>
38   <td><%#Container.DataItem("StudentEnrolYear")%></td>
39   </tr>
40  </ItemTemplate>
41  <FooterTemplate>
42   </table>
43  </FooterTemplate>
44  </asp:Repeater>
45 </form>
46 </body>
47 </html>
```

Listing 11.6 Example of use SQL in ADO.NET for Web applications (ADOAccess.aspx).

Lines **1–2** are heading lines of the ASP.NET Web page that claims to use VB.NET and ADO.NET. Lines **3–17** are the VB part. Line **5** defines variables for the database process. Lines **6–7** are a single sentence that makes the database connection. The database name is specified in line **7**. When editing the program in practice, try to avoid any line break and type the sentence in a single line without the line break sign in this case. Line **8** opens the database connection. Apparently, a beginner of ADO.NET may simply follow these lines except for the database name.

Line **9** is the SQL for this example that selects all fields from the table tblStudent. Lines **10–13** read the table using the SQL and make data binding. Lines **14–15** stop the access and close the database connection. Again, a beginner might use these lines for a simple application and change the table name in lines **12–13**.

In the Web page part, line **23** specifies database connection control. Commonly, there are two connection control methods in ASP.NET: `Repeater` and `DataList`. In this example, the Repeater control is applied. The table of the database is also declared here. Lines **24–44** create an HTML table to present the data to the client. Lines **35–38** place the data items into the table cells. The syntax of the ASP.NET sentences in these lines looks unfamiliar. Again, a beginner may simply follow these sentences but specify the particular data item names here. Another feature new to us is templates defined in lines **24**, **32**, **33**, **40**, **41**, **43**. Without including these templates, the ASP.NET Web page does not work.

As discussed in Chapter 9, ASP.NET Web pages can be tested on the IIS Server or in the Microsoft Visual Studio 2005 environment. Figure 11.3 show the execution result of this ASP.NET Web page.

The program in Listing 11.7 is an extension of Listing 11.6 that allows the client to input a number to search a specific student record.

```
<%@ Page Language="VB" %>
<%@ import Namespace="System.Data.OleDb" %>
<script runat="server">

  Public Sub Page_Load()
  End Sub

  Public Sub abc(sender As Object, e As EventArgs)
  label1.text="The inquired record for" + textbox1.value + "is:"

  dim dbconn,sql,dbcomm,dbread
  dim var1 as integer
  var1=textbox1.value

  dbconn=New OleDbConnection("Provider=Microsoft.Jet.OLEDB.4.0; data source=" _
        & server.mappath("Student.mdb"))
  dbconn.Open()

  sql= "SELECT * FROM tblStudent WHERE StudentID=" & var1
  dbcomm=New OleDbCommand(sql,dbconn)
  dbread=dbcomm.ExecuteReader()
  tblStudent.DataSource=dbread
  tblStudent.DataBind()
  dbread.Close()
  dbconn.Close()
```

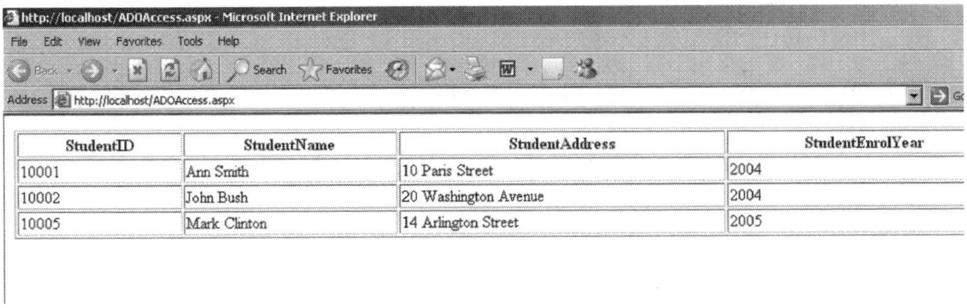

StudentID	StudentName	StudentAddress	StudentEnrolYear
10001	Ann Smith	10 Paris Street	2004
10002	John Bush	20 Washington Avenue	2004
10005	Mark Clinton	14 Arlington Street	2005

Figure 11.3 SQL execution result of the Web application in Listing 11.6.

```
   End Sub
</script>
<html>
<head>
</head>
<body>
  <form runat="server">
    Type the student number for inquiry:
    <input id="textbox1" type="text" runat="server" />
    <br />
    <input id="submit1" type="submit" value="Search"
            runat="server" onserverclick="abc" />
    <br />
    <asp:Label id="label1" runat="server"></asp:Label>
    <asp:Repeater id="tblStudent" runat="server">
      <HeaderTemplate>
       <table border="1" width="100%">
          <tr>
            <th>StudentID</th>
            <th>StudentName</th>
            <th>StudentAddress</th>
            <th>StudentEnrolYear</th>
          </tr>
      </HeaderTemplate>
      <ItemTemplate>
       <tr>
       <td><%#Container.DataItem("StudentID")%></td>
       <td><%#Container.DataItem("StudentName")%></td>
       <td><%#Container.DataItem("StudentAddress")%></td>
       <td><%#Container.DataItem("StudentEnrolYear")%></td>
       </tr>
      </ItemTemplate>
      <FooterTemplate>
       </table>
      </FooterTemplate>
    </asp:Repeater>
  </form>
</body>
</html>
```

Listing 11.7   Use SQL in ADO.NET for search (ADOSearch.aspx).

11.8   Self-Review Exercise

1.   Write SQL to include selected fields of one table.
2.   Write SQL to include selected fields with conditions.
3.   Write SQL to group and sort data of selected field of one table.
4.   Write SQL with built-in functions such as COUNT, SUM, and AVG.
5.   Write SQL to join two tables.
6.   Write SQL to join three tables with conditions.
7.   Write an ASP.NET Web page that contains SQL to access an Access database.

Appendix 11.1 Guideline for SQL Project Report

1. Front page

   Course name
   Title of the project
   Group members (names and ID)
   Date

2. Text

   Introduction and the purposes of SQL
   Application of SQL for database query

3. Source code of the SQL
4. Screen shots of SQL queries

Six Key Concepts Shared by All Procedural Programming Languages

1. Variable/Data Item

A variable or data item is the name of a piece of CPU memory that holds data. The data is called the value of the variable/data item. The original value of a variable could be a default value (such as 0). The value of a variable can be changed through operations, but can never be lost.

2. Arithmetic Operation

Arithmetic operations in procedural programming are similar to day-to-day arithmetic calculation, but use reverse expression. For instance, instead of $a + b = c$, $c = a + b$ is used in programming, which means: let c equal to a plus b.

3. Execution Sequence

During the execution of the procedure of a program, instructions are executed one after another in a sequence (so called execution sequence) in which they are encountered, but not in the order they are listed in the program. Statements of if-then and loops can control the execution sequence of the program.

4. If-Then-Else Logic

An if-then-else statement controls the computer execution sequence based on a current condition. The logic is illustrated in figure.

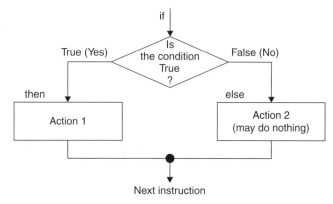

5. Loop

A loop is a group of instructions which is specified once but are carried out several times in succession. A loop statement defines such an iteration procedure, as illustrated in the figure. The common loops include for-loop and do-loop.

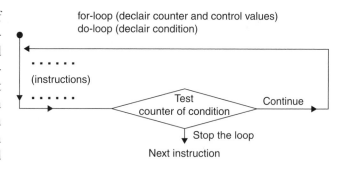

6. Call Module

A large program must be divided into modules for better quality and re-use. Here, a module could be a paragraph of instructions, a function, a method, a subroutine, depending upon a specific language. An instruction can call a module to accomplish a specific task carried out by the module, as illustrated in the figure.

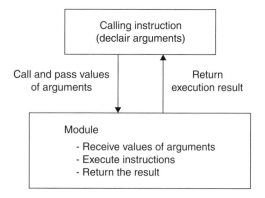

Index

Symbols

\#
  (C/C++), 53
  (Java), 181
  (Perl), 240
  (XML), 320

?
  (PHP), 270
  (XML), 311

$
  (COBOL), 18
  (Perl), 241
  (PHP), 274

%
  (C/C++), 55
  (Perl), 242, 249

@
  (Perl), 242

&
  (C/C++), 57
  (VBA), 226
  (Perl), 246, 249
  (PHP), 276

|
  (C/C++), 57
  (PHP), 276

*
  (COBOL), 10, 18, 32
  (C/C++), 55
  (SQL), 341

  (VB.NET), 211
  (XML), 320

/
  (COBOL), 32
  (C/C++), 53, 55, 57
  (VB.NET), 211

\\
  (C/C++), 52, 56
  (PHP), 277

:
  (XML), 312, 313

::
  (C++), 67

;
  (C/C++), 52
  (PHP), 271
  (SQL), 340

.
  (COBOL), 10, 18

.=
  (Perl), 248

{
  (C/C++), 53
  (JavaScript), 105
  (Java), 121
  (PHP), 273

}
  (C/C++), 53
  (JavaScript), 105
  (Java), 121
  (PHP), 273